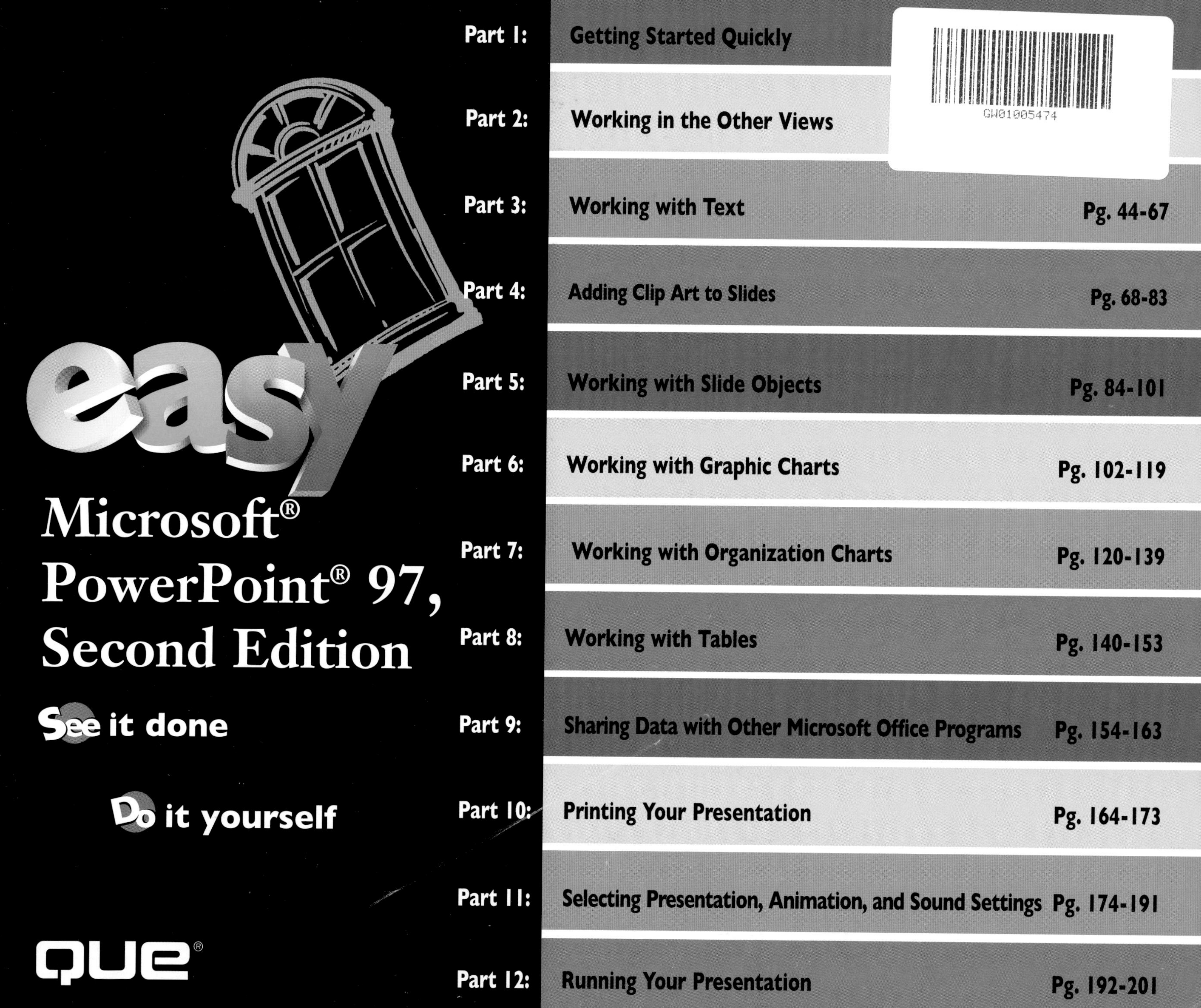
easy
Microsoft® PowerPoint® 97, Second Edition
See it done
Do it yourself
QUE®
Part 1: Getting Started Quickly
Part 2: Working in the Other Views
Part 3: Working with Text Pg. 44-67
Part 4: Adding Clip Art to Slides Pg. 68-83
Part 5: Working with Slide Objects Pg. 84-101
Part 6: Working with Graphic Charts Pg. 102-119
Part 7: Working with Organization Charts Pg. 120-139
Part 8: Working with Tables Pg. 140-153
Part 9: Sharing Data with Other Microsoft Office Programs Pg. 154-163
Part 10: Printing Your Presentation Pg. 164-173
Part 11: Selecting Presentation, Animation, and Sound Settings Pg. 174-191
Part 12: Running Your Presentation Pg. 192-201
GW01005474

## Part 1: Getting Started Quickly

## Part 2: Working in the Other Views

## 3: Working with Text

## 4: Adding Clip Art to Slides

## Part 5: Working with Slide Objects

## Part 6: Working with Graphic Charts

## Part 10: Printing Your Presentation

## Part 11: Selecting Presentation, Animation, and Sound Settings

## Part 12: Running Your Presentation

# Easy Microsoft® PowerPoint® 97, Second Edition


Library of Congress Catalog No.: 98-85094

ISBN: 0-7897-1716-6



99 98 6 5 4 3 2 1

Interpretation of the printing code: the rightmost double-digit number is the year of the book's printing; the rightmost single-digit number, the number of the book's printing. For example, a printing code of 98-1 shows that the first printing of the book occurred in 1998.



Screen reproductions in this book were created using Collage Plus from Inner Media, Inc., Hollis, NH.

## Acknowledgments

Publishing a book like this has been a unique and enjoyable challenge for me. Several people have been key in ensuring this is the most complete and comprehensive visual learning PowerPoint 97 book possible, and they deserve my thanks. Stephanie McCombs led the team of Que professionals who defined and edited this book. Her assistance and flexibility in its production allowed me to concentrate on creating realistic presentation examples and writing. Stephanie coordinated all the rest.

Several other important people instrumental in developing this book are Lorna Gentry, Malinda McCain, and Jim Grey. They did a superb job of editing the grammatical, logical, and technical content of this book, making several significant suggestions which have greatly improved the final book you now hold.

## Dedication

Though I've only met Betty Harris in person one time, her open and friendly manner impressed me immediately and we became fast friends. We have continued that friendship through wonderful, humorous letters and phone calls. This book is dedicated to her and her spirit as she struggles with cancer. Chin up, girl!

**Executive Editor**
Angie Wethington

**Acquisitions Editor**
Stephanie McComb

**Development Editor**
Lorna Gentry

**Technical Editor**
Jim Grey

**Managing Editor**
Thomas F. Hayes

**Copy Editor**
Malinda McCain

**Indexer**
Chris Barrick

**Production Designer**
Lisa England

**Proofreaders**
John Etchison
Jeanne Clark

**Book Designer**
Jean Bisesi

**Cover Designer**
Anne Jones

# How to Use This Book

## It's as Easy as 1-2-3

Each part of this book is made up of a series of short, instructional lessons, designed to help you understand basic information that you need to get the most out of your computer hardware and software.

**Click:** Click the left mouse button once.

**Double-click:** Click the left mouse button twice in rapid succession.

**Right-click:** Click the right mouse button once.

**Pointer Arrow:** Highlights an item on the screen you need to point to or focus on in the step or task.

**Selection:** Highlights the area onscreen discussed in the step or task.

**Click & Type:** Click once where indicated and begin typing to enter your text or data.

1 Each step is fully illustrated to show you how it looks onscreen.

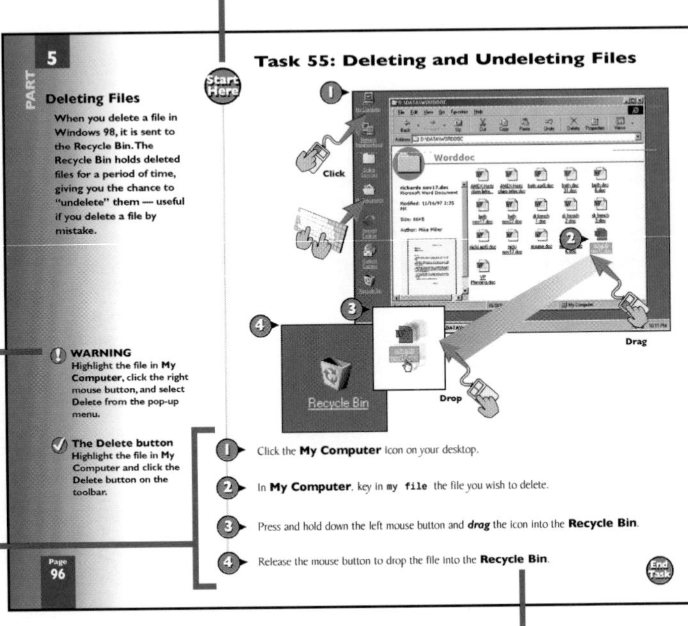

PART 5

**Deleting Files**

When you delete a file in Windows 98, it is sent to the Recycle Bin. The Recycle Bin holds deleted files for a period of time, giving you the chance to "undelete" them — useful if you delete a file by mistake.

**Task 55: Deleting and Undeleting Files**



**WARNING**
Highlight the file in **My Computer**, click the right mouse button, and select Delete from the pop-up menu.

**The Delete button**
Highlight the file in My Computer and click the Delete button on the toolbar.

1. Click the **My Computer** icon on your desktop.
2. In **My Computer**, key in `my file` the file you wish to delete.
3. Press and hold down the left mouse button and ***drag*** the icon into the **Recycle Bin**.
4. Release the mouse button to drop the file into the **Recycle Bin**.

End Task

Page 96

Tips and Warnings give you a heads-up for any extra information you may need while working through the task.

2 Each task includes a series of quick, easy steps designed to guide you through the procedure.

3 Items that you select or click in menus, dialog boxes, tabs, and windows are shown in **bold**. Words in ***bold italic*** are defined in the Glossary. Information you type is in a `special font`.

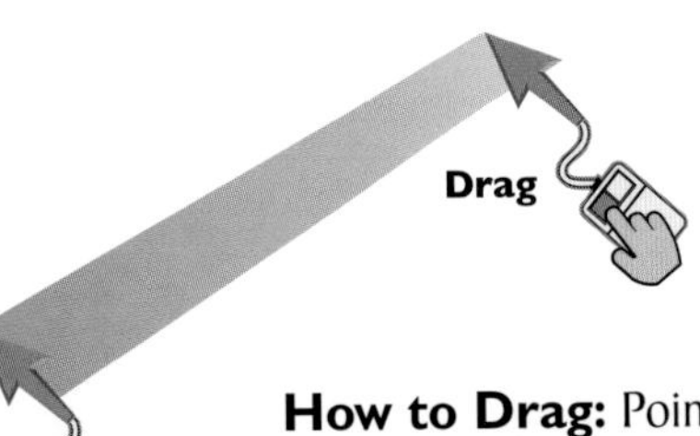



**How to Drag:** Point to the starting place or object. Hold down the mouse button (right or left per instructions), move the mouse to the new location, then release the button.

**Next Step:** If you see this symbol, it means the task you're working on continues on the next page.

**End Task:** Task is complete.

# Introduction

Learning to use PowerPoint is simple and quick with *Easy Microsoft PowerPoint 97, Second Edition.* This book approaches learning *visually*. It is designed so you can look at and follow the steps necessary to complete a task, without having to read paragraphs and paragraphs of information found in other computer reference books!

PowerPoint can be used to create formal presentations or briefings for clients, supervisors, and colleagues. It can also be used to prepare bulletin board flyers or signs. Once created, a presentation or flyer can be displayed on an overhead projection system, shipped off to have 35mm slides created, printed on acetate, or printed as handouts for your audience.

This book is designed for the person who is not familiar with PowerPoint, but knows a little about Windows and how to use a mouse. With that background, we will show you how to create and modify dynamic PowerPoint presentations quickly and easily.

This book is divided into 12 distinct color-coded parts. Within each part there are a series of 1–2 page tasks. Each task contains a brief description of the task and a series of visual steps, represented by PowerPoint screen samples, to guide you. By following the visual steps, you will learn how to accomplish the task. One or two sentences at the bottom of each page describe each step. In the page margins are tips, notes, and warnings. Tips provide hints on performing a task. Notes are additional information about the steps you are learning or references to other, related tasks. Warnings help you to avoid complications or pitfalls as you work with the PowerPoint.

You can use this book as a tutorial for learning PowerPoint and read it front to back, or use it as a reference guide to look up the steps for a specific task.

PART I

# Getting Started Quickly

Welcome to PowerPoint! PowerPoint is an exciting program you can use to create presentations, briefings, or flyers. You can print acetate slides, audience handouts, and notes pages.

This part is designed to help you quickly create, save, and print a simple PowerPoint presentation. You learn about the various parts of the PowerPoint screen, how to move from slide to slide in your presentation, and how to use the built-in Help screens. Additionally, this part shows you how to add a professional design to the background of your slides and provides useful tips on creating effective presentations.

# Tasks

| Task # | | Page # |
|---|---|---|
| 1 | Starting Microsoft PowerPoint | 4 |
| 2 | Creating a Simple Presentation | 5 |
| 3 | Understanding the PowerPoint Screen | 6 |
| 4 | Working with "Click" Placeholders | 8 |
| 5 | Adding New Slides | 9 |
| 6 | Changing the Slide Layout | 10 |
| 7 | Moving from Slide to Slide | 11 |
| 8 | Applying a Presentation Design | 12 |
| 9 | Saving Your Presentation | 13 |
| 10 | Printing Your Slides | 14 |
| 11 | Using the AutoContent Wizard to Create a New Presentation | 16 |
| 12 | Starting a New Presentation | 18 |
| 13 | Opening an Existing Presentation | 19 |
| 14 | Using the Office Assistant to Get Help | 20 |
| 15 | Closing a Presentation | 22 |
| 16 | Exiting Microsoft PowerPoint | 23 |
| 17 | Tips for Improving the Content of Your Slides | 24 |
| 18 | Tips for Improving the Design of Your Slides | 26 |

# Task 1: Starting Microsoft PowerPoint

## Opening PowerPoint

**You can get to Microsoft PowerPoint through the Start button on the Windows taskbar.**

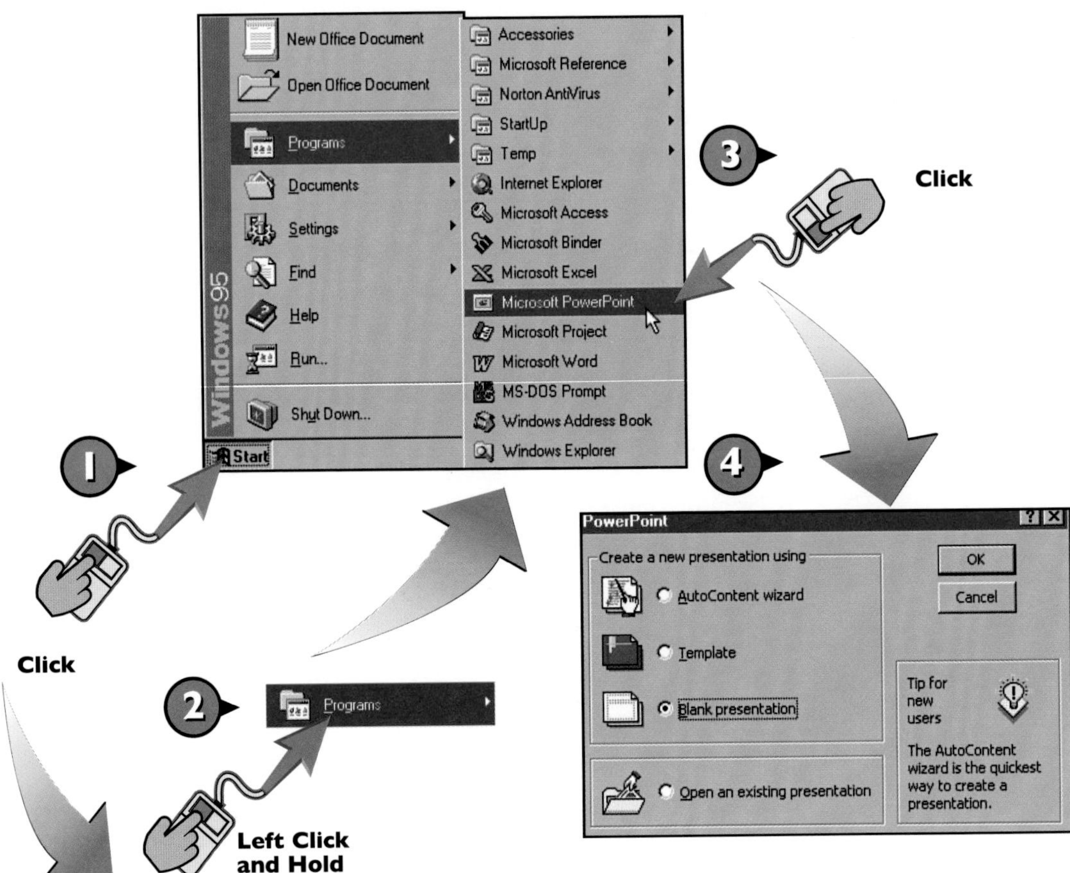


1. Click the **Start** button on the taskbar.
2. Position the mouse pointer on **Programs**.
3. Slide the mouse pointer to the right and click on **Microsoft PowerPoint**.
4. The initial **PowerPoint** screen appears.

### Understanding the Taskbar

**The programs you have open appear as buttons on the Windows taskbar (next to the Start button).**

# Task 2: Creating a Simple Presentation

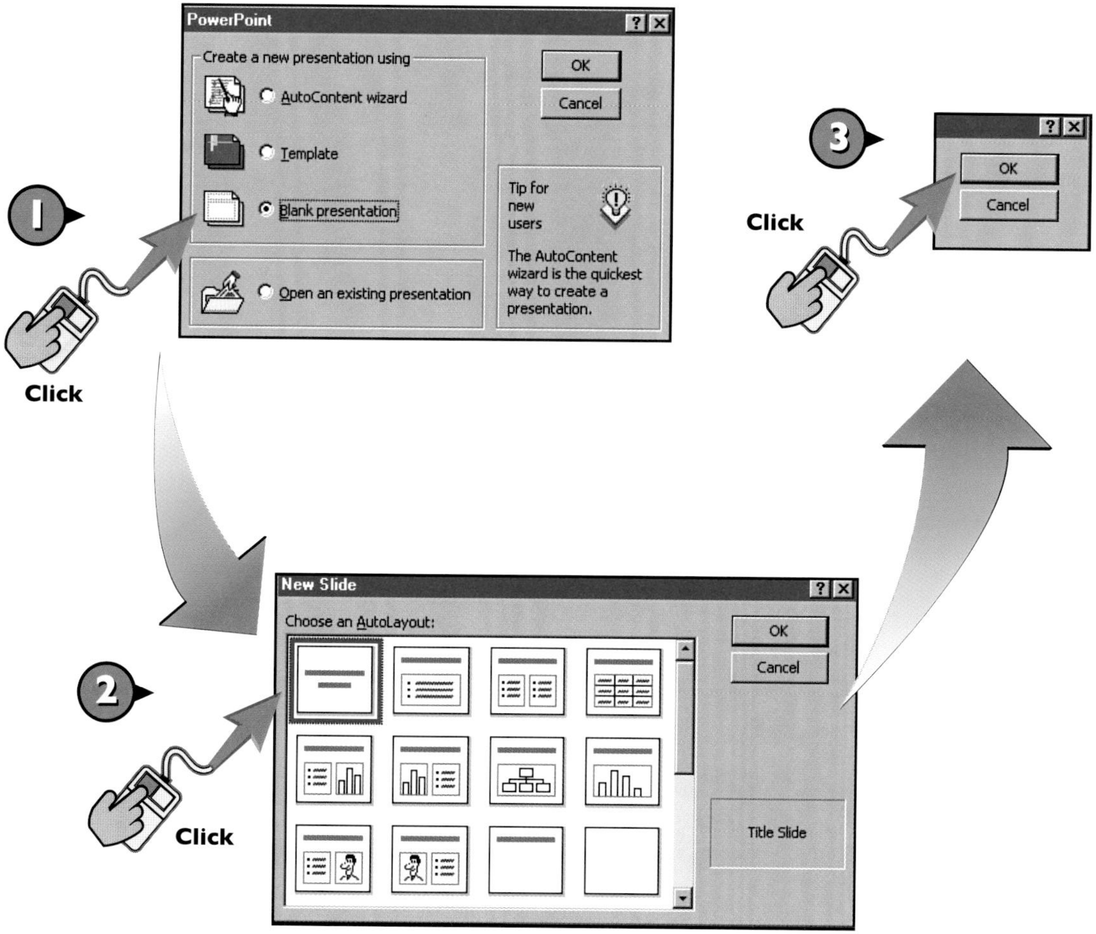

1. Click **Blank Presentation** to create a new PowerPoint presentation.
2. Choose an **AutoLayout** from the samples displayed. Scroll to see additional layout options.
3. Choose **OK**. The first slide in your presentation appears with the layout you selected.

## Starting a New Presentation from the Initial PowerPoint Screen

You have the option of creating a new presentation or opening an existing presentation from the initial PowerPoint screen.

### Identifying Slide Layouts

When you click on a layout, a description appears in the lower-right corner of the dialog box.

### Creating More Presentations

See Task 12 to learn how to create additional presentations while working in PowerPoint.

# Task 3: Understanding the PowerPoint Screen

## Getting Acquainted with PowerPoint

**The PowerPoint screen has features similar to other Microsoft Office programs (such as Word or Excel); for example, the menu bar, toolbars, and scrollbars.**

Start Here

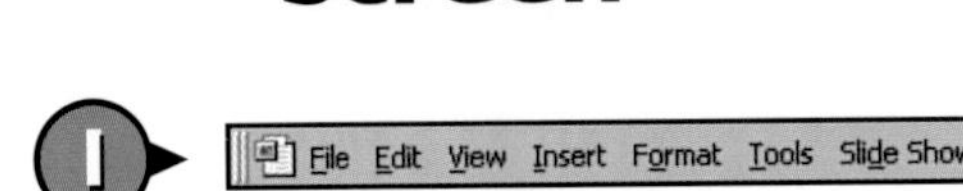


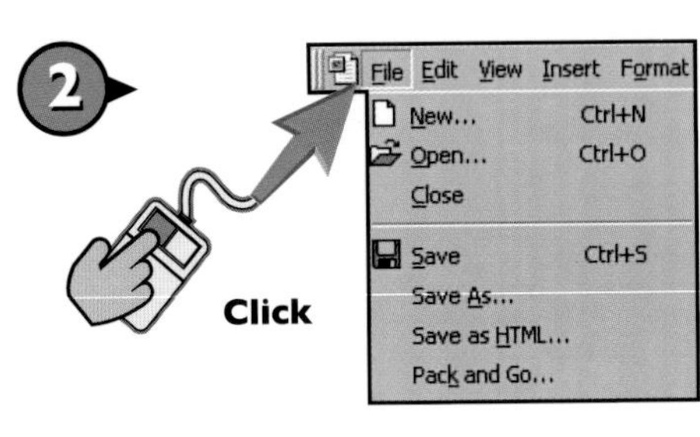


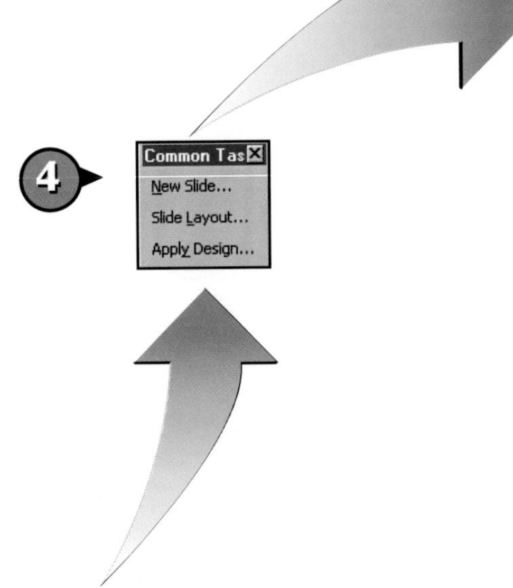

The ***menu bar*** appears at the top of the PowerPoint screen and organizes PowerPoint commands, or activities.

Click on a menu to see the list of available commands. Toolbar icons appear in front of menu commands, and keyboard shortcuts appear after the commands.

The Standard and Formatting toolbars appear below the menu bar. Position the mouse pointer over a toolbar icon button until you see a ***ScreenTip*** showing the command icon.

The Common Tasks toolbar also appears on the screen. Drag the colored title to move the toolbar.

### Displaying Inactive Icons

**Some menu choices and toolbar icons might appear grayed out, indicating they are inactive at this time.**

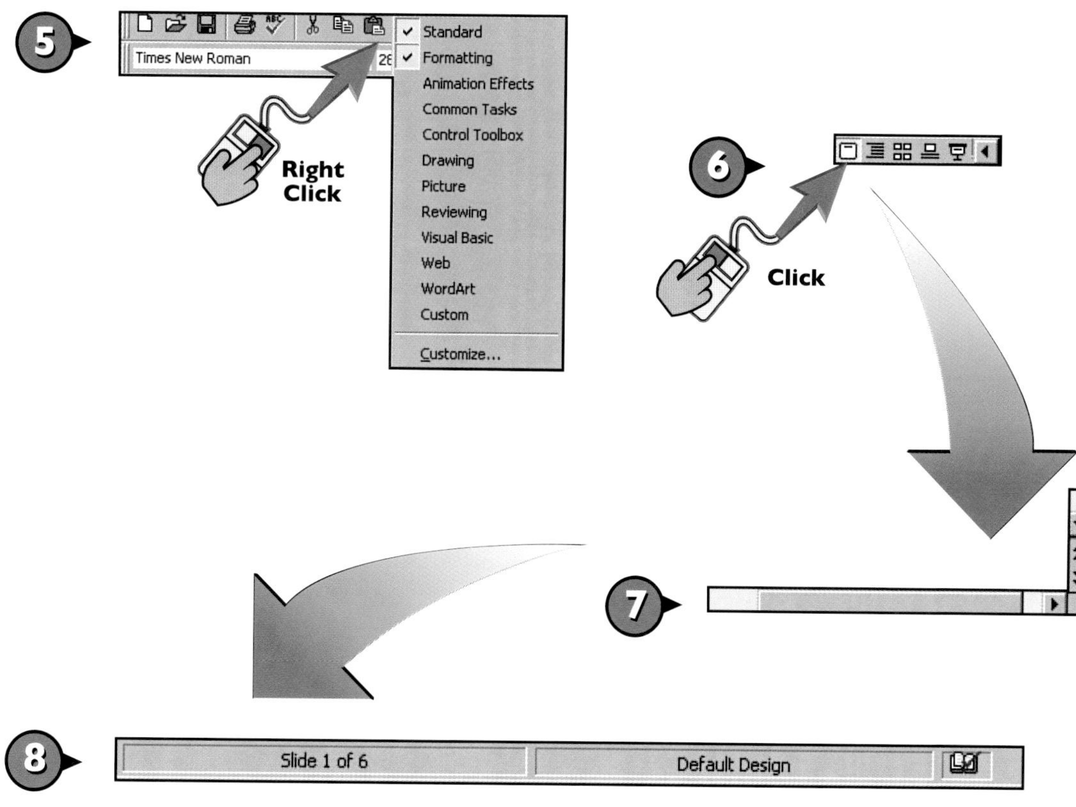


5. Right-click on parts of the screen or on slide objects to see shortcut menus.

6. Use the View buttons (located in the lower-left corner of the PowerPoint screen) to switch among the PowerPoint Views—Slide, Outline, Slide Sorter, Notes Pages, or Slide Show.

7. The scrollbars appear to the right and bottom of the PowerPoint screen.

8. The status bar indicates the current slide number, the total number of slides, and the design being used on the presentation.

**Right Click to Display Shortcut Menus**

**Use Shortcut menus to display a specific set of commands used with parts of the screen or with slide objects.**

**Displaying Other Slides**

**See Task 7 for specific steps on moving from slide to slide. See Task 8 for information on changing the presentation design.**

# Task 4: Working with "Click" Placeholders

## Understanding Slide Placeholders

**Most slide layouts contain placeholders where you can add text, chart, or clip art objects. These placeholders control the size and format of the objects.**

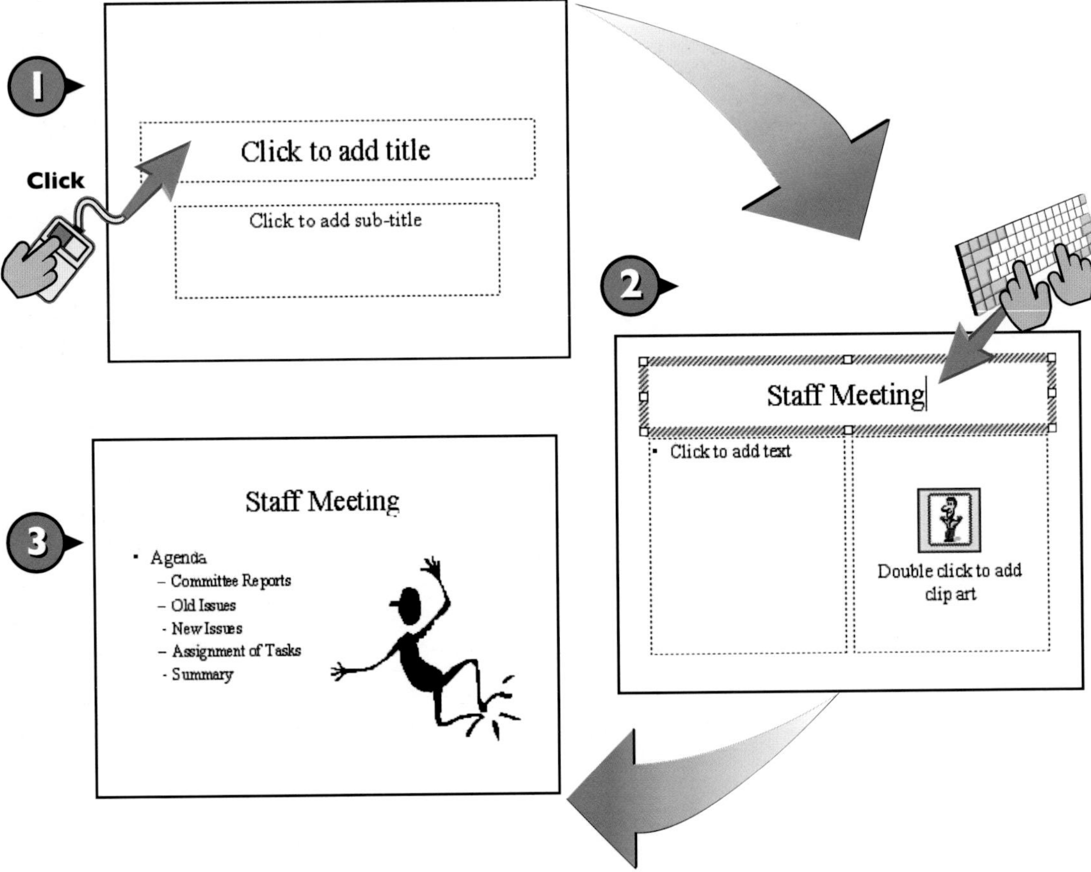


1. The Title Slide Layout contains two placeholders, one for the title and the other for a sub-title; click anywhere inside a placeholder.
2. Begin typing the desired text (this slide shows three "click" placeholders).
3. This figure shows a slide that contains a completed title, bulleted list, and clip art placeholder.

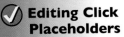

### Editing Click Placeholders

**When you click in a text placeholder such as a title or bulleted list, a flashing cursor appears to indicate you are editing the placeholder.**

# Task 5: Adding New Slides

Start Here

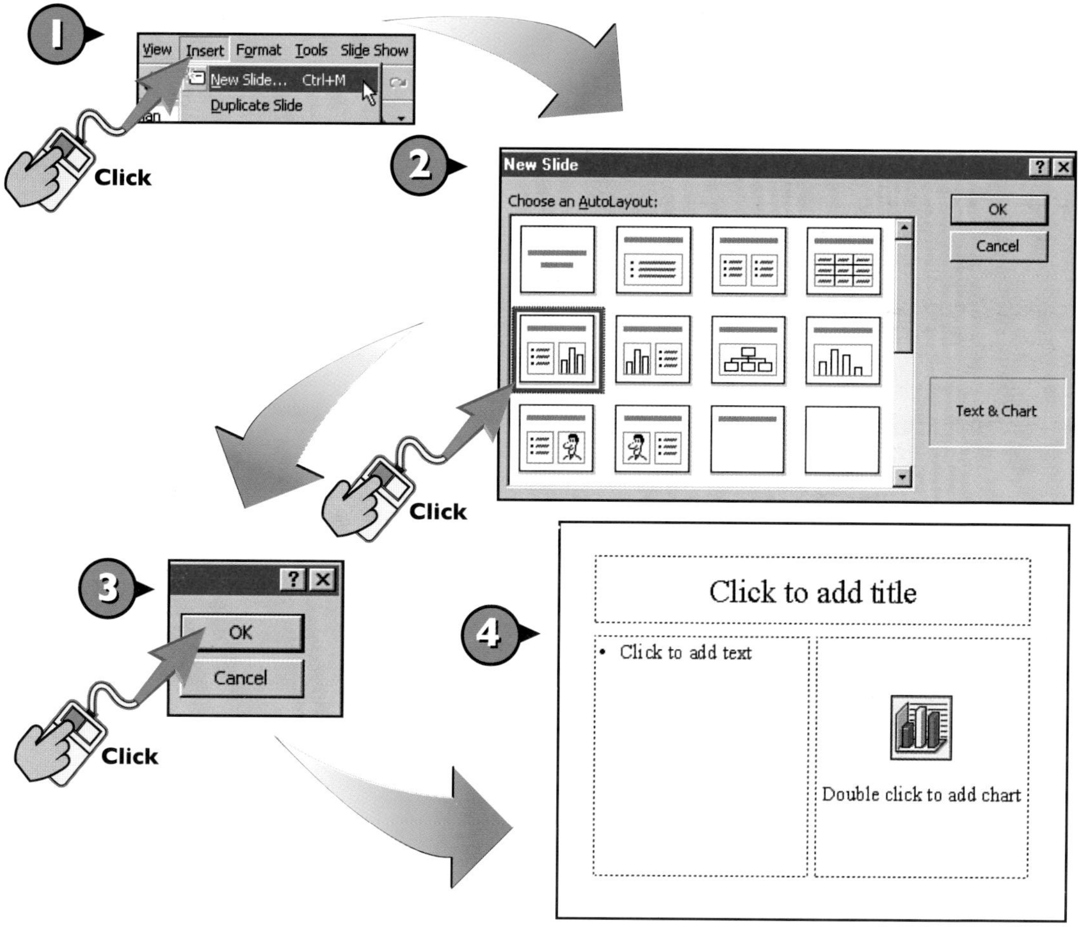

1. Choose **Insert, New Slide**.

2. Select a slide layout; a brief description appears in the lower-right corner of the dialog box.

3. Choose **OK**.

4. The new slide is added to your presentation with the layout you selected.

## Adding More Slides to Your Presentation

Each slide you create can have a different layout.

### Scroll to See Additional Slide Layouts

Drag the scrollbar in the New Slide dialog box to see other slide layout choices.

### Creating Graphic Charts

See Part 6, "Working with Graphic Charts," to learn how to create graphic charts in PowerPoint.

# Task 6: Changing the Slide Layout

## Choosing a Different Slide Layout

You can easily change the arrangement and type of "click" placeholders on a slide by selecting a different slide layout.

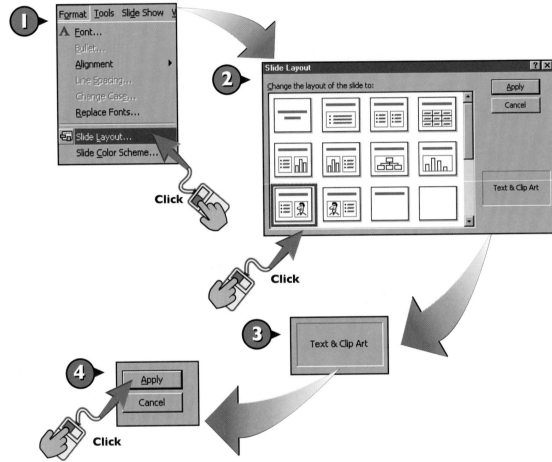

1. Choose **Format, Slide Layout**.
2. In the Slide Layout dialog box, the layout currently being used is selected. Choose a new layout.
3. Read the description for the selected layout in the lower-right corner to ensure you selected the correct layout.
4. Choose **Apply** to change the slide layout.

### Adding Clip Art Images to Slides

See Part 4, "Adding Clip Art to Slides," Task 1, to learn how to add clip art to your presentation.

# Task 7: Moving from Slide to Slide

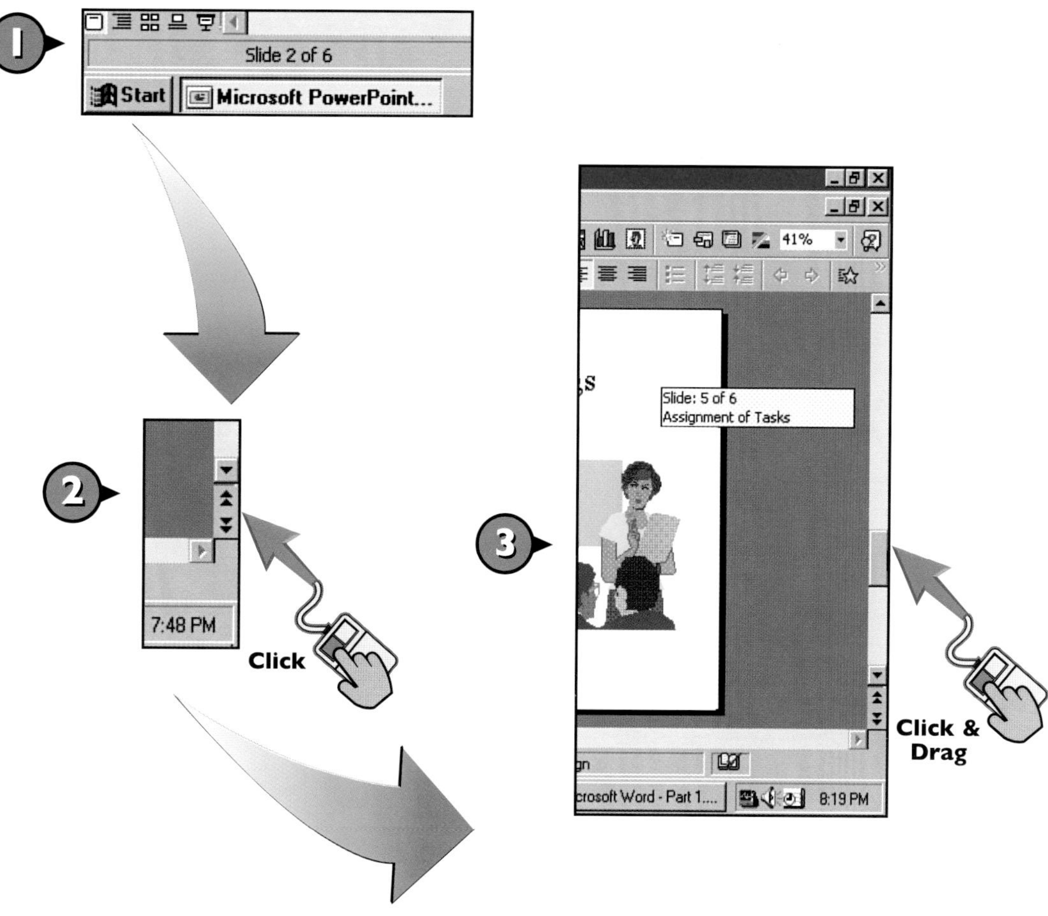


## Displaying Other Slides

**Most presentations consist of several slides. You can move forward or backward in your presentation with a few simple mouse clicks.**

Look at the slide indicator on the status bar to determine which is the active slide.

To move forward or backward one slide at a time in the presentation, click on the **Next Slide** or **Previous Slide** button in the lower-right corner of the PowerPoint screen.

To move to a specific slide in the presentation, drag the **scroll box** until the yellow pop-up box displays the slide title and number you want.

**Dragging the Scroll Box**

**If you have not added titles to your slides, the yellow pop-up ScreenTip displays only the slide numbers as you drag the scroll box.**

PART I

# Task 8: Applying a Presentation Design

## Changing the Appearance of the Presentation

**PowerPoint includes a set of presentation design templates that quickly give your presentation a professional appearance.**

Start Here

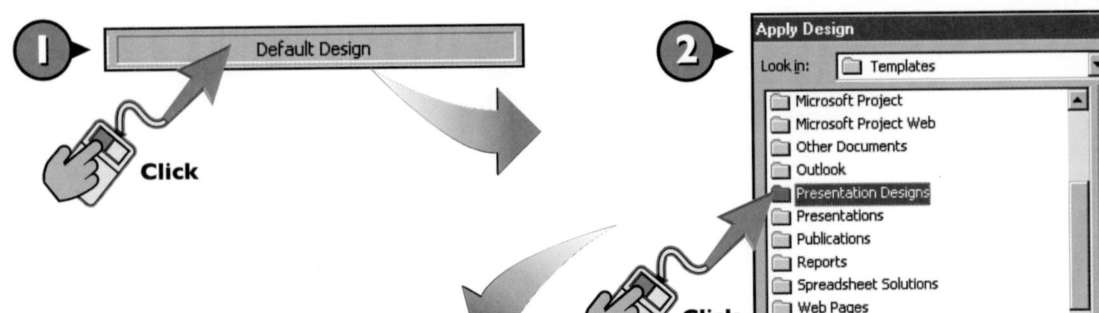


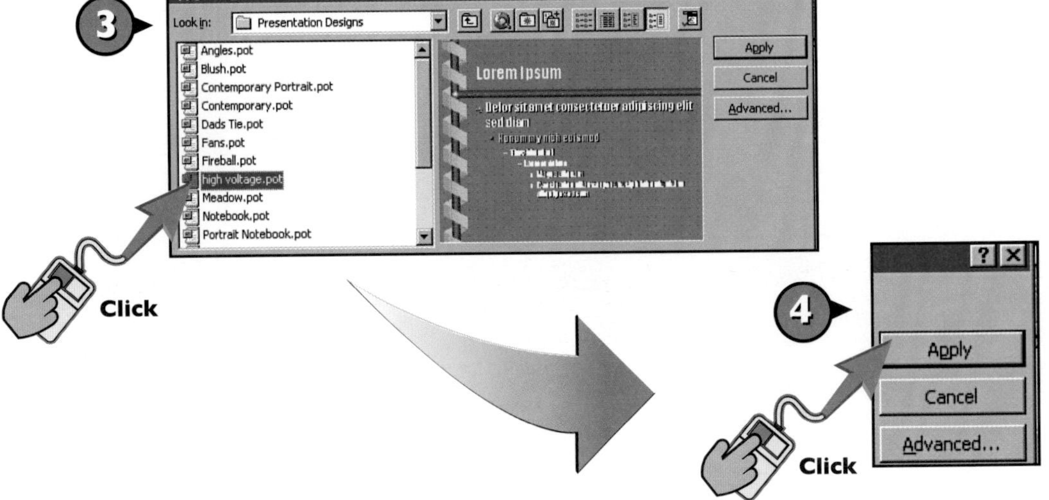


Apply
Cancel
Advanced...
Click

1. Double-click the design name indicator on the status bar.
2. Double-click the **Presentation Designs** folder in the Apply Design dialog box.
3. Choose a design to apply to your presentation; a sample of the design appears in the preview box.
4. Choose **Apply**.

### Locating Other Design Templates

**Additional design templates are available in the ValuPak folder on the Microsoft Office 97 CD. Or click Help, Microsoft on the Web, Free Stuff if you have access to the Internet.**

End Task

# Task 9: Saving Your Presentation

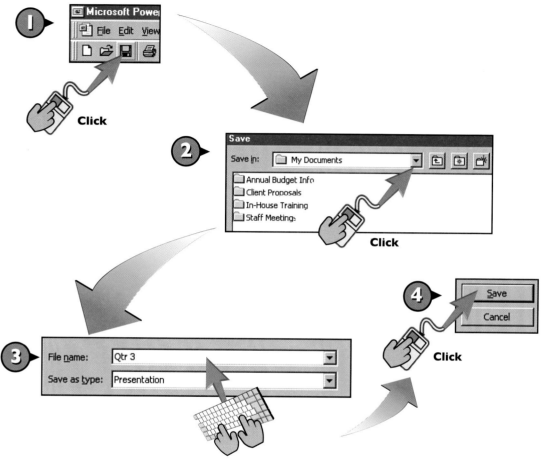


1 Click the **Save** button. This is the only step necessary if the file has already been saved.

2 From the **Save In** drop-down list, choose the folder where you would like to store the presentation.

3 Click in the **File Name** box and type the name for the presentation; maximum name length is 255 characters.

4 Choose **Save**.

## Saving Your Work

Whether you have created a new file or are simply making changes to an existing presentation, be sure you save your presentations often.

### Saving a Copy of the Presentation

To save a copy of a file and keep the original unchanged, use the **File, Save As** command, and give the copy a new name.

### Invalid File Name Characters

The following characters cannot be used in filenames:

/ \ > < * ? " | : ;

# Task 10: Printing Your Slides

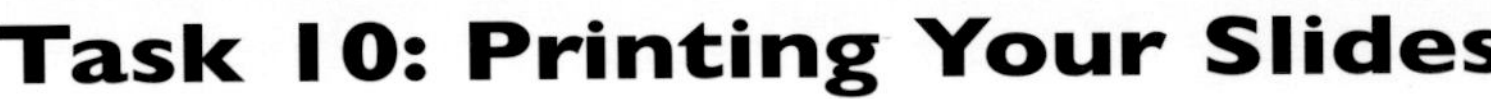

## Previewing and Printing Slides

**Use the Slide Show feature to preview your PowerPoint presentation, to make sure it is correct before you waste paper printing it. Then choose the print options you need.**

Start Here

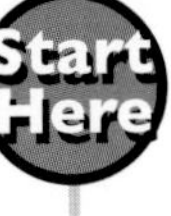

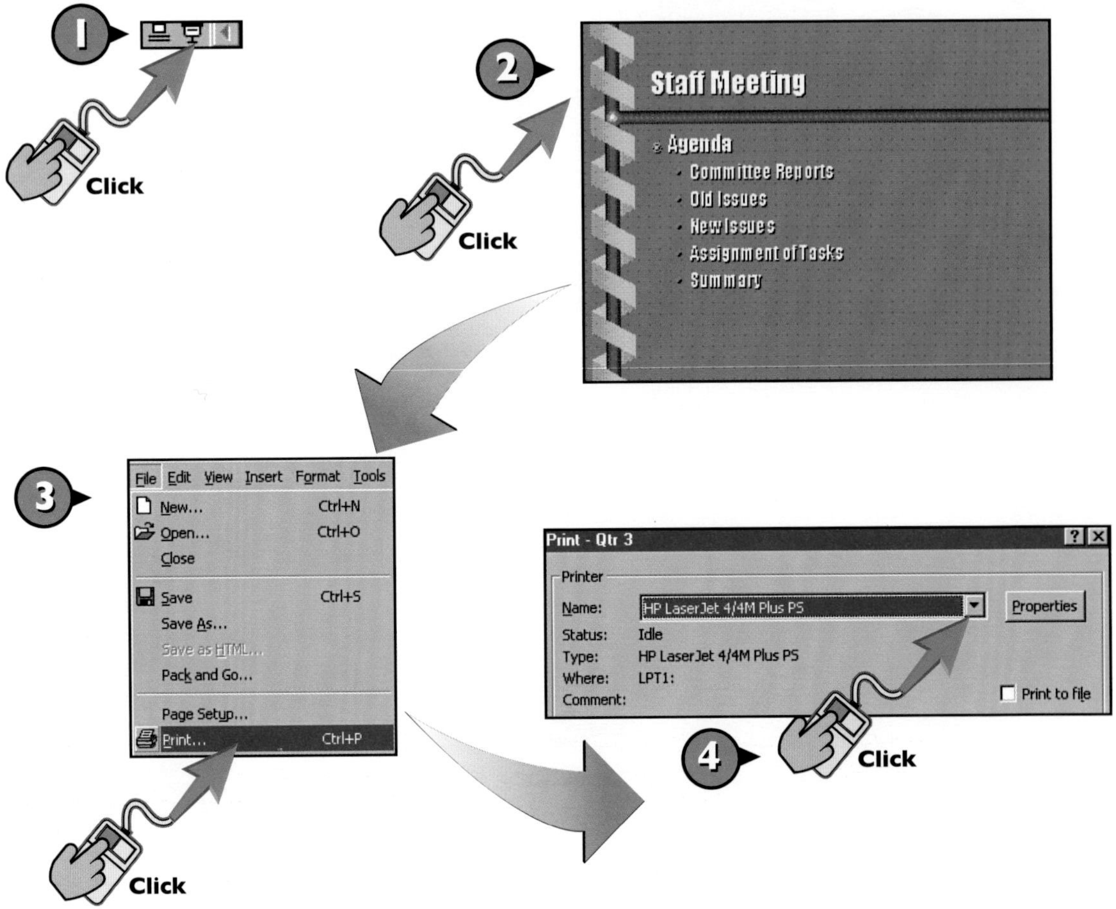

1. Click the **Slide Show** button, located in the lower-left corner of the screen, to preview your presentation slides.
2. Click the left mouse button once or press **Page Down** to advance to the next slide in the presentation. On the last slide, clicking the mouse exits the Slide Show.
3. Choose **File, Print** to display the Print dialog box, where you can designate the print options.
4. The default printer is listed at the top of the Print dialog box. If necessary, choose another printer.

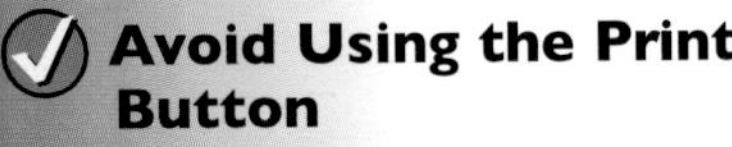

**Avoid Using the Print Button**
**If you click the Print button located on the Standard toolbar, your presentation is sent to the printer immediately, with no prompts for any print information.**

Next Step

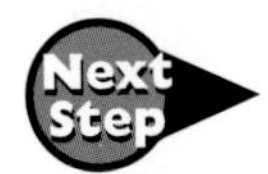

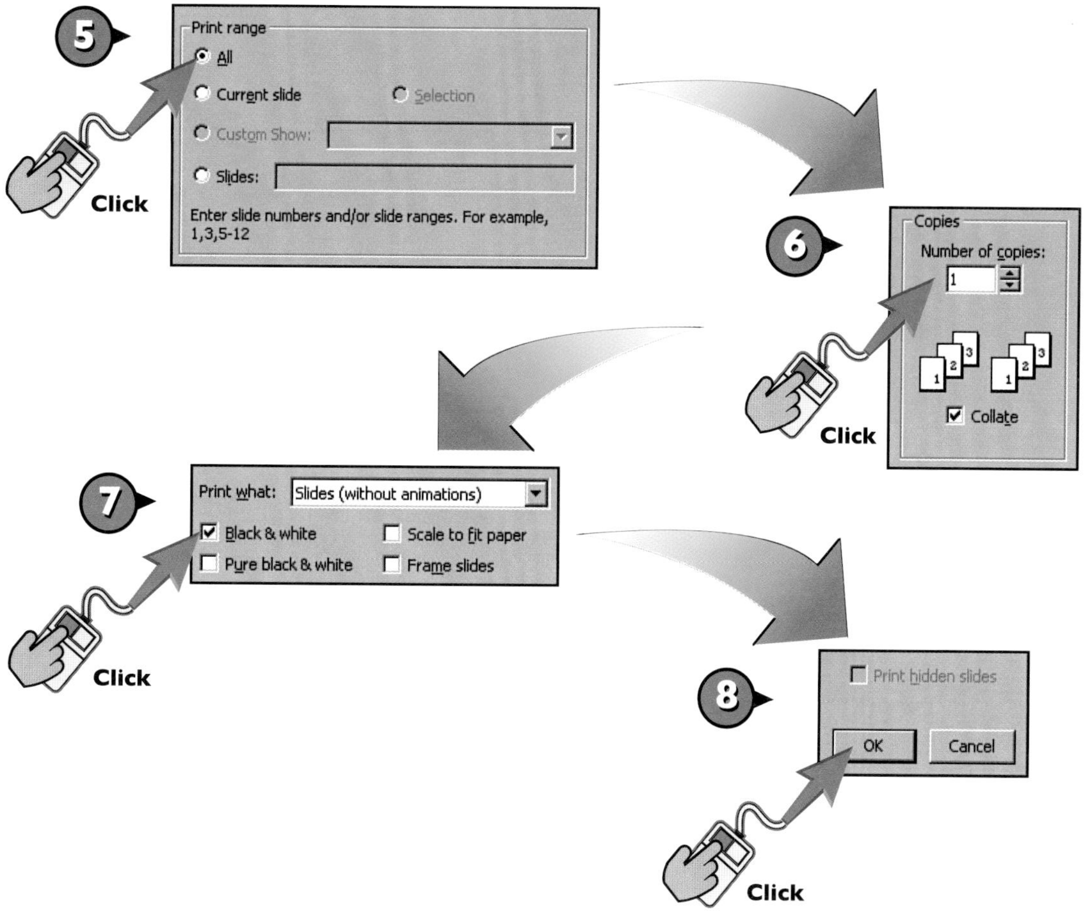

5

Print range
All
Current slide
Selection
Custom Show:
Slides:
Enter slide numbers and/or slide ranges. For example, 1,3,5-12

Click

6

Copies
Number of copies:
1
Collate

Click

7

Print what: Slides (without animations)
Black & white
Scale to fit paper
Pure black & white
Frame slides

Click

8

Print hidden slides
OK
Cancel

Click

5 You can print all the slides in your presentation, the slide currently displayed, or only slides you specify.

6 To print more than one copy of the slides, use the up arrow button or type the number of copies.

7 When printing draft copies of your slides, choose **Black & White** to print with shades of gray.

8 When you have selected the print options, choose **OK**.

**Getting Help in Dialog Boxes**

**To learn more about options in dialog boxes, click the Help button, represented by a question mark (?) in the upper-right corner of the dialog box. Then click the option.**

**Other Printing Alternatives**

**See Part 10, "Printing Your Presentation," for the steps to print audience handouts, speaker's notes, and an outline of your presentation.**

## Getting Started with Professionally Designed Presentations

**Do you need help deciding what topics to include in your presentation? Use the AutoContent Wizard and select from 23 presentation templates.**

**Another Way to Access the Wizard**
**You can also access the wizard through the initial PowerPoint screen. Refer to Task 1, Step 4.**



# Task 11: Using the AutoContent Wizard to Create a New Presentation

Start Here

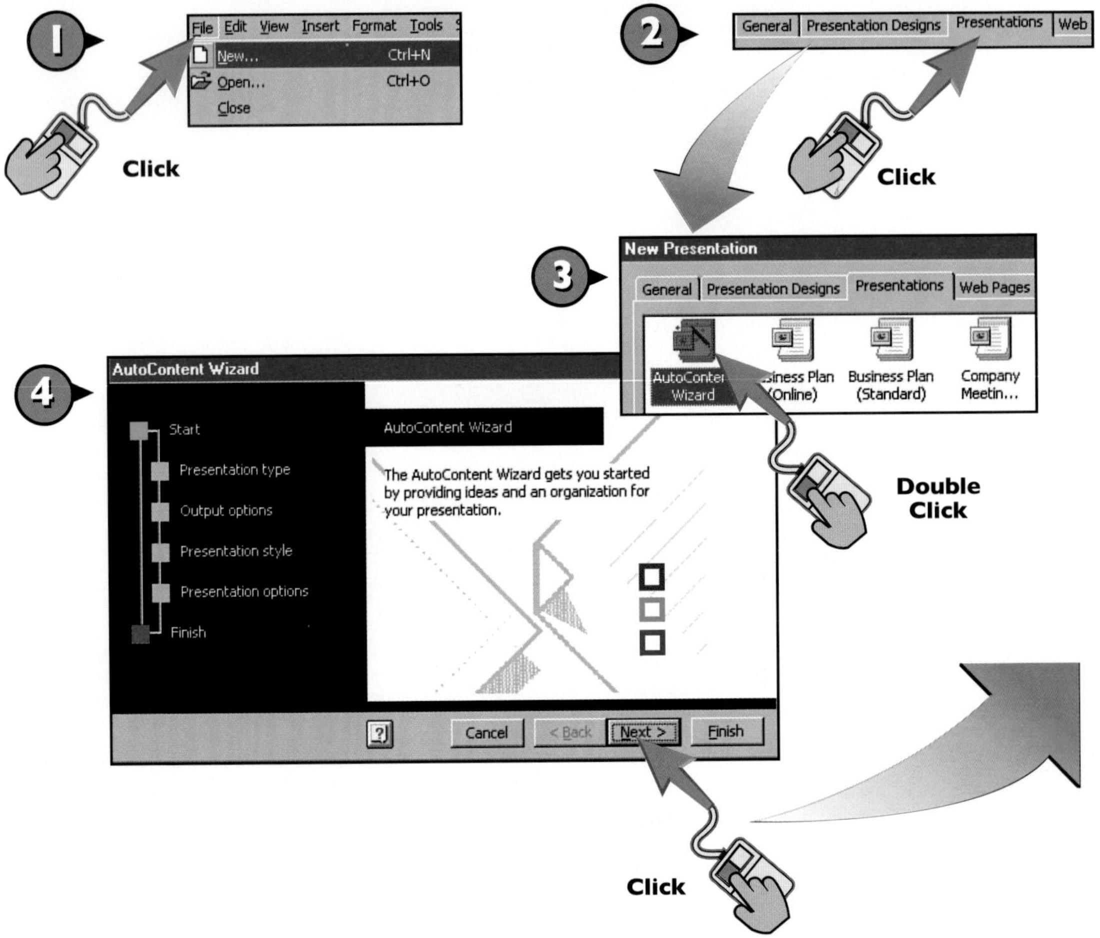

1. Choose **File, New**.
2. Select the **Presentations** tab in the New Presentations dialog box.
3. Double-click the **AutoContent Wizard** icon. (This icon might be labeled AutoContent Wizard.pwz.)
4. The initial screen appears; click **Next** to advance to the next step in the wizard.

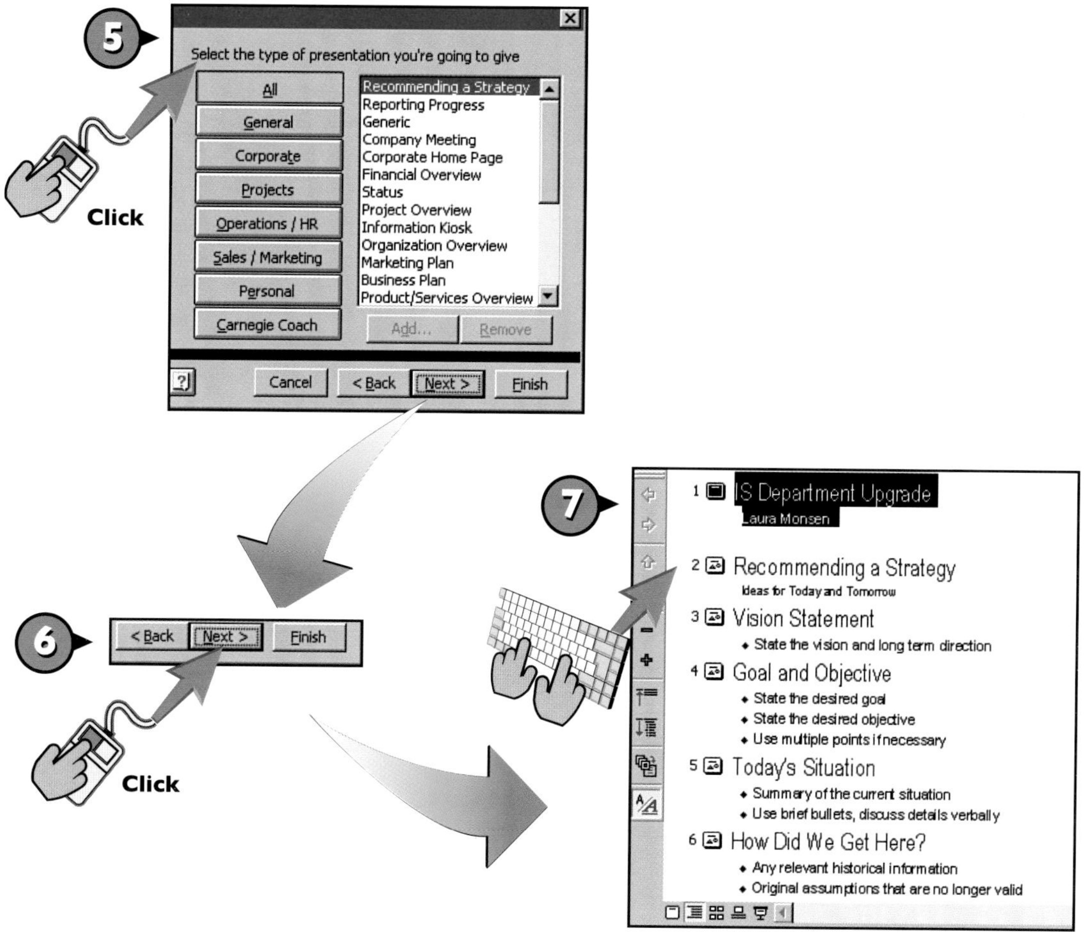

5 Choose a category and presentation type from the list.

6 Choose **Next** to advance through each step in the wizard. Choose the **Finish** button to complete the wizard on the last step.

7 After you complete the wizard, the new presentation is displayed in the Outline View.

**Skipping Steps in the AutoContent Wizard**
**Use the Roadmap in the AutoContent Wizard to quickly move to the steps you need.**

**Internet and Intranet Presentations**
**You can use the AutoContent Wizard to create online presentations to use on the Internet or your company's intranet.**

**Exploring the Outline View**
**Refer to Part 2, "Working in the Other Views," for information on using the Outline View.**

# Task 12: Starting a New Presentation

## Creating a Blank Presentation While in PowerPoint

You can create new, blank presentations while you are working on other presentations in PowerPoint.

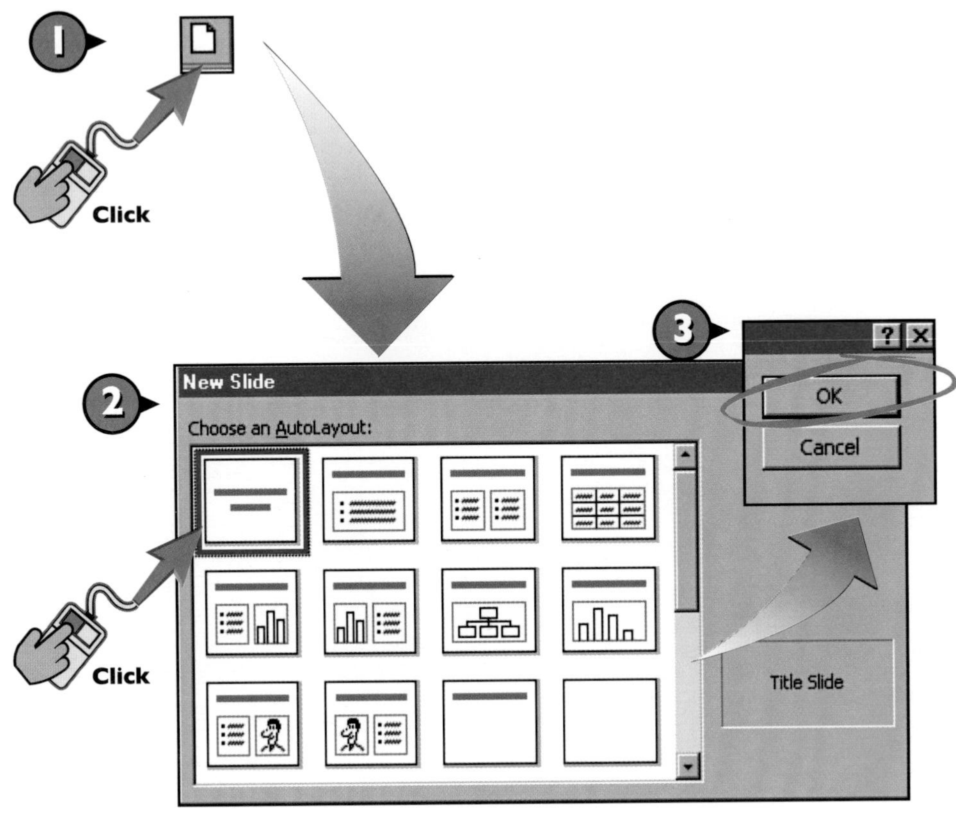


1. Click the **New** button on the Standard toolbar.
2. In the New Slide dialog box, choose a slide layout for the first slide in your new presentation.
3. Click **OK**. The new presentation is created, with the first slide displayed.

**Working with Several Open Presentations**
Use the Window menu to switch back and forth between the presentations you have open.

# Task 13: Opening an Existing Presentation

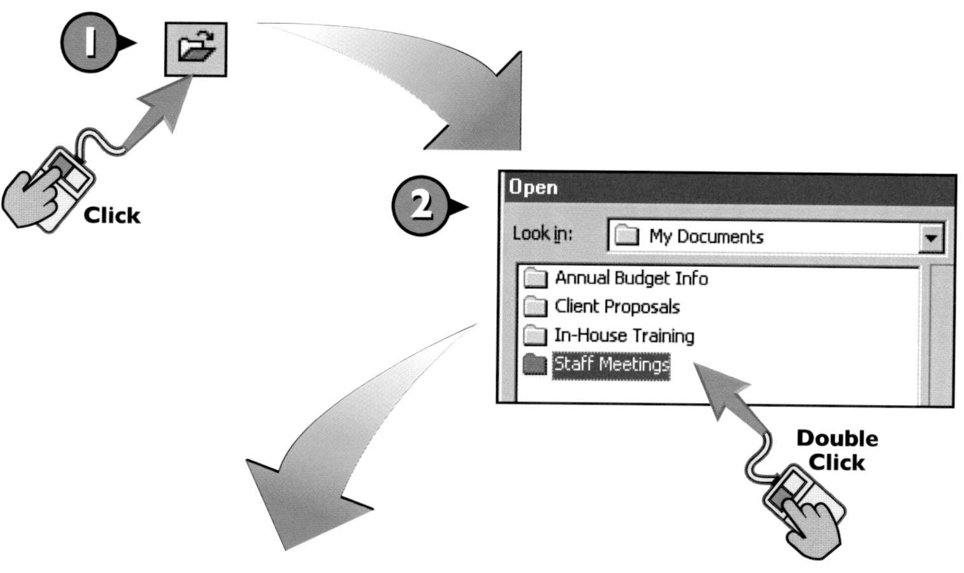

1. Click the **Open** button on the Standard toolbar.
2. In the Open dialog box, if the file is located in a folder under My Documents, double-click the folder that contains the file you are looking for.
3. Double-click the name of the file you want to open.

## Viewing Presentations You've Already Created

**Opening a PowerPoint presentation is similar to opening other Windows files.**

**Searching for Files**
**If the file you want to open is not in the My Documents folder, you can use the Advanced button in the Open dialog box to search for the file.**

## Working with the Built-in Help Screens

**One of the easiest ways to get help while using PowerPoint is to ask the Office Assistant. If you type in a few words—such as creating charts or printing slides—the Office Assistant will list several Help topics you can choose from.**

# Task 14: Using the Office Assistant to Get Help

Start Here

Click

What would you like to do?

Open a presentation

Type your question here, and then click Search.

Search

Tips Options Close

What would you like to do?

Open a presentation

create slides

Search

Click

What would you like to do?

Make a new slide

Create multiple slides from items on a single slide

Create a new slide from titles of other slides

Create an agenda slide

Copy a file

See more...

create slides

Search

Tips Options Close

Click

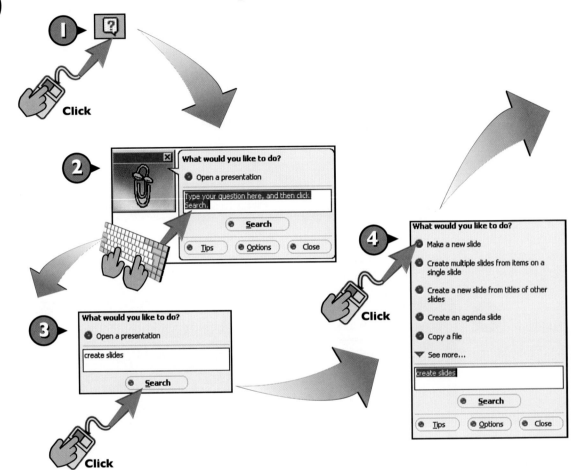

1. Click the **Office Assistant** button on the Standard toolbar.
2. In the **What would you like to do?** dialog box, type a description of what you are seeking help on.
3. Click **Search** or press **Enter**.
4. A list of Help topics appears. Click the topic you want to view, or type another description.

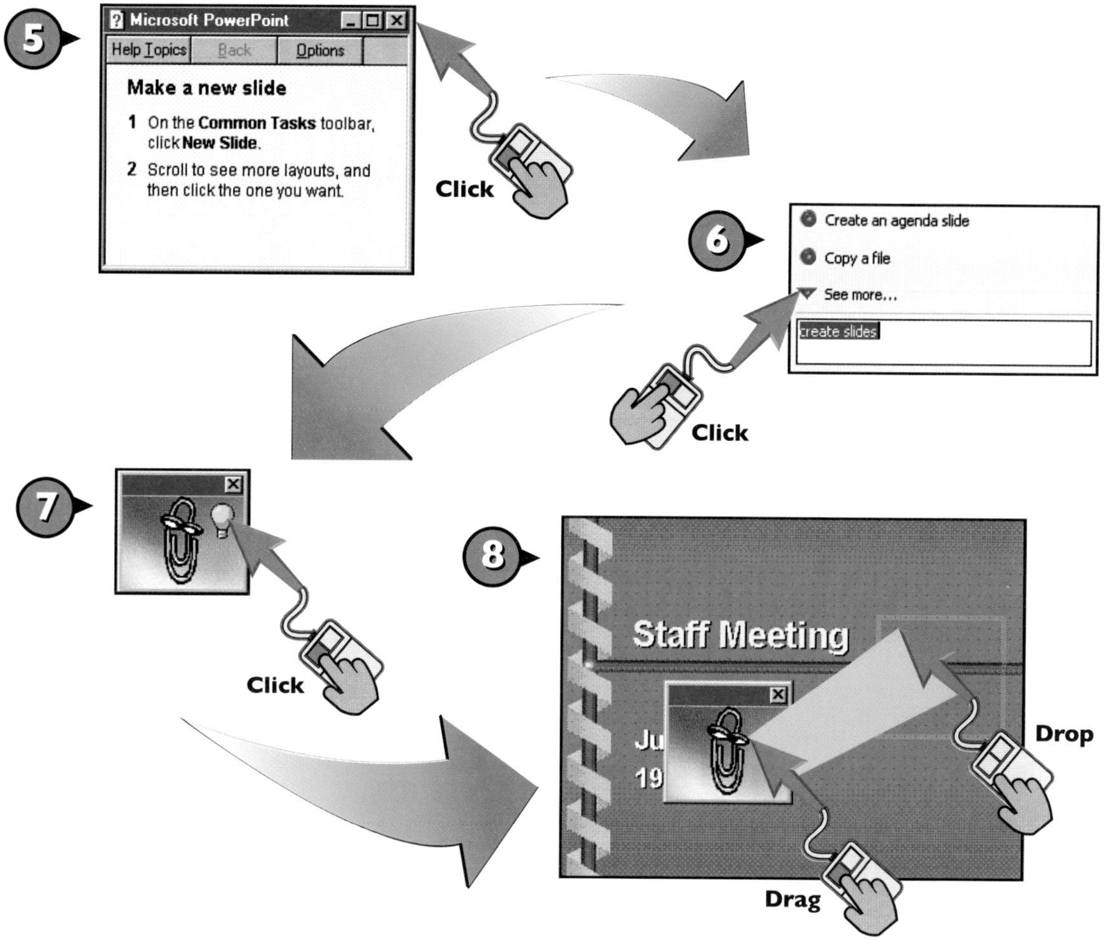

5 You can minimize or close the Help topic after you read it.

6 The list of Help topics (shown in step 4) often includes a **See more** option; click it to view additional topics.

7 When a lightbulb appears next to the Office Assistant, click it to see a relevant **TIP**.

8 You can drag and drop the Office Assistant window to any part of the PowerPoint screen.

**Understanding the Office Assistant**
**Want to see the Help topics for the last description you typed? Simply click the Office Assistant; the description is still displayed. Then click Search in the Office Assistant Help window.**

**Getting Help from Microsoft's Web Site**
**If you have access to the Internet, choose Help, Microsoft on the Web to see a list of PowerPoint Help topics on Microsoft's Web site.**

# Task 15: Closing a Presentation

## Clearing the Presentation Off the Screen

**Closing a presentation is like placing it in a file cabinet. You should close presentations you no longer need to work with or display.**

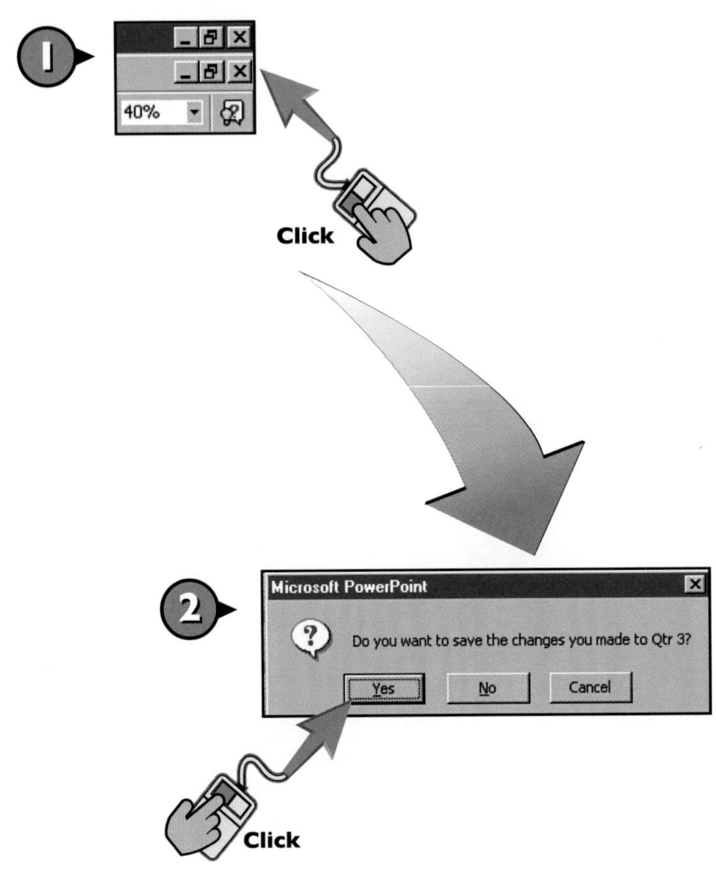


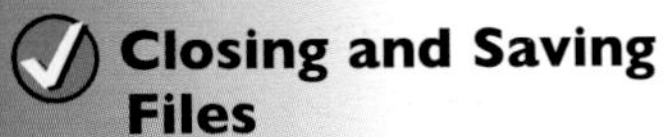

**Closing and Saving Files**

**You can also choose File, Close to close your active presentation.**

**If the file has not been saved previously, PowerPoint displays the File Save dialog box. See Task 9 for the steps to save a file.**

1. Click the lower **Close** button (the one in the PowerPoint menu bar) in the upper-right corner of the PowerPoint screen.

2. If you have made changes to the presentation, PowerPoint prompts you to save the changes. Choose **Yes** to save the changes and close the presentation. Choose **No** to close the presentation without saving the changes. Choose **Cancel** to cancel the command to close the presentation.

# Task 16: Exiting Microsoft PowerPoint

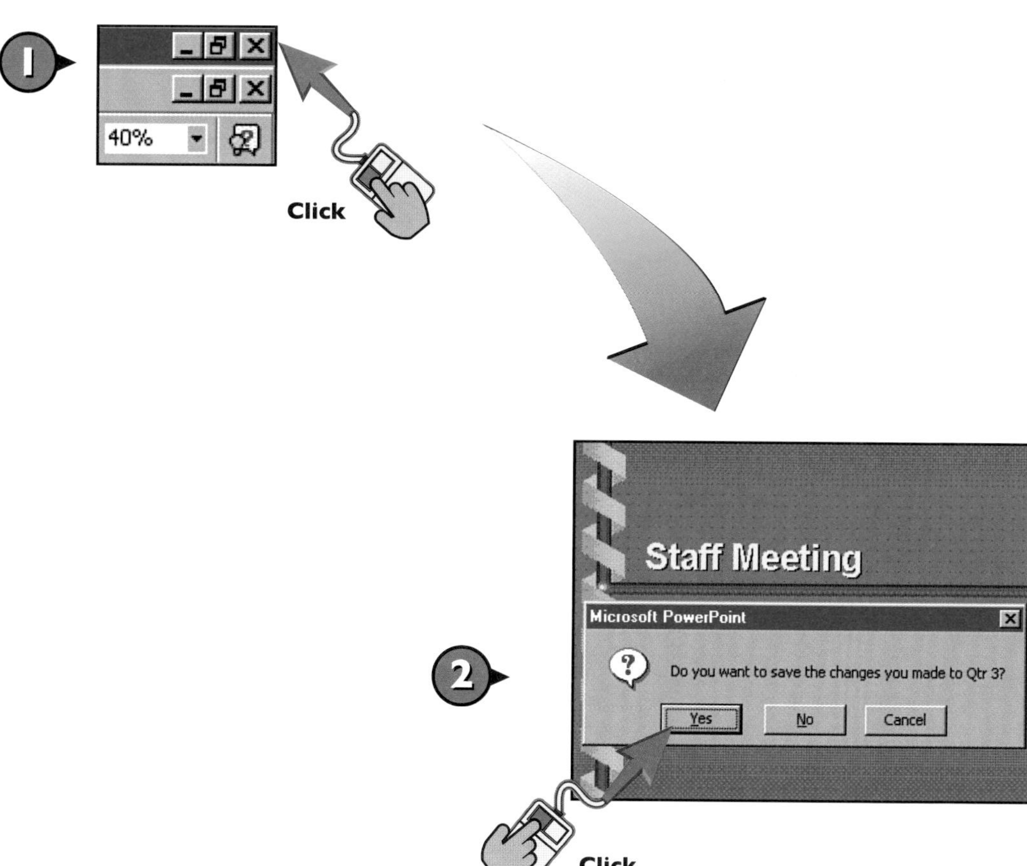


1 Click the top **Close** button (the one in the PowerPoint title bar) in the upper right corner of the PowerPoint screen.

2 If you made changes but have not saved them, a prompt appears for each presentation, asking about saving the changes. Choose **Yes** to save the changes. Choose **No** to exit without saving the changes. Choose **Cancel** to cancel the command to exit PowerPoint.

## Closing the PowerPoint Program

**Closing PowerPoint is similar to closing any program.**

**Using the Menu to Close PowerPoint**
You can also choose **File, Exit** to close PowerPoint.

**Minimizing PowerPoint**
If you want to keep PowerPoint open but need to work in another program, minimize PowerPoint instead of closing it.

## Validating the Presentation Content

**Part of creating effective presentations is to step back from the details and determine the overall impression your presentation will make on the audience. Is it clear? Does it flow logically?**

# Task 17: Tips for Improving the Content of Your Slides

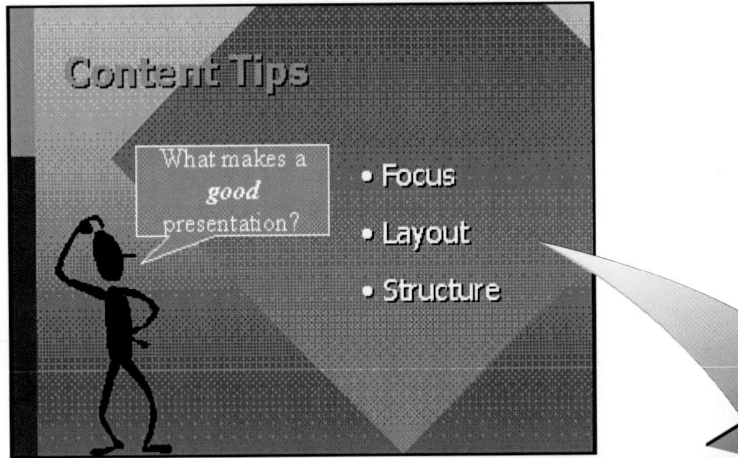


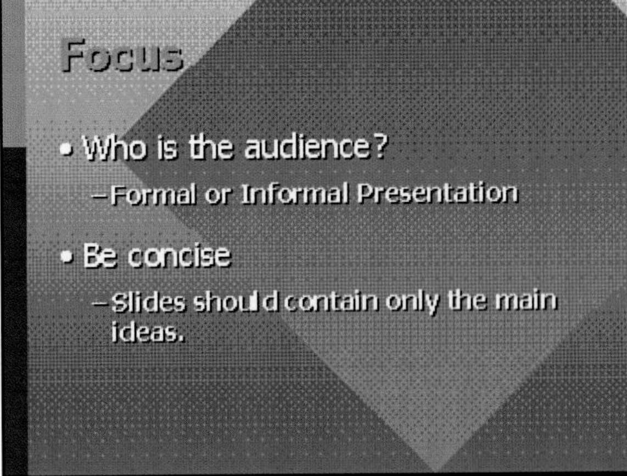

1. When you have a short list of bullets, use a slide layout that combines bullets and clip art or bullets and a chart for more effective use of the slide space.

2. The language and humor you use for casual, internal presentations is very different from what you use for external, formal presentations.



Next Step

**Layout**

- Balance
  - –Use a variety of slide types.
- Simplicity
  - –Use "Blank Space" effectively

**Structure**

- Introduce each topic
- Transition smoothly from topic to topic
- Summarize the main points presented

Sometimes a graphic chart or table can convey more information than paragraphs of text. Place the most important information in the upper-left corner of the slide.

Use the Title slide layout to introduce or conclude a topic. Make sure you present the topics in a logical order; don't jump from topic to topic.

**How Detailed Should the Slide Text Be?**

**It is not necessary to include paragraphs of explanations in your slides. Instead, use Speaker's Notes Pages to write explanations for each topic you will discuss. The text on the slides should summarize the topics.**

## Checking the Presentation Design

**The design choices you make can enhance or degrade the information you are presenting. Legibility is essential—text case, font type, and color are critical elements that lend legibility to the overall design of your slides.**

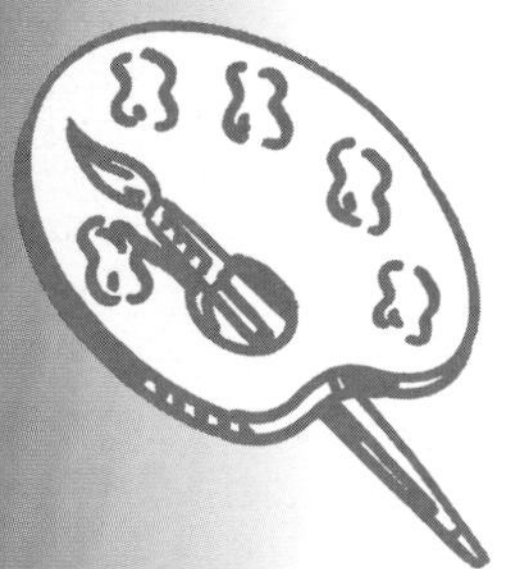

# Task 18: Tips for Improving the Design of Your Slides

Design Tips
• Uppercase vs Mixed Case
• Serif vs Sans Serif
• Using Colors Effectively

UPPERCASE vs Mixed Case

• IT WILL TAKE YOUR AUDIENCE LONGER TO READ SLIDES THAT ARE IN ALL UPPERCASE.

• Instead, use uppercase to EMPHASIZE specific text in your slides.

1 One of the most common design mistakes is adding too many objects to your slides.

2 Another mistake is to use only uppercase letters in your slides.

Serif vs Sans Serif

- Serif font

  Times New Roman, font size 36

- Sans Serif font

  Arial, font size 36

Choosing the Right Colors

- Some people cannot distinguish red from green.
- Avoid using similar colors next to one another.

Serif fonts are formal fonts, but somewhat difficult to read quickly. Sans serif fonts are less formal, and a better choice if your presentation is given in a large room or auditorium.

If you decide to change the colors of text or chart data, make sure you choose contrasting colors.

**Changing Text Appearance**

**See Part 3, "Working with Text," Task 9 and Task 11, for steps to change the font type and text color.**

PART 2

# Working in the Other Views

In Part 1, "Getting Started Quickly," we worked exclusively with the Slide View. PowerPoint has three other views you can use to create and modify your presentations. Part 2 introduces you to these views and the ways in which you can use them.

The Slide Sorter View is used to move, copy, and delete slides. Use the Outline View to create presentations that are mostly text or bulleted lists. In the Notes Pages View, you can create printed notes to use when you give presentations.

# Tasks

Task 1: Introducing the Views in PowerPoint

## Getting Acquainted with the PowerPoint Views

**Four views are PowerPoint available in PowerPoint for creating and enhancing your presentations. You use the View buttons at the lower-left corner of the PowerPoint screen to switch views.**

Start Here

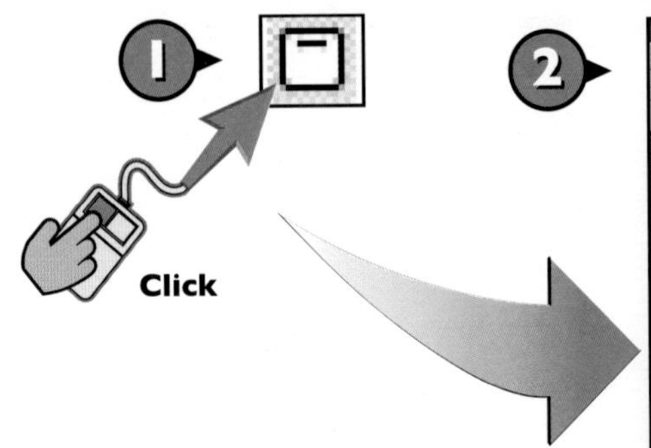
1
Click

2
Microsoft PowerPoint - [Annual Meeting]
Hughes, Funches, and Harris
Annual Meeting
1998
Slide 1 of 5
Whirlpool
1:07 AM

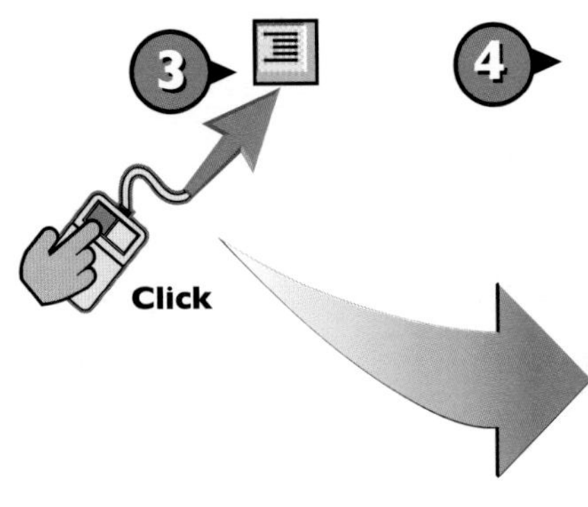
3
Click

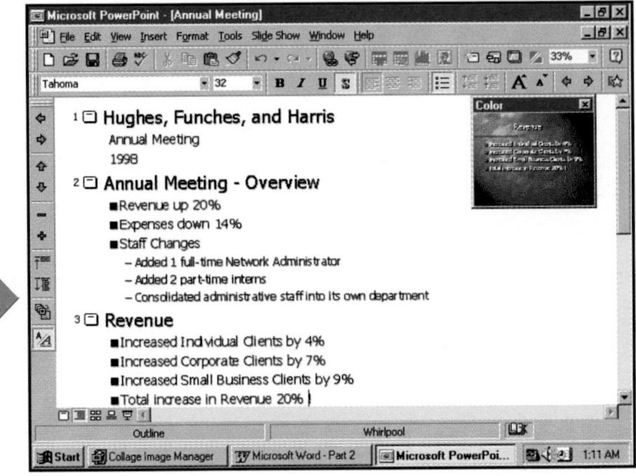
4
Microsoft PowerPoint - [Annual Meeting]
1 Hughes, Funches, and Harris
Annual Meeting
1998
2 Annual Meeting - Overview
Revenue up 20%
Expenses down 14%
Staff Changes
– Added 1 full-time Network Administrator
– Added 2 part-time interns
– Consolidated administrative staff into its own department
3 Revenue
Increased Individual Clients by 4%
Increased Corporate Clients by 7%
Increased Small Business Clients by 9%
Total increase in Revenue 20%
Outline
Whirlpool
1:11 AM

**Limitations of the Outline View**

**You cannot view or edit clip art, drawn objects, or graphic charts in the Outline View.**

1. Click the **Slide View** button.

2. In the Slide View, you can work with the text, clip art, and graphic charts—one slide at a time.

3. Click the **OutlineView** button.

4. In the Outline View, you can add or edit the title and bullet text in all of your slides.

Next Step

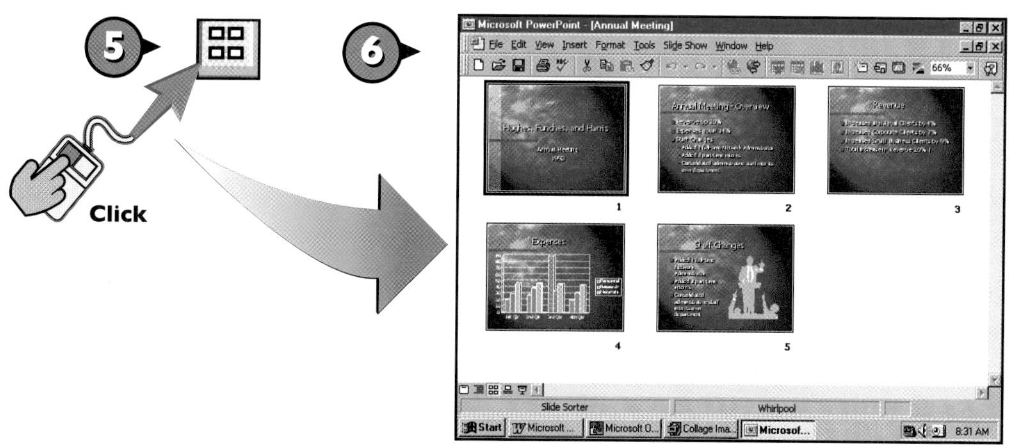


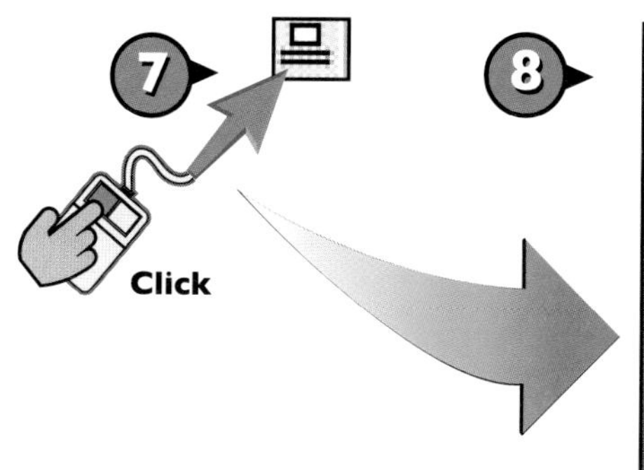


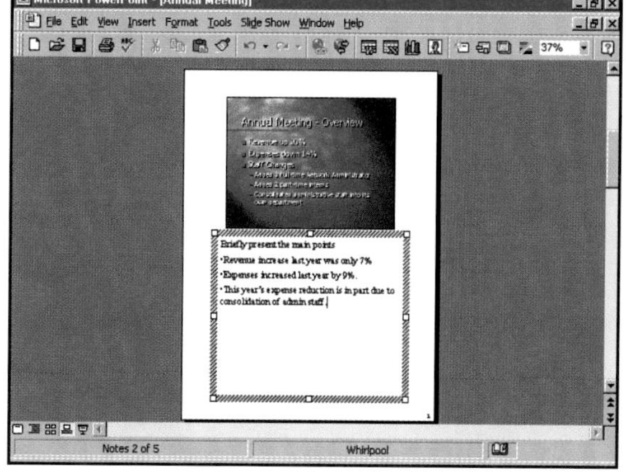


5. Click the **Slide Sorter View** button.

6. In the Slide Sorter View, you can move, copy, and delete slides, but you cannot edit the slides.

7. Click the **Notes Pages View** button.

8. In the Notes Pages View, you can create notes for each slide, to use when you give the presentation.

**Seeing More Slides in the Slide Sorter View**
**Change the Zoom percent in the Slide Sorter View to see more (or fewer) slides. The Zoom control is located on the right side of the toolbar.**

**Limitations of the Notes Pages View**
**You cannot edit slides in the Notes Pages View. This view is used to create printed speaker's notes.**

## Moving Slides Around

From time to time you will need to reorder the slides in your presentation. Whether you want to move one or several slides, the Slide Sorter View is the best view to use.

# Task 2: Rearranging the Slide Order in the Slide Sorter View

Start Here

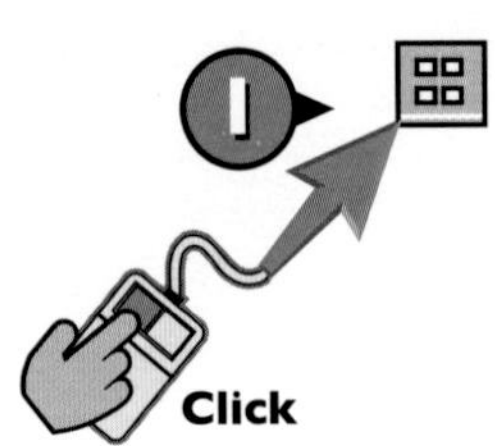


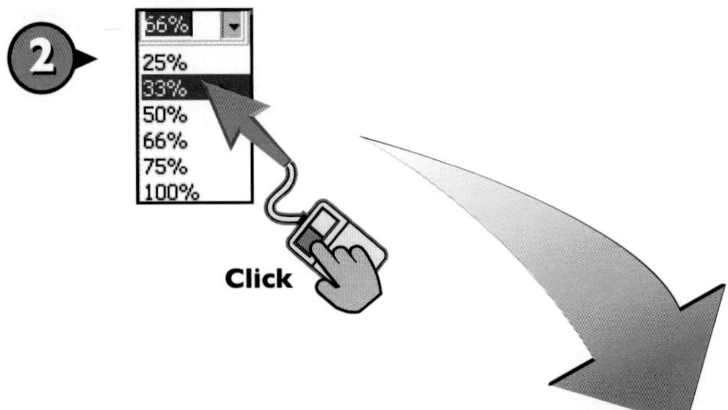


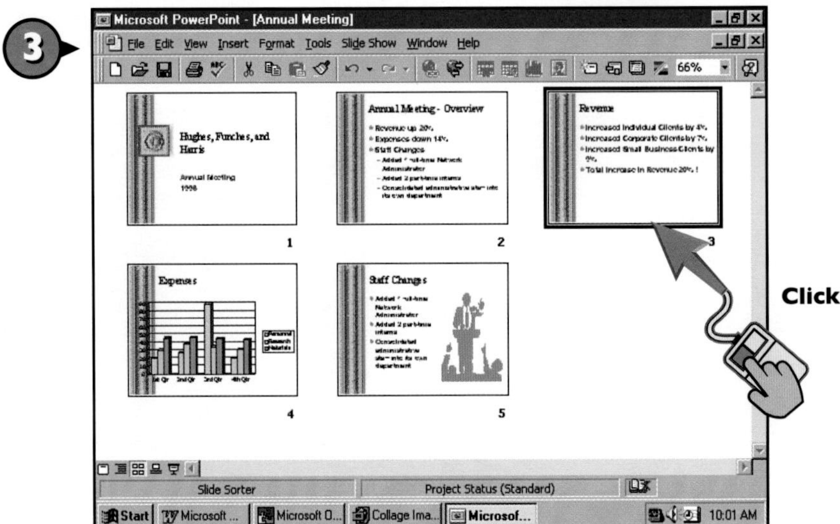


1. Click the **Slide Sorter View** button.
2. To see more slides on the screen, use the **Zoom** control and select a lower percentage.
3. Click on the slide you want to move. A heavy border appears around the slide.

**Scrolling to See More Slides**
If you have a lot of slides in your presentation, use the scrollbar on the right side of the Slide Sorter View to scroll through the slides.

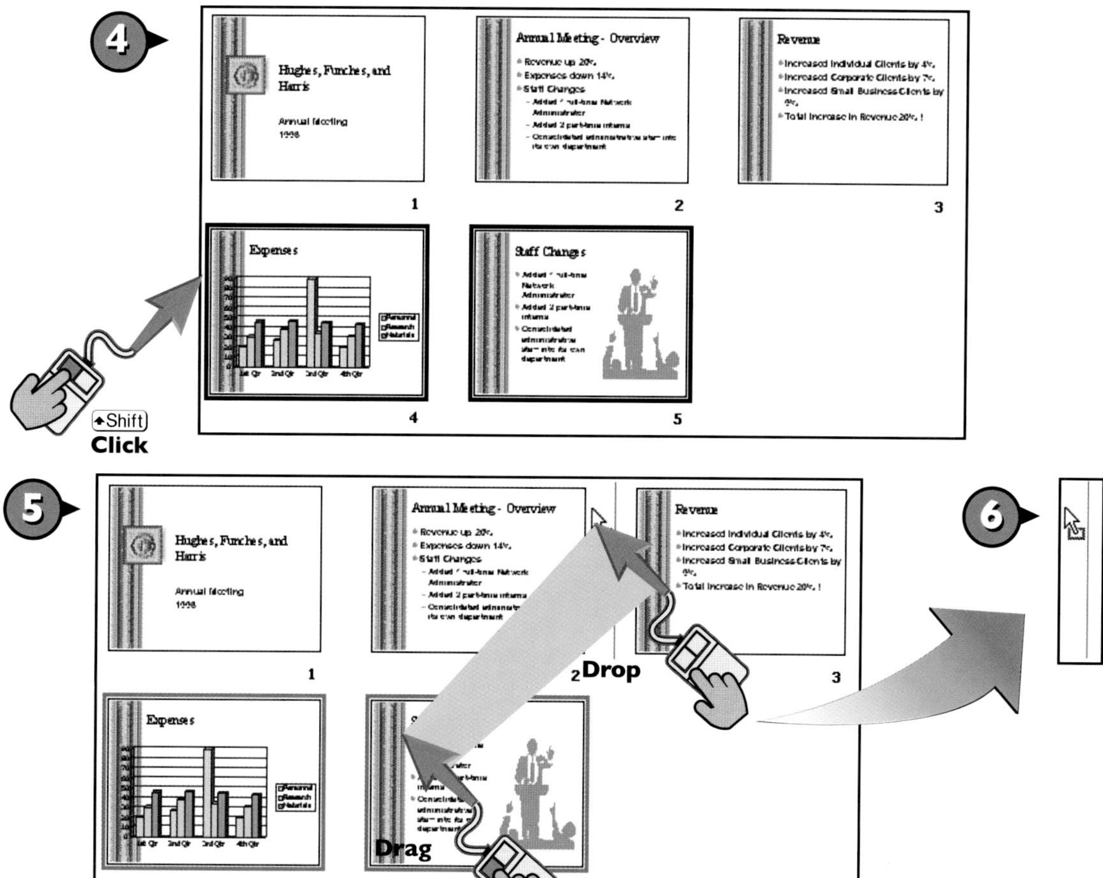


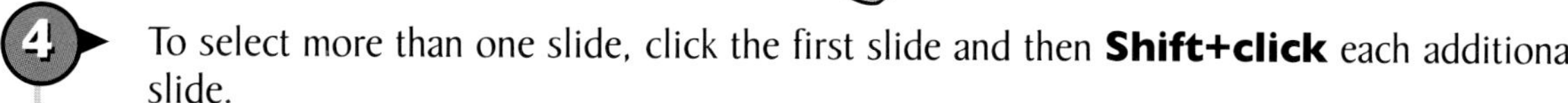

**4** To select more than one slide, click the first slide and then **Shift+click** each additional slide.

**5** After all the slides are selected, drag and drop the slides to the new position.

**6** A gray line indicates where you are moving the slides. A box is displayed next to the mouse pointer.

### When to Use the Cut and Paste Commands

**If the position you want to move the slides to is not visible on the screen, you can select the slides and choose Edit, Cut. Then click at the position where you want to move the slides and choose Edit, Paste.**

# Task 3: Deleting Slides in the Slide Sorter View

## Removing Slides from Your Presentations

**Unwanted slides can easily be deleted from a presentation. The Slide Sorter View enables you to see many slides at one time, making it the ideal view in which to remove slides from a presentation.**

Start Here

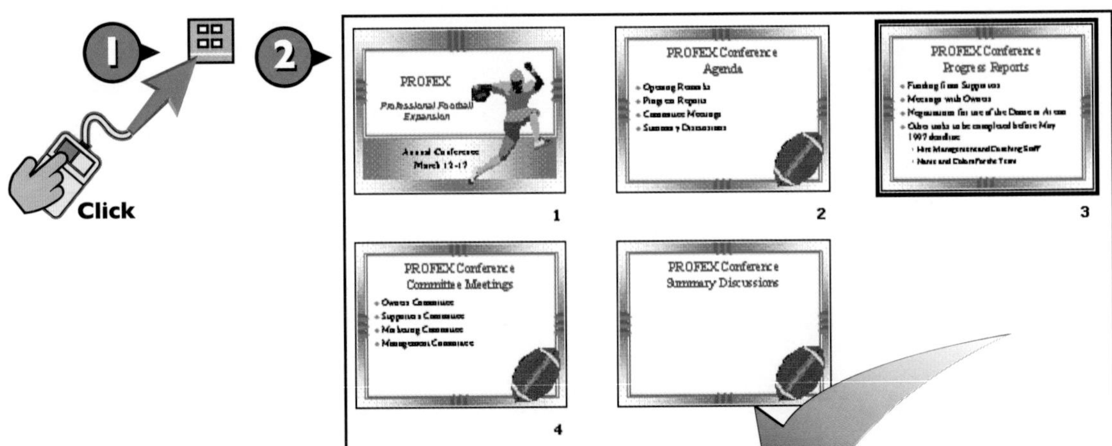


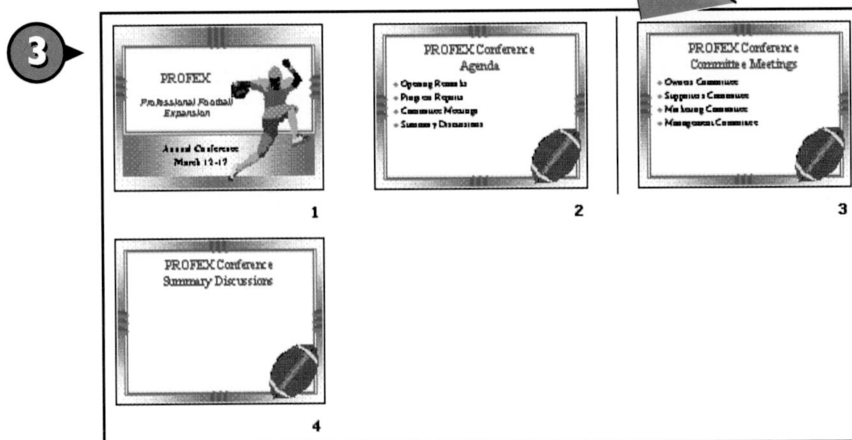

**Recovering a Deleted Slide**

**Choose Edit, Undo to recover a slide you have accidentally deleted.**

1. Click the **Slide Sorter View** button.
2. Click the first slide you want to delete. Use **Shift+click** to select additional slides. A heavy border appears around the selected slides.
3. Press **Delete**. Any selected slides are deleted and the remaining slides are renumbered.

# Task 4: Copying Slides in the Slide Sorter View

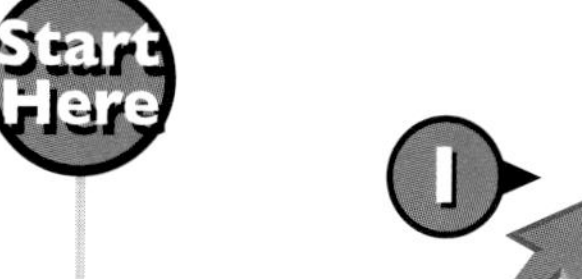


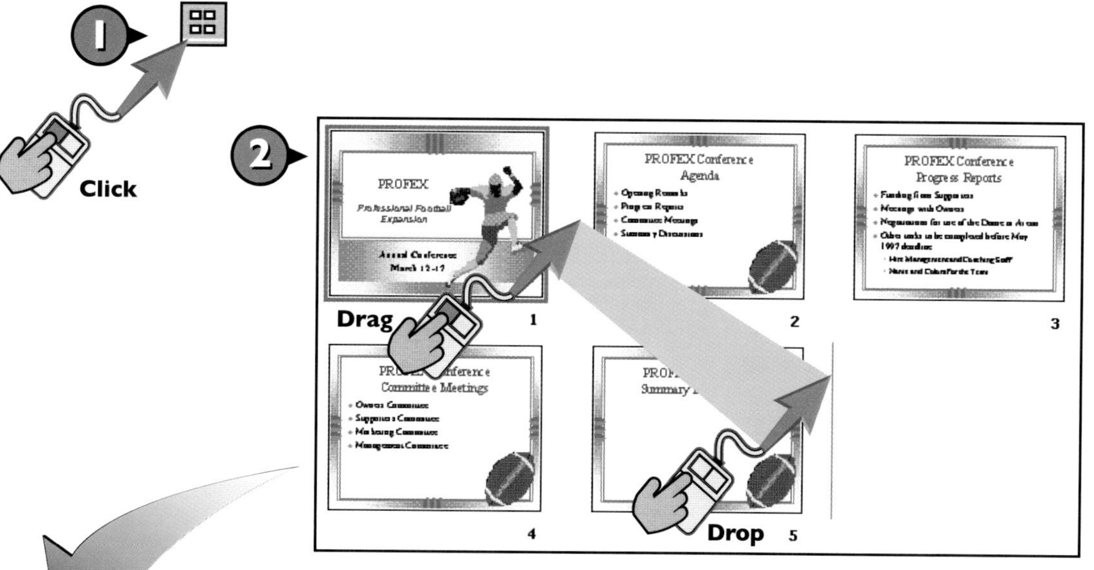


## Creating Copies of Slides in a Presentation

**Copying is handy when you need to repeat a slide, such as an agenda, or use one slide as the basis for another slide.**

1. Click on the **Slide Sorter View** button.

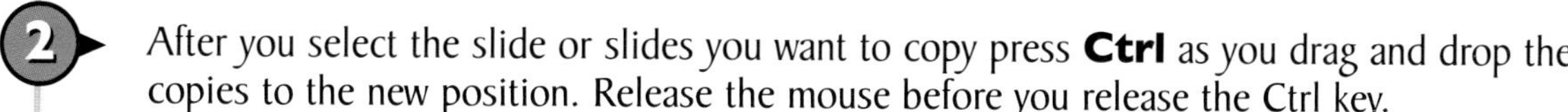

2. After you select the slide or slides you want to copy press **Ctrl** as you drag and drop the copies to the new position. Release the mouse before you release the Ctrl key.

3. A gray line indicates the placement of the slides. A box with a plus (+) sign displays next to the mouse pointer.

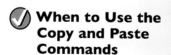

### When to Use the Copy and Paste Commands

**If the position to which you want to copy the slide is not visible on the screen, you can select the slide and choose Edit, Copy. Then click at the position where you want the copy and choose Edit, Paste.**

# Task 5: Copying Slides Between Presentations

## Using the Same Slides in Multiple Presentations

**Copying a slide from one presentation to another is easy, using drag and drop, but first you must display both presentations in the Slide Sorter View.**

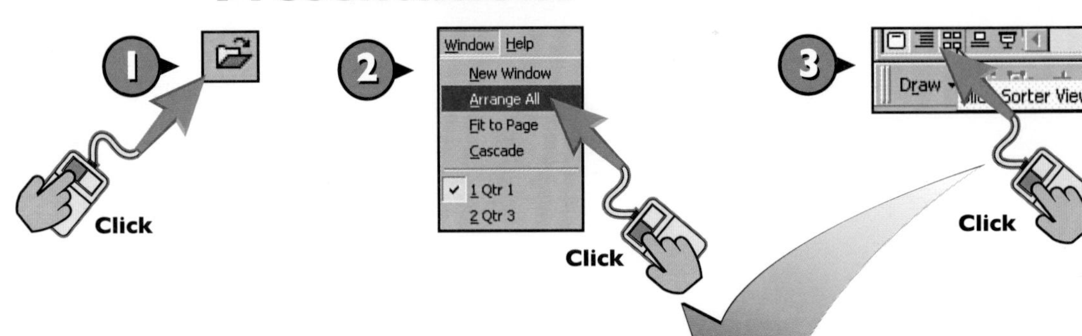


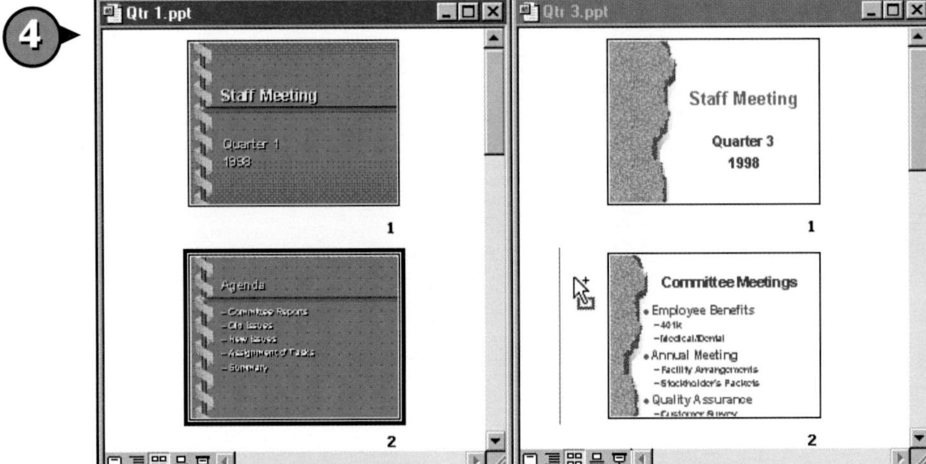


1. Open the source and target presentations.
2. Choose **Window, Arrange All** to display all open presentations side by side.
3. Change to the **Slide Sorter View** in both source and target presentations.
4. Click to select the slide you want to copy. Then press **Ctrl** as you drag and drop the copy to the new position.

**To select more than one slide, Shift+click each additional slide. A heavy border appears around the selected slides.**

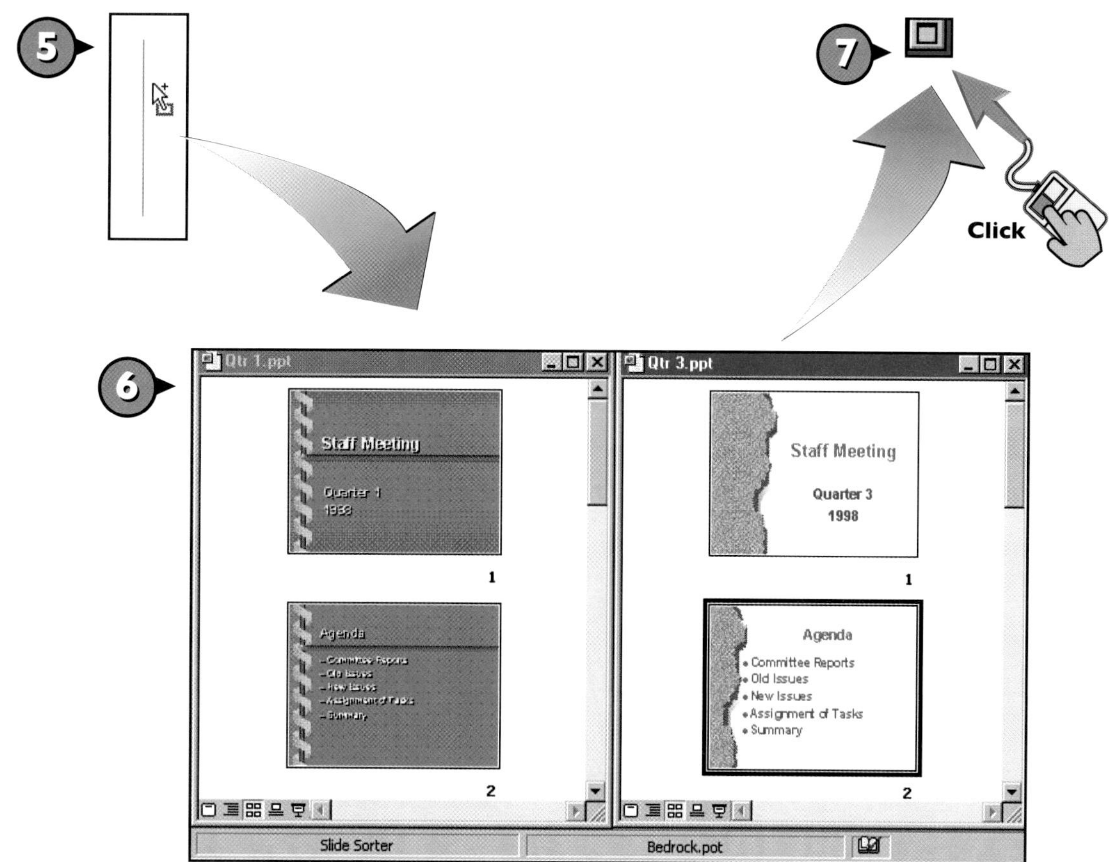


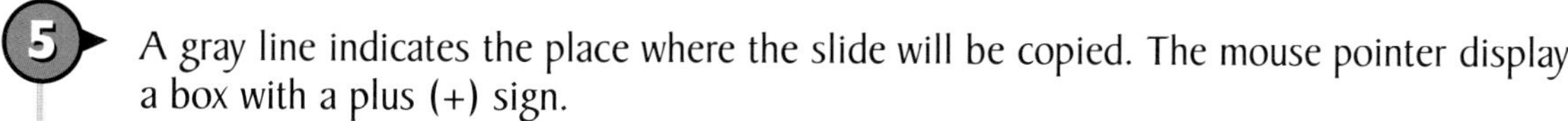

5 A gray line indicates the place where the slide will be copied. The mouse pointer displays a box with a plus (+) sign.

6 The copied slide takes on the design used in the target presentation.

7 Click the **Maximize** button to display the presentation window full screen.

**WARNING**

**When using drag and drop to copy slides, make sure you release the mouse button before you release the Ctrl key. If you don't, the slides will be moved instead of copied!**

# Task 6: Creating Slides Quickly in the Outline View

## Using the Outline View to Build a Presentation

**If you prefer to jot down the main topics of your presentation and fill in the details later, use the Outline View in PowerPoint.**

Start Here

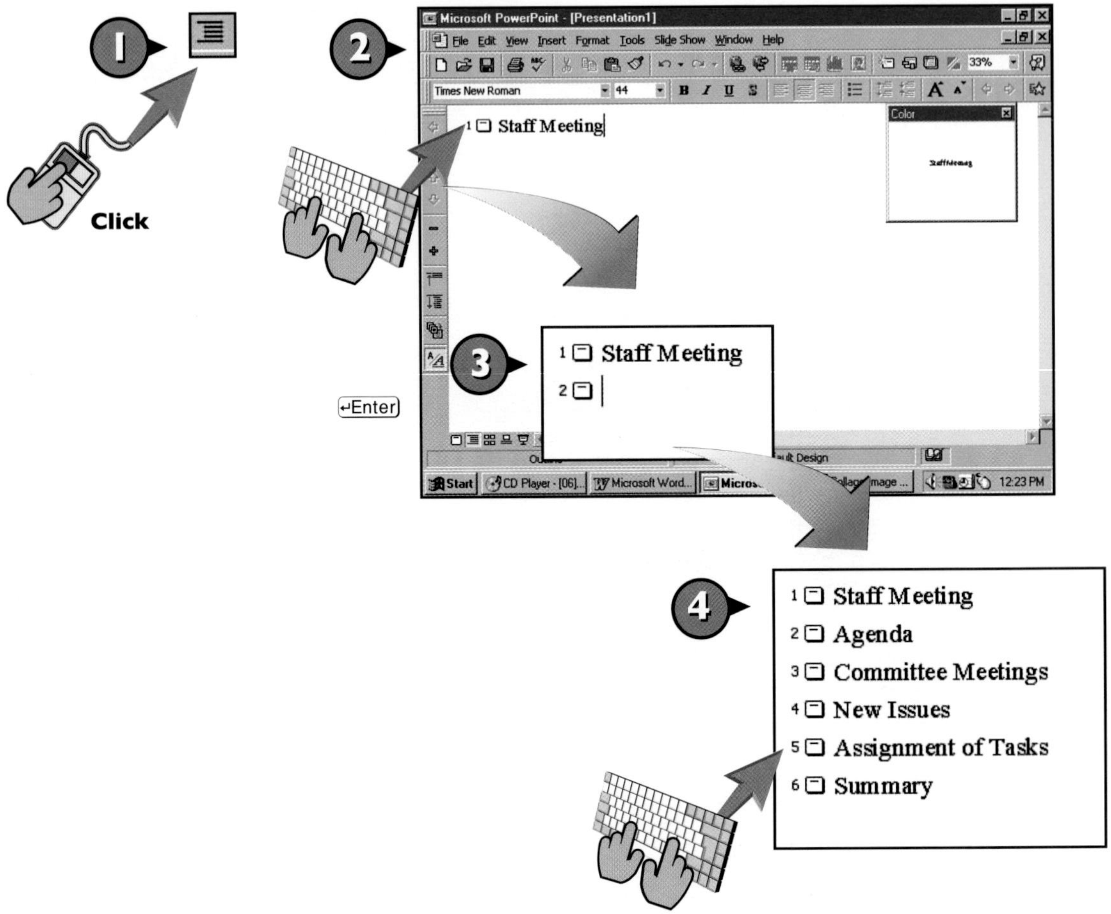

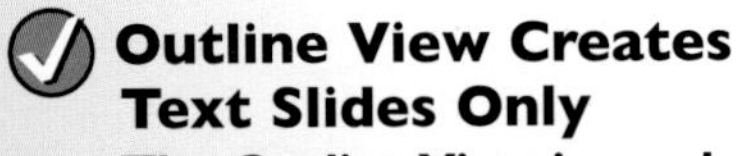

### Outline View Creates Text Slides Only

**The Outline View is used to create text slides, especially those made up of bulleted lists. You cannot create graphic charts in the Outline View. Use the Slide View to create slides with charts.**

1. Click the **Outline View** button.
2. Each slide displays a slide number and symbol; type the title for the first slide.
3. Press **Enter** to create the next slide.
4. Continue to create new slides by typing a title or subject.

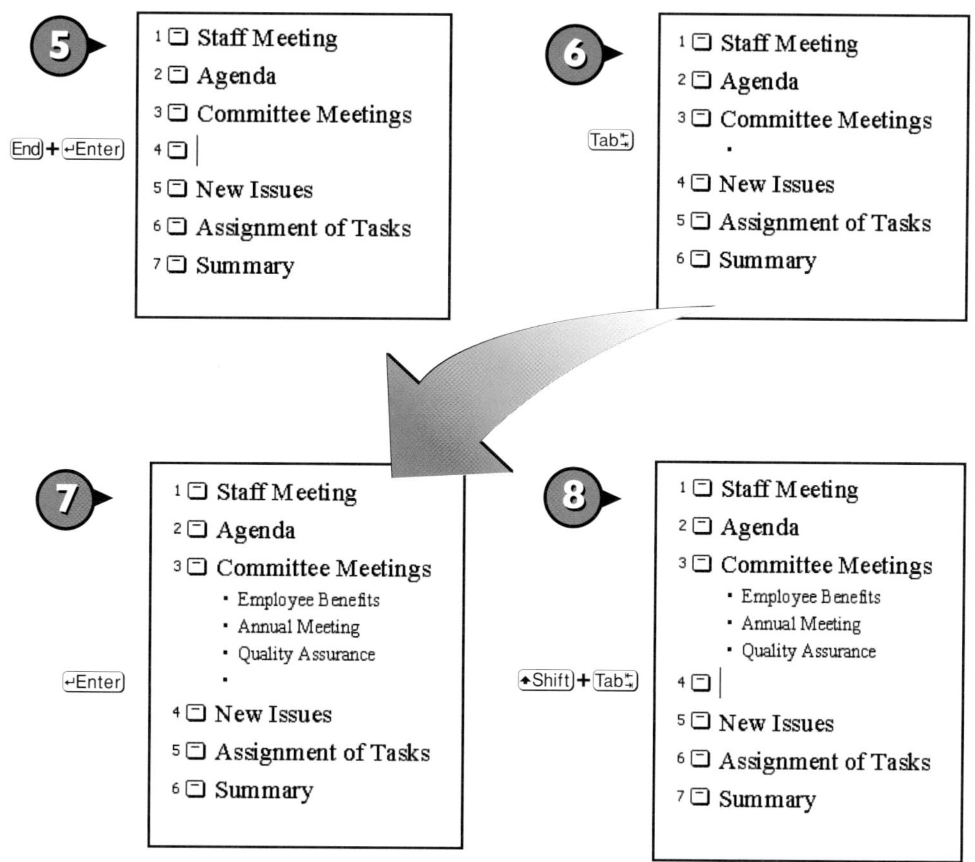


5. To insert a slide, click the slide above where you want the new slide. Press **End** and then **Enter**.
6. To create a list of bullets on the slide, press **Tab** to indent one level.
7. Each time you press **Enter**, a new bullet appears at the same level.
8. To change an indented bullet to a slide, press **Shift+Tab**.

### Creating and Modifying Bullets

**You can create five levels of bullets. To learn more about creating a bulleted list or changing the shapes of the bullet symbols, see Part 3, "Working with Text."**

### The Outline View Toolbar

**The Outline View has a special toolbar that appears on the left side of the screen. To find out what each toolbar button will do, rest your mouse over a button until a description appears.**

# Task 7: Selecting Text in the Outline View

## Selecting Slides, Bullets, and Individual Words

**Before you can move, copy, or delete items in the Outline View, you must first select them.**

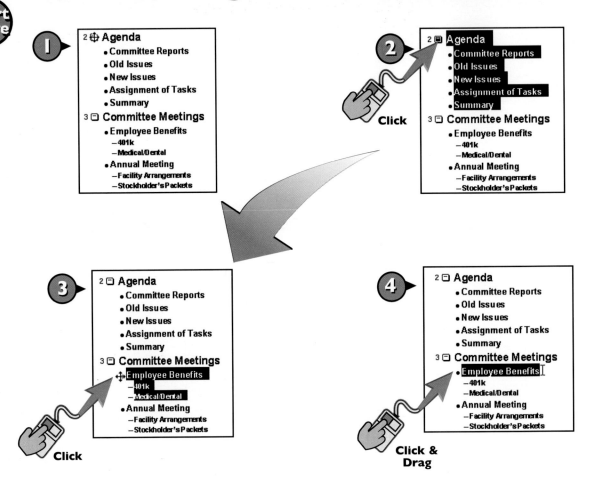

Start Here



1. To select an entire slide, position the mouse pointer over the slide symbol; the pointer becomes a four-headed arrow.
2. Click the slide symbol to select the entire slide.
3. When you select a bullet, any sub-bullets are also selected.
4. To select individual words, position the pointer over the first word (the mouse pointer becomes an "I" shape) and drag over the text you want to select.

**Selecting Text Quickly**
**Double-click in the middle of a word to select the entire word. Triple-click a slide title to select the entire slide. Triple-click a bullet to select the bullet (and any sub-bullets).**

# Task 8: Hiding and Displaying Text in the Outline View

Start Here

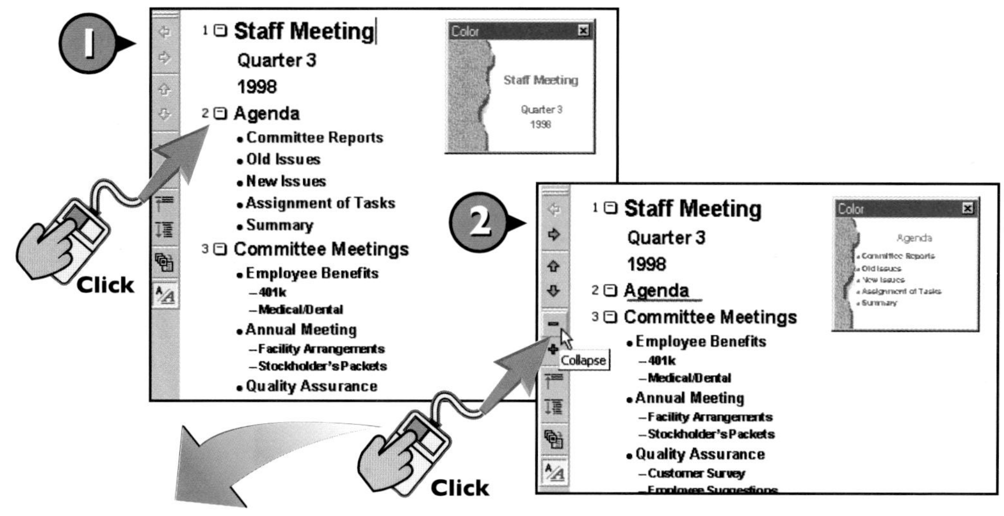


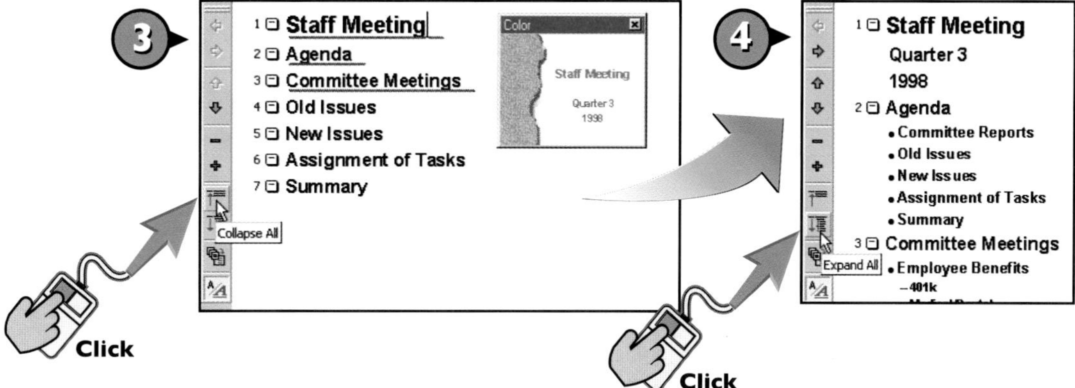


1. In the Outline View, click the text of the slide you want to hide.

2. Click the **Collapse** button on the Outline View toolbar; the slide collapses to show just the slide title.

3. To hide the bulleted text in all slides, click the **Collapse All** button on the toolbar.

4. To display the bulleted text in all slides, click the **Expand All** button on the toolbar.

## Collapsing and Expanding Slides in the Outline View

You can hide all but the slide titles in the Outline View to clearly see the flow of topics in the presentation.

### Knowing an Outline Is Collapsed

A gray underline indicates a collapsed slide that contains bulleted text.

### Printing a Collapsed Outline

It is especially useful to be able to print the collapsed outline. See Part 10, "Printing Your Presentation," for steps on printing your outline.

# Task 9: Creating Speaker's Notes in the Notes Pages View

## Preparing Presentation Notes in the Notes Pages View

**Each slide has its own notes page, and you should use it. Having a set of printed notes with you when you give a presentation ensures you won't forget the points you want to make.**

Start Here

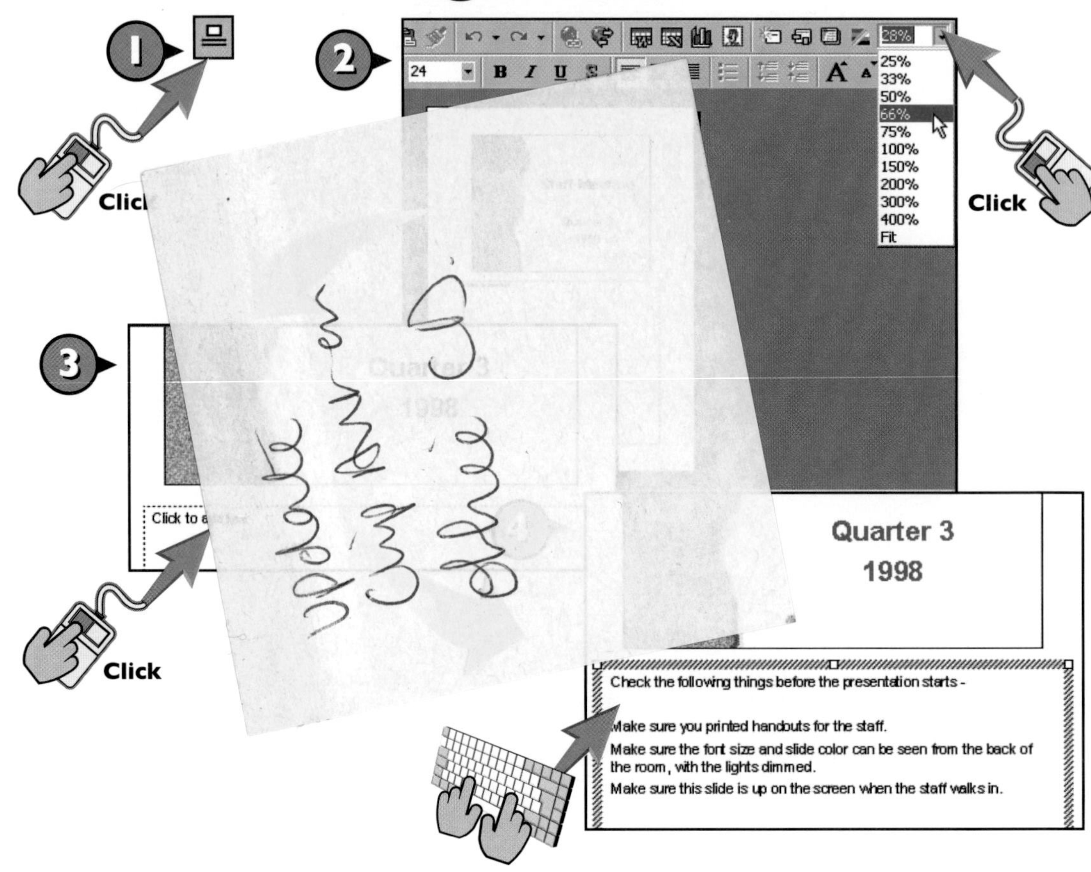

### Formatting Notes Pages

**See Task 10 for steps on creating bullets and applying other formats to the text in the Notes Pages.**

1. Click the **Notes Pages View** button.
2. Use the **Zoom control** to select a higher percentage so you can see the notes as you type them.
3. Each Notes Page displays a miniature of the slide and a "click" placeholder for notes; click in the placeholder.
4. Type in your notes.

End Task

# Task 10: Formatting Text in the Speaker's Notes

Start Here

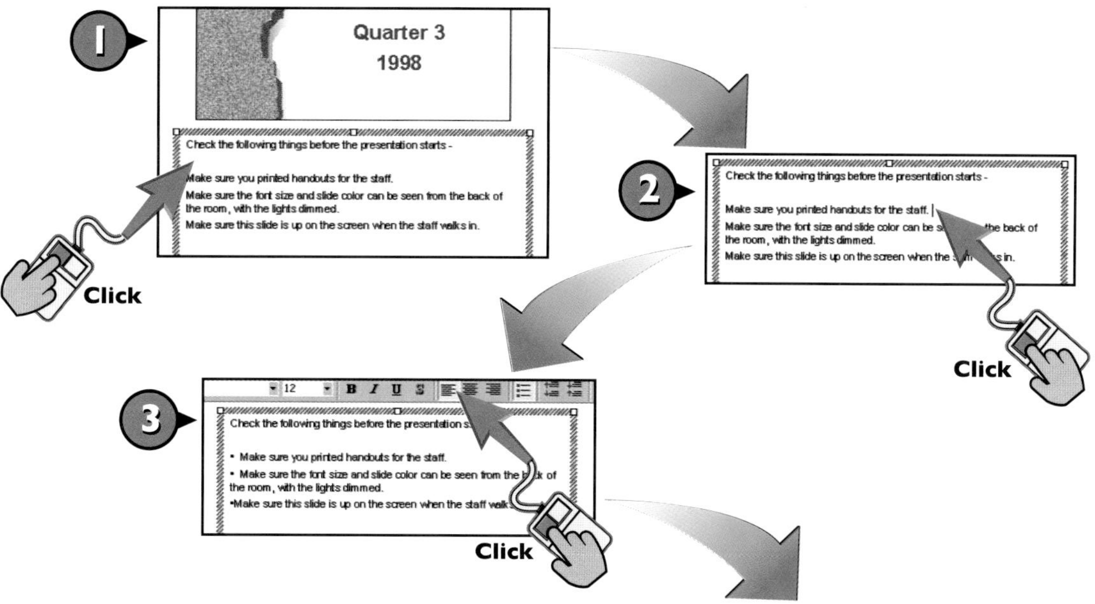


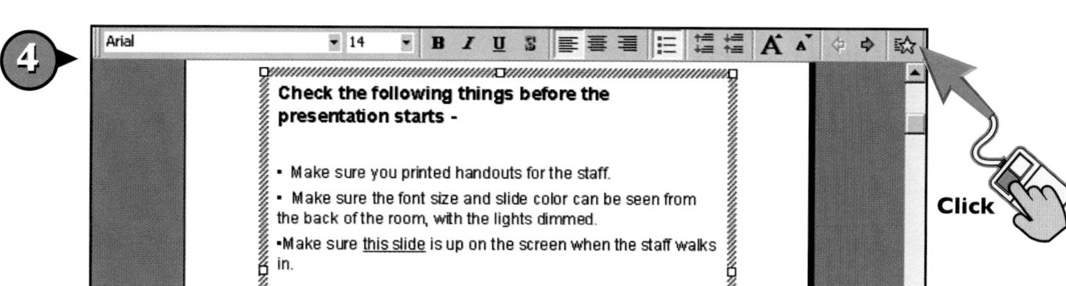


1. Display the Notes Page you want to format, and click in the notes area.
2. To show bullets next to a line of text, click anywhere in that line.
3. Click the **Bullets** button on the Formatting toolbar to insert a bullet symbol.
4. Use the **Formatting toolbar** buttons to change the font type or size, or to bold or underline text in the notes pages.

## Adding Bullet Symbols and Using the Formatting Toolbar

You can enhance the readability of the text in your notes pages by applying a few simple formats. This is especially useful when you are giving a presentation in a room with the lights dimmed.

**Creating Space Between the Bullet and the Note**
When you insert a bullet, it appears immediately to the left of the text. Press the spacebar once or twice to create space between the bullet and the text.

PART 3

# Working with Text

In this part we focus on the text components of your presentations. Along with editing, moving, copying, and deleting slide text, this part shows you how to apply formats such as bold, italic, and color to enhance the appearance of the text and how to choose from many font styles and sizes.

You also learn to create and modify bulleted lists—an important element in many slide presentations. These lists can appear by themselves or can be paired with graphic charts or clip art images in other slide layouts.

# Tasks

# Task 1: Creating a Bulleted List

## Adding a List of Bullets to a Slide

One of the most popular types of slides in a presentation is a list of `bullets`. You can create a single list, a double list, a list paired with a graphic chart, or a list paired with `clip art`.

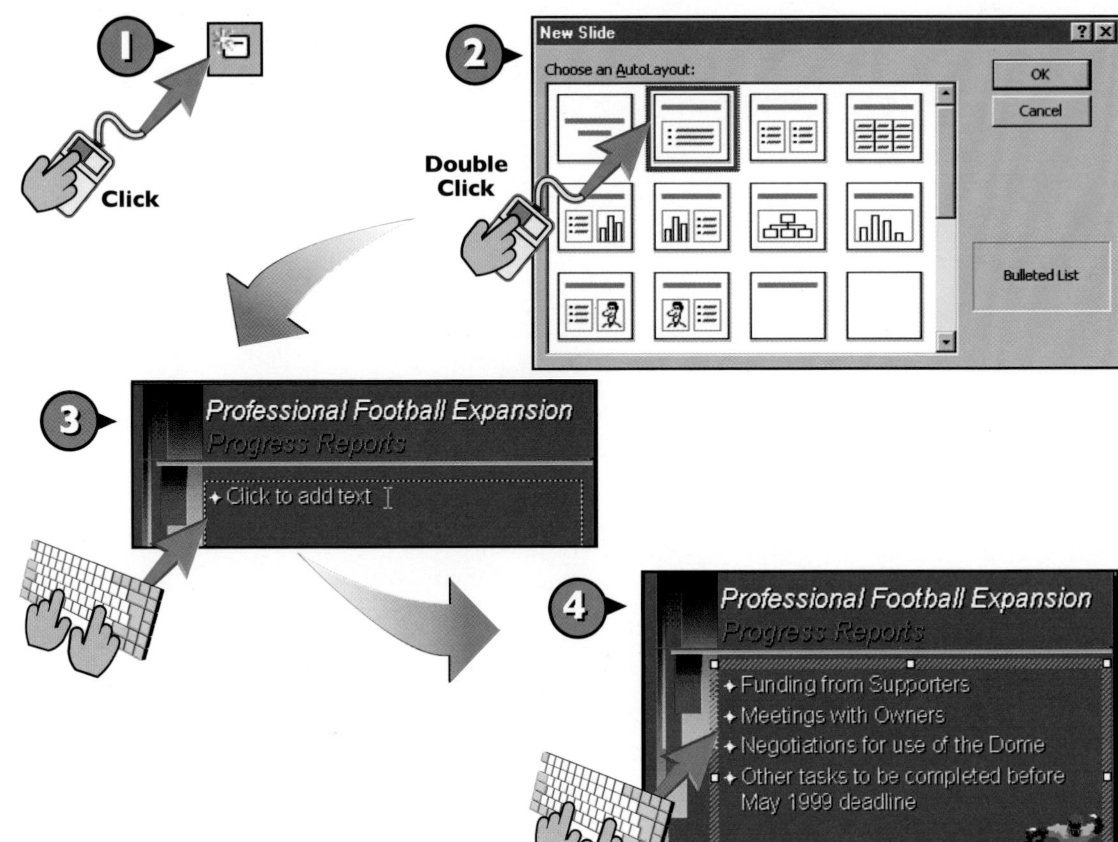


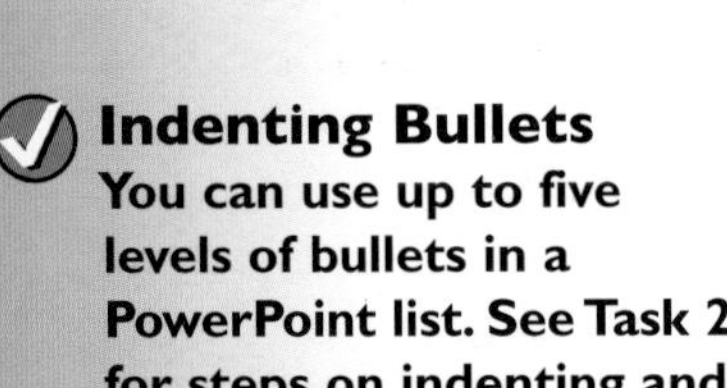

**Indenting Bullets**
You can use up to five levels of bullets in a PowerPoint list. See Task 2 for steps on indenting and `outdenting` bullets.

1. Click the **New Slide** button on the Standard toolbar.
2. Double-click the **Bulleted List** slide layout or one of the other layouts that includes a bulleted list.
3. When the new slide appears, click in the title placeholder and type a title.
4. After you click in the bulleted list's "click" placeholder, type the text for your first bullet. The text wraps to the next line if necessary. Press **Enter** for each new bullet.

# Task 2: Indenting and Outdenting Bullets

1 Click

2 Enter Tab

3 Shift+ Tab

4

## Creating Lists that Contain Sub-bullets

**Each slide layout that includes a bulleted-list "click" placeholder is capable of displaying up to five levels of bullets and sub-bullets.**

1. Click in the line above where the new bullet is to appear. Press **End** to move the cursor to the end of the line.
2. Press **Enter** to create another bullet. Press **Tab** to indent the bullet one level; continue to use Tab to indent farther.
3. Each time you press **Enter**, a new bullet appears at the same level.
4. To outdent a bullet, press **Shift+Tab**.

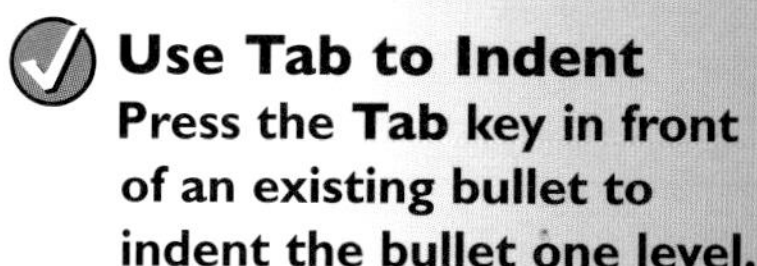

### Use Tab to Indent

**Press the Tab key in front of an existing bullet to indent the bullet one level.**

### Formatting the Bullet Shape

**See Task 3 for steps on changing the bullet shape.**

# Task 3: Modifying Bullet Symbols on a Single Slide

## Changing the Shape of Several Bullets

**You can change the shape of a single bullet or group of bullets on a slide.**

Start Here

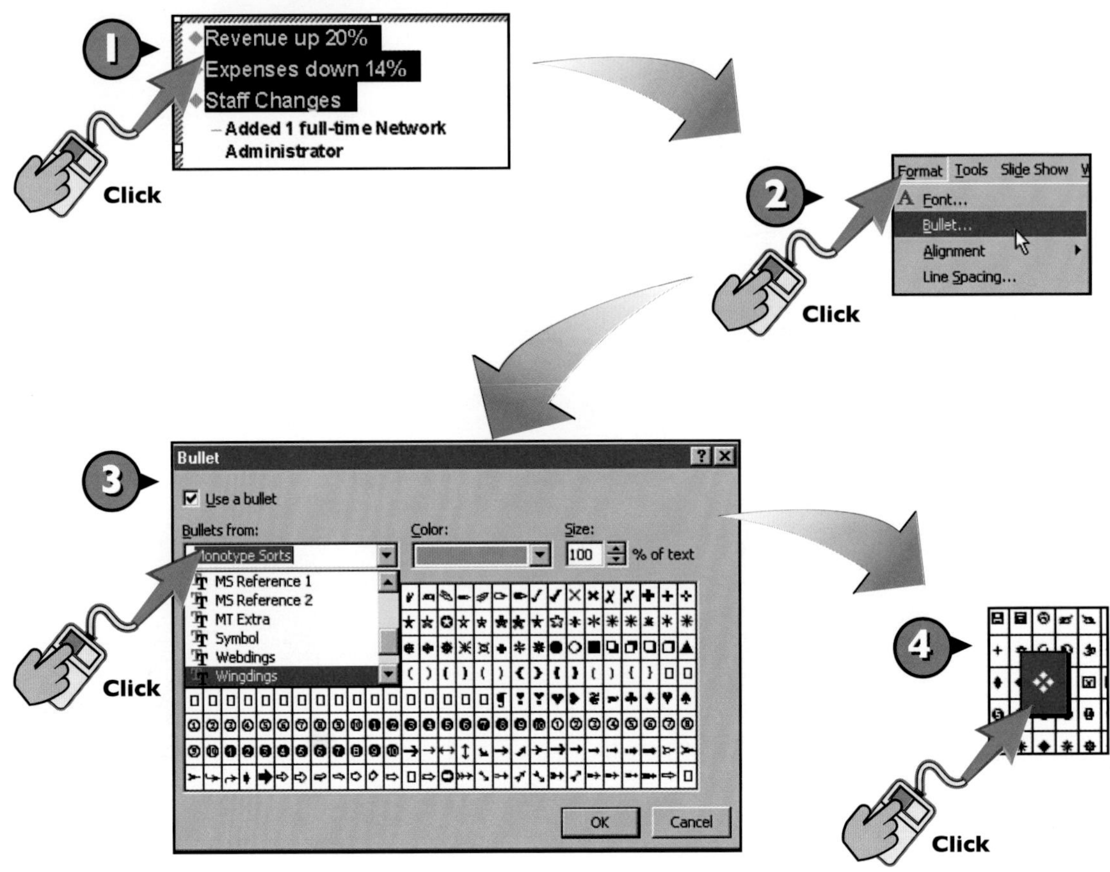


1. Click and drag to select the text for which you want to change the bullets.
2. Choose **Format, Bullet**.
3. Click the arrow at the end of the Bullets From box and choose the font to use.
4. Click a bullet in the grid to see the shape more clearly.

### The Best Bullet Shapes

**The Bullets From drop-down list shows the font types available on your computer. Each font contains special shapes. The most interesting shapes are in the Monotype Sorts, Symbol, and Wingdings groups.**

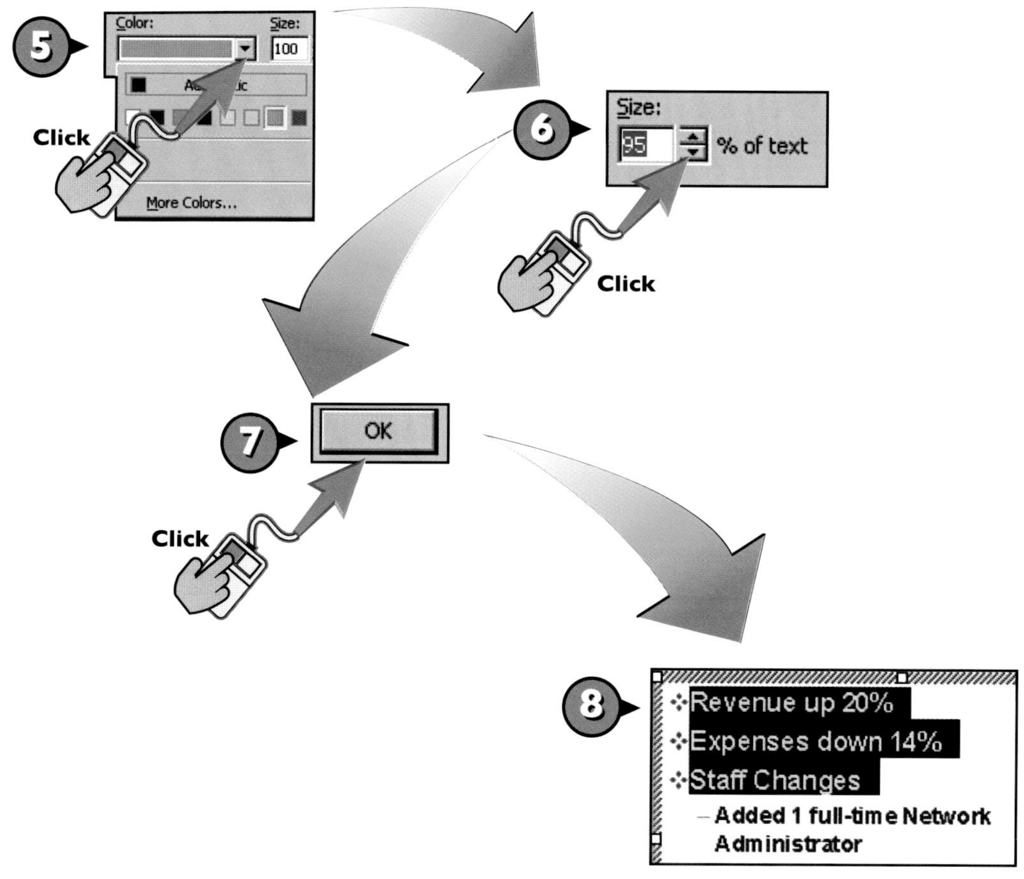


5 Click the **Color** option to change the bullet color.

6 Click the **Size** option to enlarge or reduce the size of the bullet in relation to the size of the text.

7 Choose **OK** to apply your changes.

8 The new bullet shape appears next to the highlighted text.

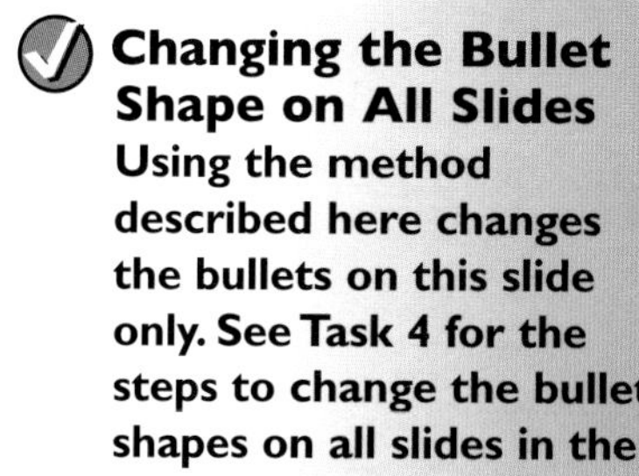

**Changing the Bullet Shape on All Slides**
**Using the method described here changes the bullets on this slide only. See Task 4 for the steps to change the bullet shapes on all slides in the presentation.**

# Task 4: Modifying Bullet Symbols on All Slides

## Changing the Bullet Shape on Slide Layouts that Include Bulleted Lists

Using the `Slide Master`, you can change the shape of bullets at each level. The Slide Master controls the shapes for the Bulleted List layout and for Two Columns of Bullets, Bullets with a Chart, and Bullets with Clip Art.

Start Here

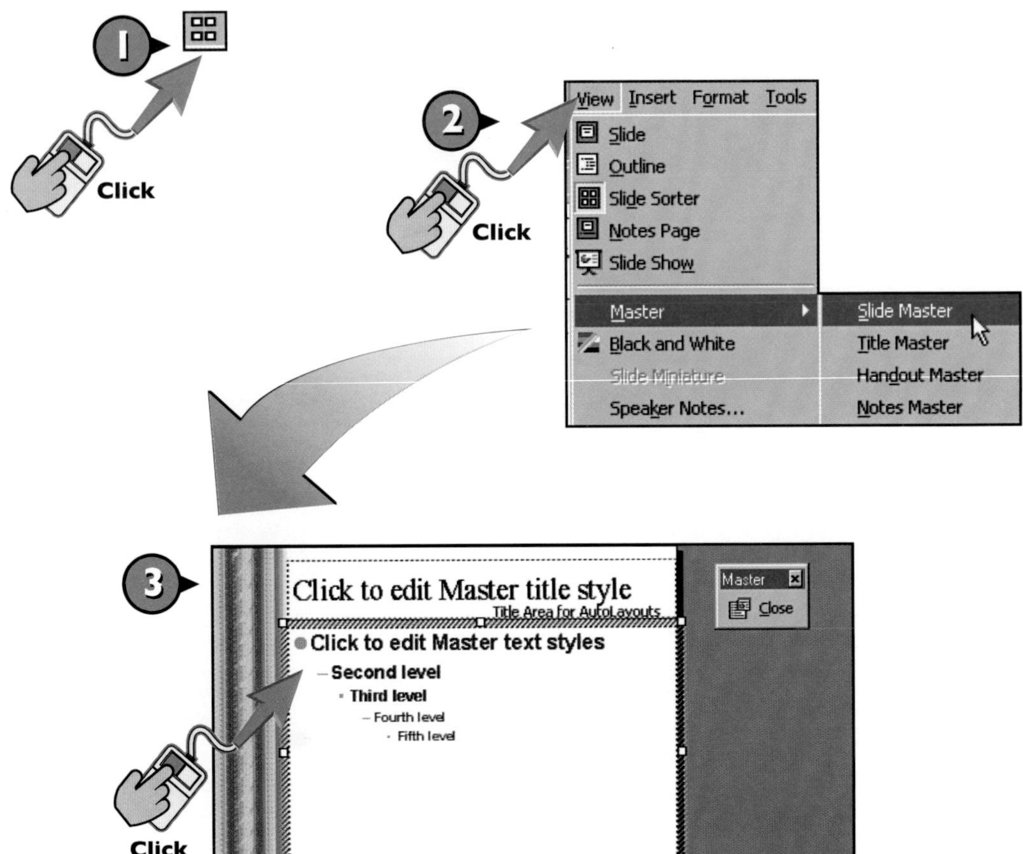


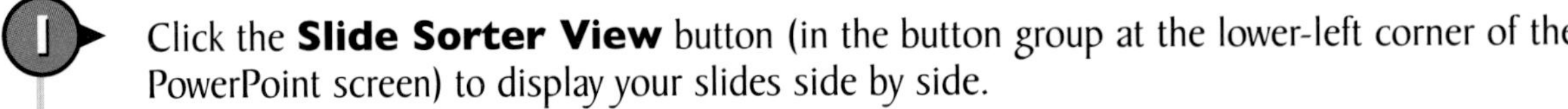

1. Click the **Slide Sorter View** button (in the button group at the lower-left corner of the PowerPoint screen) to display your slides side by side.
2. Choose **View, Master, Slide Master**.
3. The Slide Master displays, showing the five bullet levels. Click the level you want to change.

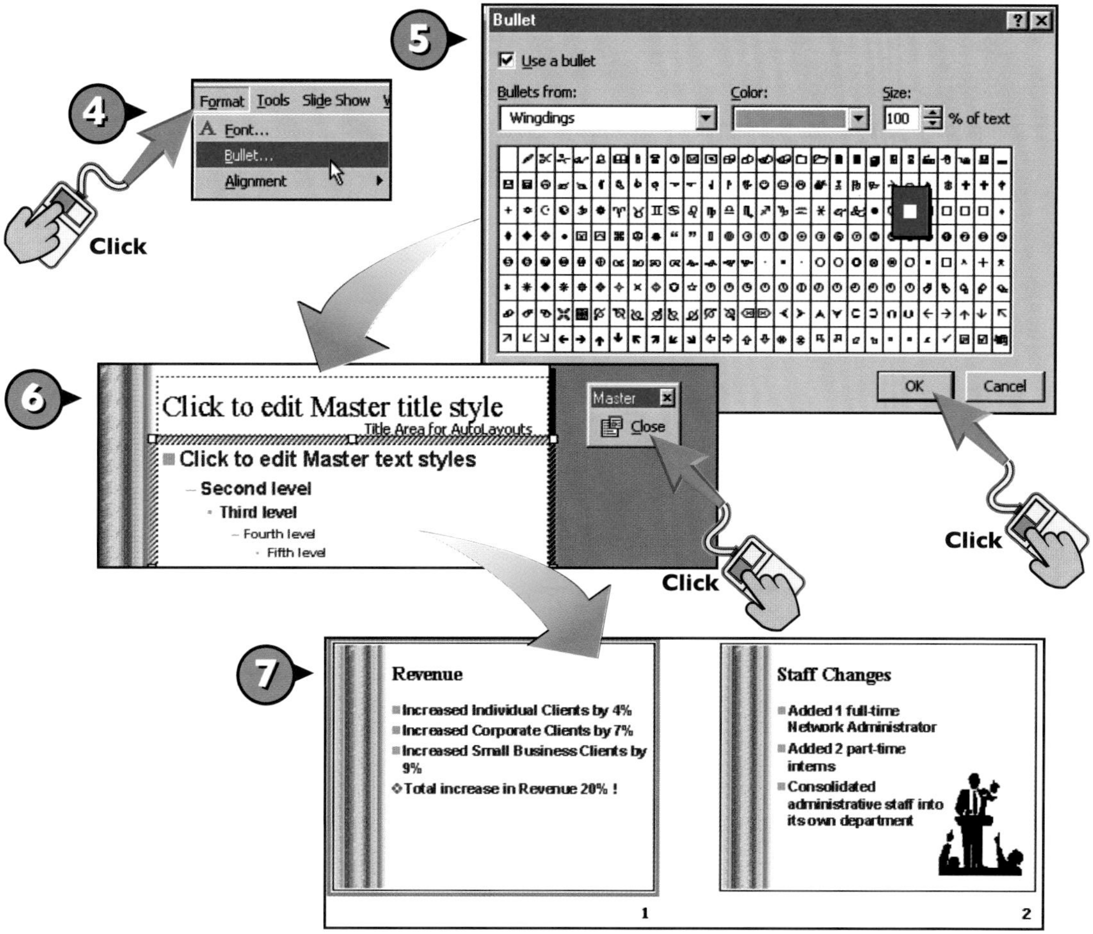

4. Choose **Format, Bullet**.

5. Select the desired bullet shape, color, and size; then choose **OK**.

6. The new bullet shape appears in the Slide Master. Choose **Close** to exit the Slide Master.

7. The new bullet shape is applied to all slides.

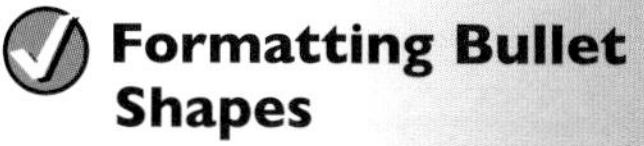

### Formatting Bullet Shapes

You don't remember how to change the bullet shape, color, or size? Refer to Task 2 for these steps.

### Converting Previously Customized Bullets

If you had previously changed the shape of a single bullet or group of bullets, they retain the previous shape (see step 7). To convert them to the shape you applied on the Slide Master, choose **Format, Slide Layout,** and click the **Reapply** button.

# Task 5: Changing the Text in a "Click" Placeholder

## Inserting and Replacing Text in "Click" Placeholders

**You can add or change the text in the title, sub-title, or bulleted list placeholders in any of your slides.**

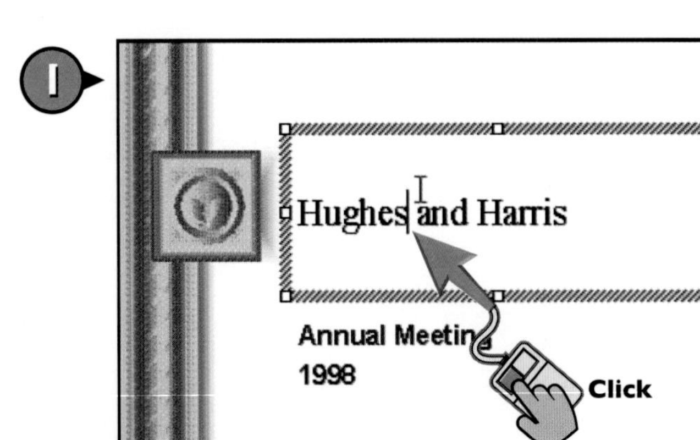


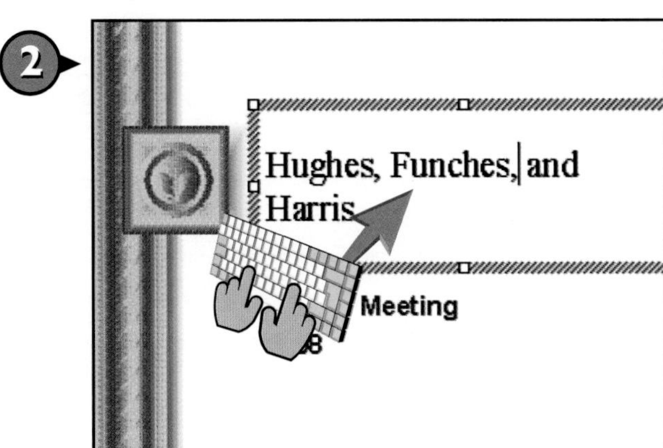

1. To insert text in a "click" placeholder, click at the point where you want to add text. The mouse pointer becomes an "I" shape, and a flashing cursor appears where you clicked.

2. Type the text you want to add; the placeholder automatically wraps the text. Press **Enter** for a new line or bullet.

**Editing a Placeholder**
**When you are entering or editing text in a placeholder, the border around the placeholder appears as slash marks.**



Next Step

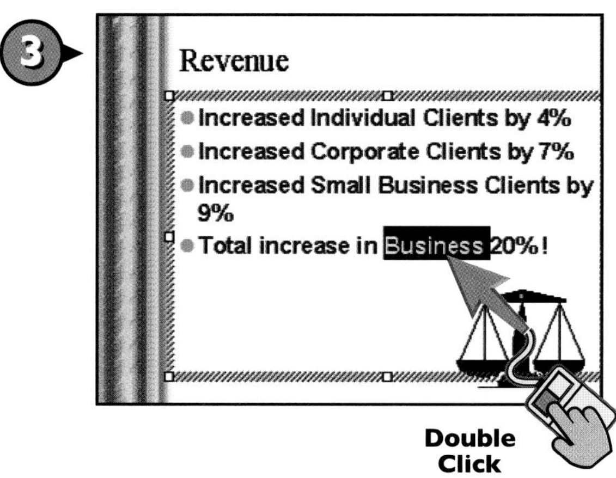
Revenue
Increased Individual Clients by 4%
Increased Corporate Clients by 7%
Increased Small Business Clients by 9%
Total increase in Business 20%!
Double Click

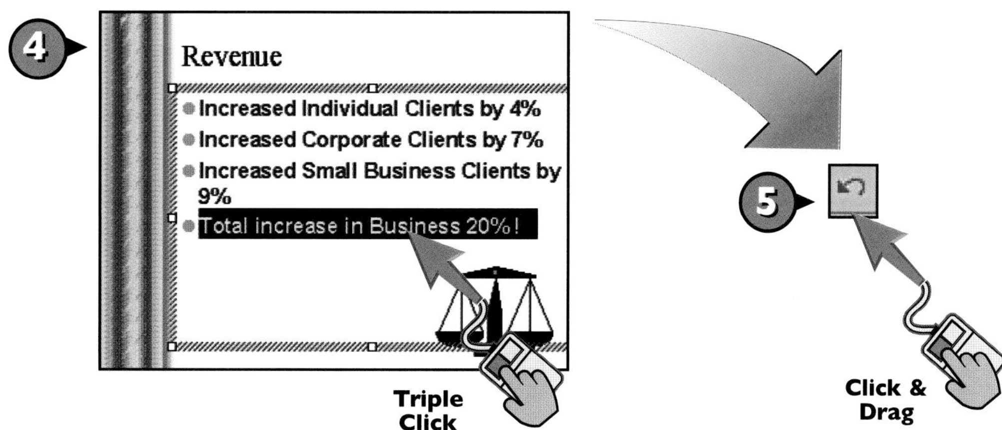
Revenue
Increased Individual Clients by 4%
Increased Corporate Clients by 7%
Increased Small Business Clients by 9%
Total increase in Business 20%!
Triple Click
Click & Drag

3 Double-click the word to select it; then type the new word.

4 To change an entire bullet or paragraph, triple-click in the bullet or paragraph; then type the new text.

5 If you accidentally delete the text in a "click" placeholder, click the **Undo** button.

**Selecting Text Quickly**
Double-clicking and triple-clicking can be used to select text in other Microsoft Office programs, such as Word.

**Undoing Your Changes**
You can undo more than just your last action in PowerPoint. The default is set to track and undo the last 20 actions. Click the **drop-down arrow** next to the Undo button to see a list of actions you can undo.

# Task 6: Removing Text in a "Click" Placeholder

## Deleting Words, Paragraphs, or the Entire Text in a Placeholder

The first step in removing text from a "click" placeholder is to select it. You can use both mouse and keyboard methods for selecting text.

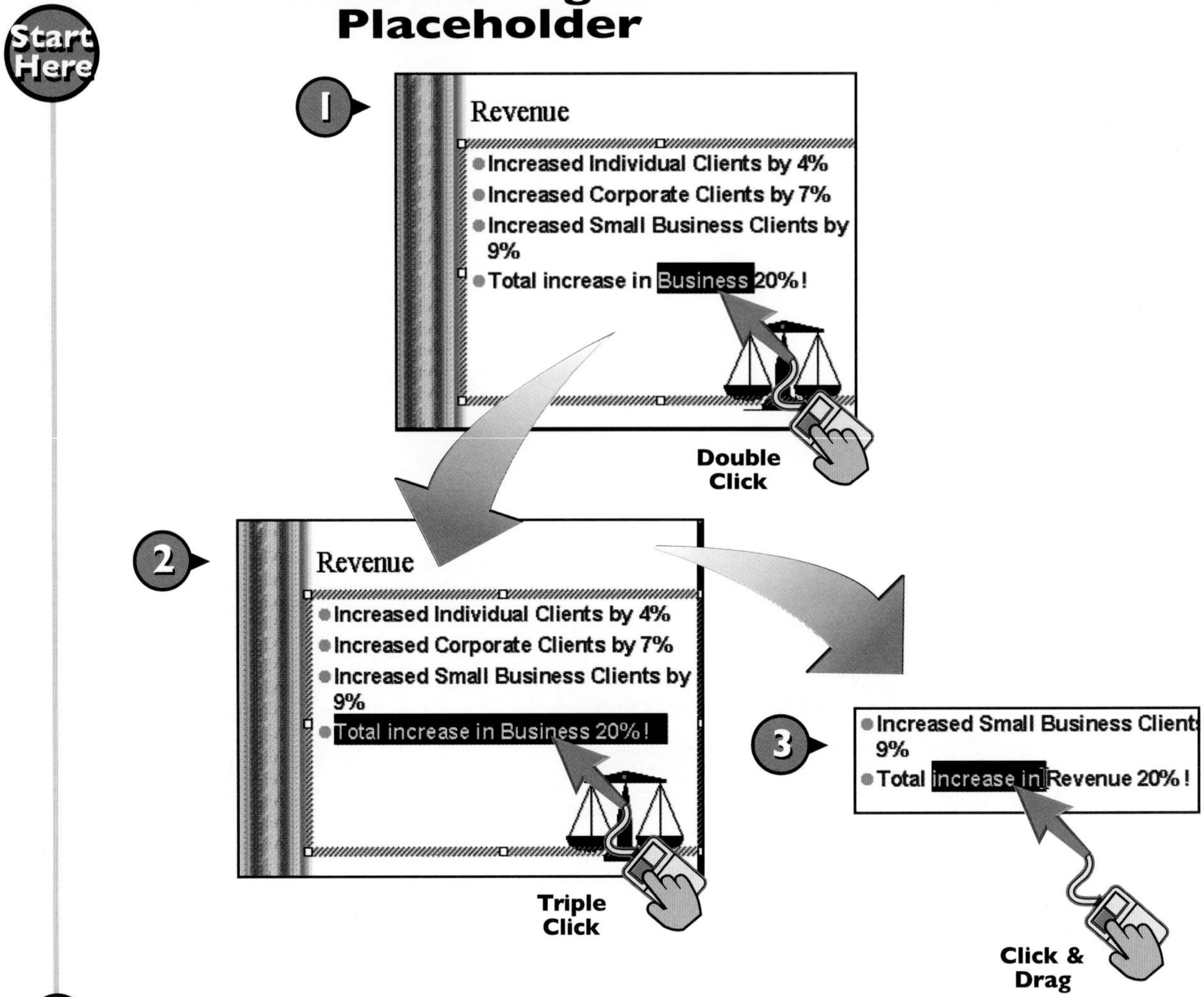

Start Here

1. To remove a single word in a "click" placeholder, double-click the word and press **Delete**.

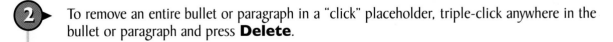

2. To remove an entire bullet or paragraph in a "click" placeholder, triple-click anywhere in the bullet or paragraph and press **Delete**.

3. To select several words, click in front of the first word and drag across them.

**Removing Text Deletes the Text Box**

**You can remove words from a text box just as you do from a placeholder; however, when you remove all of the text in a text box, the text box is also deleted.**

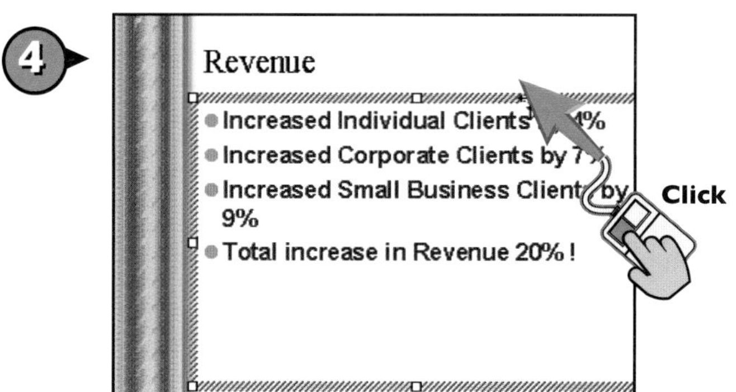
4
Revenue
Increased Individual Clients
Increased Corporate Clients by 7
Increased Small Business Client
9%
Total increase in Revenue 20%!
Click

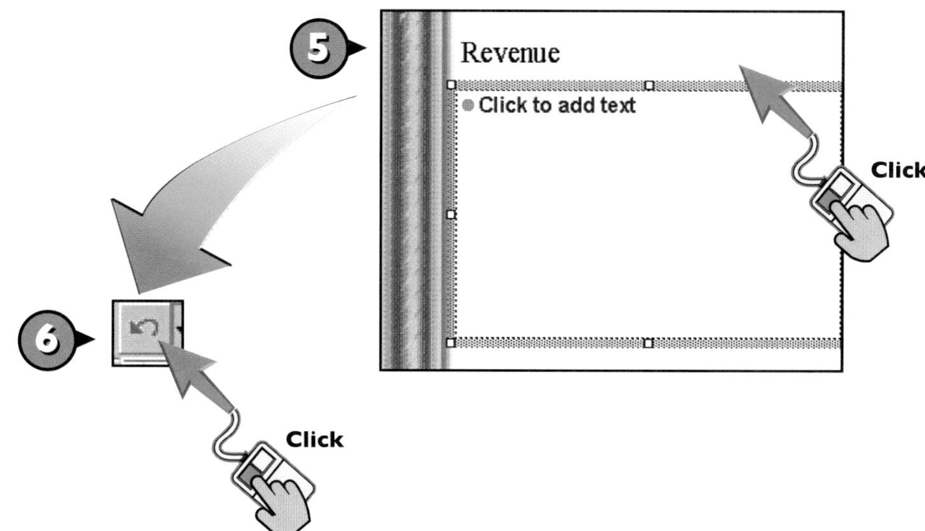
5
Revenue
Click to add text
Click
6
Click

4 To remove all text in a "click" placeholder, click anywhere inside the placeholder. Then press **Esc** to select the placeholder.

5 Press **Delete**. The click prompt reappears in the placeholder.

6 If you accidentally delete the "click" placeholder, select the **Undo** button on the Standard toolbar.

**Selecting Text with the Arrow Keys**

**You can use the arrow keys on the keyboard to select text. Position the flashing cursor at the beginning of the text you want to select. Then press and hold the Shift key while you press an arrow key. Continue to press the arrow key until all of the text is selected.**

End Task

## Rearranging Text in a Slide

**Use the Cut, Copy, and Paste toolbar buttons to move or copy text from one part of a slide to another part.**

# Task 7: Moving and Copying Text in a "Click" Placeholder

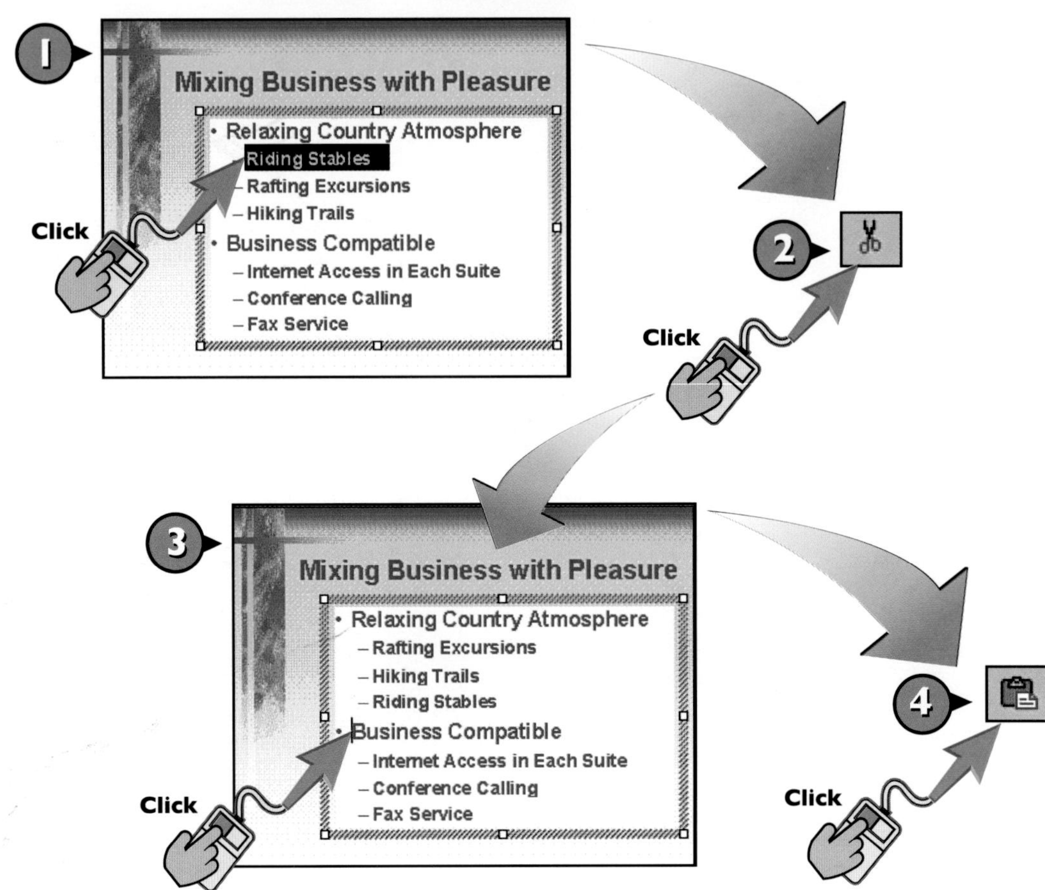
1
Mixing Business with Pleasure
• Relaxing Country Atmosphere
Riding Stables
– Rafting Excursions
– Hiking Trails
• Business Compatible
– Internet Access in Each Suite
– Conference Calling
– Fax Service
Click
2
Click
3
Mixing Business with Pleasure
• Relaxing Country Atmosphere
– Rafting Excursions
– Hiking Trails
– Riding Stables
• Business Compatible
– Internet Access in Each Suite
– Conference Calling
– Fax Service
Click
4
Click

Drag the mouse pointer across the text to select the text you want to move.

Click the **Cut** button to remove the text from its current location.

Click to position your cursor where you want to move the text; the flashing cursor indicates the position.

Click the **Paste** button to move the text to the new location.

### Double- and Triple-Click to Select Text

**You can use several methods for selecting text. In addition to dragging the mouse pointer across the text, you can double-click to highlight a word or triple-click to highlight a bullet or paragraph.**

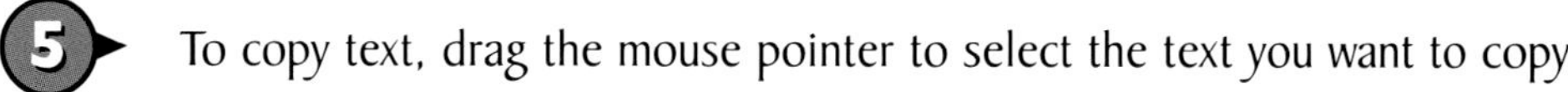

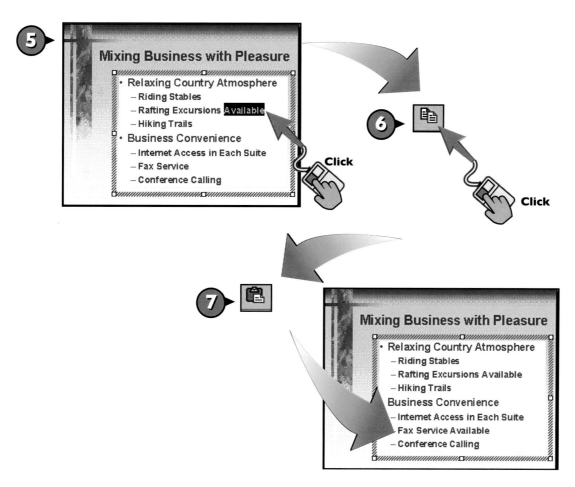

5 To copy text, drag the mouse pointer to select the text you want to copy.

6 Click the **Copy** button.

7 Click the location where you want to copy the text, and click the **Paste** button. The text is copied to the new location.

**Using the Edit Menu Commands**

**You can also use the Cut, Copy, and Paste commands in the Edit menu to rearrange text in a slide.**

# Task 8: Adding Independent Text to a Slide

## Inserting Text Anywhere on a Slide

**You can add text to a slide, separate from the placeholders, by using text boxes and AutoShapes. This type of text is sometimes referred to as "graphic text" or "independent text."**

Start Here

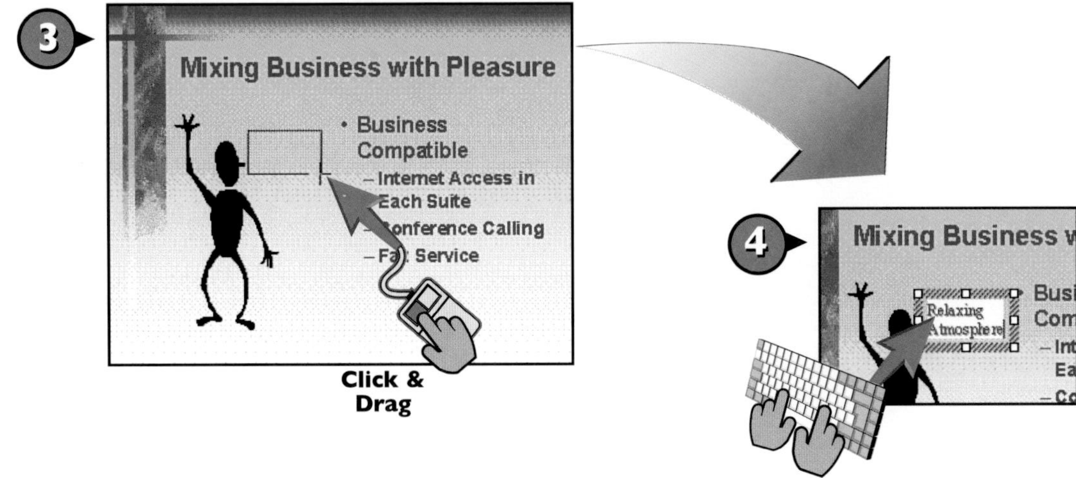


**Adding Independent Text to Slides**
**You must use the Slide View to add independent text to slides.**

1. Click the **Slide View** button, located in the lower left-corner of the PowerPoint screen.
2. One way to add independent text is to click the **Text Box** button on the Drawing toolbar.
3. The mouse pointer becomes a large plus sign (crosshairs). Click and drag where you want the text box to appear.
4. Type the desired text. The text is left aligned in the text box. The text automatically wraps. Press **Enter** to force a new line.

Next Step

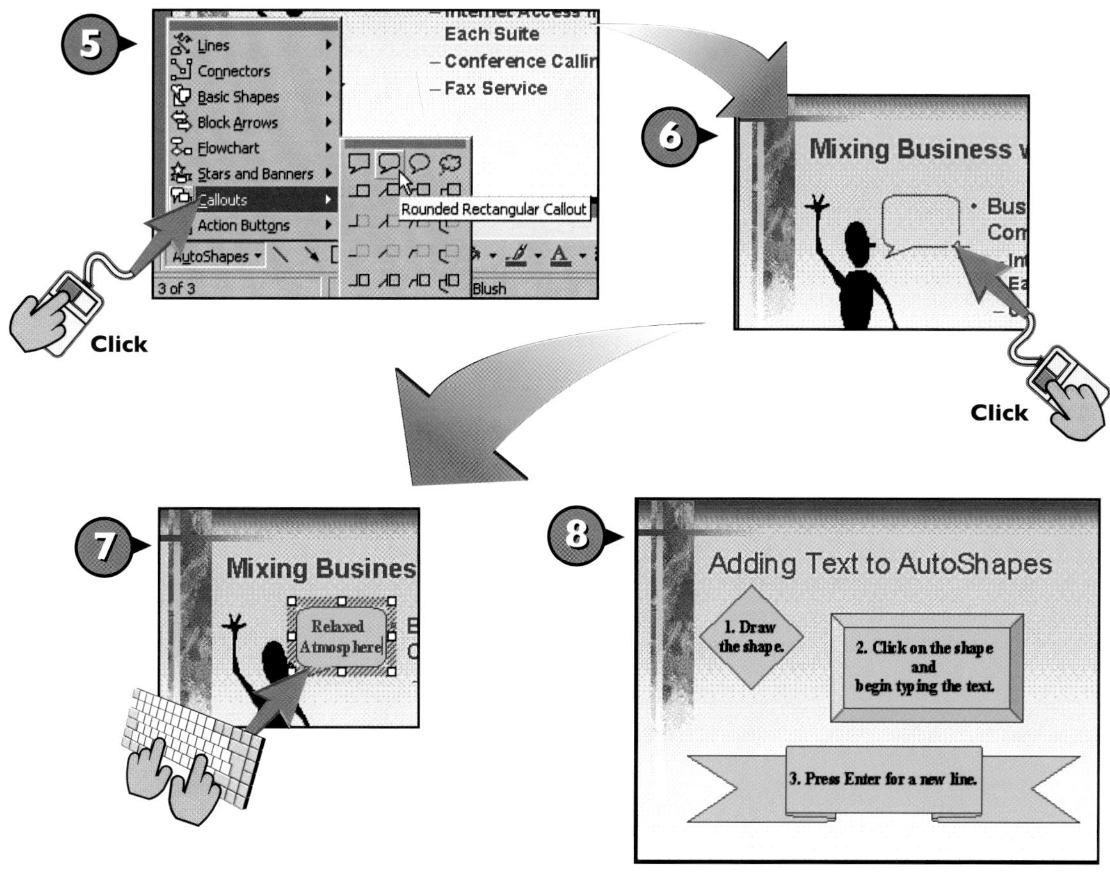

**Formatting Independent Text**

**See Task 9 for information about formatting the text font type and size.**

**See Task 10 for information about applying formats such as bold and italic.**

**See Task 11 for information about changing the color of the text.**

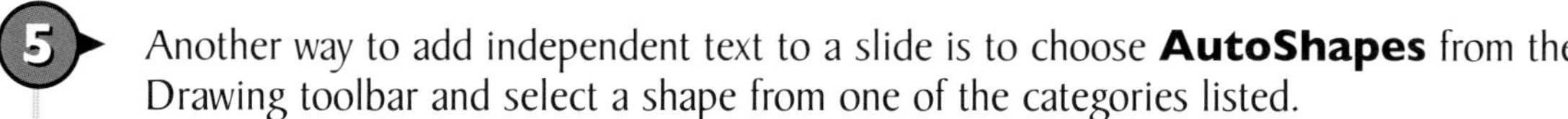

5 Another way to add independent text to a slide is to choose **AutoShapes** from the Drawing toolbar and select a shape from one of the categories listed.

6 The mouse pointer becomes a large plus sign (crosshairs). Click and drag to create the AutoShape.

7 Type the desired text. The text is centered in the shape. Press **Enter** for a new line.

8 You can add text to many of the AutoShapes.

## Formatting the Slide Text

**You can greatly alter the appearance of your slides by changing the font type and font size of their text.**

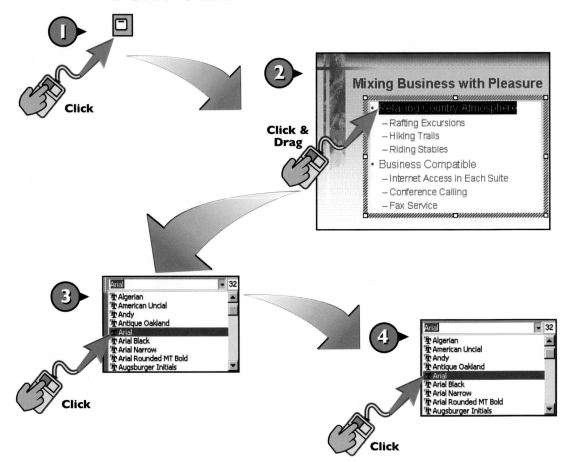

# Task 9: Changing the Font Type and Font Size

Start Here

Click

Click & Drag

Mixing Business with Pleasure

- Relaxing Country Atmosphere
  - Rafting Excursions
  - Hiking Trails
  - Riding Stables
- Business Compatible
  - Internet Access in Each Suite
  - Conference Calling
  - Fax Service

Arial 32
Algerian
American Uncial
Andy
Antique Oakland
Arial
Arial Black
Arial Narrow
Arial Rounded MT Bold
Augsburger Initials

Click

Click

1. Click the **Slide View** button in the lower-left corner of the PowerPoint screen.

2. Drag the mouse pointer across the text to select the text you want to change.

3. Click the **Font Type** drop-down button to see a list of fonts (scroll down to see additional font types).

4. Click the font type name you want to use.

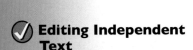

### Editing Independent Text

**You can use the Outline View to change the font type and size in a "click" placeholder. You must use the Slide View to change independent text—text *outside* a "click" placeholder.**

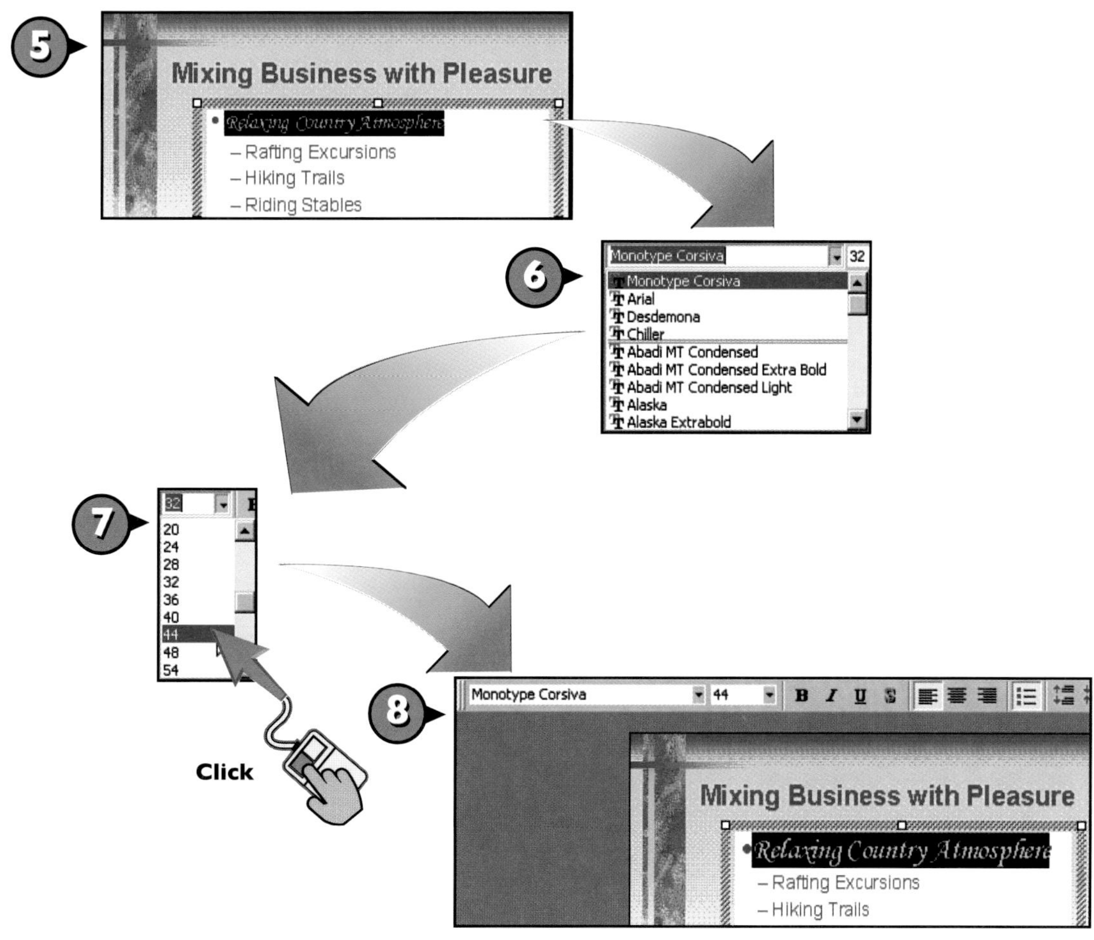


5 The font type is applied to the selected text.

6 The font types you have recently selected are listed at the top of the Font Type drop-down list so you can quickly apply the same font to other text in your presentation.

7 Click the **Font Size** drop-down button and select a font size. Scroll to see additional font sizes.

8 The new font type and font size are applied to the selected text.

**End Task**

### Entering Your Own Font Size

**If the font size you want does not appear on the list, type the size in the drop-down box and press Enter.**

### Selecting Text Quickly

**You can use several methods for selecting text. In addition to dragging the mouse pointer across the text, you can double-click to select a word or triple-click to select a bullet or paragraph.**

## Enhancing Text Through Formatting

You can use several methods to change the way text appears on your slides. You can apply formats such as bold and italic, or change characters to `superscript` or `subscript`.

# Task 10: Applying Special Formats to Text

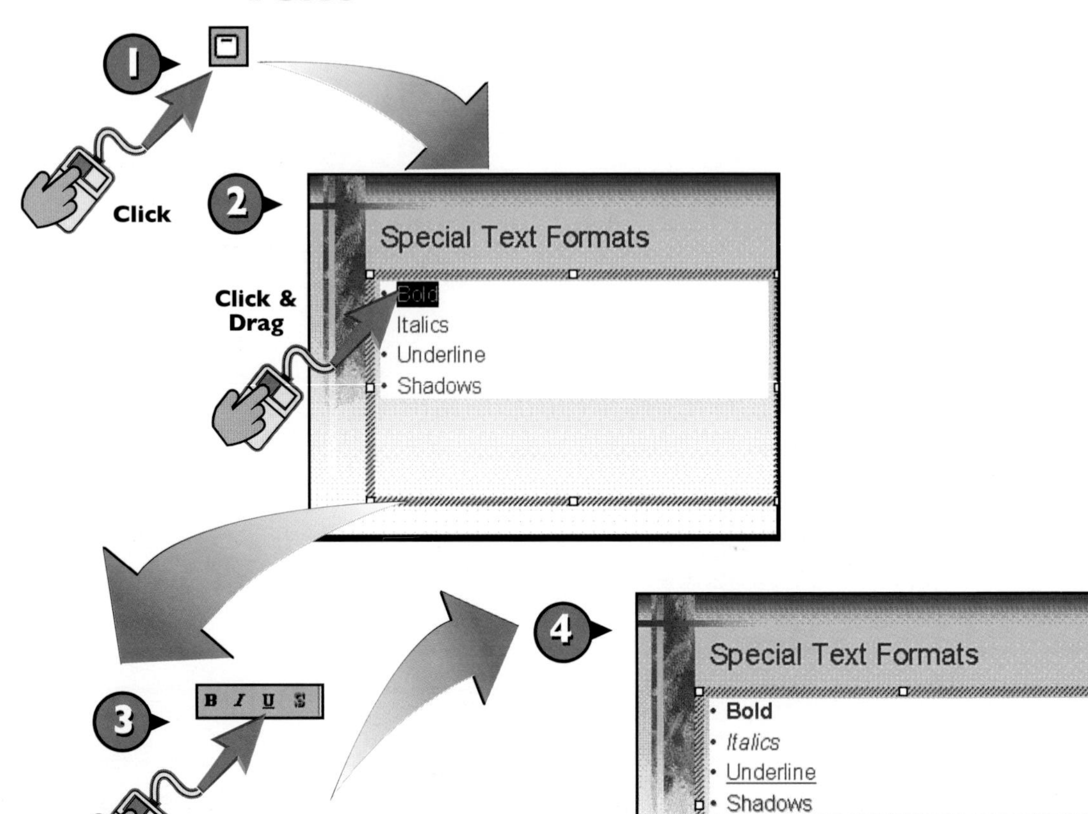


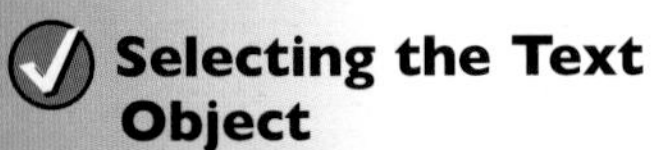

### Selecting the Text Object

To apply the same format to all the text in a "click" placeholder, text box, or AutoShape, click anywhere on the text and press **Esc**. When the text object is selected, its border displays dots instead of slash marks.

Click the **Slide View** button in the lower left-corner of the PowerPoint screen.

Drag the mouse pointer across the text to select the text you want to change.

Bold, underline, italic, and shadow text formats can be applied quickly by using the buttons on the Formatting toolbar.

When you use a format button, you see the text changes immediately.

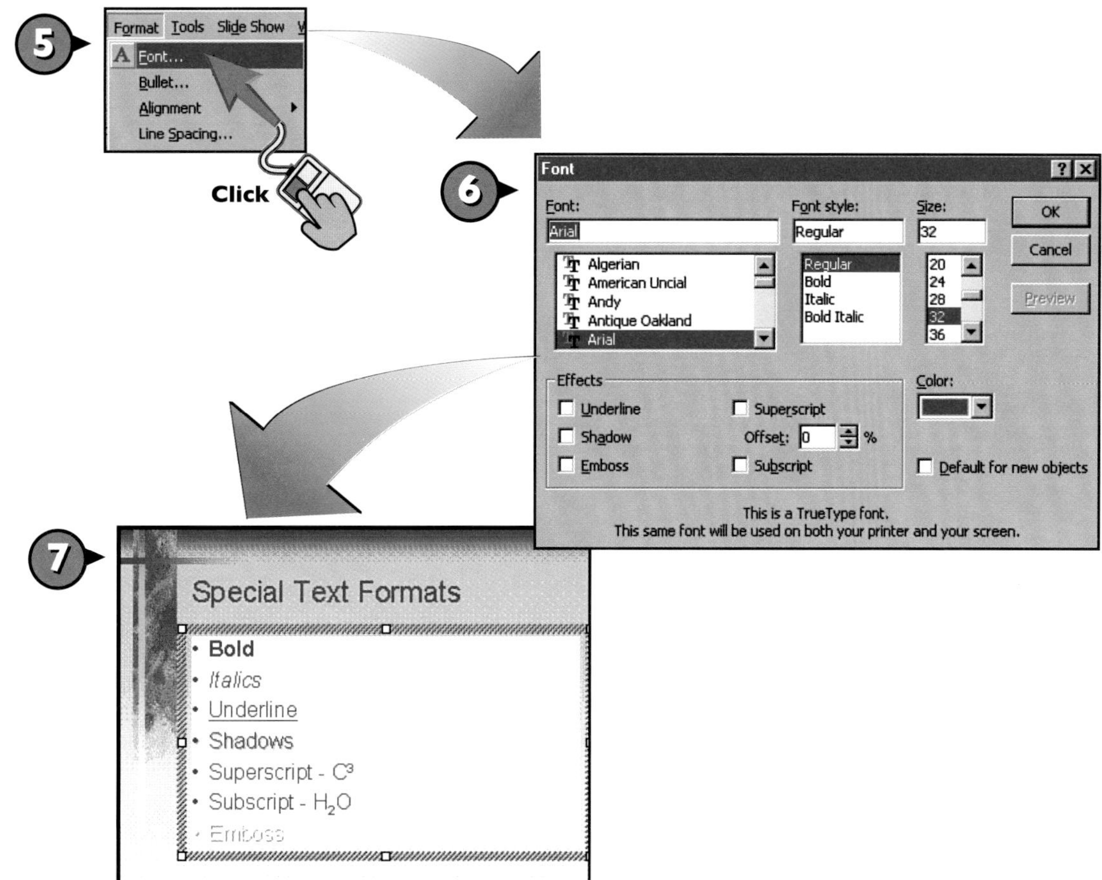


5. Another way to apply text formats is to choose Format, Font.

6. Use the **Font** dialog box to apply **Superscript**, **Subscript**, and **Emboss** formats to your text.

7. You can experiment with the various text formats to see how they can enhance your slide text.

**Applying Several Formats at One Time**
You can also use the Font dialog box to apply several formats all at once.

**Formatting Text**
See Task 9 for the steps to change the text font type and font size.

See Task 11 for the steps to change the color of the text.

# Task 11: Changing the Text Color

Start
Here

## Altering the Color of Text

Each presentation design uses eight coordinating colors in the presentation. You can use one of these colors or select any color you want from the color wheel.

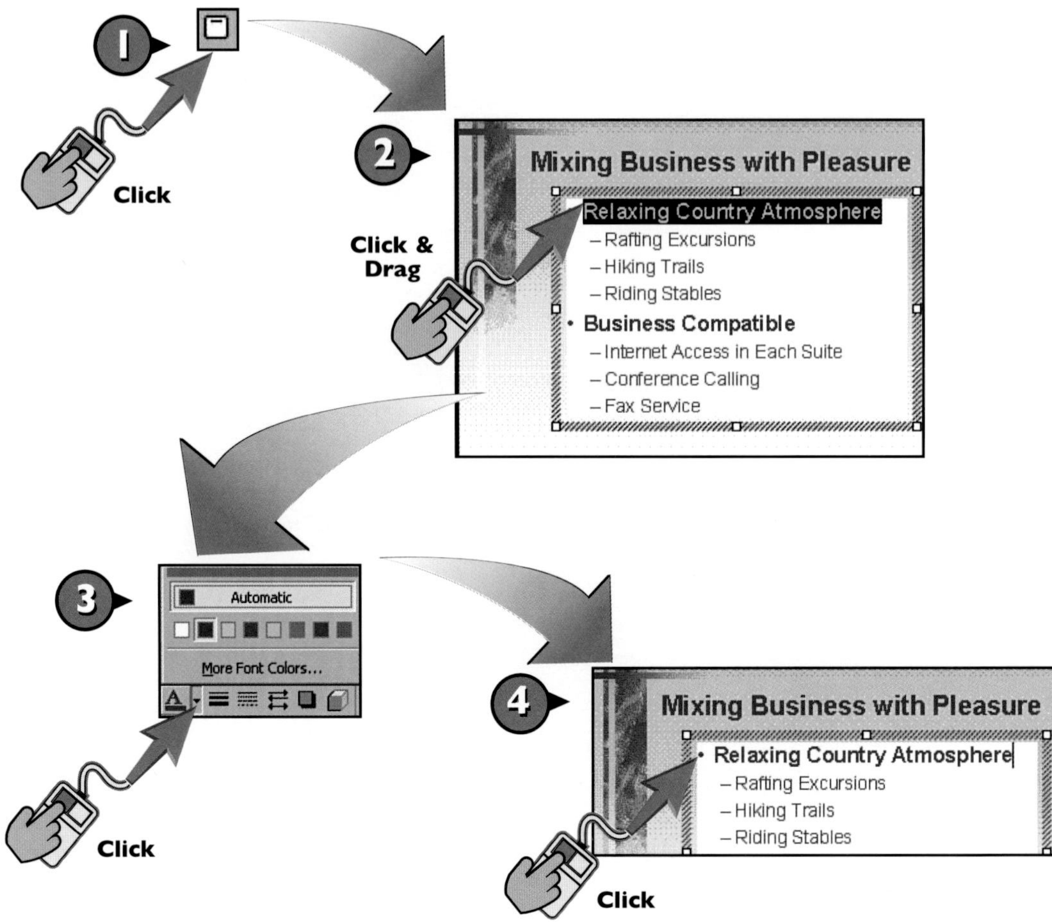
Click
Click &
Drag
Mixing Business with Pleasure
Relaxing Country Atmosphere
– Rafting Excursions
– Hiking Trails
– Riding Stables
• Business Compatible
– Internet Access in Each Suite
– Conference Calling
– Fax Service
Automatic
More Font Colors...
Click
Mixing Business with Pleasure
• Relaxing Country Atmosphere
– Rafting Excursions
– Hiking Trails
– Riding Stables
Click

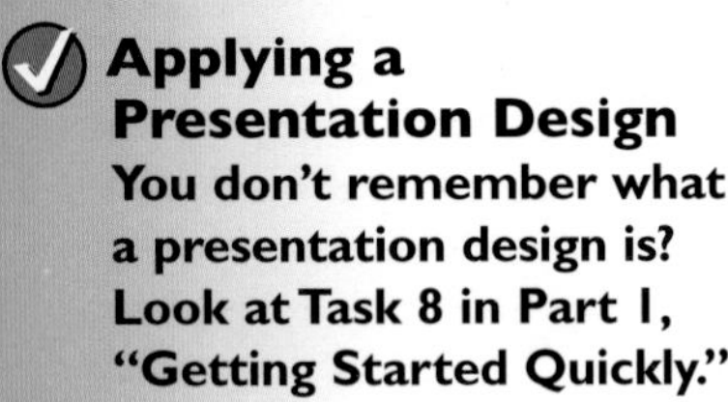

**Applying a Presentation Design**
You don't remember what a presentation design is? Look at Task 8 in Part 1, "Getting Started Quickly."

1. Click the **Slide View** button in the lower-left corner of the PowerPoint screen.
2. Drag the mouse pointer across the text to select the text you want to change.
3. Click the **Font Color** drop-down button. Choose one of the eight default colors.
4. The selected text changes color.

Next
Step

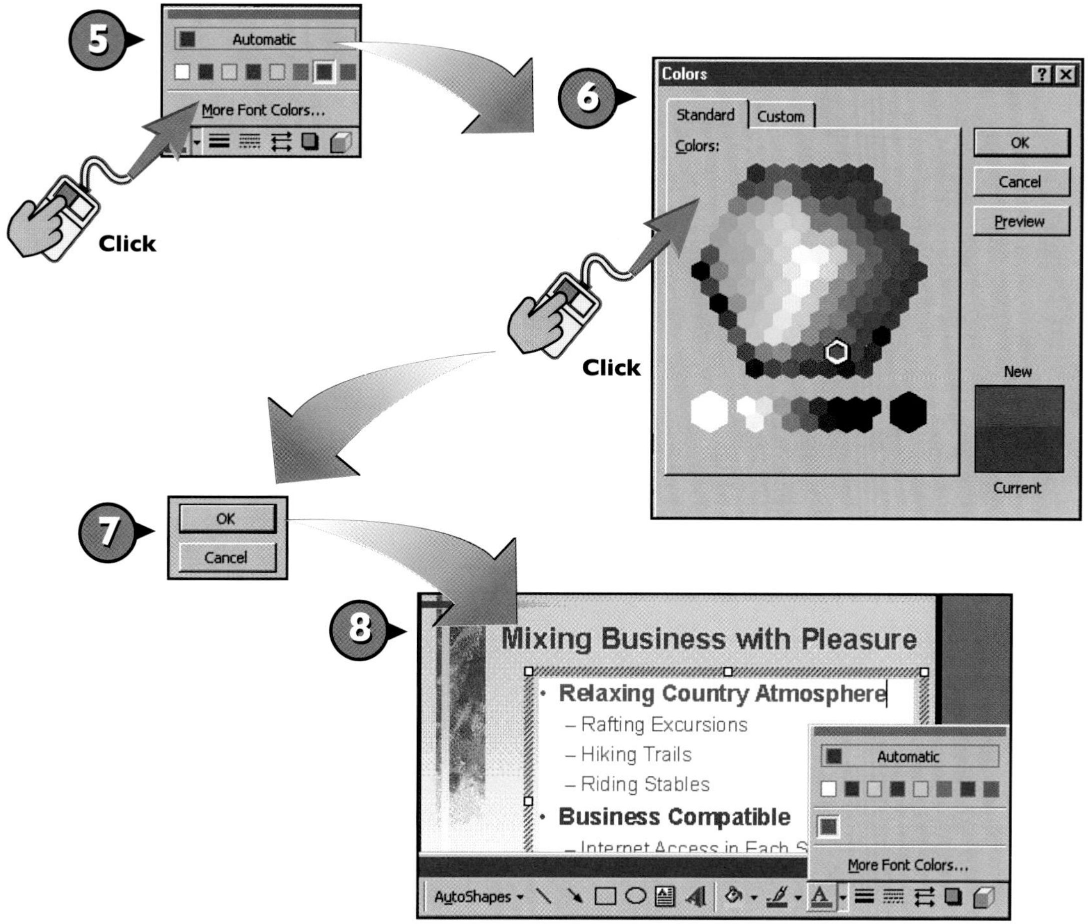

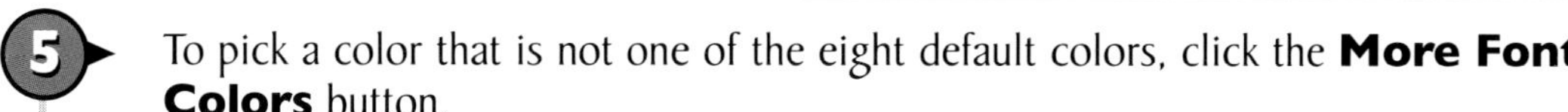

5. To pick a color that is not one of the eight default colors, click the **More Font Colors** button.

6. Select a color from the **Colors** dialog box; the current and new colors are displayed in the lower-right corner.

7. Choose **OK** to apply the selected color.

8. Colors used in the presentation now appear in the **Font Colors** drop-down list for quick access.

### Changing the Color on All Text in an Object

**To apply the same color to all the text in a "click" placeholder, text box, or AutoShape, click anywhere on the text and press Esc. When the text object is selected, its border displays dots instead of slash marks.**

# Task 12: Checking Your Spelling

## Identifying and Correcting Spelling Errors

**Avoid embarrassment by spell-checking your presentation before you print or show it to others!**

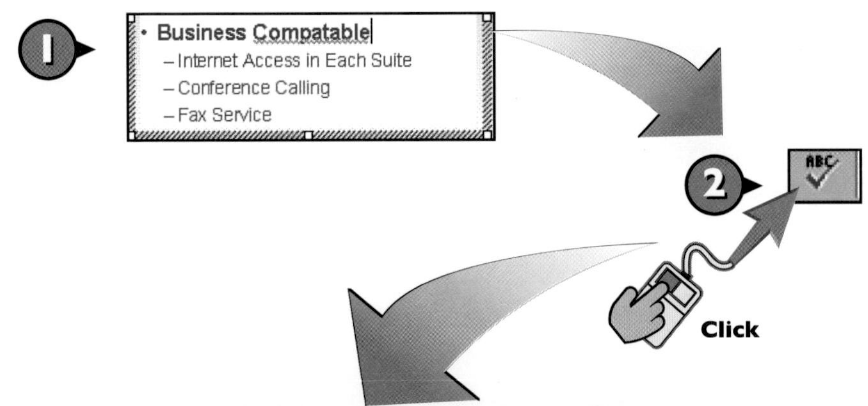


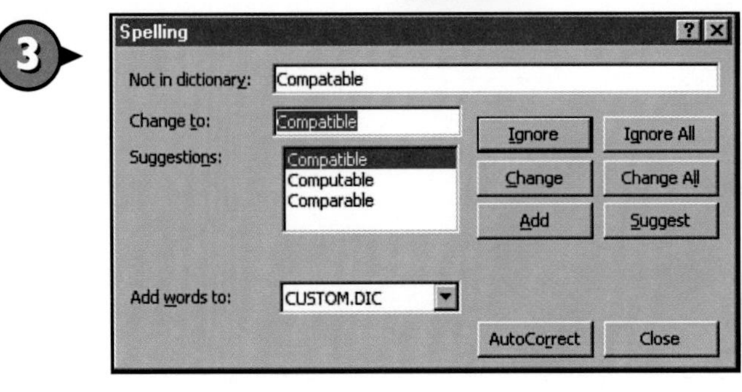

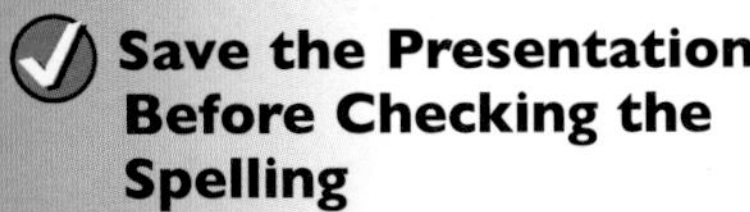

**Save the Presentation Before Checking the Spelling**

**Save your presentation before you use the spell checker. If you make a mistake during the spell-check process, you can close your file (without saving the changes) and open it to spell check again.**

1. Whenever PowerPoint does not recognize a word you have typed, the word is underlined in red so you can correct it immediately if necessary.
2. To spell-check your entire presentation, click the **Spelling** button on the Standard toolbar.
3. The Spelling dialog box appears.
4. PowerPoint identifies the first word in your presentation it believes is not spelled correctly.

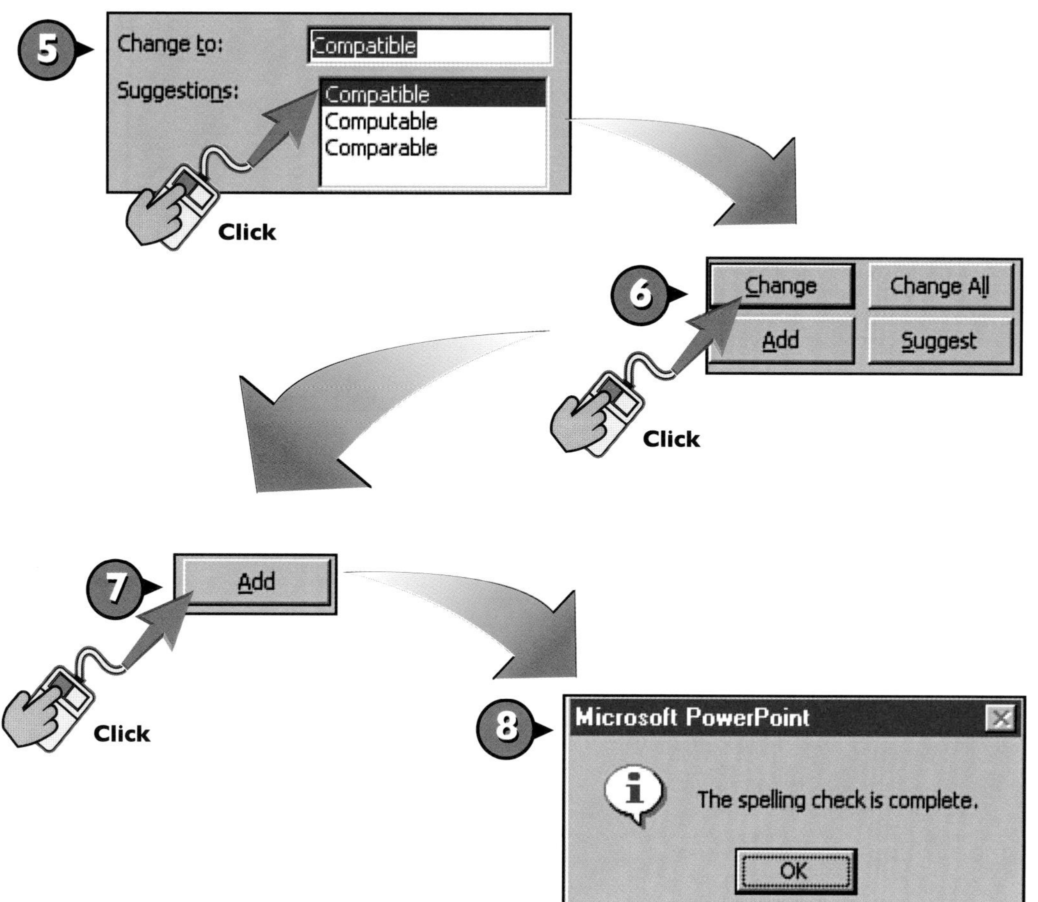

5 A correction is proposed in the **Change To** box and alternatives are listed in the **Suggestions** box.

6 Choose **Ignore** if the word is spelled the way you want, or select a suggested spelling and choose **Change**.

7 **Add** words to the dictionary, such as acronyms or people's names; these will not be flagged as misspelled again.

8 When PowerPoint has finished checking the spelling, a dialog box appears. Choose **OK**.

**Typing Your Own Correction**
**If the word you want does not appear in the Suggestions box, type the correction in the Change To box.**

**Spelling Checks All Text**
**All text in your entire presentation is verified when you spell check, including text in text boxes, speaker's notes, and AutoShapes.**

PART 4

# Adding Clip Art to Slides

PowerPoint contains many techniques for enlivening your presentations, including the use of images and drawings.

*Clip art* includes colorful illustrations, symbols, and cartoons. Many clip art images are installed with PowerPoint. Additional clip art can be found on the Microsoft Office CD.

*WordArt* is a technique of curving or angling the text of words or phrases. WordArt also adds special colors and shadows to the text.

The Microsoft Office CD contains dozens of photographs ranging from the Golden Gate Bridge to a tropical sunset to an action shot of bicycle racing.

You can also create a wide range of shapes in PowerPoint, such as starbursts, callout boxes, and flowchart symbols, by using the Drawing toolbar.

# Tasks

# Task 1: Adding a Clip Art Image to a Single Slide

## Using Clip Art Images on Slides

**One way to improve the appearance of a slide is to add a clip art image. Images can be added to any slide, even if it doesn't have a placeholder for a clip art image.**

Start Here

**Modifying Clip Art Objects**

**See Part 5, "Working with Slide Objects," Tasks 2 and 3, to learn more about moving and resizing clip art images.**

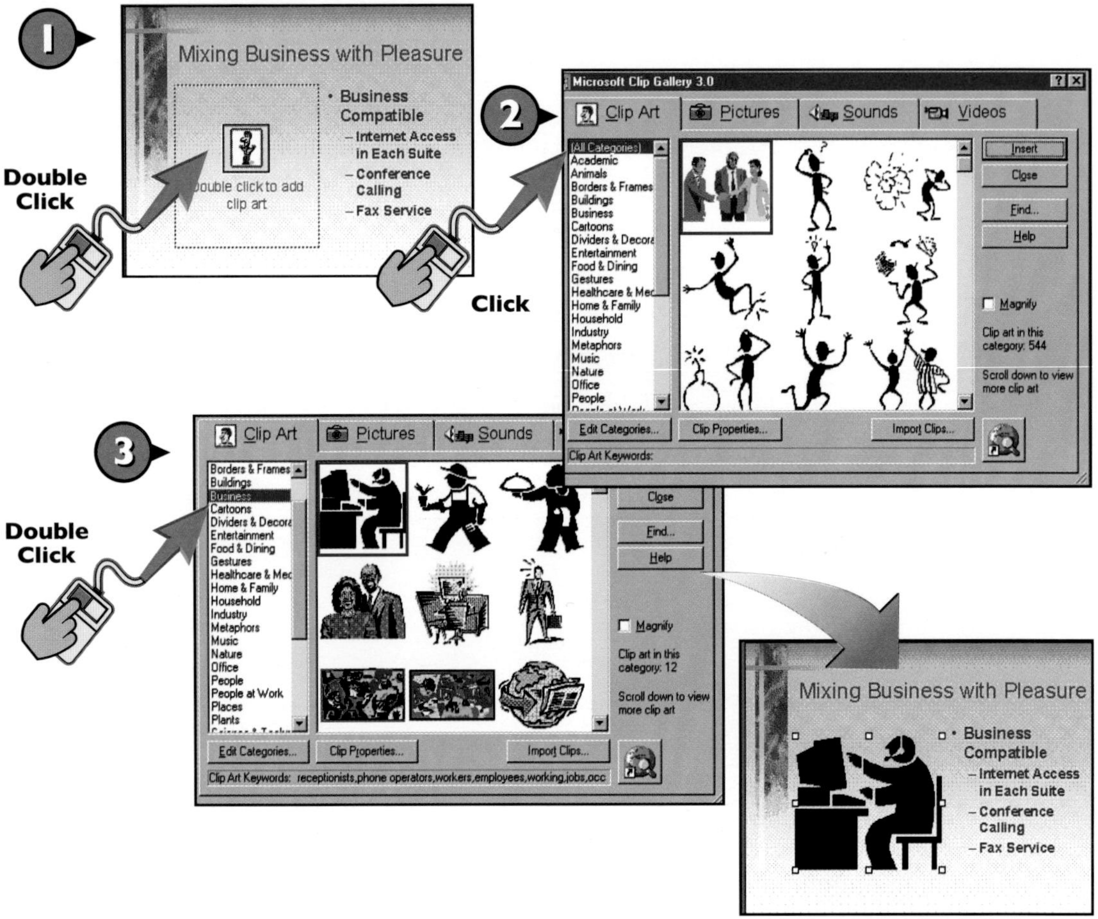

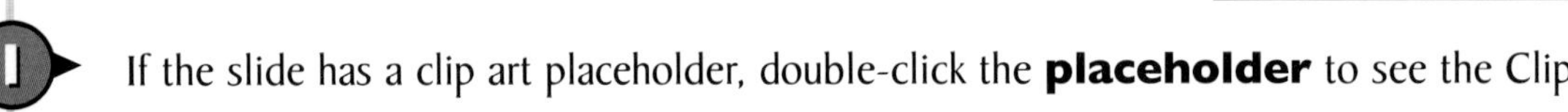

1. If the slide has a clip art placeholder, double-click the **placeholder** to see the Clip Gallery.
2. From the list on the left side of the dialog box, choose a category. Scroll to see additional categories.
3. If necessary, scroll to see more images; then double-click the image you want. The clip art image appears in the placeholder on the slide.

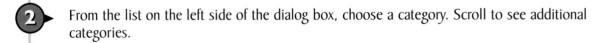

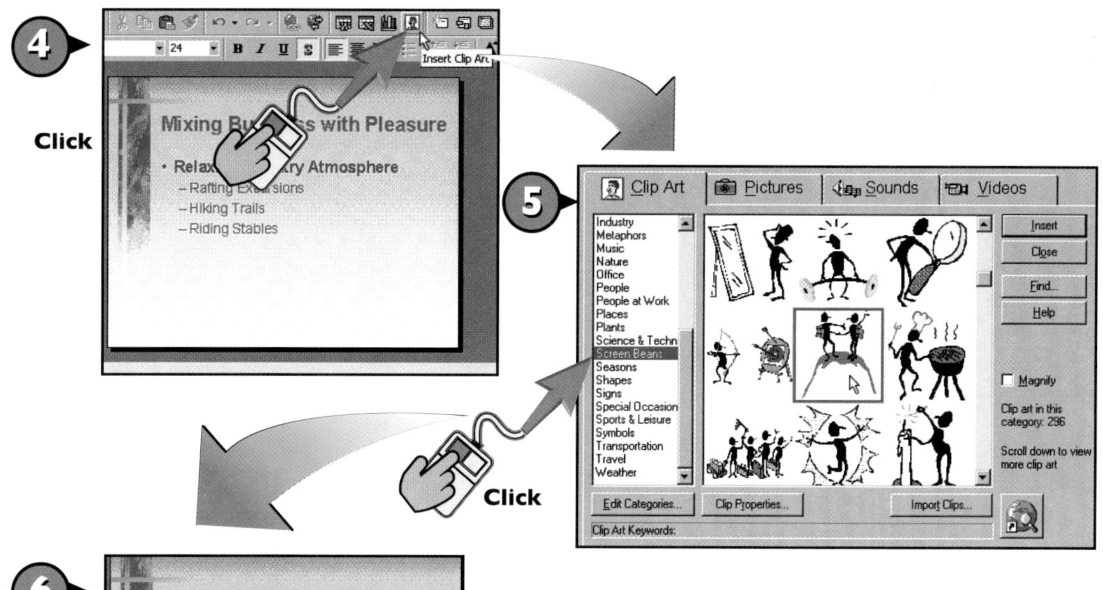


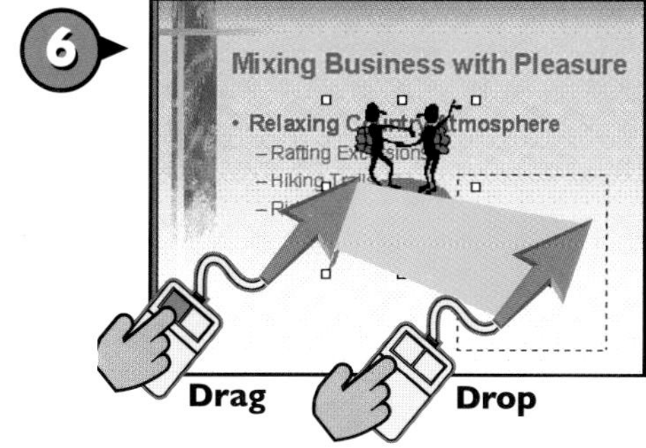


**4** If the slide does not have a clip art placeholder, click the **Insert Clip Art** button on the Standard toolbar.

**5** Select the category and the clip art image you want to display on your slide.

**6** The clip art is placed in the middle of the slide. Use drag and drop to move the image.

**Finding Clip Art on the Office CD**

**The Microsoft Office CD comes with additional clip art images. Using Microsoft Explorer, locate the Clip Art folder on the CD. Double-click the Setup.exe file to add the additional clips to your hard drive.**

**Then, in the Clip Gallery dialog box, right-click on any image and choose Update Clip Previews, Update All to bring these additional images into the Gallery.**

# Task 2: Adding the Same Clip Art Image to All Slides

Start Here

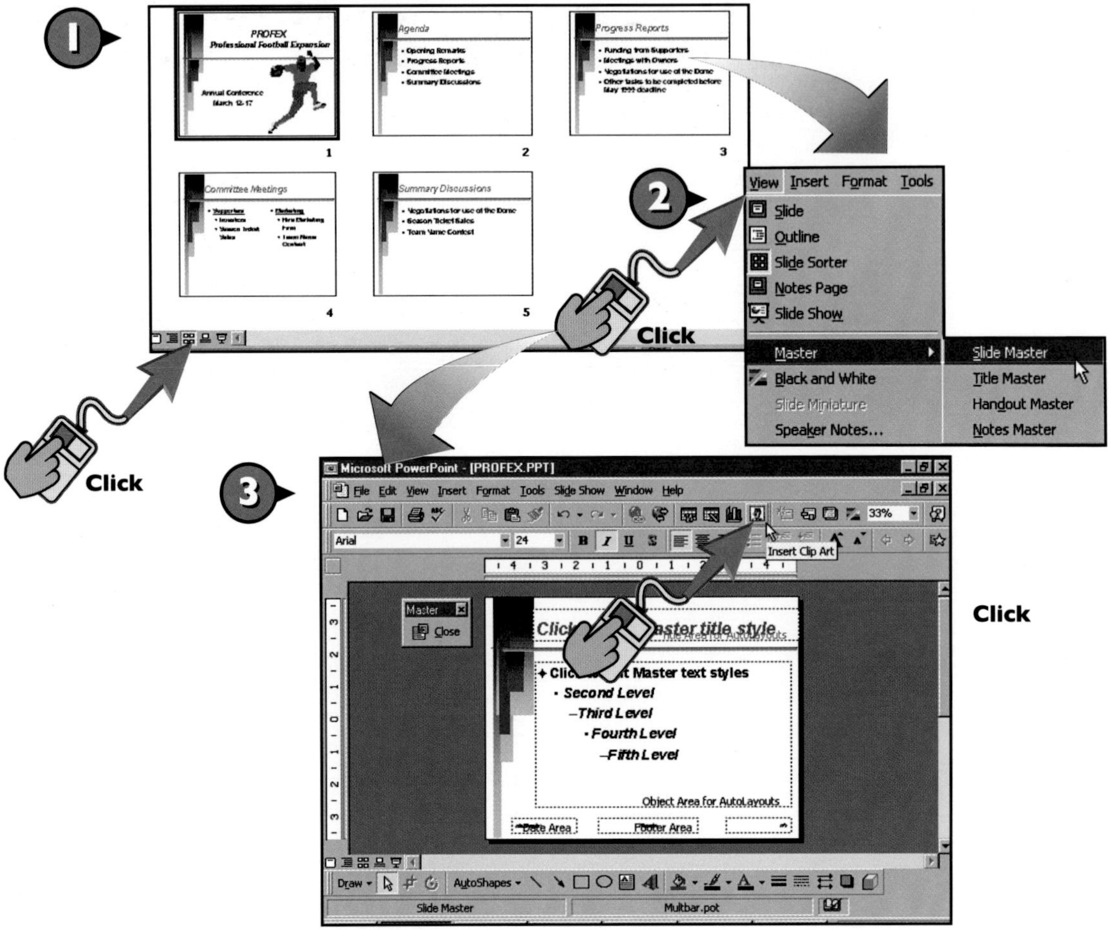

## Placing a Clip Art Image on the Slide Master

If you want the same clip art image to appear on all slides, you can add the image to the Slide Master.

Images added to the **Slide Master** appear on all slides except those that have a title layout.

1 Switch to the **Slide Sorter View**.

2 Choose **View, Master, Slide Master**.

3 In the Slide Master, click the **Insert Clip Art** button on the Standard toolbar.

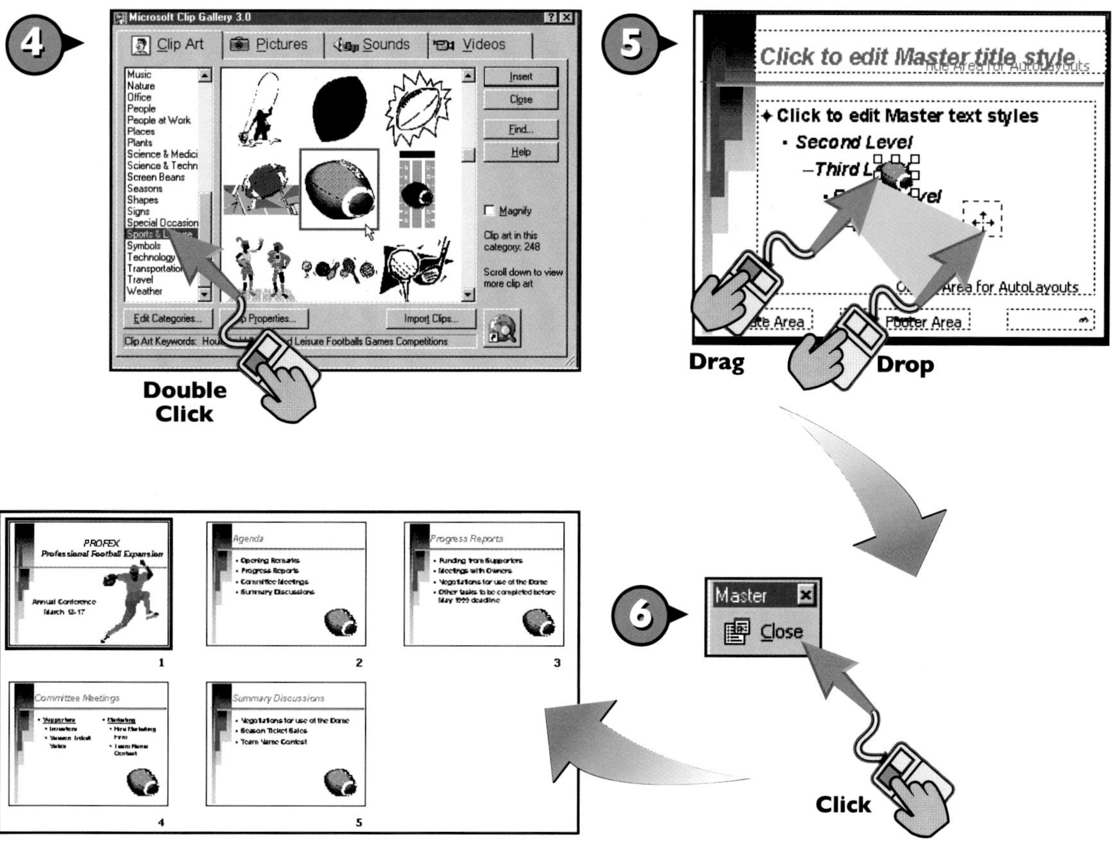


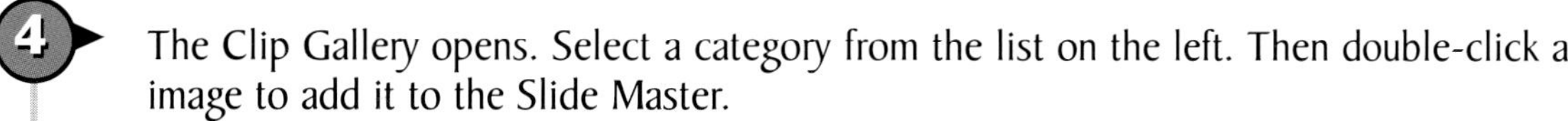

4 The Clip Gallery opens. Select a category from the list on the left. Then double-click an image to add it to the Slide Master.

5 Drag the image to the desired location and drop it. Resize the image as necessary.

6 Click the **Close** button to close the Slide Master. The clip art image appears on all slides except those using the title slide layout.

**Modifying Clip Art Images**
**See Part 5, Tasks 2 and 3, to learn more about moving and resizing clip art images.**

**Removing Clip Art Images**
**You must display the Slide Master to modify or remove the clip art image.**

# Task 3: Recoloring Clip Art

## Changing the Default Colors of a Clip Art Image

**If you don't like the colors on the clip art image you want to use, change them!**

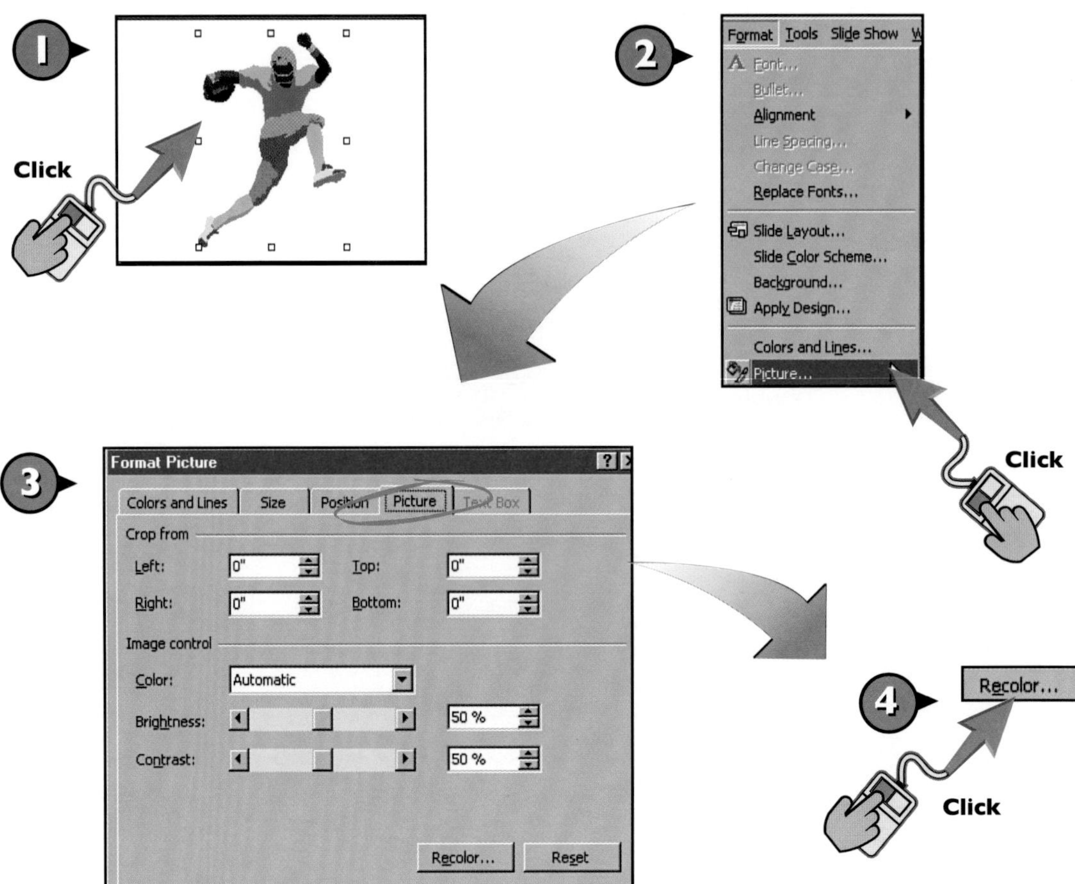


1. After you add a clip art image to your presentation, click on the image you want to recolor. The selection handles appear, indicating the image has been selected.
2. Choose **Format, Picture**.
3. The Format Picture dialog box appears. Select the **Picture** tab.
4. Click the **Recolor** button on the Picture tab.

**Making Sure the Image is Selected**
**When you click on a clip art image, a set of *selection handles* appears around the image, indicating it is selected.**

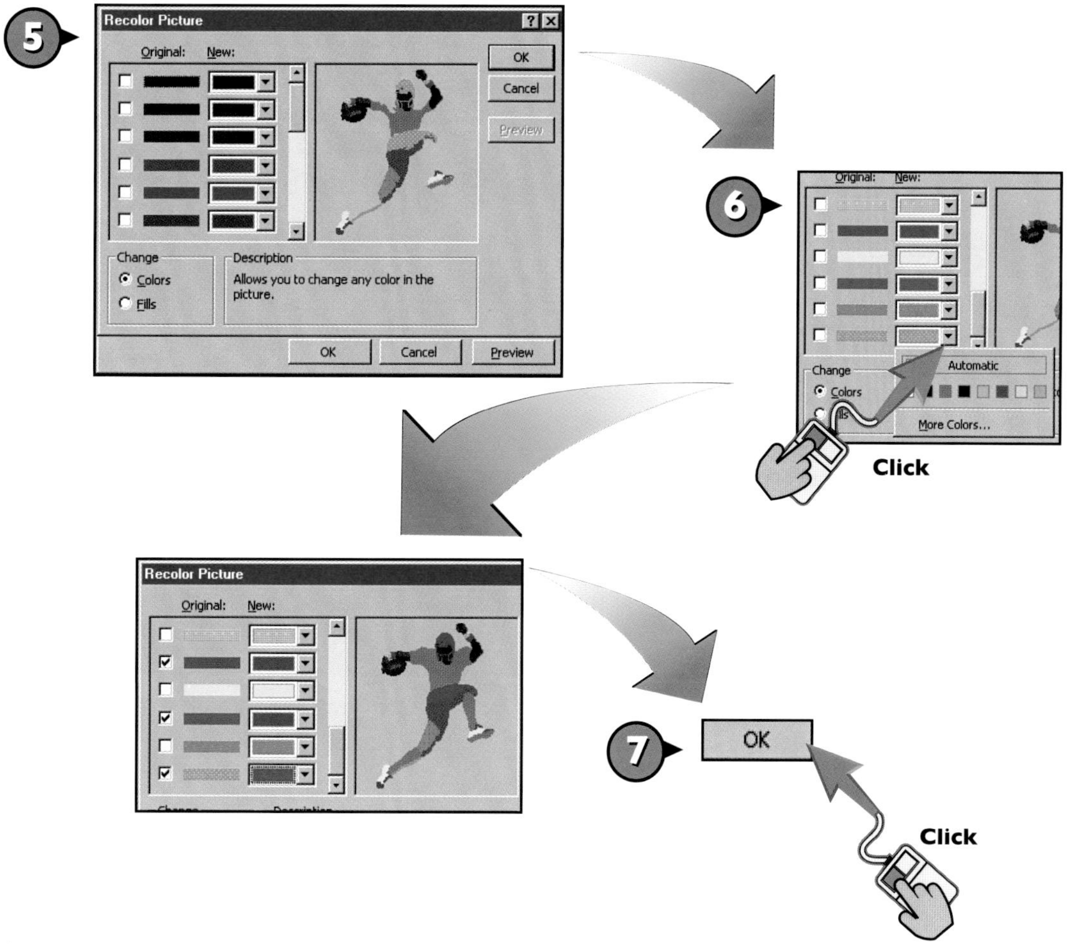

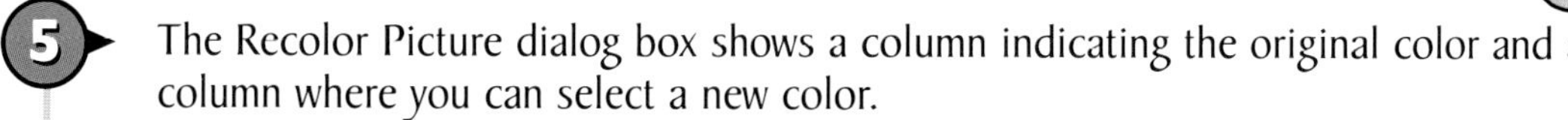

5. The Recolor Picture dialog box shows a column indicating the original color and a column where you can select a new color.

6. Click the **drop-down arrow** next to the color you want to change. Choose a default color or click on **More Colors**.

7. Choose **OK** to accept the changes in the Recolor Picture dialog box. Choose **OK** again to exit the Format Picture dialog box.

### Identifying All the Image Colors

**Sometimes you may have to scroll in the Recolor Picture dialog box to see all the colors used in the clip art image.**

### Selecting a New Image Color

**When you click on a drop-down arrow to change a color, the eight default colors that are part of the presentation design appear, along with the More Colors button. Choose More Colors to display a dialog box with two tabs. Choose the Standard tab to select a new color from a color wheel.**

# Task 4: Adding WordArt to a Slide

## Using WordArt to Enhance Your Slides

Another way to liven up slides is to use WordArt, frequently seen on flyers or bulletin board notices.

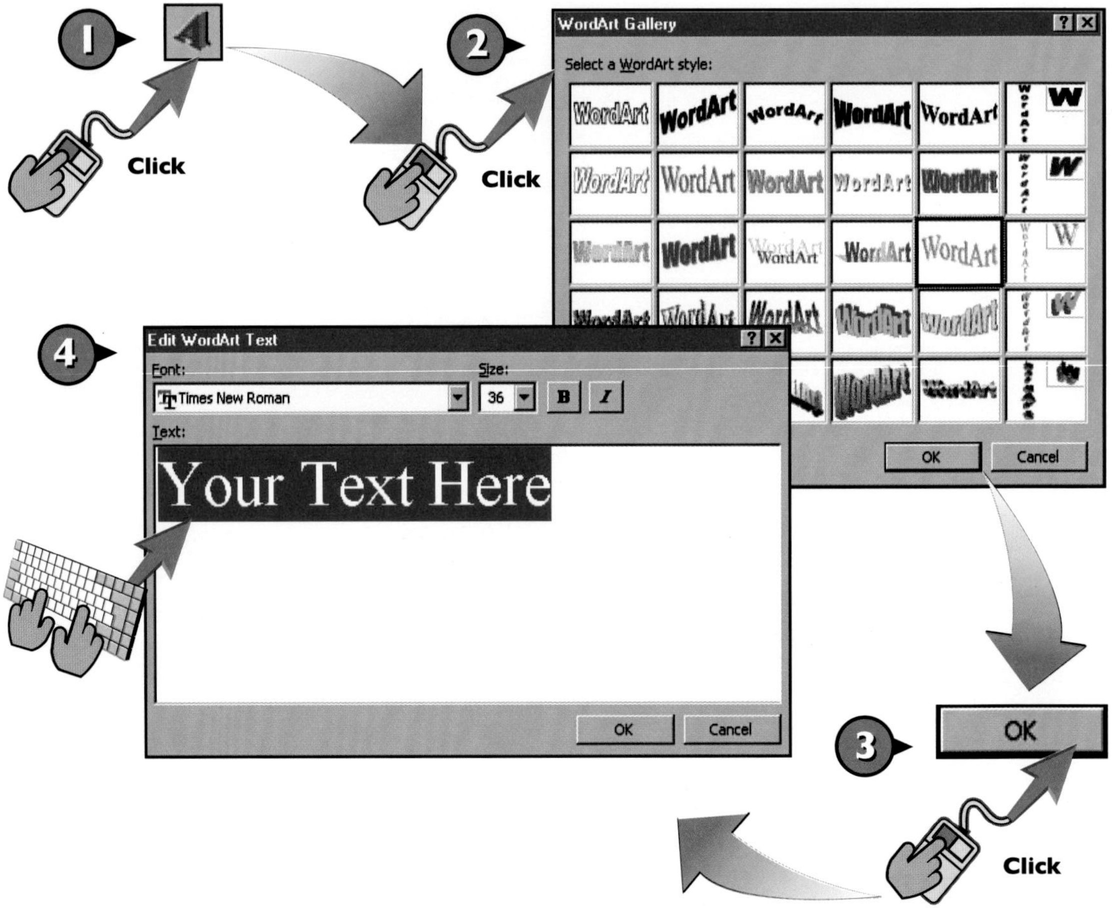

1. Click the **WordArt** button on the Drawing toolbar.
2. Choose the style you want for the WordArt. The styles include shape, direction, shadow, and color.
3. Choose **OK**.
4. The Edit WordArt Text dialog box appears. Type the text you want for the WordArt.

**Modifying WordArt Objects**
You can modify the WordArt styles. See Task 5 for steps on changing WordArt shape, direction, and color.

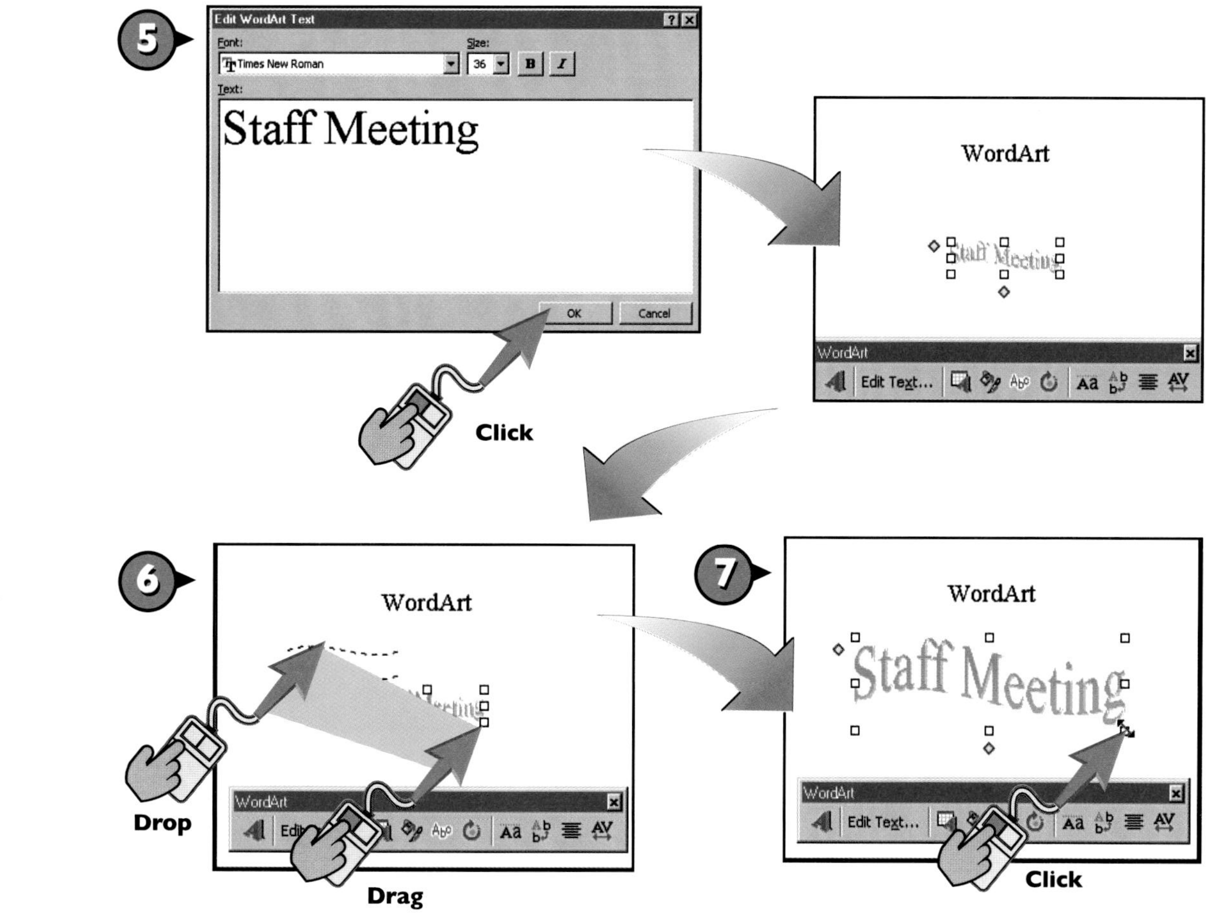

5. Choose **OK** to create a WordArt object using the text you typed. The WordArt object appears in the middle of the slide, along with the WordArt toolbar.

6. Drag and drop from the middle of the object to move it.

7. Drag a corner selection handle to resize the WordArt object.

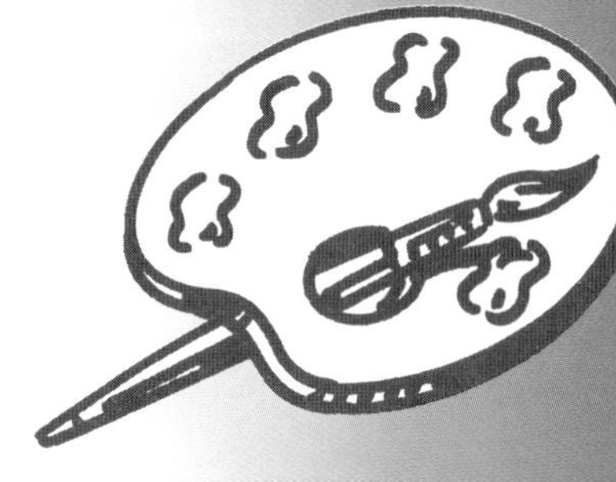

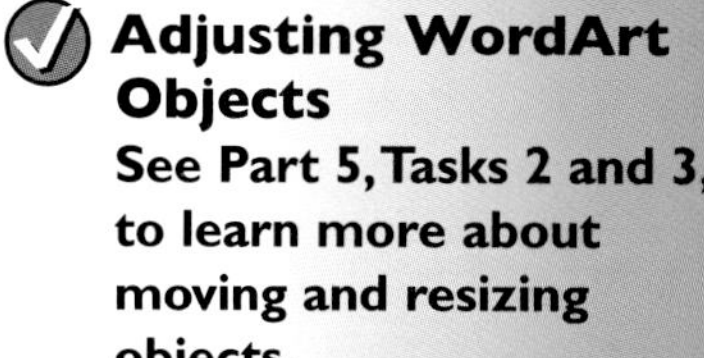

**Adjusting WordArt Objects**
**See Part 5, Tasks 2 and 3, to learn more about moving and resizing objects.**

# Task 5: Changing the WordArt Style

## Altering the Appearance of WordArt Objects

**You can easily change the style or shape used for the WordArt by using the buttons on the WordArt toolbar.**

**Selecting WordArt Objects**

**To select the WordArt object, make sure the mouse pointer is a four-headed arrow before you click on the object.**

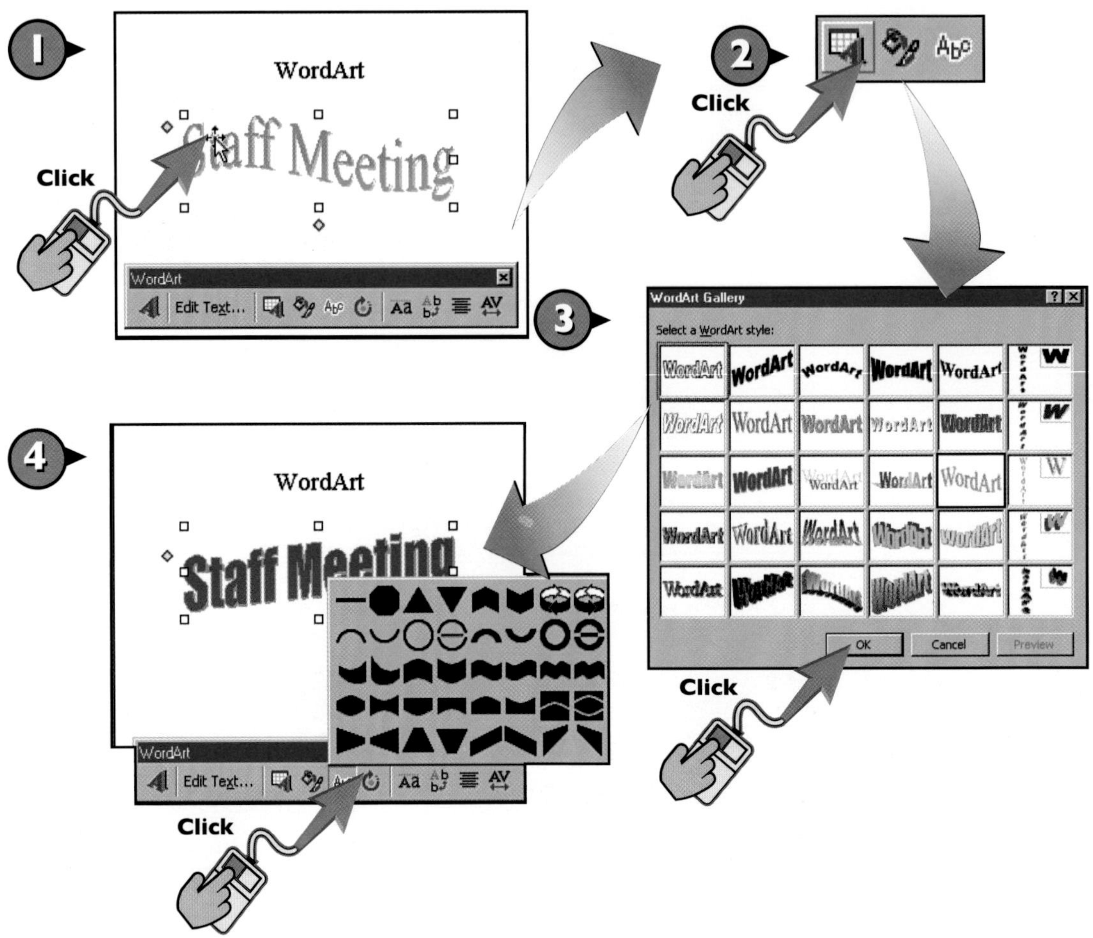

1. Select the WordArt object you want to change.
2. Click the **WordArt Gallery** button on the WordArt toolbar.
3. Select a new style from the Gallery and then choose **OK** to apply the new WordArt style.
4. Click the **WordArt Shape** button to select a different shape for the display of the words.

# Task 6: Editing the WordArt Text

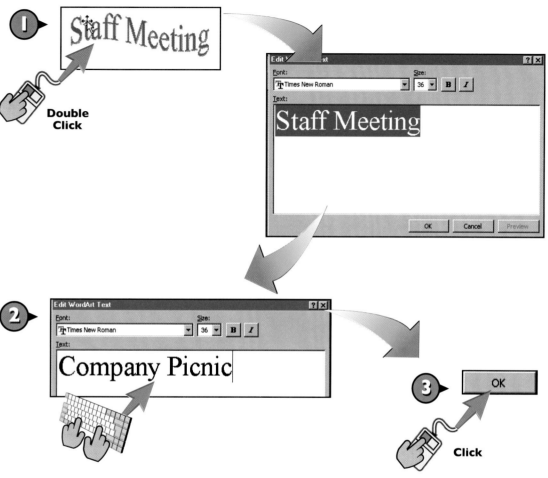


## Change or Edit the Text in a WordArt Object

You can quickly modify or format the WordArt text by double-clicking on the WordArt object.

1. Position the mouse pointer over the WordArt object. When the pointer changes to a four-headed arrow, double-click.
2. Type the new text. Use the Font and Size drop-down boxes or the Bold and Italic buttons to format the text.
3. Choose **OK** to apply the changes to the WordArt text.

**Editing WordArt Text**
You can use common Windows editing techniques in the text area of the Edit WordArt Text dialog box. For example, you can double-click to highlight a word or use the backspace key to delete one character to the left of the flashing cursor.

# Task 7: Drawing Shapes on a Slide

## Adding Lines, Arrows, and Other Shapes to Your Slides

**PowerPoint has a Drawing toolbar that contains all the tools necessary to create and enhance drawn objects.**

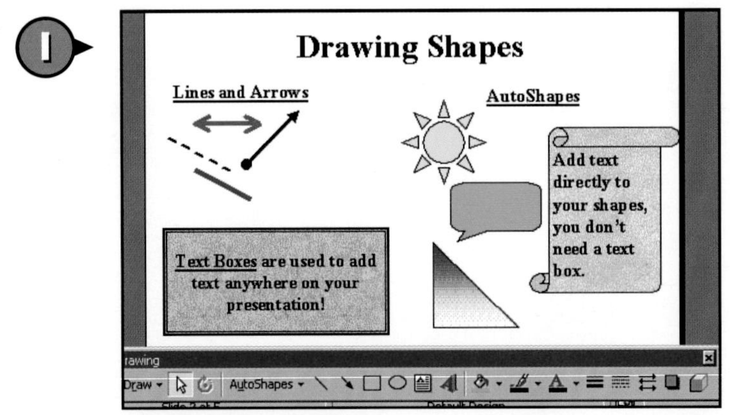


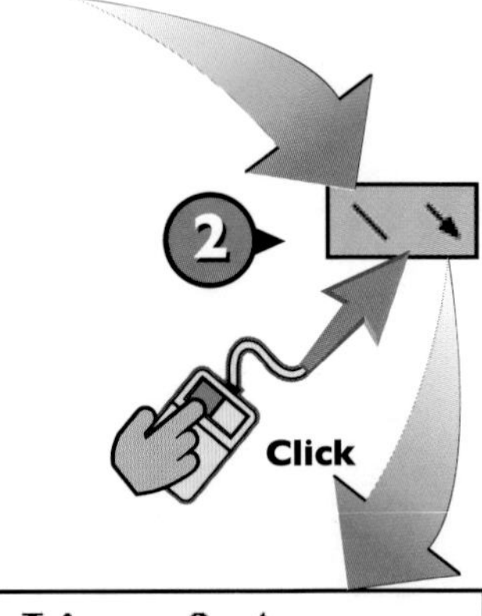


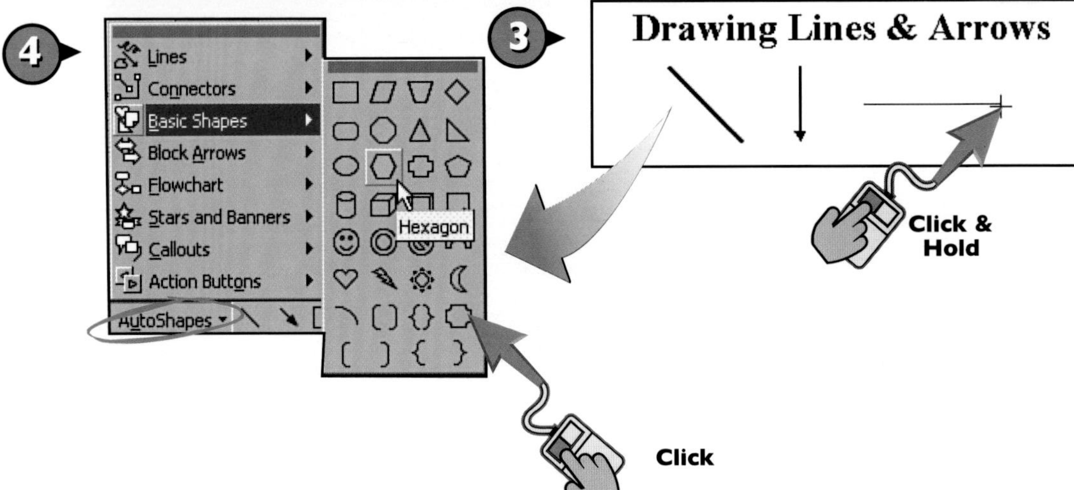

**Removing Unwanted Objects**
**If you make a mistake while drawing an object, simply select it, press the Delete key, and try again!**

1. The Drawing toolbar is the starting point for drawing lines, arrows, and shapes.

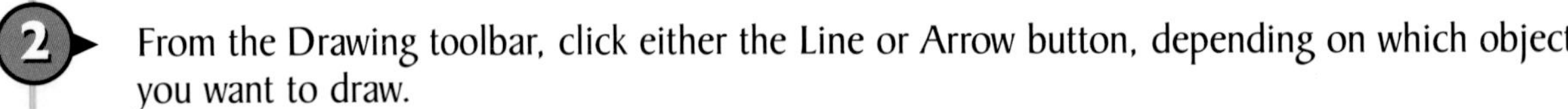

2. From the Drawing toolbar, click either the Line or Arrow button, depending on which object you want to draw.
3. Drag the mouse pointer from the beginning of the line or arrow to the end point.
4. To draw an AutoShape, start by selecting a shape from one of the groups listed on the AutoShape menu.

5 Drawing AutoShapes

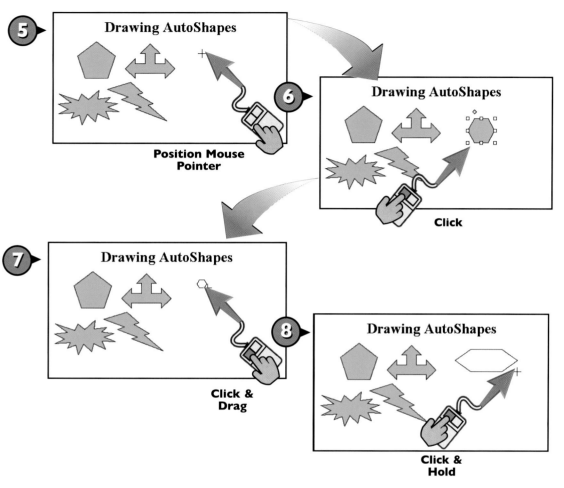

Position Mouse Pointer

6 Drawing AutoShapes

Click

7 Drawing AutoShapes

Click & Drag

8 Drawing AutoShapes

Click & Hold

 One way to draw a shape is to position the mouse pointer where you want the shape to begin.

 Then click once to draw a sample of the shape.

 Alternatively, you can click and drag the mouse pointer to start drawing the shape.

 Drag in the direction where you want to create the shape, and release the mouse button when the shape looks the way you want it.

**Formatting Drawn Objects**

**See Part 5, Task 9, to change the fill and border color of drawn objects.**

# Task 8: Adding Pictures to a Slide

## Using Pictures from the Microsoft Office CD

**In addition to clip art images for enhancing your slides, the Microsoft Office CD contains many picture images you can add as backgrounds to slides.**

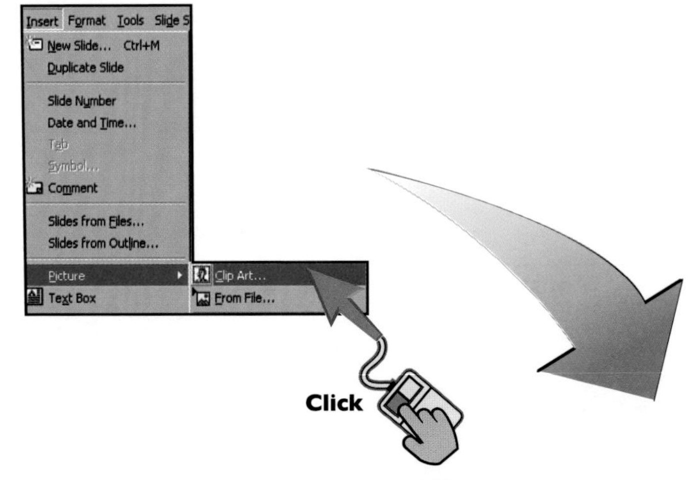

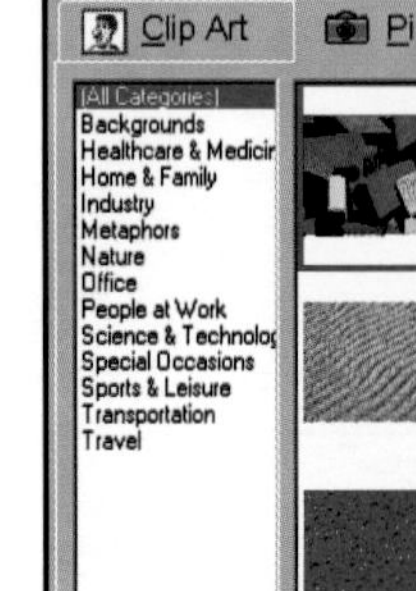

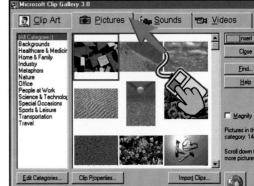

### Accessing PowerPoint Picture Files

**Picture files are very large. Because of this, the picture files are not placed on your machine when PowerPoint is installed. Instead, you access pictures through the Microsoft Office 97 CD.**

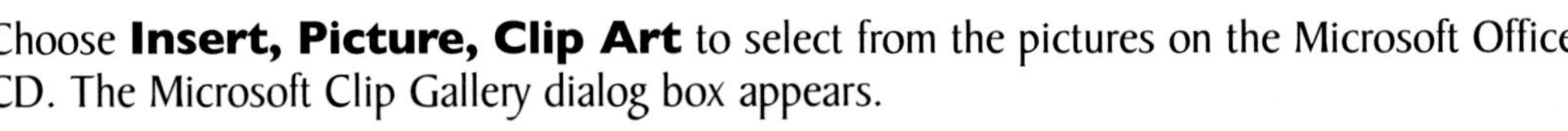

1. Choose **Insert, Picture, Clip Art** to select from the pictures on the Microsoft Office CD. The Microsoft Clip Gallery dialog box appears.

2. Click the **Pictures** tab. If you have the Microsoft Office 97 CD loaded in the CD-ROM drive, the list of categories and miniature pictures appears.

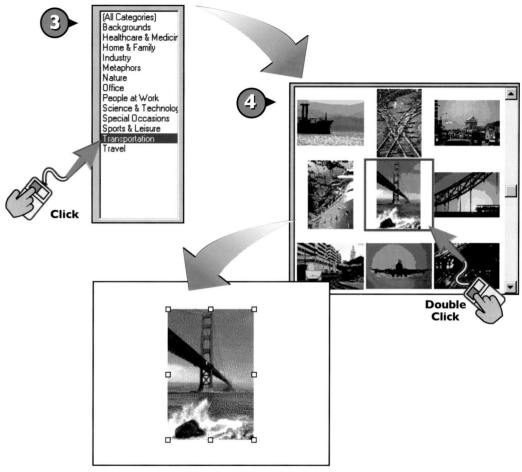

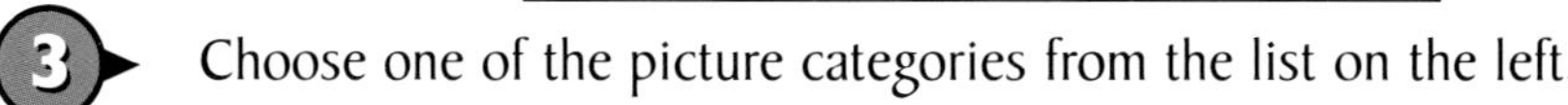

**3** Choose one of the picture categories from the list on the left.

**4** Double-click one of the pictures. The picture appears in the center of the slide. Move or resize as necessary.

### Copying Picture Files to Your Machine

**If you don't have regular access to the Microsoft Office CD, you can copy some (or all) of the picture files onto your computer's hard drive.**

**The picture files on the CD are located in the Clip Art folder. Use Windows Explorer to copy them to the Clipart folder on your machine—located in the Program Files\Microsoft Office subdirectory.**

**See Task 9 for steps on adding pictures to the Clip Gallery.**

PART 5

# Working with Slide Objects

Any item you can select on a slide is considered a slide ***object***. This includes "click" placeholders, independent text boxes, clip art, pictures, and drawings. The way you manipulate slide objects is similar, regardless of the type of object; that is, you move and resize a text object much in the same way you move and resize clip art.

In this part, you learn how to rearrange objects by moving, aligning, layering, and grouping. Additionally, this part shows you how to format, resize, copy, and delete slide objects.

# Tasks

# Task 1: Selecting Objects

## Selecting Text and Image Objects

**Before you can move, copy, resize, or delete an object, you must first select it. The procedures for selecting a text object are slightly different than those for selecting an image object.**

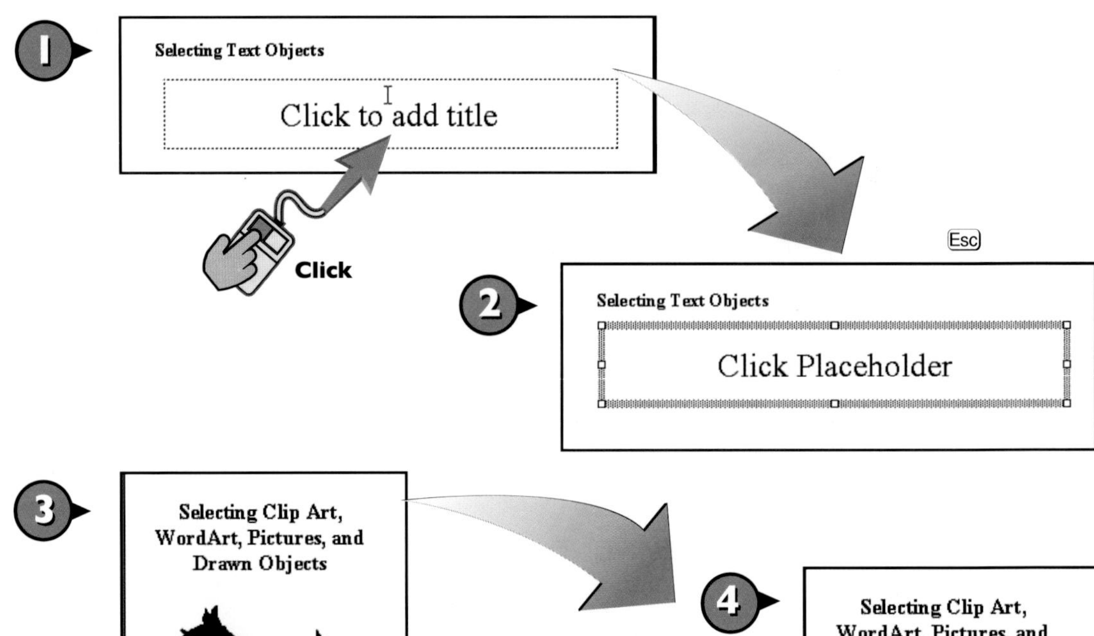


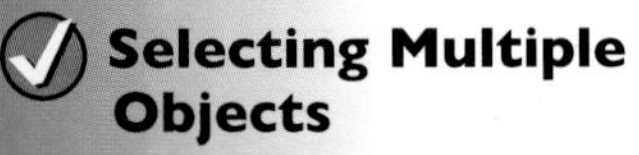

**Selecting Multiple Objects**

**To select more than one object, click the first object. Then press Shift and click each additional object you want to select.**

1. To select a text object, position the mouse pointer in the middle of the text. The pointer changes to an "I" shape or a thin plus sign. Click once.

2. Press **Esc**. A set of ***selection handles*** appears around the text object, indicating it is selected.

3. To select an image object, position the mouse pointer in the middle of the object. The pointer changes to a four-headed arrow. Click once.

4. A set of selection handles appears around the object, indicating it is selected.

# Task 2: Moving Slide Objects

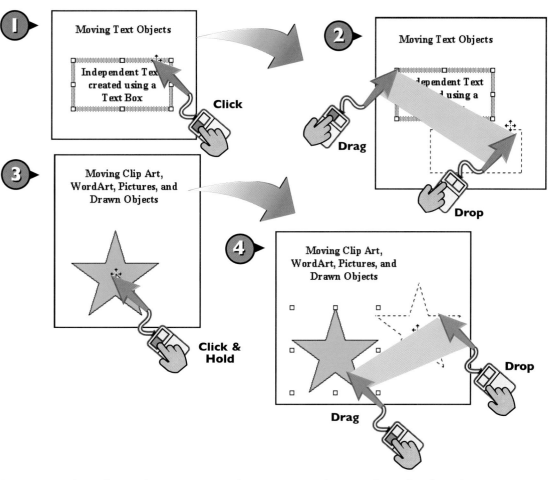

## Rearranging Selected Objects

You can use the ***drag and drop*** method to move selected text or image objects on your slides (you learned how to select objects in the previous task). You drag an object by clicking on it and then holding the mouse button down while you drag the object to its new location. When the object is in the new location, release the mouse button to "drop" the object.

To move a selected text object, position the pointer on the text object border. The pointer becomes a four-headed arrow.

Hold the mouse button down while you move the mouse to drag the text object to its new location. Then release the mouse button to drop the object.

To move a selected image object, position the pointer in the middle of the object. The mouse pointer changes to a four-headed arrow.

Hold the mouse button down while you move the mouse to drag the image object to its new location. Then release the mouse button to drop the object.

**Moving Objects to Other Slides**

**To move an object from one slide to another slide, see Task 5.**

# Task 3: Resizing Slide Objects

## Altering the Size and Shape of Slide Objects

**You can enlarge a slide object by dragging a selection handle away from the opposite corner. To shrink the object, drag toward the opposite corner.**

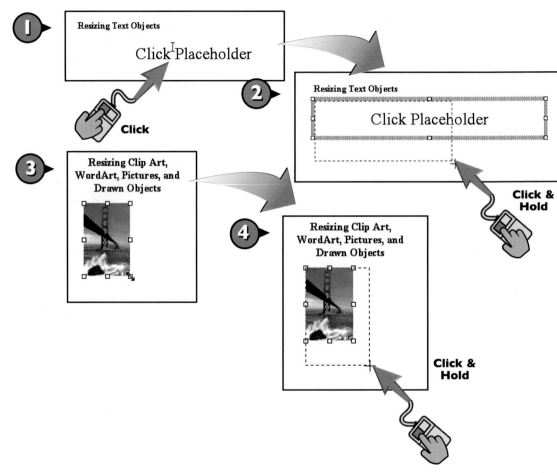

Start Here



1. To resize a text object, click anywhere on the text object. You can resize an object in the Edit mode or with the object selected.
2. Drag the object by any of its selection handles to change its dimensions. A dashed outline indicates the new size.
3. To resize a selected image object, position the mouse pointer on a corner selection handle.
4. To keep the image proportional as you resize it, drag the image from a corner selection handle.

### Resize Using Corner Selection Handles

**If you attempt to *resize* image objects by using the top, bottom, or side selection handles, the image becomes distorted. You can avoid this by always resizing from a corner selection handle.**

# Task 4: Copying Slide Objects

Copying Text Objects

Independent Text created using a Text Box

Click

Copying Text Objects

Independent Text created using a Text Box

Ctrl Drag

Drop

Copying Clip Art, WordArt, Pictures, and Drawn Objects

Copying Clip Art, WordArt, Pictures, and Drawn Objects

Ctrl Drag

Drop

Position the pointer on the border of the selected text object but not on a selection handle. The selection handle becomes a four-headed arrow.

Hold **Ctrl** as you drag and drop to create the copy.

To copy an image object, position the pointer in the middle of the object. The pointer changes to a four-headed arrow.

Hold **Ctrl** as you drag and drop to create the copy.

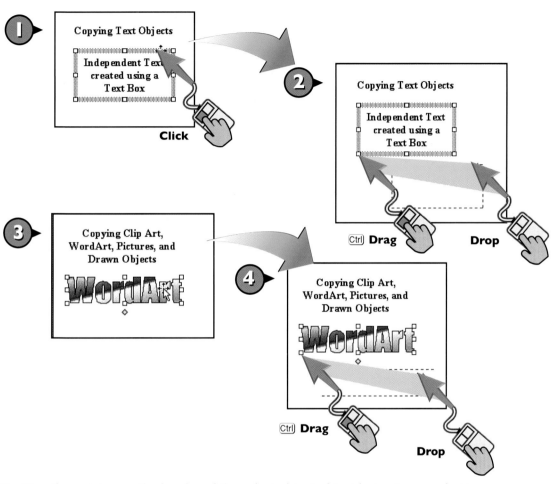

## Making Copies of Objects on Your Slides

**It is often easier to copy an object than to try to create an identical object from scratch. The key to copying an object is to make sure the mouse pointer is a four-headed arrow.**

**Copying Objects to Other Slides**

**To copy an object from one slide to another, see Task 5.**

# Task 5: Moving and Copying Objects to Other Slides

## Rearranging and Copying Objects Between Slides

The Cut, Copy, and Paste buttons on the Standard toolbar make it easy to move or copy objects to other slides.

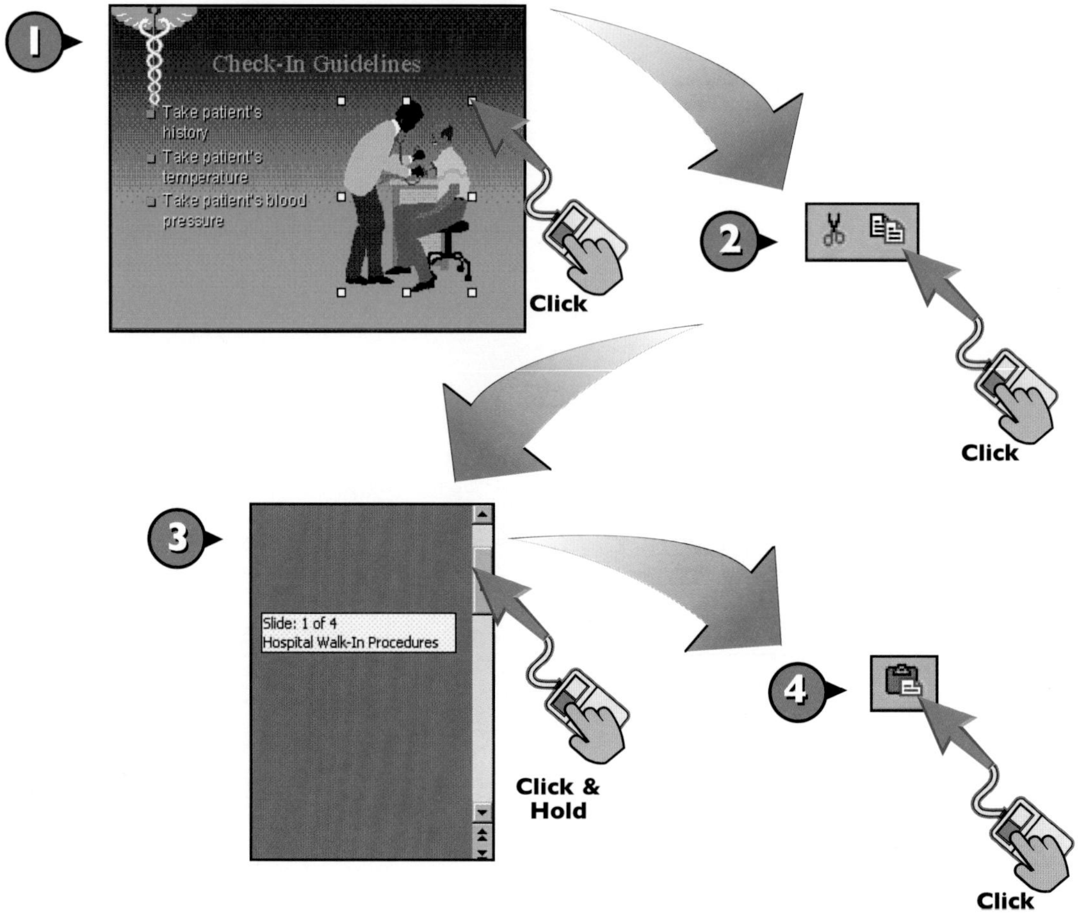

1. Click to select the object you want to move or copy.
2. Click the **Cut** button to move the object. Click the **Copy** button to copy the object.
3. Drag the scroll box on the vertical scrollbar to locate the slide you want to move or copy the object to.
4. Click the **Paste** button on the Standard toolbar.

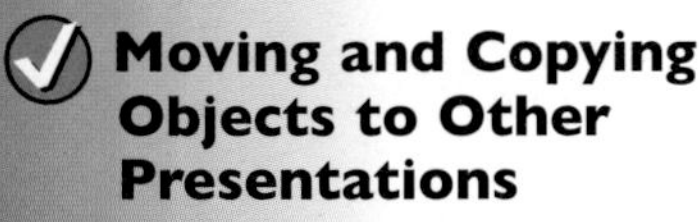

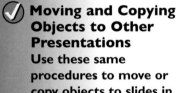

### Moving and Copying Objects to Other Presentations

Use these same procedures to move or copy objects to slides in other presentations. In step 3, open the other (target) presentation. Use the Window menu to switch back and forth between the source and target presentations.

# Task 6: Deleting Slide Objects

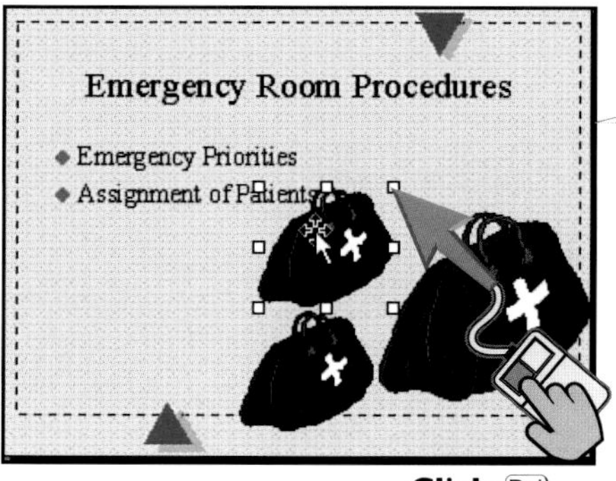


Click Del

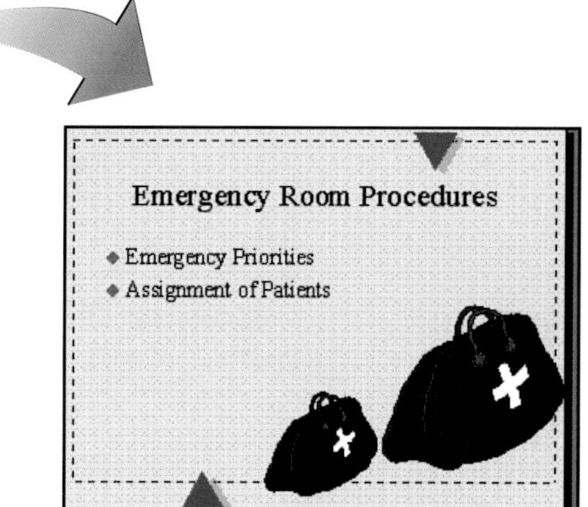


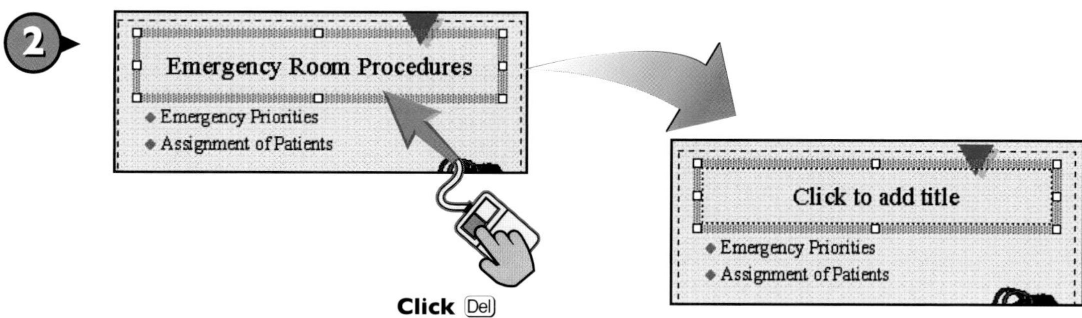


## Removing Objects from Slides

**Unwanted objects can be deleted from a slide by selecting the object and pressing the Delete key. You don't remember how to select objects? See Task 1.**

**Where's the Empty?**
**An empty placeholder does not print and does not appear when you run the Slide Show.**

**Recovering a Deleted Object**
**If you accidentally delete an object, choose Edit, Undo to recover the object.**

1 To delete an image or a text box, select the object and press **Delete**. The object is removed from the slide.

2 To delete the text in a "click" placeholder, select the placeholder and press **Delete**. The text in the placeholder is removed but the placeholder remains.

# Task 7: Aligning Slide Objects

## Lining Up Objects on Your Slides

**The Drawing toolbar contains many options for aligning objects on your slides. Among other alignment choices, you can left-, right-, or center-align objects, and you can distribute them evenly in a horizontal or vertical row.**

Start Here

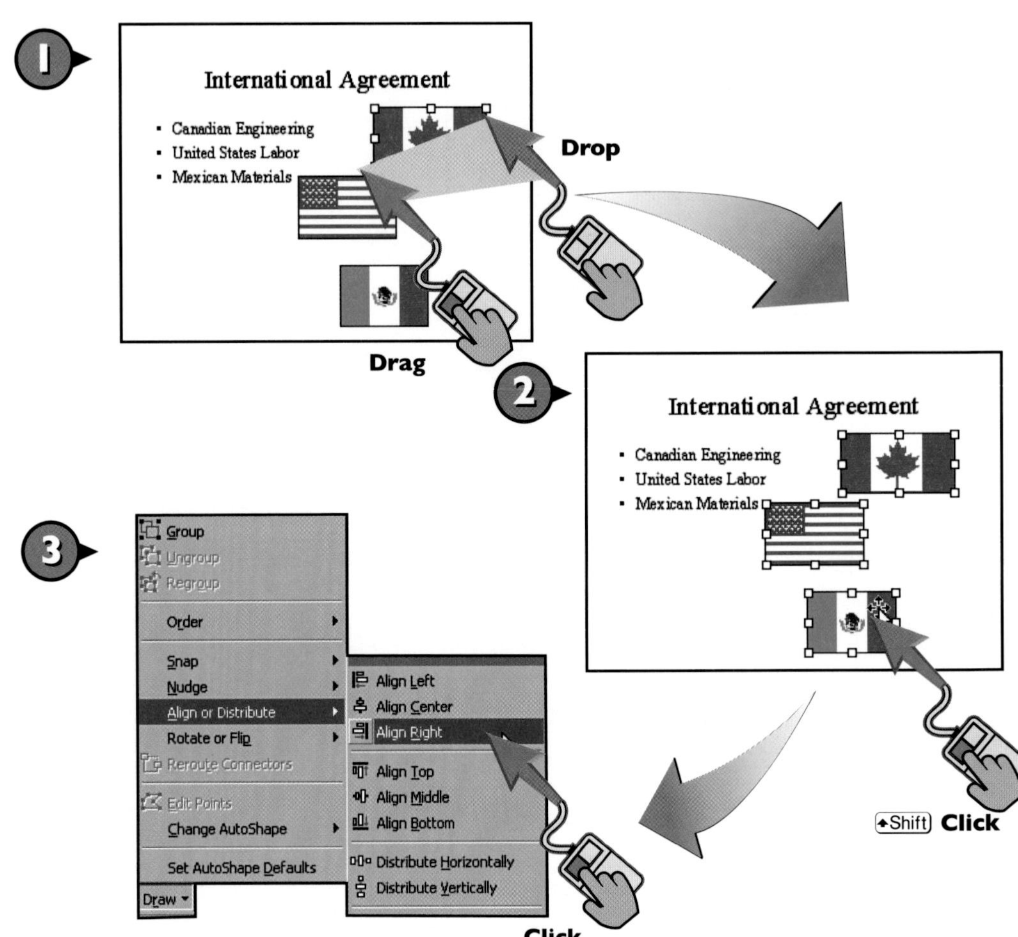


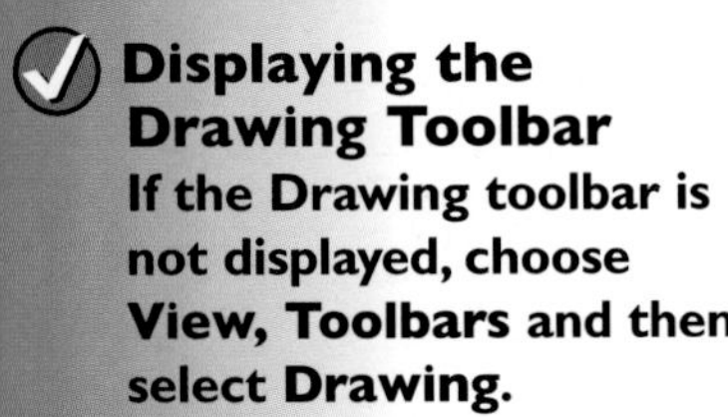

**Displaying the Drawing Toolbar**
**If the Drawing toolbar is not displayed, choose View, Toolbars and then select Drawing.**

1. To align several objects, start by dragging and dropping one of the objects to the position where you want all the objects to line up.

2. With the first object selected, press **Shift** and click on each additional object. Selection handles appear around each selected object.

3. From the Drawing toolbar, choose **Draw, Align or Distribute**. Then select the alignment option you need.

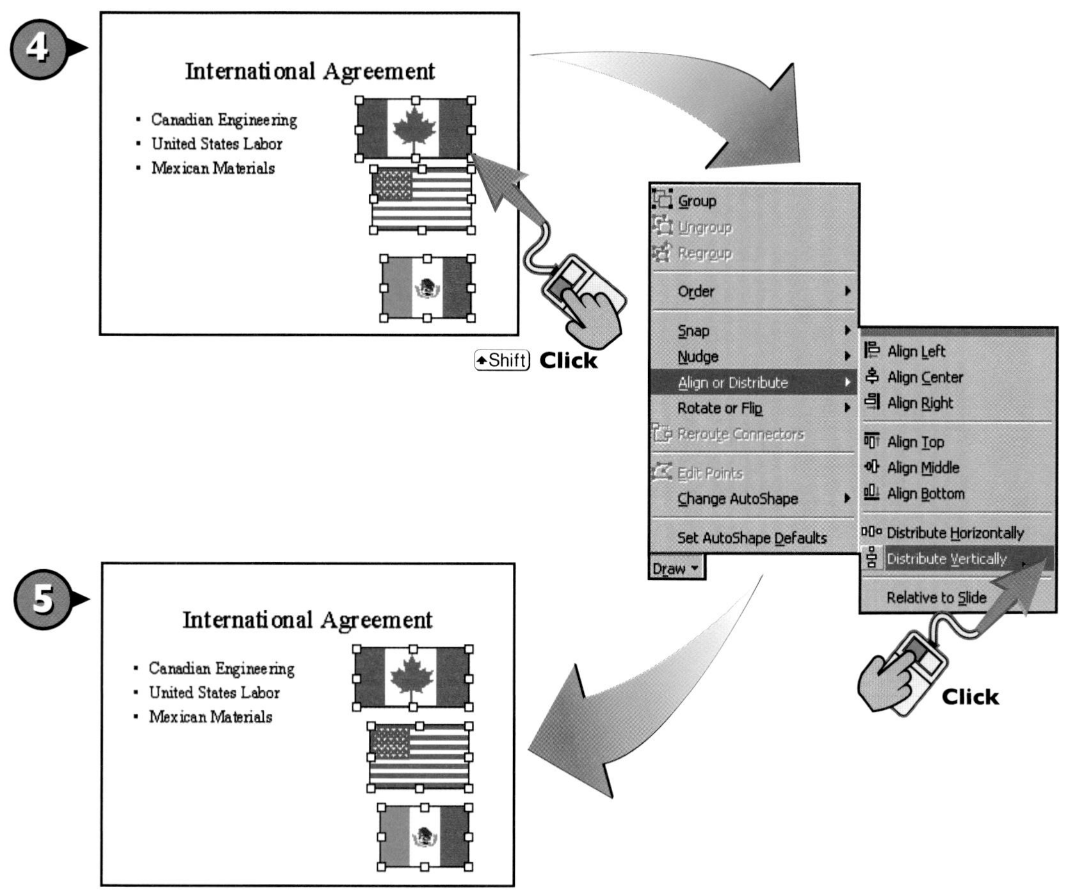


4. Make sure the outermost objects (top and bottom or farthest to the right and left) are positioned at the boundaries of the space within which you want to distribute all of the objects. The other objects will be evenly spaced between these two boundary objects. Then press **Shift** and click to select all the objects to be distributed.

5. From the Drawing toolbar, choose **Draw, Align or Distribute**. Then select the desired distribution—**Distribute Horizontally** or **Distribute Vertically**.

**Centering Objects**
**Centering several objects on top of one another is a two-step process. Select the objects and choose Draw, Align or Distribute, Align Center. Then choose Draw, Align or Distribute, Align Middle.**

# Task 8: Formatting Text Objects

## Applying a Background Color and Border to Text Objects

Any text object can be enhanced by changing its formatting. Use color and line options to add a colorful background and border to your object.

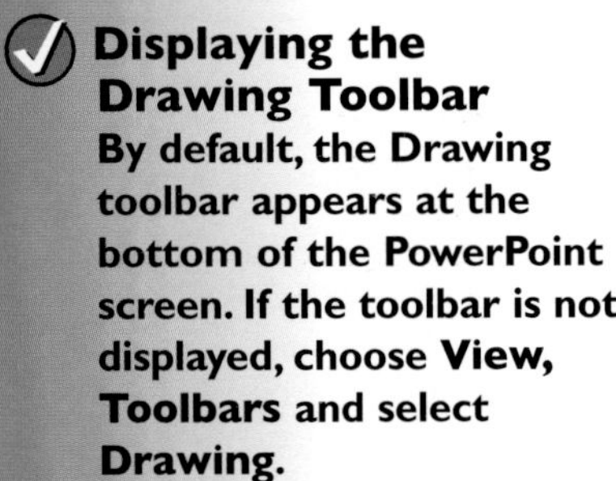

**Displaying the Drawing Toolbar**
By default, the Drawing toolbar appears at the bottom of the PowerPoint screen. If the toolbar is not displayed, choose **View, Toolbars** and select **Drawing.**

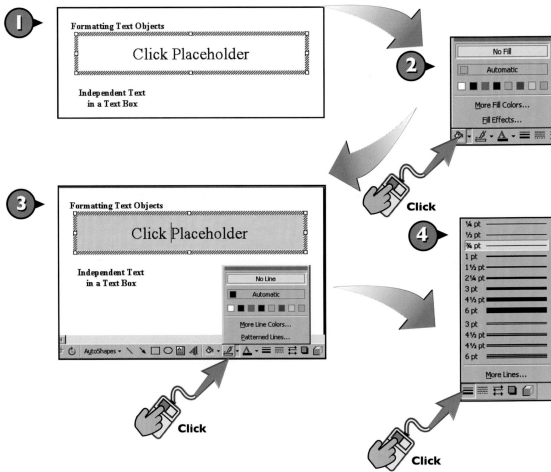

1. Select the text object you want to enhance.
2. To apply a background color behind the text, click the **Fill Color** button and choose a color.
3. To change the color of the line surrounding a text object, click the **Line Color** button and choose a color.
4. To change the thickness of the line or to display alternative styles, click the **Line Style** button and choose a style.

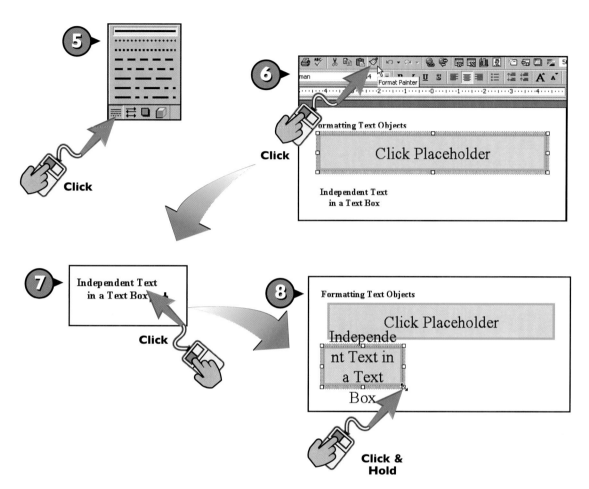

5. To apply abackground dashed or dotted line style, click the **Dash Line** button and choose a dash style.

6. To copy formats from one object to another, first select the object containing the formats and click the **Format Painter** button on the Standard toolbar.

7. Next, position the mouse pointer on the object where you want to apply the formats (the pointer has a paint brush attached) and click.

8. All of the formats from the original object are applied. Drag to enlarge the object (or change the font size).

**Coloring Slide Objects**
**See Task 9 for additional fill color (background) options you can use with slide objects.**

# Task 9: Formatting Drawn Objects

## Applying a Background Color and Border to Drawn Objects

**Any object you draw can be enhanced by formatting the object's color and line options.**

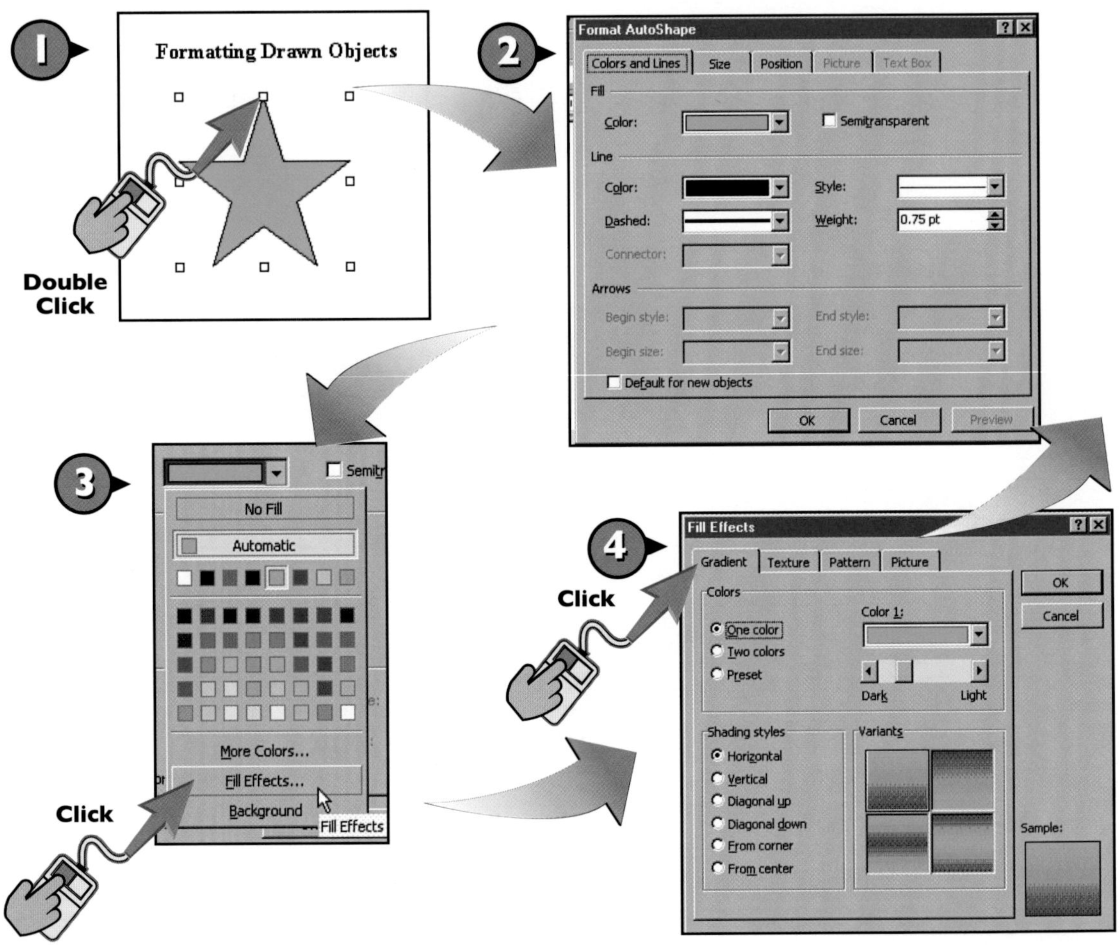

Double Click

Click

Click

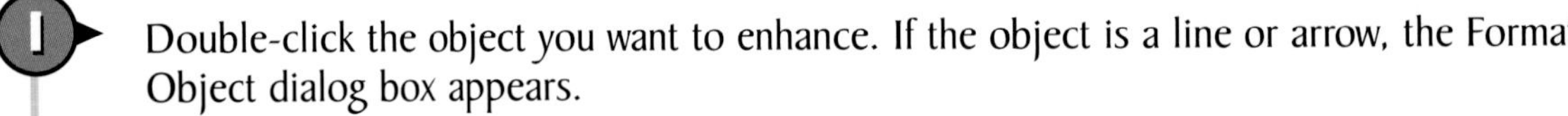

1. Double-click the object you want to enhance. If the object is a line or arrow, the Format Object dialog box appears.

2. The Format AutoShape dialog box appears with all drawn objects except lines or arrows.
3. To change the fill color, choose one of the displayed colors or select any color by choosing More Colors. Click **Fill Effects** to fill the object with a gradient, texture, pattern, or picture.
4. In the Fill Effects dialog box, select the appropriate tab to choose the type of effect you want applied to the object. See the sample fill effect options.

### Setting the Default Formats for AutoShapes

**The Format AutoShapes dialog box contains an option at the bottom to set the current formats as the default for any new objects drawn.**

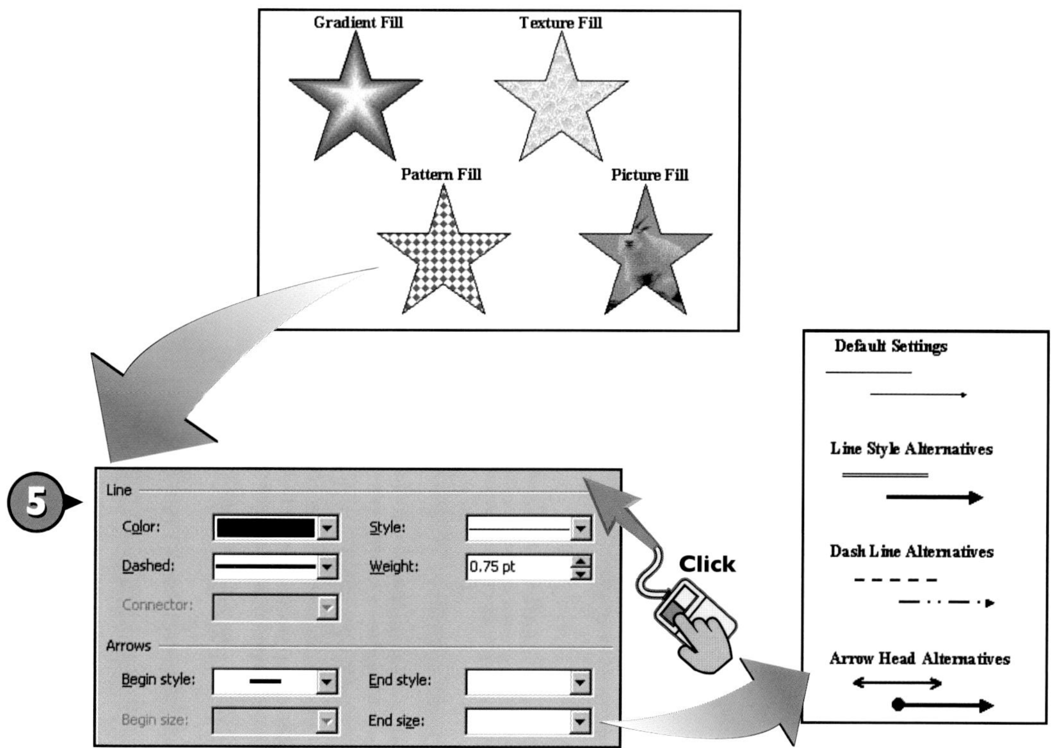

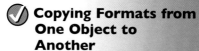

To change the border of an AutoShape or the color or style of lines and arrows, choose from the options in the Format AutoShape or Format Object dialog box. See the sample line and arrow formats.

## Copying Formats from One Object to Another

**If you want to apply the same formats to several objects, select the objects and format them all at once.**

**If one object already has the formats you want applied to other objects, select the object containing the formats you want and click the Format Painter button (paint brush) on the Standard toolbar. Then click the object you want to receive the formats.**

# Task 10: Layering Slide Objects

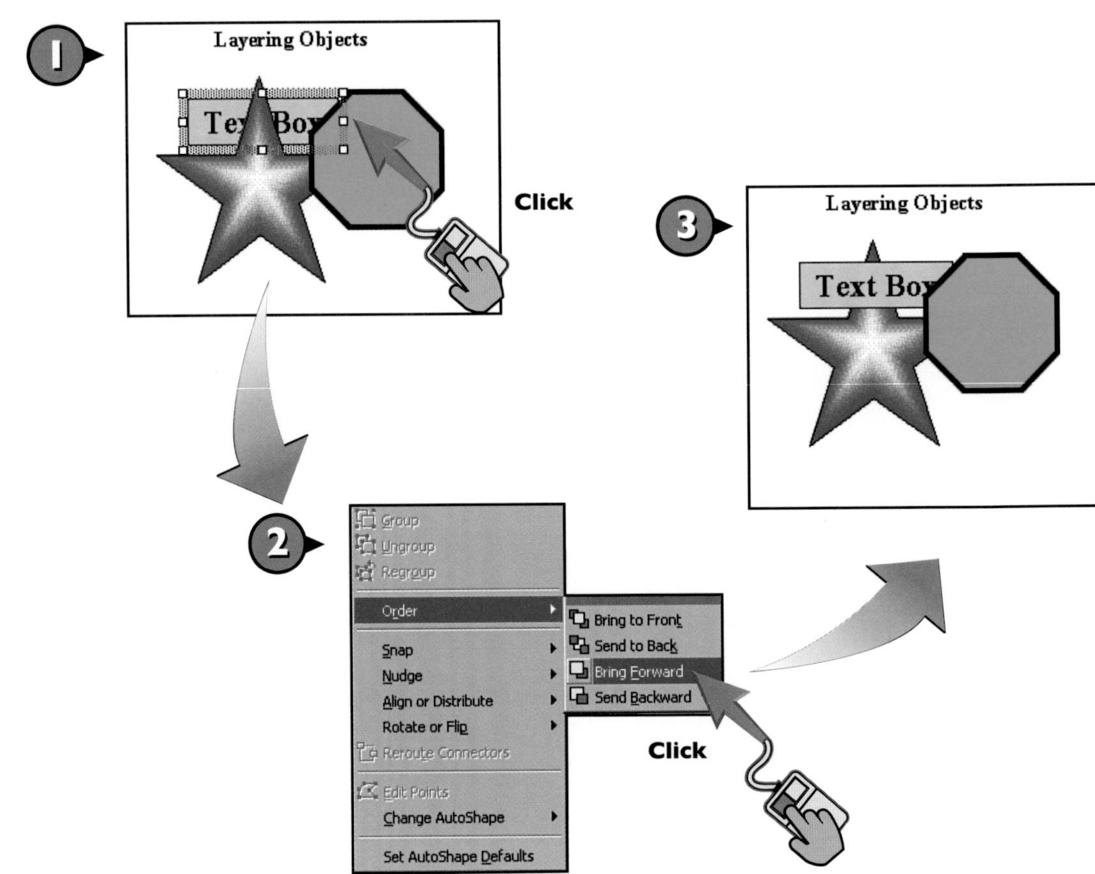


## Rearranging the Order of Slide Objects

**Each object on a slide sits on an invisible layer. The first object on the slide is on the bottom layer. The most recently added object is on the top layer. You can reorder the *layering* of the slide objects by using the Draw option on the Drawing toolbar.**

1. To change the layering of slide objects, select the object you want to reorder.
2. To bring an object forward one layer, choose **Draw, Order, Bring Forward**.
3. The object moves up one layer. To place an object behind other objects, choose **Draw, Order, Send Backward**.

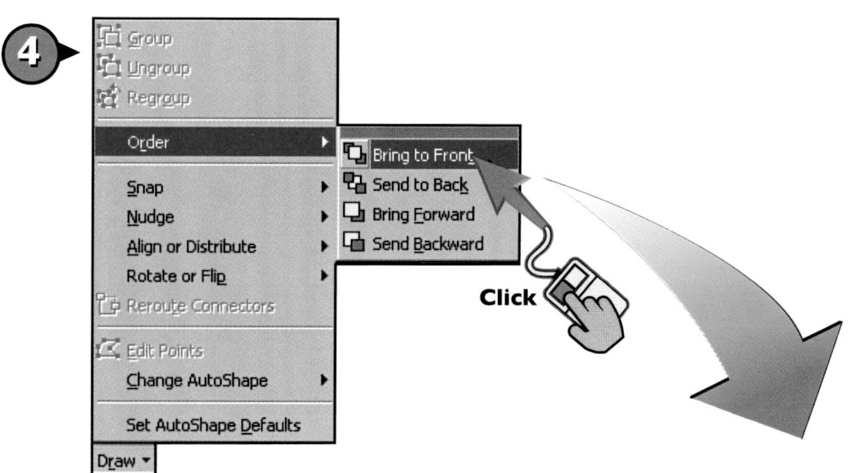


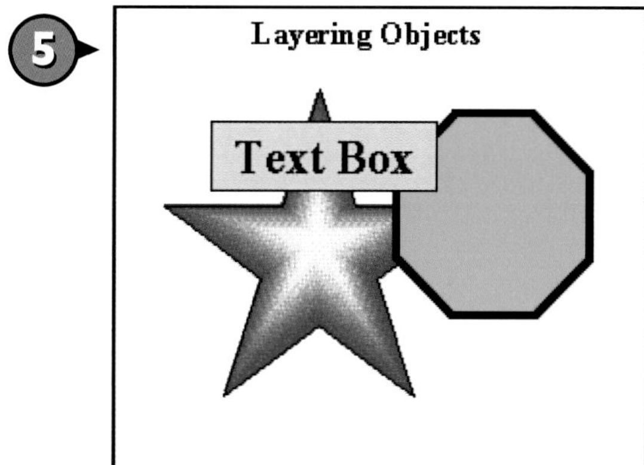


4 To bring an object in front of all the other objects, select the object and choose **Draw, Order, Bring to Front**.

5 The object moves to the top layer, above all other objects. To place an object on the bottom layer, choose **Draw, Order, Send to Back**.

**Layering Objects**
**All objects, including "click" placeholders, are on these invisible layers.**

# Task 11: Grouping Slide Objects

## Creating One Object from Several Objects

**Most often you will group objects together to make them easier to move, copy, or resize. Grouping ensures the objects maintain their positions relative to one another.**

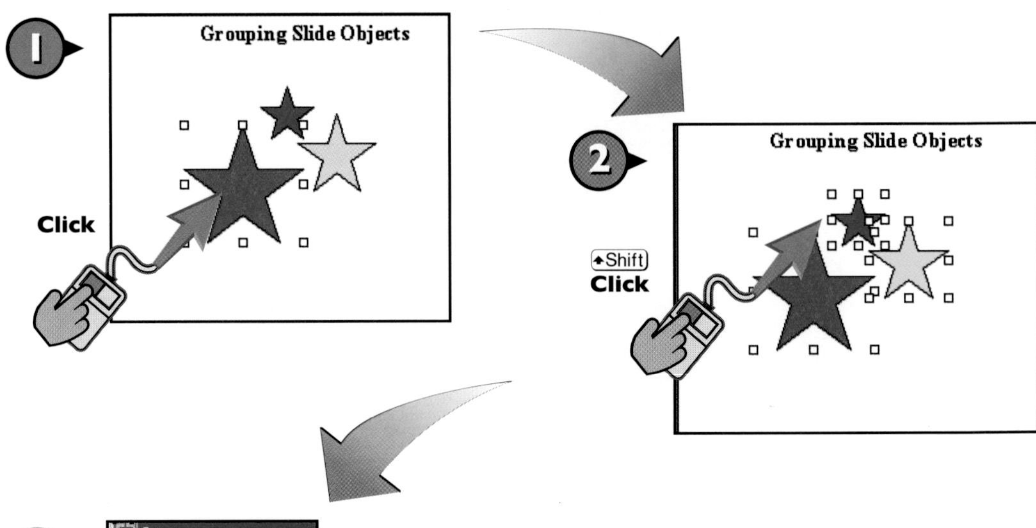


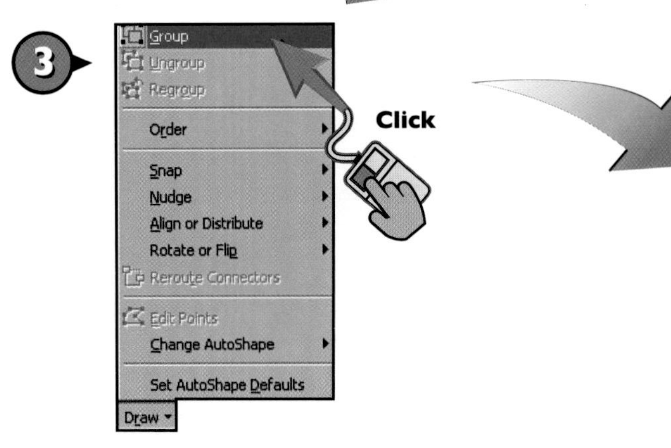


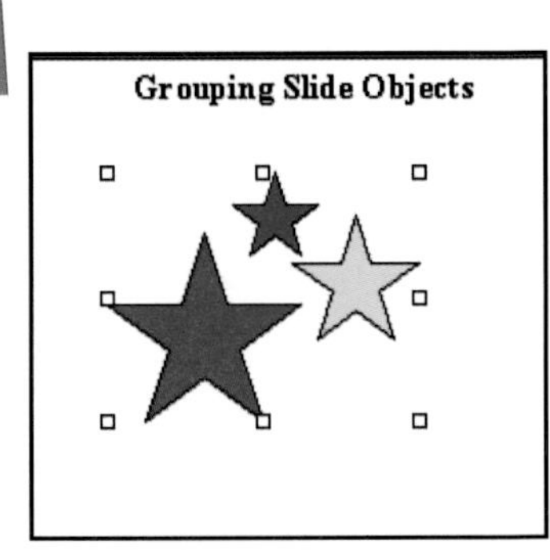


1. To group several objects into one object, select the first object.
2. Press **Shift** and click on each additional object; a separate set of selection handles appears around each selected object.
3. Choose **Draw, Group** from the Drawing toolbar. The selected objects now have one set of selection handles.

**Ungrouping Objects**
**You can ungroup objects when you no longer need to maintain the group. Choose Draw, Ungroup from the Drawing toolbar.**

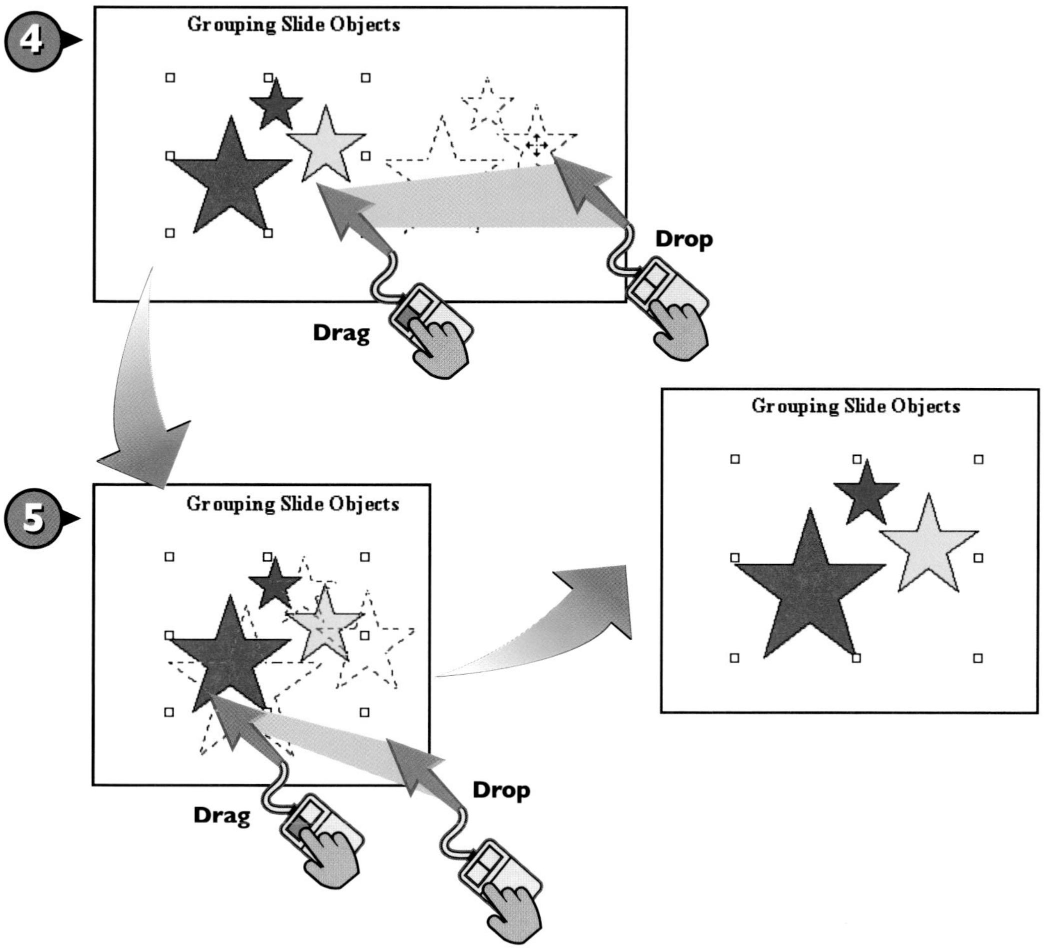

4

Grouping Slide Objects

Drop

Drag

Grouping Slide Objects

5

Grouping Slide Objects

Drop

Drag

Now if you drag and drop the grouped objects, they move together and maintain their positions relative to one another. Press **Ctrl** and drag to copy the grouped objects.

Drag from a corner selection handle to resize the grouped objects. The object sizes change in proportion to one another, without any need to resize each object separately.

**Grouping Objects**

**Any slide object can be part of a group—"click" placeholders, independent text boxes, clip art, WordArt, pictures, and drawn objects.**

PART 6

# Working with Graphic Charts

With PowerPoint, you can create a wide variety of graphic charts, including such common chart types as Column, Pie, and Line. You can also create a number of less common charts, such as Combination, Doughnut, and Bubble charts.

When you create or edit a chart in PowerPoint, you work in a separate program called Microsoft Graph. You enter the data that will be plotted on the chart in a spreadsheet-like window called the **Datasheet**. Microsoft Graph has its own menu bar and toolbars.

# Tasks

# Task 1: Creating a Graphic Chart

## Using the Chart Slide Layout

When you create a graphic chart in PowerPoint, you work in a separate program called Microsoft Graph. The commands on the menu bar and the buttons on the toolbars become Microsoft Graph commands and buttons when you start to create a graphic chart.

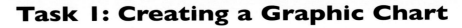

Start Here

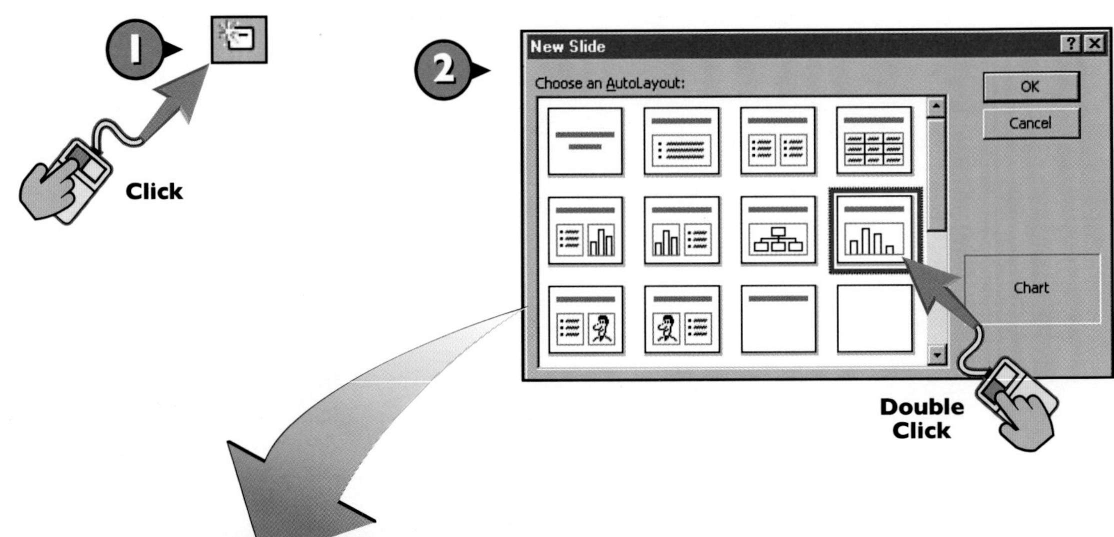


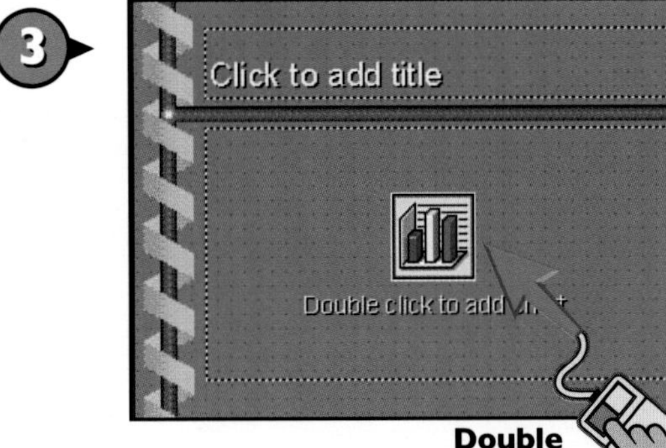


**Inserting a Chart**
To insert a chart into an existing slide, choose **Insert, Chart.**

1. Select the **New Slide** button on the Standard toolbar.
2. Double-click the Chart layout in the New Slide dialog box. The new slide appears, with the chart layout.
3. Double-click the chart placeholder to open Microsoft Graph and create the chart.

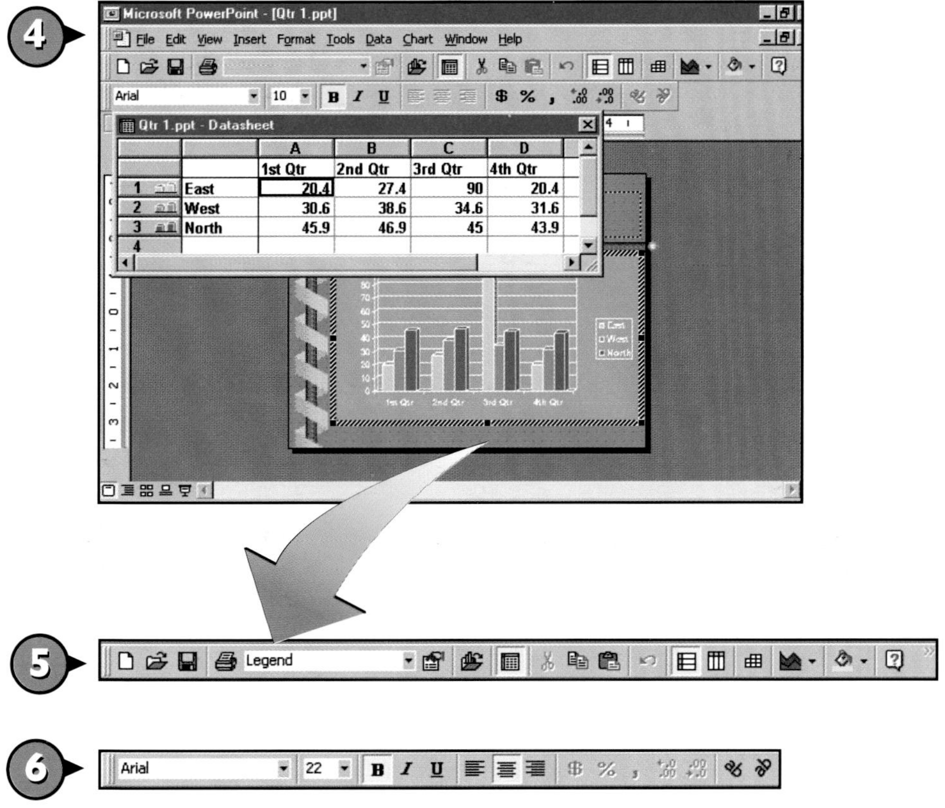

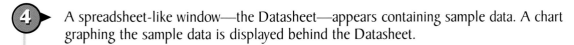

4. A spreadsheet-like window—the Datasheet—appears containing sample data. A chart graphing the sample data is displayed behind the Datasheet.

5. The buttons on the Standard toolbar have been significantly altered to include chart-specific options, such as changing the chart type and displaying a data table beneath the chart.

6. The buttons on the Formatting toolbar now include options to angle text.

**Understanding the Chart Border**
**When you are creating or editing a chart, the chart displays a slash-mark border.**

**Clearing the Sample Data**
**See Task 2 for steps on clearing the sample data in the Datasheet.**

**Filling in the Datasheet**
**See Task 3 for steps on entering your data in the Datasheet.**

# Task 2: Clearing the Sample Data from the Datasheet

## Removing All Data from the Datasheet

**When you first create a chart, data appears in the Datasheet to provide an example of how to use the Datasheet. Before you can create a chart based on your own data, you must remove the sample data. You must be in the Edit mode to remove the sample data. When you are in Edit mode, the border of the chart area is slash marks, not dots.**

Start Here

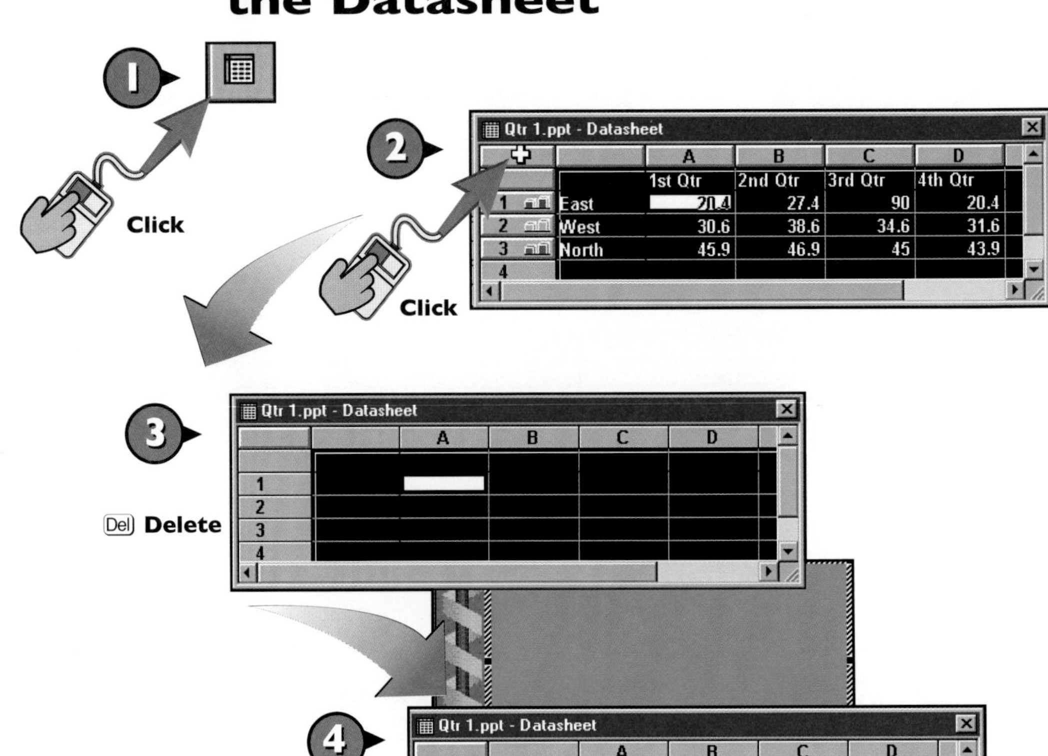


1. If the Datasheet is not displayed, click the **Datasheet** button on the Standard toolbar.

2. Click on the gray area in the upper left corner of the Datasheet to highlight every cell in the Datasheet. (Notice that your pointer becomes a white cross when it is on the Datasheet.)

3. Press the **Delete** key to clear the sample data from the cells. The sample chart disappears because there is now no data to plot.

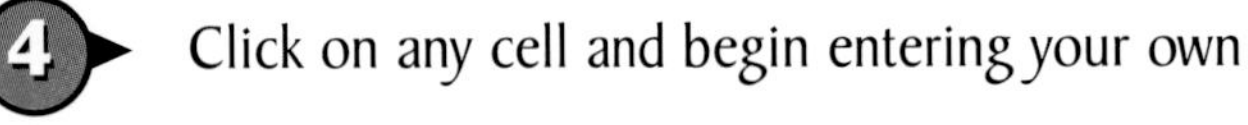

4. Click on any cell and begin entering your own data.

# Task 3: Entering Chart Data

Click

## Entering and Editing Data in the Datasheet

**The Datasheet is made up of numbered rows and columns labeled with letters from the alphabet. The intersection of a row and a column is called a cell.**

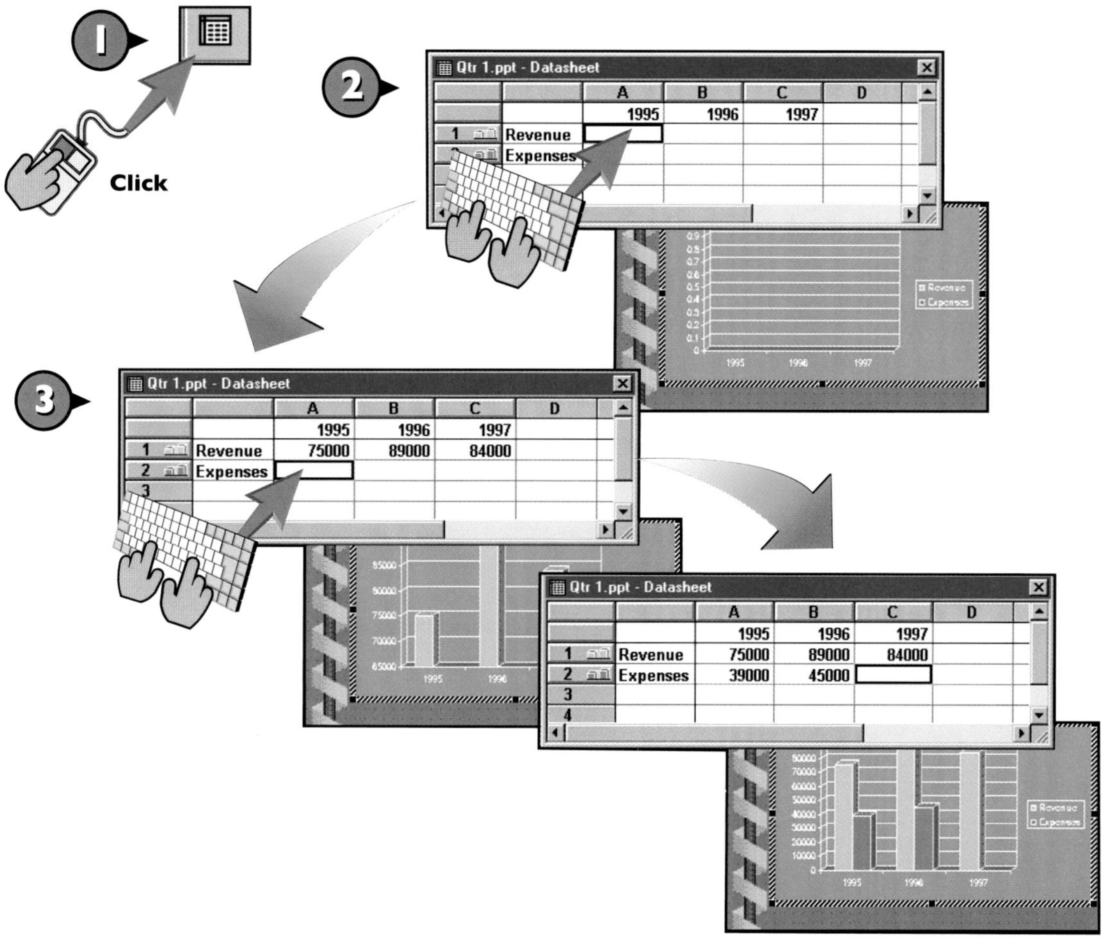

1. If the Datasheet is not displayed, click the **Datasheet** button on the Standard toolbar.

2. Use the first row and column to type the headings, or ***labels***, that describe the data you are going to chart. As you type the headings, the legend and frame for the chart appear.

3. As you type each row of data, a series of columns is plotted on the chart. To change any of the data, select the cell and type over the old data.

### Moving Around in the Datasheet

**To move to another cell in the Datasheet, press Enter to move down or use the keyboard arrow keys to move in the direction you want.**

## Using Excel Data to Create a PowerPoint Chart

**If the data you want to use for a PowerPoint chart already exists in an Excel worksheet, you can save time by copying the data instead of retyping it.**

# Task 4: Importing Data from Excel into the Datasheet

Start Here

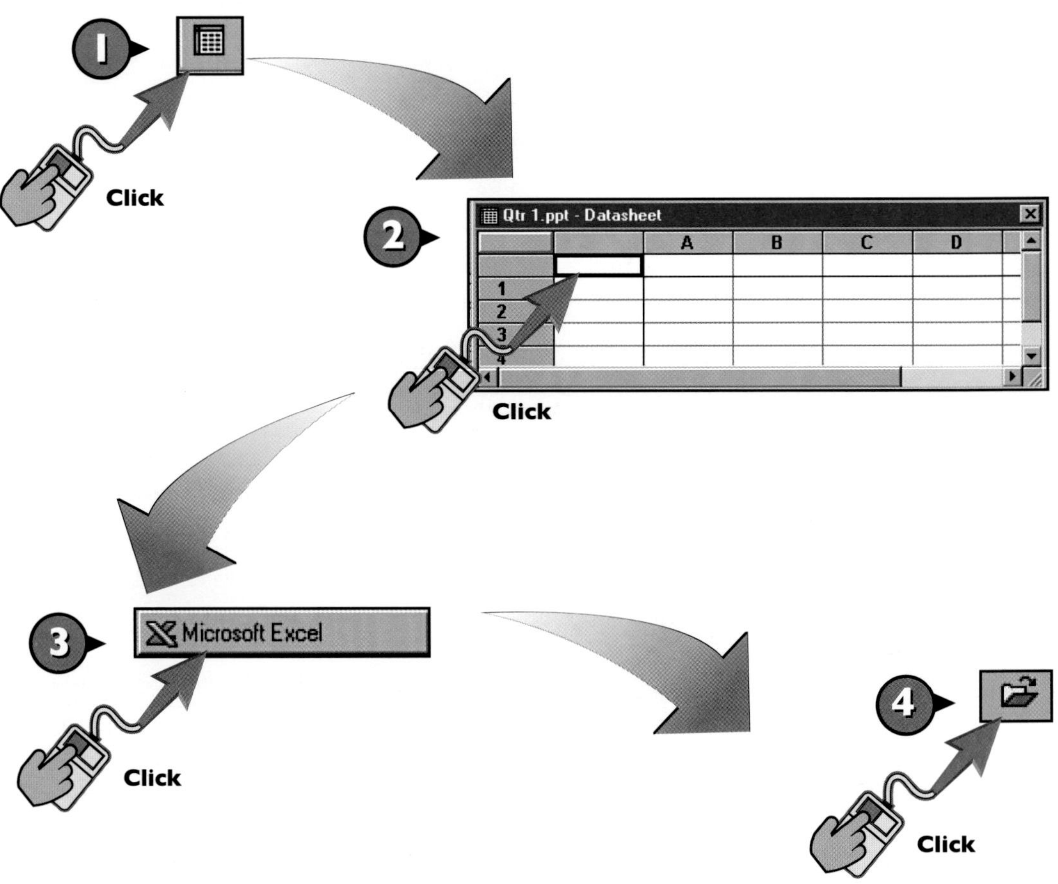


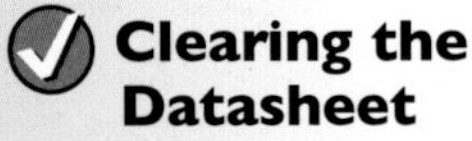

**Clearing the Datasheet**
**Unless you are adding Excel data to an existing PowerPoint chart, it is recommended you clear all data from the Datasheet. See Task 2 for the steps to clear the data.**

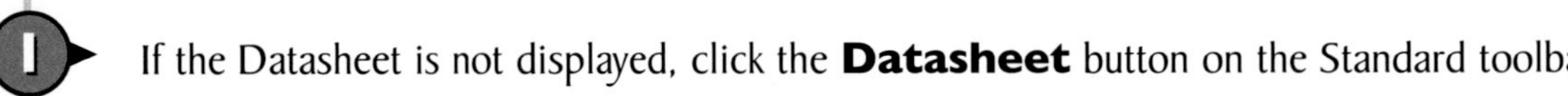

1. If the Datasheet is not displayed, click the **Datasheet** button on the Standard toolbar.
2. Select the cell in which you want the first piece of Excel data to appear—usually the cell that intersects the header row and column.
3. Open or switch to Excel.
4. Open the Excel file containing the data you want to bring into PowerPoint.

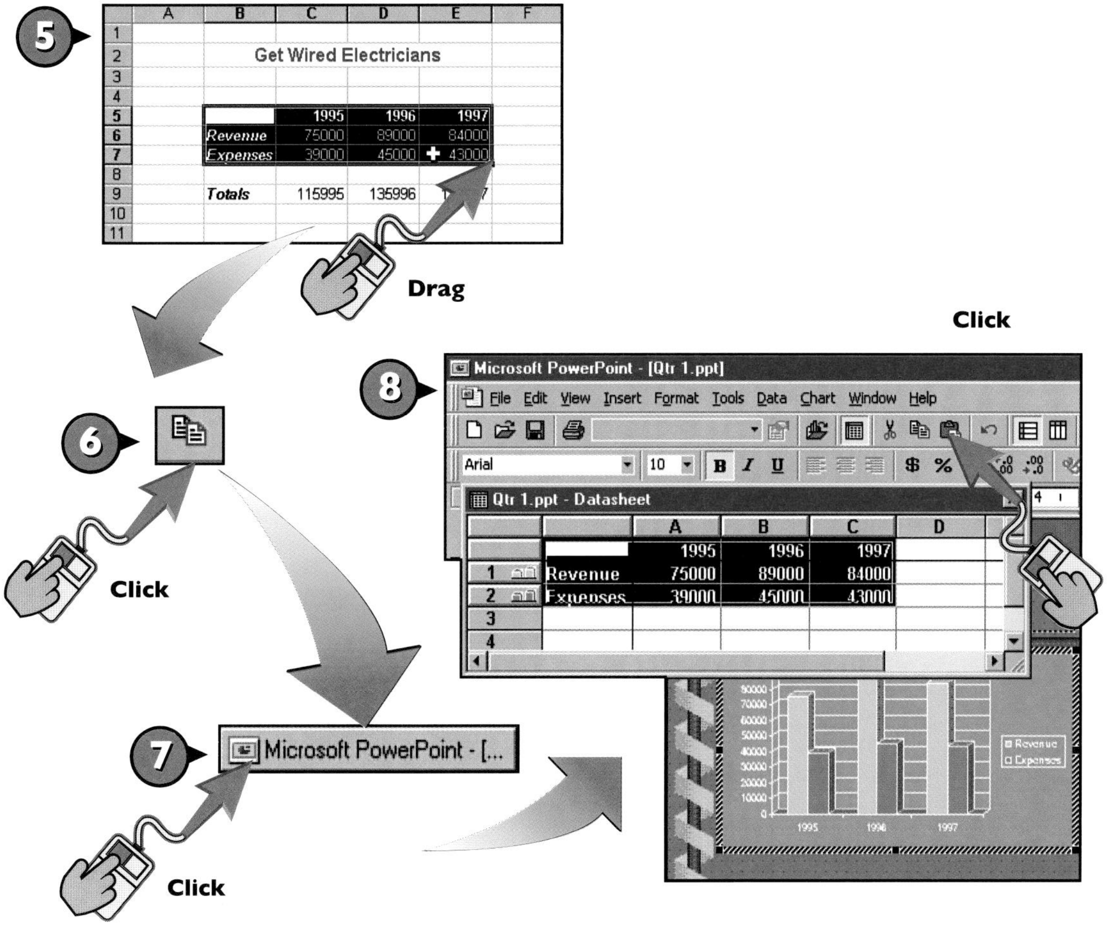

5. Drag to select the data in Excel that you want to copy into the PowerPoint Datasheet.

6. Click the **Copy** button on the Standard toolbar.

7. Switch back to PowerPoint by clicking the **Microsoft PowerPoint** button on the taskbar.

8. Click the **Paste** button to insert the data from Excel.

### Linking Data Between Excel and PowerPoint

**If you want the PowerPoint chart to be revised automatically when the data in Excel is changed, you can link the data. In step 8, instead of clicking the Paste button, choose Edit, Paste Link.**

# Task 5: Inserting Rows and Columns in the Datasheet

## Adding Rows or Columns to Your Datasheet

Make room for new data by inserting extra rows or columns in the Datasheet.

Start Here

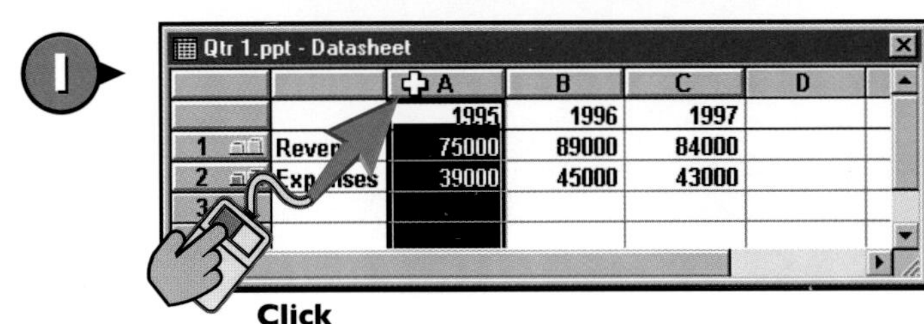


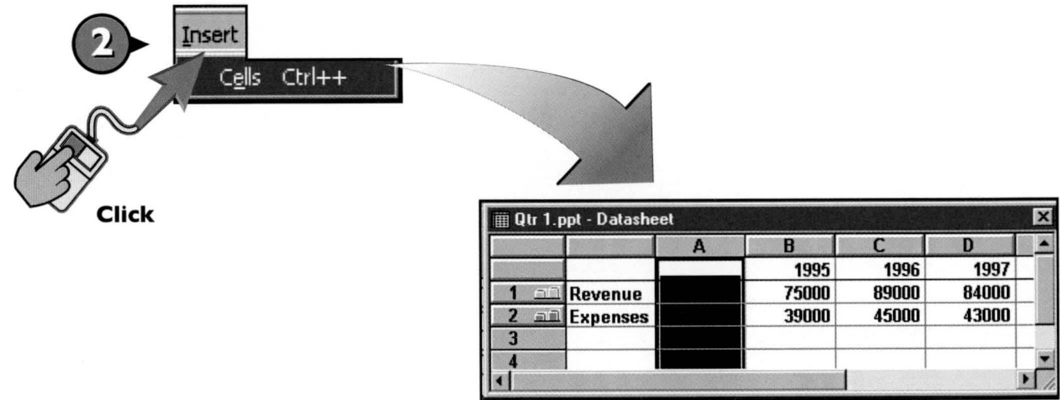


**Adding New Columns on Rows**
New columns are inserted to the left of the selected column and new rows are inserted above the selected row.

**Selecting Multiple Rows or Columns**
To select more than one row or column, drag the mouse pointer across the gray area displaying the row or column labels.

1. Click on the column to the right of where you want the new column or on the row below where you want the new row.
2. Choose **Insert, Cells**. The new column or row is inserted.

End Task

# Task 6: Deleting Rows and Columns in the Datasheet

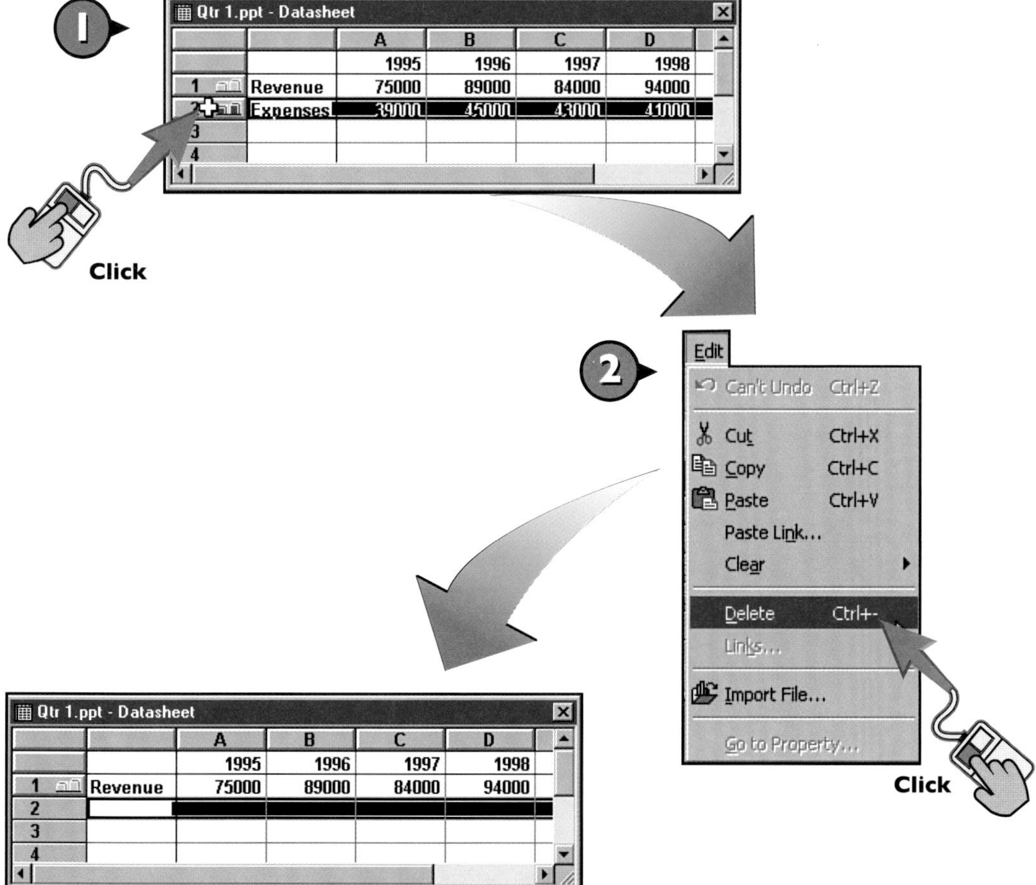


## Removing Rows or Columns in Your Datasheet

When you no longer need a row or column in the Datasheet, delete it.

Click on the label of the row or column you want to delete. To select more than one row or column, drag the mouse pointer across the labels of the rows or columns.

Choose **Edit**, **Delete**. The selected row or column is deleted.

**Accidentally Deleting a Row or Column**

If you delete a row or column accidentally, choose **Edit, Undo.**

# Task 7: Switching the Plot of the Chart Data

## Plotting the Data by Rows or Columns

**Depending on the information you are trying to convey to your audience, you might prefer to switch the way the data is plotted in the chart.**

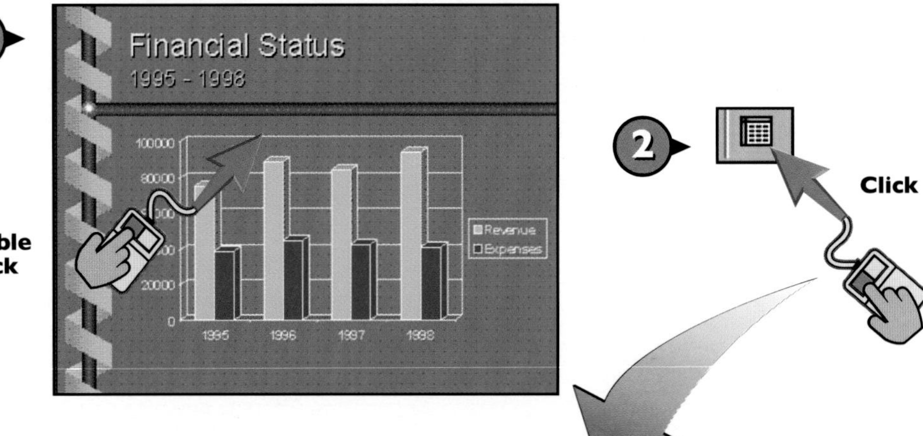


Qtr 1.ppt - Datasheet

| | | A | B | C | D |
|---|---|---|---|---|---|
| | | 1995 | 1996 | 1997 | 1998 |
| 1 | Revenue | 75000 | 89000 | 84000 | 94000 |
| 2 | Expenses | 39000 | 45000 | 43000 | 41000 |
| 3 | | | | | |
| 4 | | | | | |

### Understanding Chart Terminology

**The data being plotted is referred to as the data series. The groups of data along the x-axis are referred to as the data categories. In the Datasheet in this example, the data series are Revenue and Expenses. The data categories are the years.**

1. Position the mouse pointer in the middle of the chart. The pointer changes to a four-headed arrow. Double-click the chart to get into the Edit mode.

2. Click the **Datasheet** button on the Standard toolbar to display the Datasheet. Notice each row number also has a colored chart symbol and the data in each row is plotted in the chart.

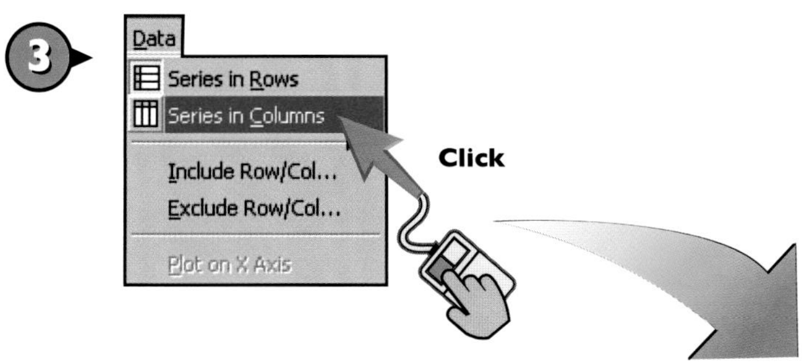


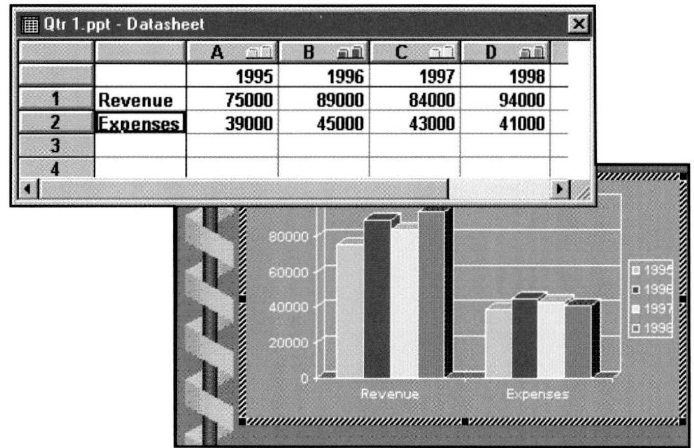


3 To plot the column data in the chart, choose **Data, Series in Columns**. Now the data in each column is plotted, and each column letter has a colored chart symbol.

**Seeing the Series Being Changed**

**You do not have to display the Datasheet to change which data is plotted in the chart, but doing so makes it easier to identify the data series.**

**Using Toolbar Buttons to Switch the Plot**

**Notice the button icons displayed in step 3 next to the Series in Rows and Series in Columns commands. These buttons are on the Standard toolbar.**

# Task 8: Selecting a Chart Type

## Changing the Chart Type

You can choose from 14 different chart types in PowerPoint, each with its own uses. The default chart type is a three-dimensional column chart. Most types have two-dimensional and three-dimensional variations.

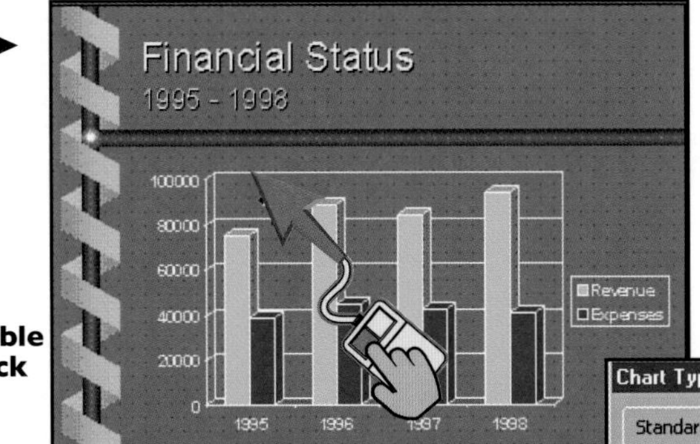

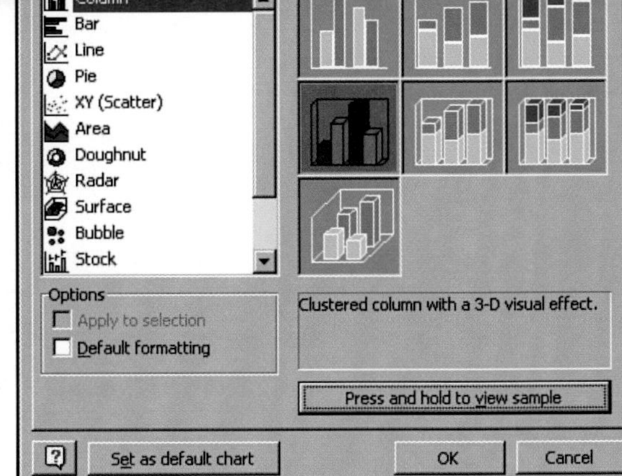

### Using Built-In Custom Chart Types

Several unique chart types are available on the Custom Types tab in the Chart Type dialog box, including charts that combine columns and lines.

1. Position the mouse pointer in the middle of the chart. The pointer changes to a four-headed arrow. Double-click the chart to get into the Edit mode.

2. Choose **Chart, Chart Type**. The Chart Type dialog box appears, with the active chart type highlighted.



Next Step

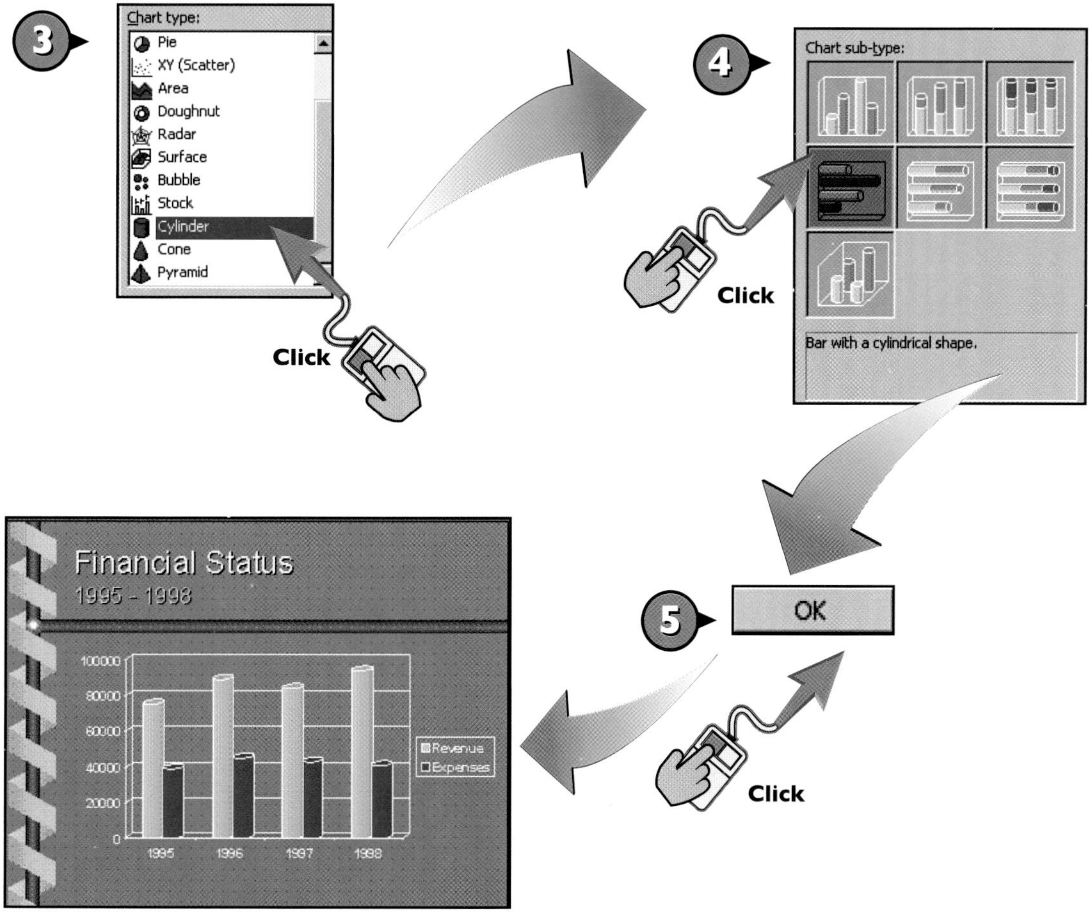

3 In the Chart Type list, scroll to see the list of chart types available in PowerPoint. Then select the type of chart you want.

4 The Chart sub-type list displays all the variations of the chart type you selected. Click to select a sub-type.

5 Choose **OK** to change the chart type.

**Choosing the Right Chart Type**

**Line charts are a good choice when you have more than four or five data series or data categories.**

**Pie charts plot only one data series—for example, revenue for each year (but no expenses) or revenue and expenses for 1998 (but not the other years).**

**Cylinder, Cone, and Pyramid charts are attractive variations of column and bar charts.**

# Task 9: Working with Chart Options

## Adjusting the Chart Features

Through the Chart Options dialog box, you can choose and customize the features that appear on a chart. These features include chart titles, gridlines, legend, data labels, and data table. You must be in Edit mode to access the Chart Options dialog box; double-click the chart to switch to Edit mode.

Start Here

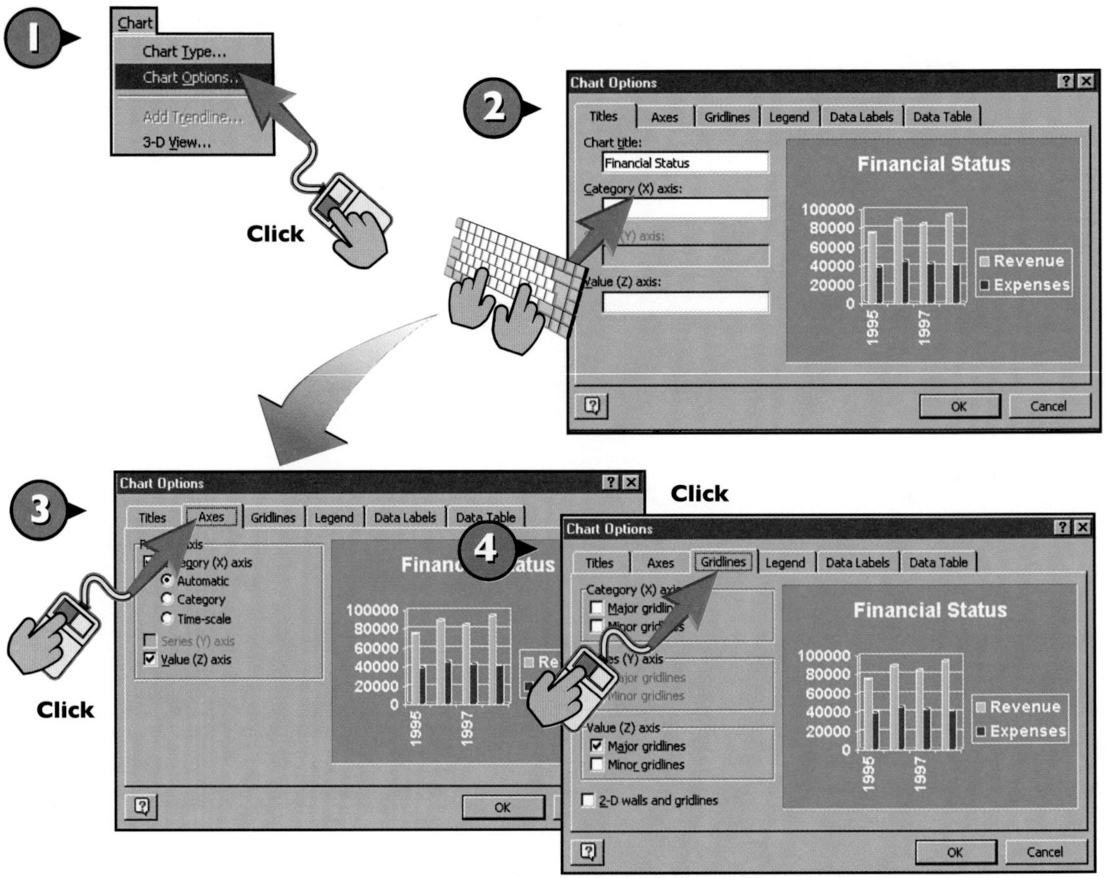

1. Choose **Chart, Chart Options** to display the Chart Options dialog box.
2. On the Titles tab, you can type a title for the chart or one of the axes.
3. The Axes tab has options for showing the chart axes. Generally, the Value and Category axes should be displayed. Click to select or deselect options on this tab.
4. The Gridlines tab includes options for displaying chart gridlines. Most charts show the major value axis gridlines. Click to select or deselect options.

Next Step

Click

Click

Click

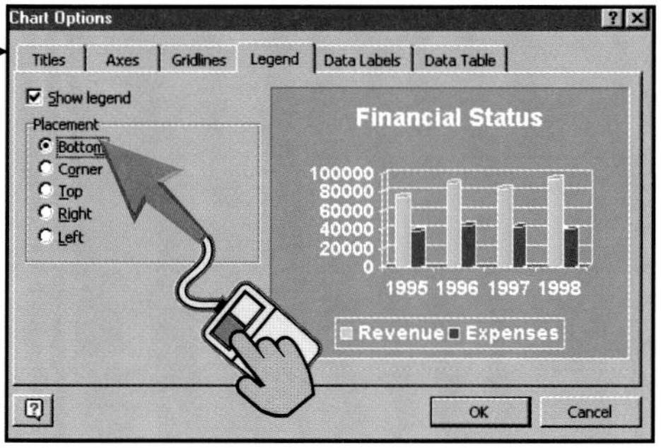

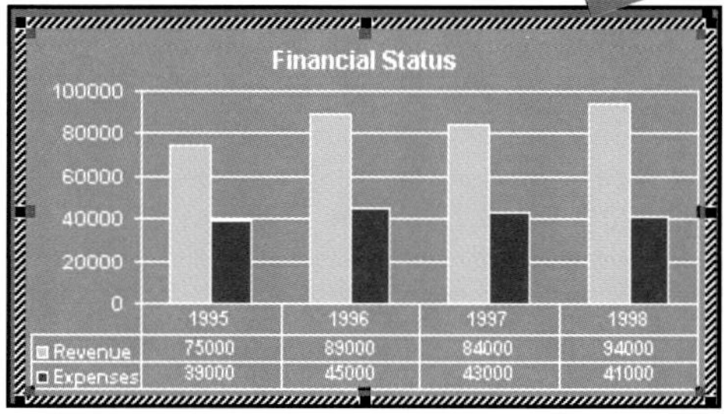

5. On the Legend tab, choose a location for the legend. The most common placements are Right and Bottom.

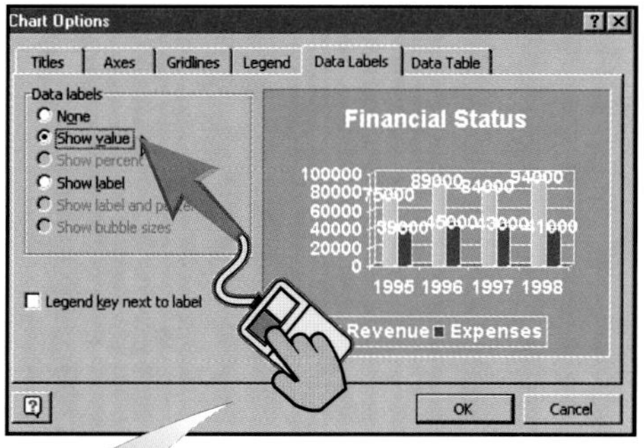

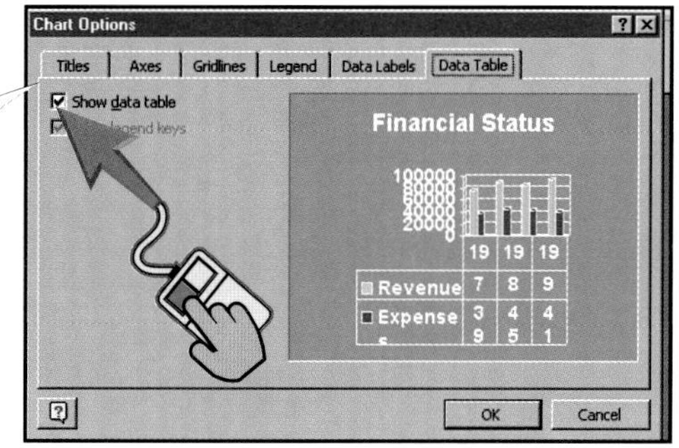

6. On the Data Labels tab, choose **Show Value** to display the plotted number next to each data series.

7. On the Data Table tab, choose **Show Data Table** to display a table below your chart, similar to the Datasheet. Use a data table instead of data labels.

### Chart Formatting Options

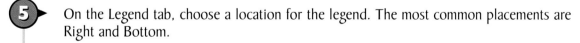

**See Task 10 for steps on formatting the parts of the chart, including the color of the data series, the scale of the axes, and the legend.**

### Chart Preview Is Just a Sample

**The preview in the Chart Options dialog box attempts to show as much data as possible, given its limited space. Choose OK to see the full chart.**

End Task

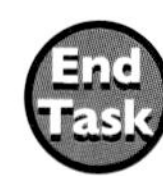

# Task 10: Formatting Chart Components

## Changing the Appearance of the Chart

**Options in the Format dialog box enable you to change the appearance of your chart. For example, you can change the color for the data series, unclutter the scale of the Value axis, and add a drop shadow and background color to the legend. When you right-click on a part of the chart you want to change, the shortcut menu appears; use it to access the Format dialog box.**

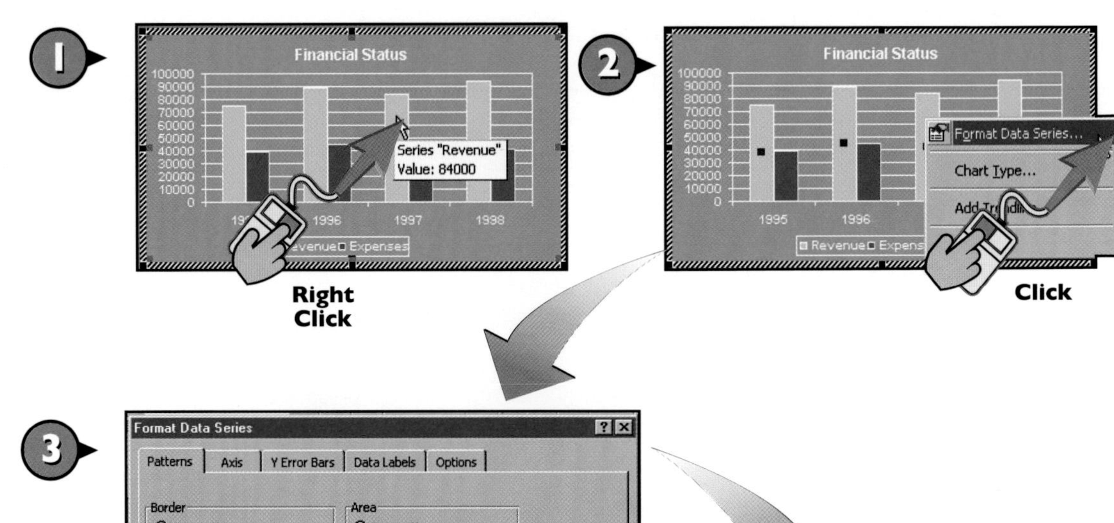


1. To format a data series, right-click on the data series.

2. Choose **Format Data Series** from the shortcut menu.

3. Use the options on the Patterns tab of the Format Data Series dialog box to adjust the color of the series. Choose **OK** to see the changes on the chart.

4. To format an axis, right-click on the axis and choose **Format Axis** from the shortcut menu.

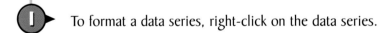

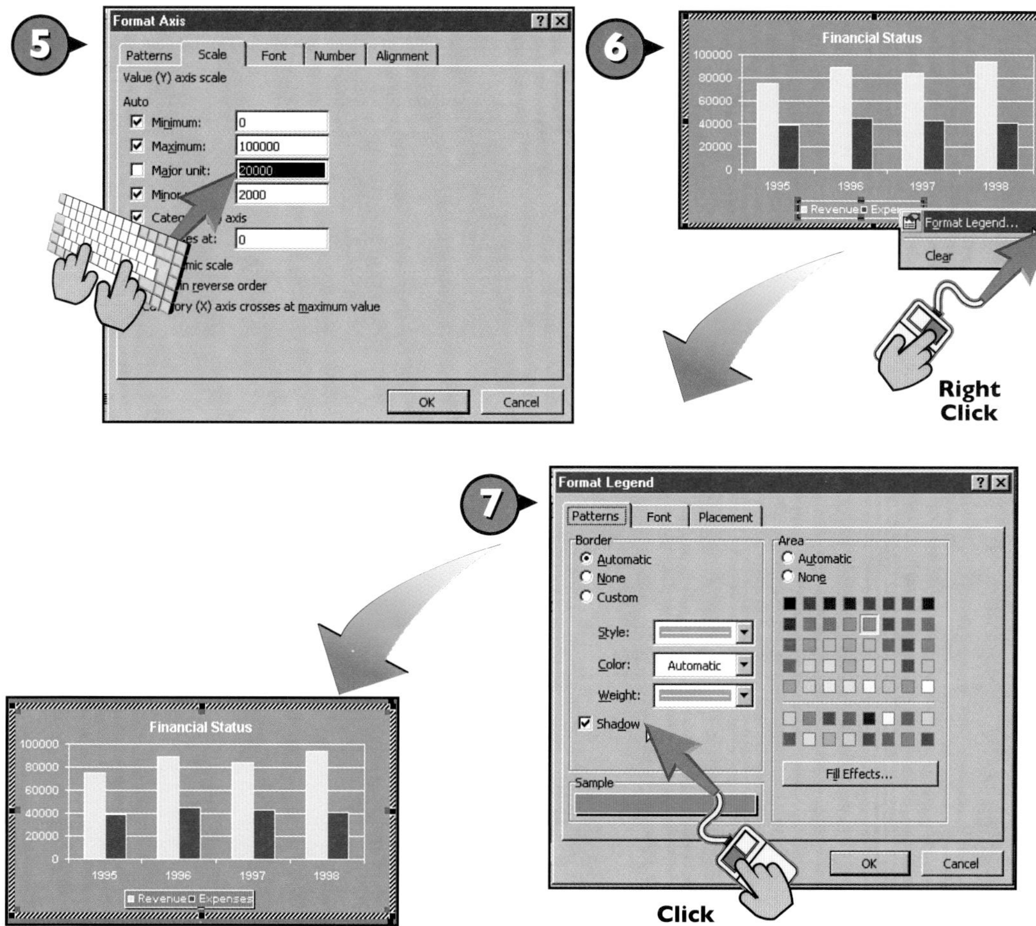


**5** Use the options on the Scale tab of the Format Axis dialog box to adjust the scale of the Value axes. Type the values and choose **OK** to see the changes on the chart.

**6** Right-click anywhere on the legend and choose **Format Legend** from the shortcut menu.

**7** Use the options on the Patterns tab of the Format Legend dialog box to format the border and background color of the legend. Choose **OK** to see the changes on the chart.

### Identifying the Parts of a Chart

**Whenever you rest the mouse pointer over a part of the chart, a ScreenTip identifies the part, as shown in step 1.**

### Understanding the Value Axis

**The Value Axis in any chart is the axis showing a range of numbers corresponding to the numbers plotted in the data series. The range is usually from zero to a number slightly higher than the largest number being plotted.**

PART

# Working with Organization Charts

PowerPoint includes a program specifically designed for creating organization charts. The program—called Microsoft Organization Chart—appears in its own window, separate from PowerPoint. Through the Microsoft Organization Chart program, you create and enhance organization charts by using the menu bar commands and toolbar buttons that are unique to that program.

The information about each person or position in an organization chart is placed in a box, which can be formatted by changing colors and fonts or by adding drop shadows. You can even change the display of the boxes to be vertical instead of the traditional horizontal arrangement seen in most organization charts.

# Tasks

| Task # | | Page # |
|---|---|---|

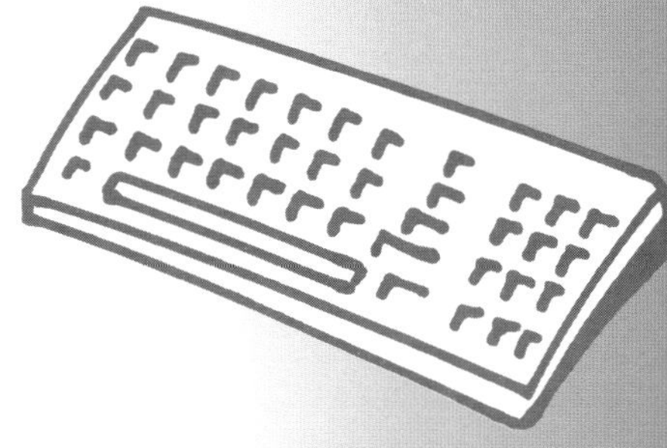

# Task 1: Creating an Organization Chart

## Using the Organization Chart Slide Layout

When you create an organization chart in PowerPoint, you work in a separate program called Microsoft Organization Chart. This program appears in a separate window.

Start Here

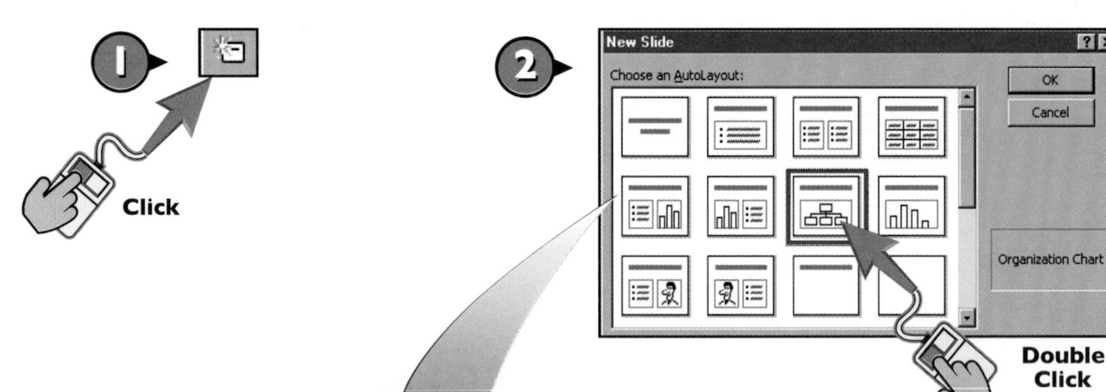


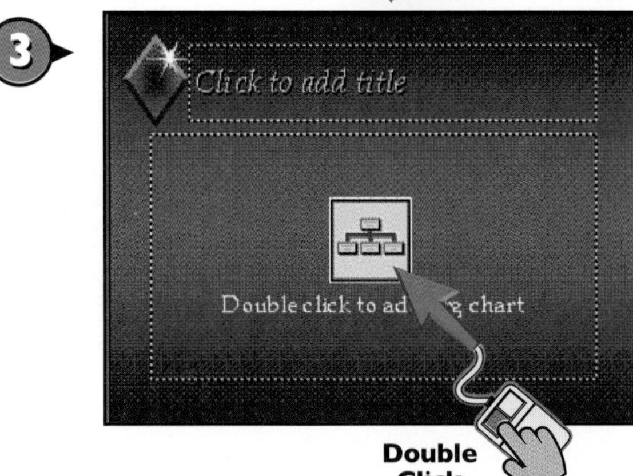

1. Select the **New Slide** button on the Standard toolbar.
2. Double-click the **Organization Chart** layout in the New Slide dialog box.
3. The new slide appears, with the chart layout. Double-click the organization chart placeholder to create the chart.

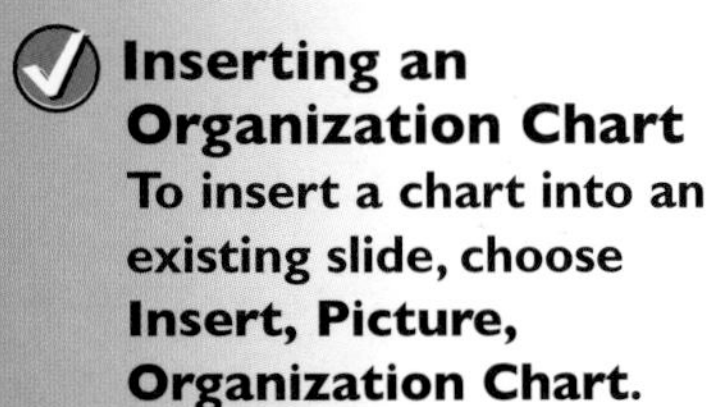

**Inserting an Organization Chart**
To insert a chart into an existing slide, choose **Insert, Picture, Organization Chart.**

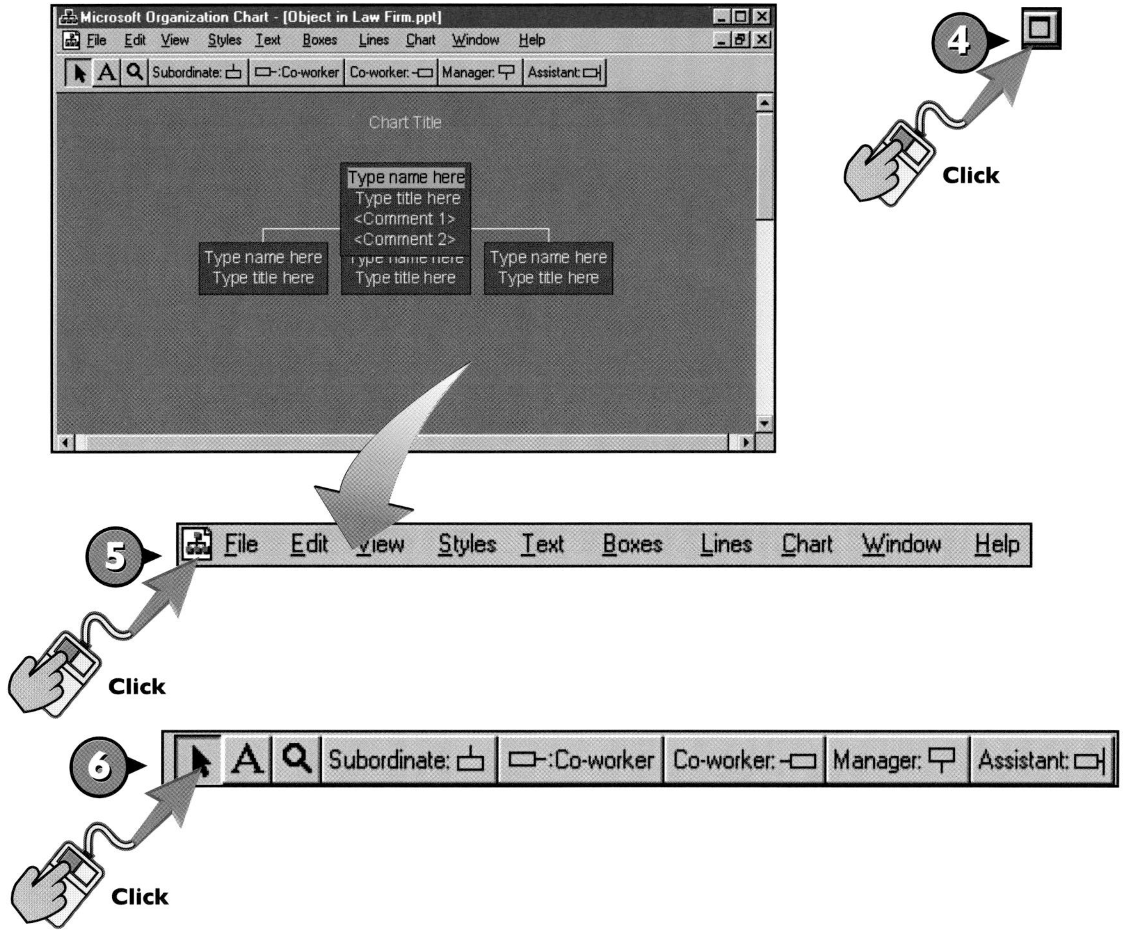

4. The Microsoft Organization Chart program appears in a separate window, with a new organization chart started. Click the **Maximize** button to make the window full-screen.

5. The Organization Chart program has its own menu bar containing commands you can use to create and modify organization charts.

6. The Organization Chart toolbar is used primarily to add people to your organization chart.

**Filling in the Organization Chart**
**See Task 2 for steps on entering names and titles in the Organization Chart boxes.**

**Adding More Positions to an Organization Chart**
**See Task 3 for steps on adding more people to your Organization Chart.**

# Task 2: Entering Names and Titles into an Organization Chart

## Start Building Your Organization Chart

**The organization chart is made up of a series of boxes that hold information about the people or positions in your organization. Each box can contain the name and pertinent information for one person or position. The box can hold up to four lines of text.**

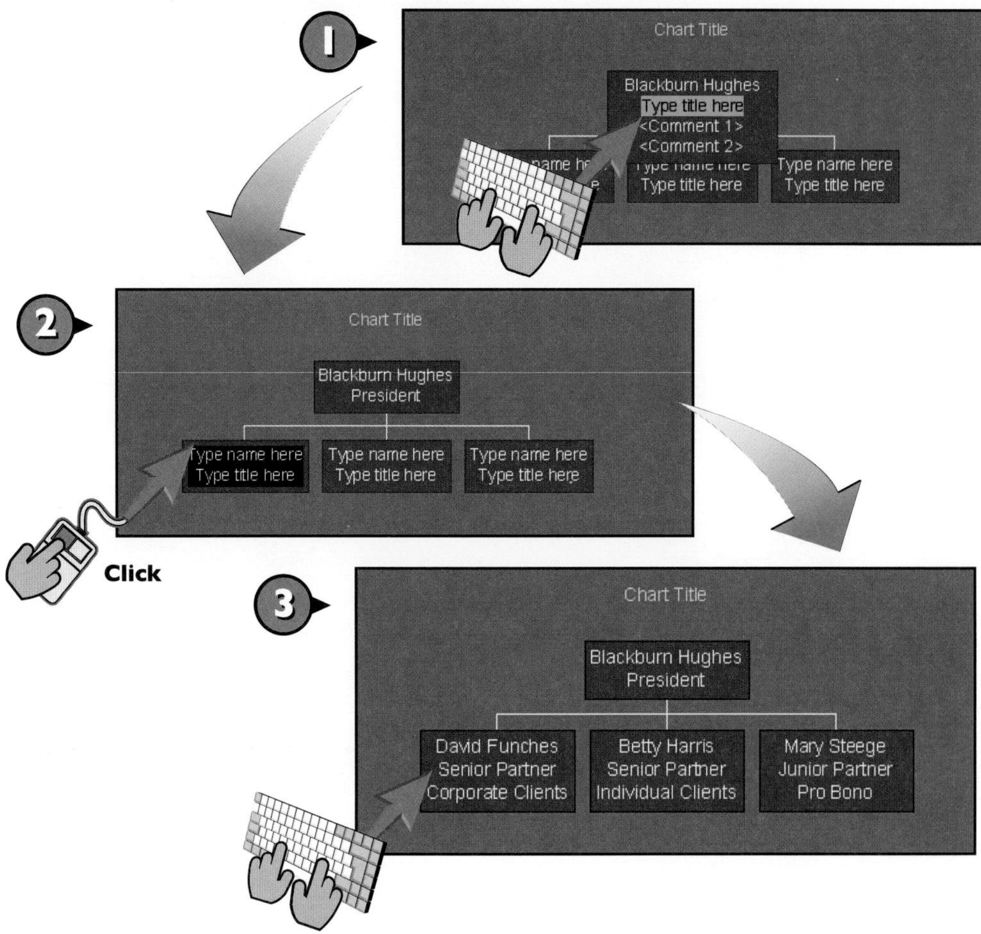

### Adding More Positions to the Organization Chart

**See Task 3 for how to add more people to your chart.**

1. When you create an Organization Chart, the first box is active. Type the first line, then press **Enter** to activate the next line. Type the remaining information, pressing **Enter** each time.

2. Click the next box in which you want to enter data, and type the information.

3. Type the information in each box.

Next Step

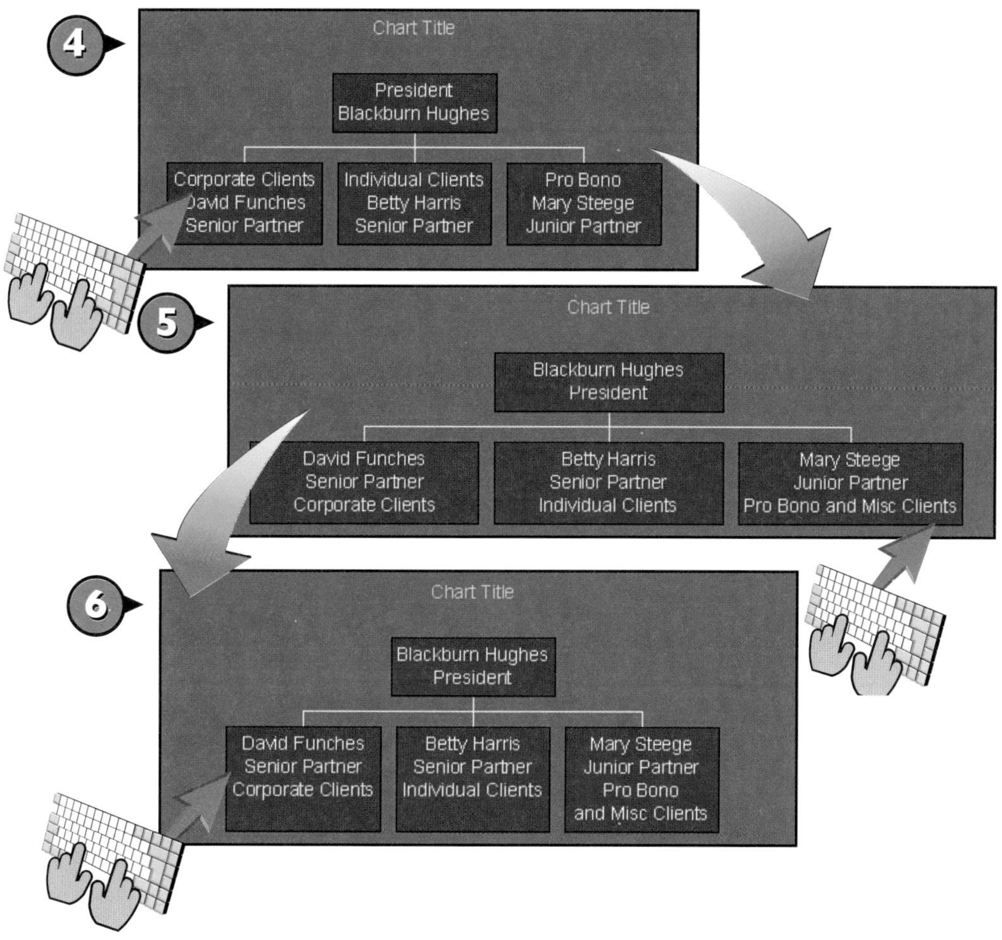


4. The boxes suggest entering the name in the first line; however, you can type the information in any order you wish.

5. The longest line in a box dictates the width of all boxes on the same level except the topmost box.

6. The box containing the most lines of information dictates the vertical height of all boxes on the same level, except the topmost box.

**Moving People in an Organization Chart**
**See Task 4 for how to move a person from one part of the Organization Chart to another.**

**Formatting Organization Chart Text and Boxes**
**See Tasks 7 and 8 for how to format the text and style of the boxes.**

## Inserting and Deleting Boxes in the Organization Chart

To add people to the organization chart, use the box buttons on the toolbar. You can add positions below (subordinates), next to (coworkers), and above (managers) other positions in the organization chart. You can even add boxes for assistants.

### Adding Multiple Positions at Once

To add more than one box at a time, use multiple clicks; the number of clicks on the box button determines the number of boxes added. For example, click three times on a box button to add three positions to your chart.

Start Here

# Task 3: Adding and Deleting People in an Organization Chart

Double Click

Click

Click

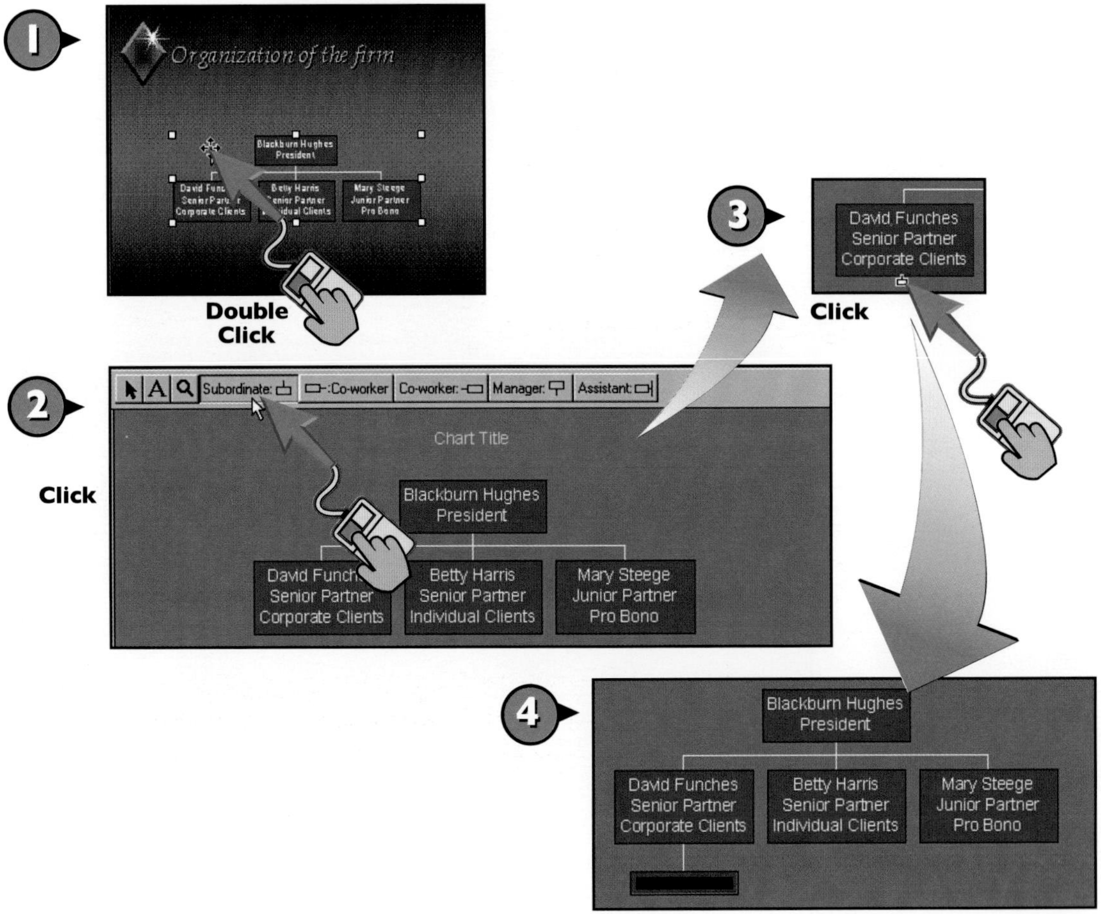

1. Double-click the chart to get into the Organization Chart program.
2. To add a person below someone on the chart, click once on the **Subordinate** button.
3. Position the mouse pointer in the box where you want to add the new person. A symbol appears, indicating the type of person being added, such as the subordinate symbol seen here.
4. Click on the box to add the person; the new box is added to the chart. Type the information in the new box.

5 Another type of box is for an assistant. The assistant branches off the selected box and can be attached to any box in the organization chart.

6 The assistant box appears below and to the left of the selected box. A box can have more than one assistant.

7 To remove a box, first click on it to select it.

8 Then press the **Delete** key to remove the box. The organization chart layout is automatically adjusted.

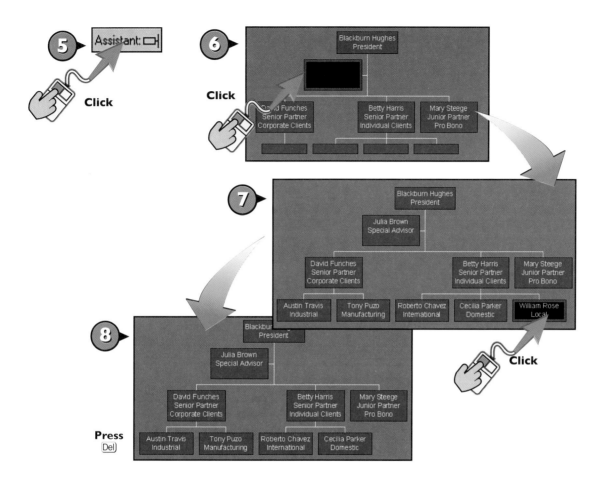

**Selecting Multiple Boxes**

**To select more than one box, click on the first box. Then press Shift and click on the other boxes you want to select.**

**WARNING**

**When you delete a "manager," all of that manager's "subordinates" are deleted as well. To keep the subordinates, move them under someone else before deleting the manager. See Task 4 to learn how to move people in your organization chart.**

# Task 4: Moving People in an Organization Chart

## Changing the Order of the Boxes in the Organization Chart

**You can move a person to different positions in the organization chart by dragging his box next to a coworker or manager.**

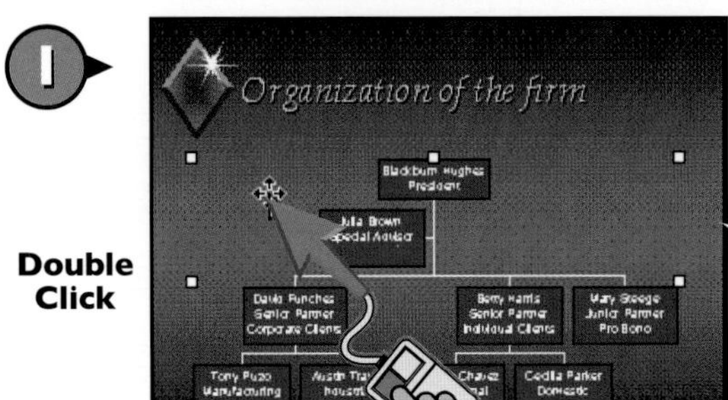


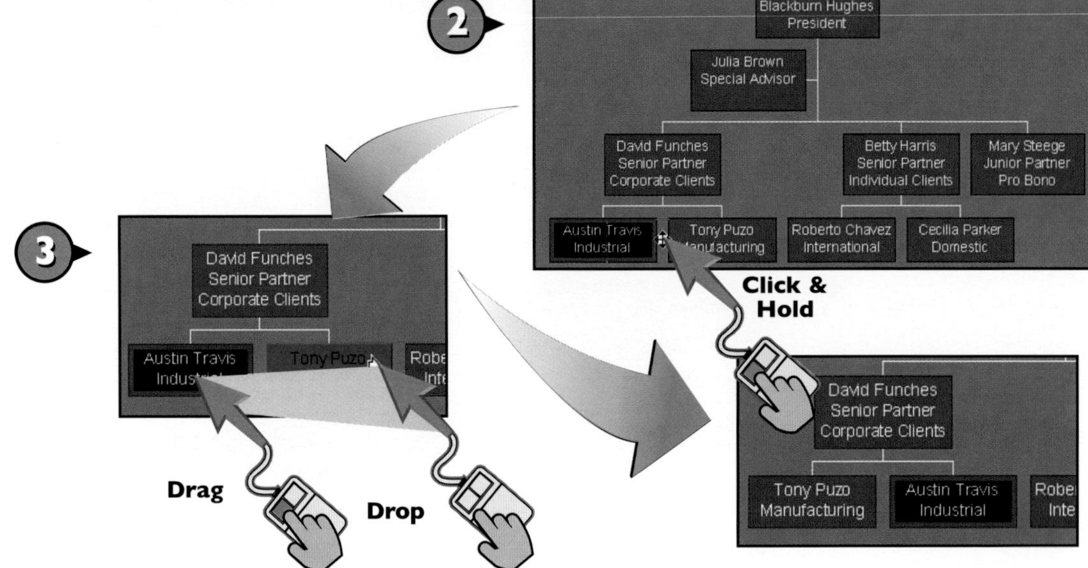

**WARNING**

**Do not select the box you are going to move. Hold the mouse pointer down on the box and immediately drag the mouse to move it. Selecting a box first makes it difficult to move.**

1. Double-click the chart to get into the Organization Chart program.

2. To move a box, position the mouse pointer over the box. Hold and drag the mouse. The mouse pointer changes to a four-headed arrow.

3. The mouse changes to a pointing arrow to indicate the placement of the box you are dragging in relation to the box your mouse pointer is resting on.



Next Step

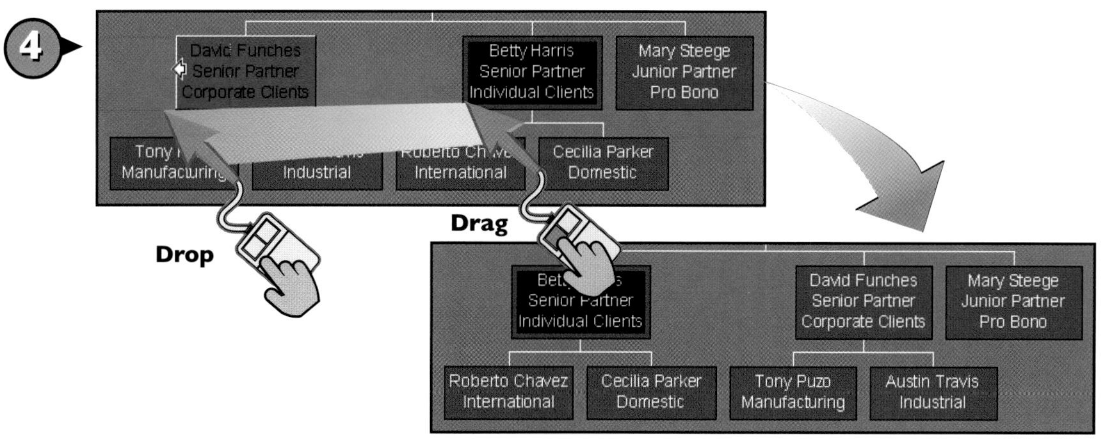


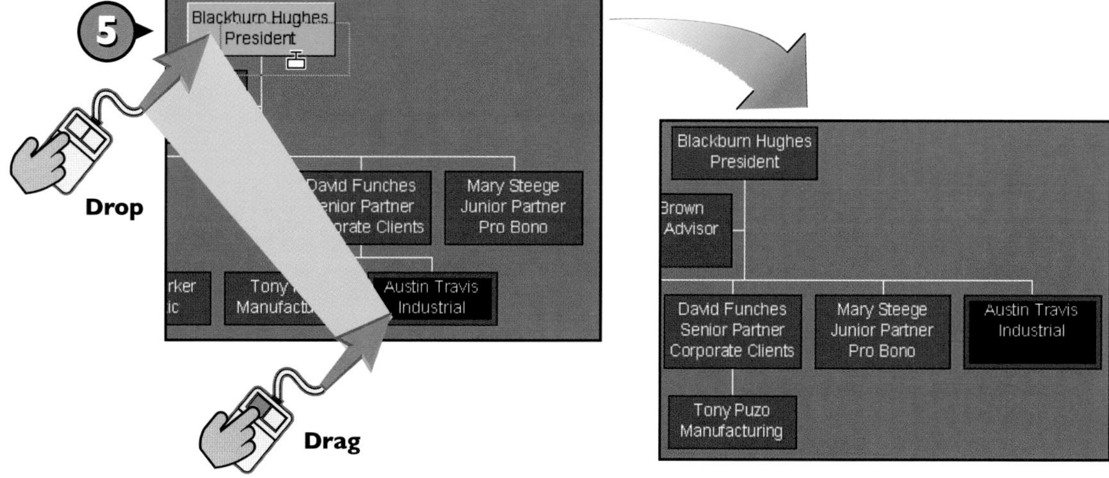


4. When you drag and drop a manager box, all the subordinate boxes follow.

5. You can also move people up (and down) levels in the organization chart. Look for the subordinate symbol (shown in step 5) or the manager symbol as you drag the box.

**Levels versus Branches**
**Each row of boxes is known as a *level*. A manager and subordinates together are called a *branch*.**

**Formatting Organization Chart Boxes**
**See Task 8 for steps to format the boxes in the organization chart.**

## Selecting Chart Components

**Before you can format the text inside the boxes, the layout of the boxes, the appearance of the boxes, or even the linking lines, you must first learn to select the boxes.**

# Task 5: Selecting People in an Organization Chart

Start Here

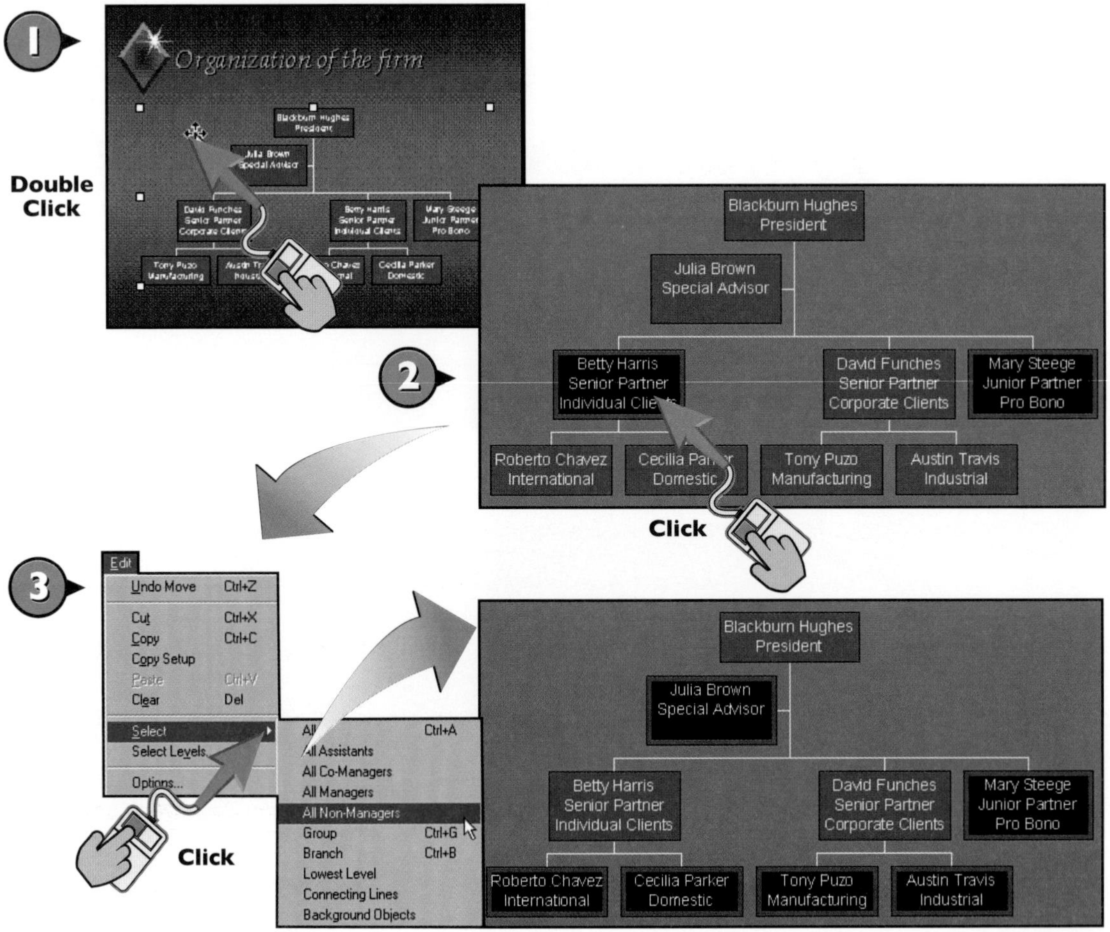

**Selecting All Boxes on a Specific Level**

**Each row of boxes in the organization chart is considered a level. The Edit, Select Levels command enables you to select boxes based on levels rather than components of the chart.**

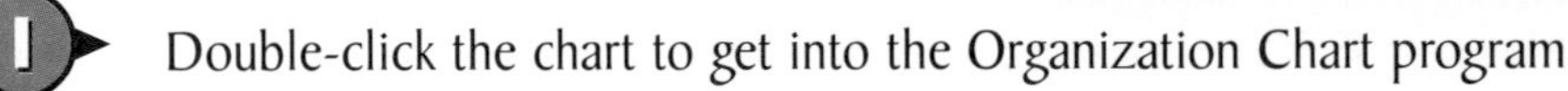

1. Double-click the chart to get into the Organization Chart program.

2. To select a person in the organization chart, simply click on the appropriate box. To select additional people, press **Shift** and click on the other people you want to select.

3. The Edit, Select command provides several useful options. For example, choose **All Non-Managers** to select every person who does not have subordinates.

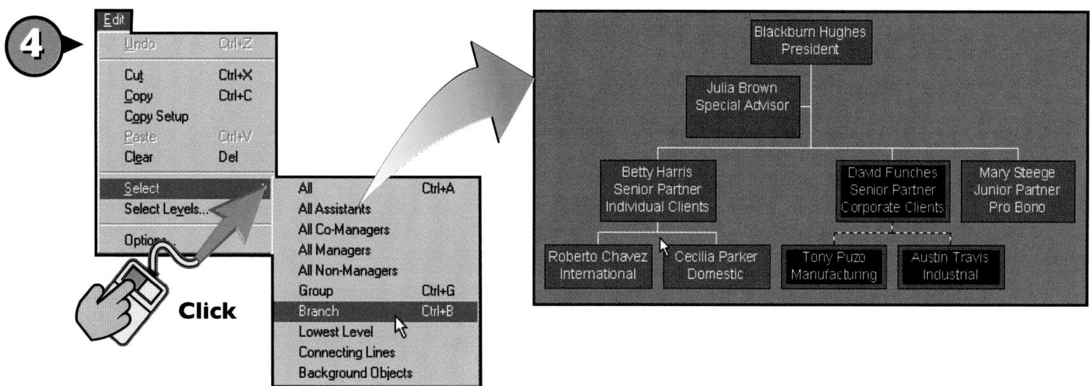


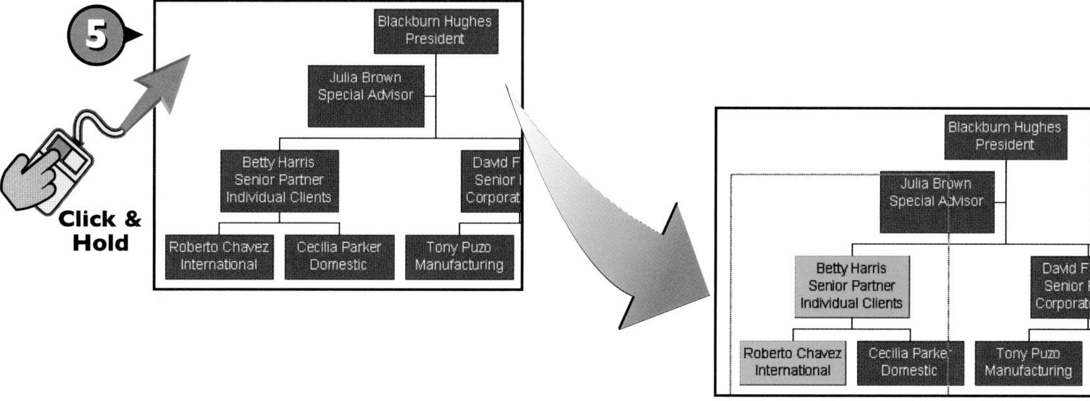


**Branches versus Groups**
A ***branch*** is the set of boxes below (subordinate to) the active box. A ***group*** is the set of boxes on the same level as the active box.

**Formatting Box Styles and Appearance**
See Task 6 for steps to format the layout of the boxes.

See Task 8 for steps to format the appearance of the boxes.

4 Choose **Edit, Select** to see a list of selection options. To use the Group or Branch option, you must first select a box.

5 Another method for selecting boxes is to drag the mouse and draw an imaginary box. Each organization chart box that falls completely within the imaginary box is selected.

# Task 6: Formatting the Box Layout in an Organization Chart

## Working with the Box Styles

The Organization Chart program includes several flexible box layout styles you can use. Some styles display the boxes vertically, horizontally, or even without borders.

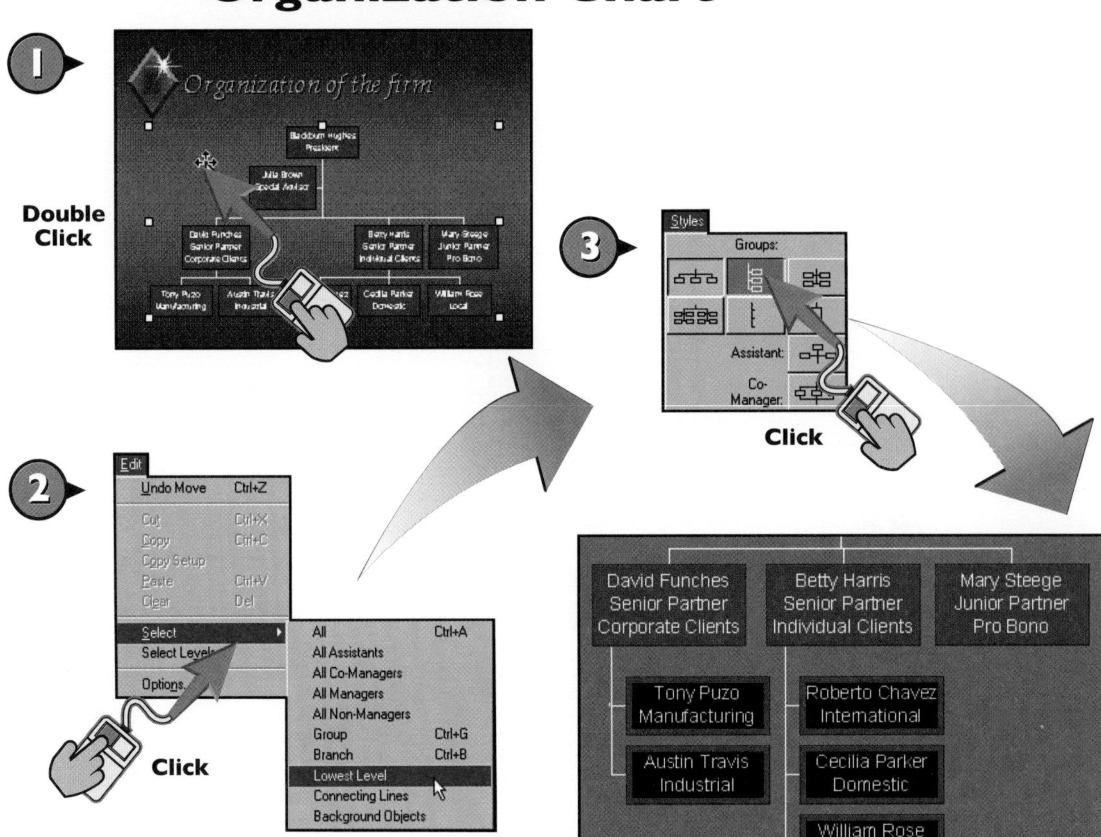


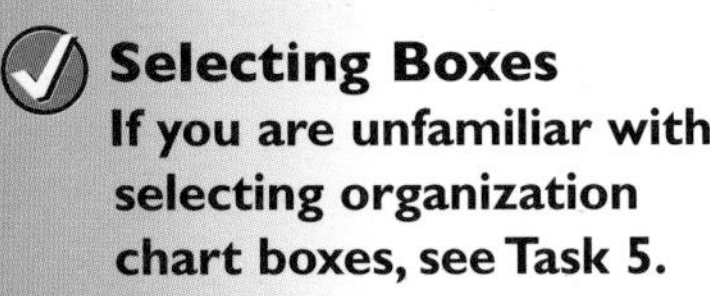

**Selecting Boxes**
If you are unfamiliar with selecting organization chart boxes, see Task 5.

1. Double-click the chart to get into the Organization Chart program.
2. Before you can alter the box styles, you must first select the boxes you want to change.
3. Then choose **Styles** and select a box style layout. This style displays the boxes in one vertical column.

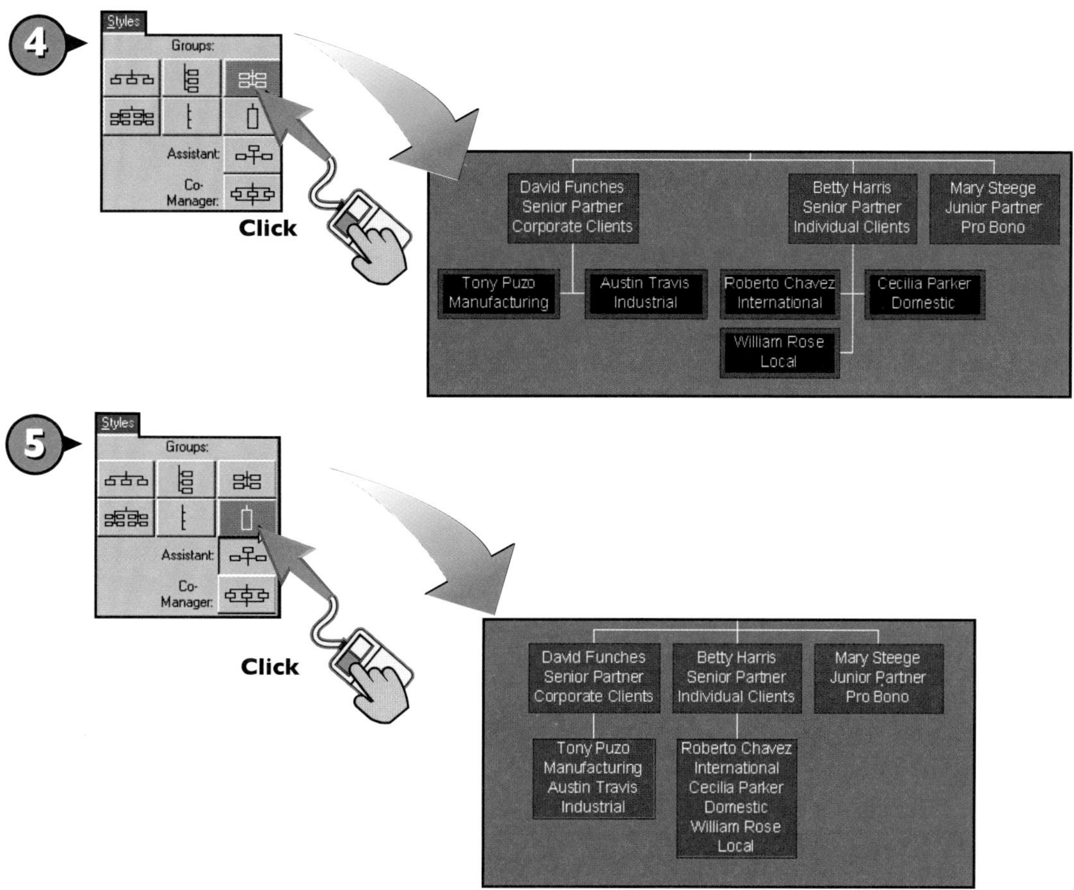


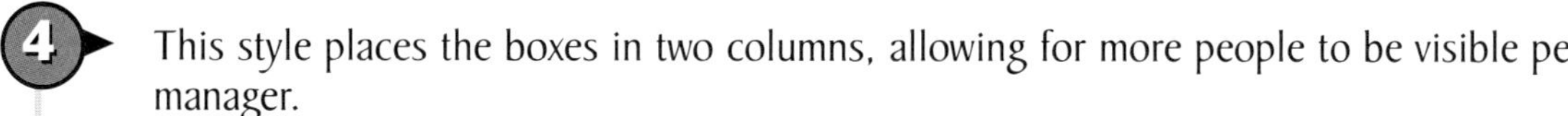

4. This style places the boxes in two columns, allowing for more people to be visible per manager.

5. With this style, everyone in each branch is pooled into a single box. This style is best used when there is only one line of information for each person, either a name or a title.

**Changing Text Size**
**In addition to changing the box styles to fit more people into the organization chart, you can also reduce the font size of the text. See Task 7 for steps to change the font size.**

# Task 7: Formatting Text in an Organization Chart

## Changing the Font and Color of the Text

You can change the text in one box or a group of boxes. You can even apply individual formats to each line in a box. You must first select the boxes or the specific text before you can change the font formats.

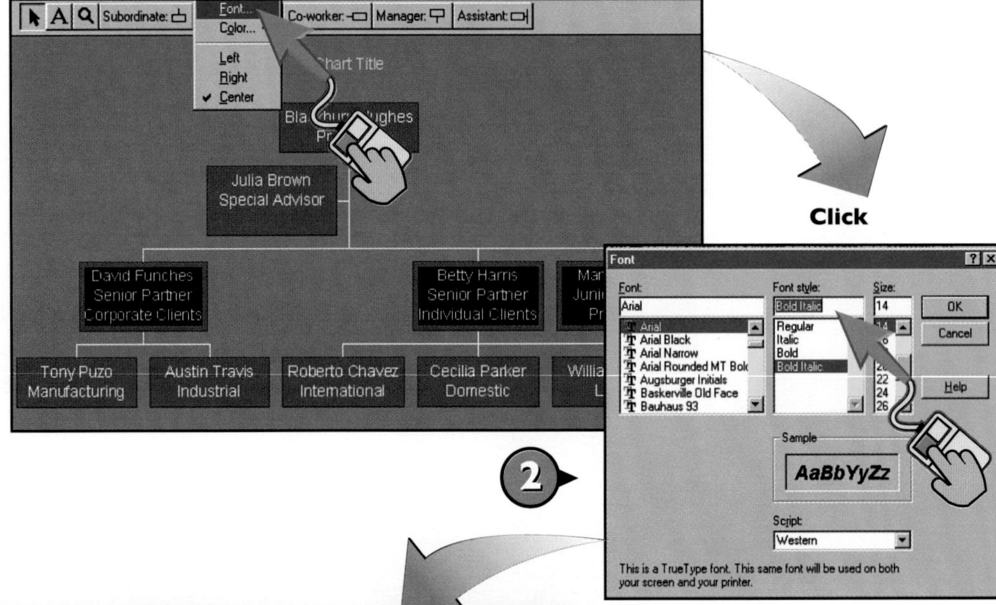


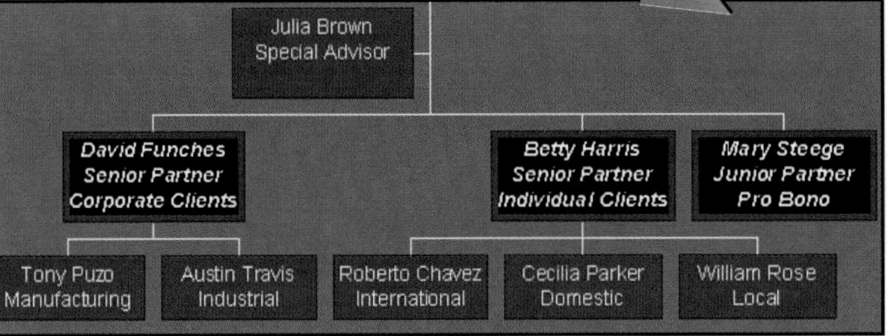


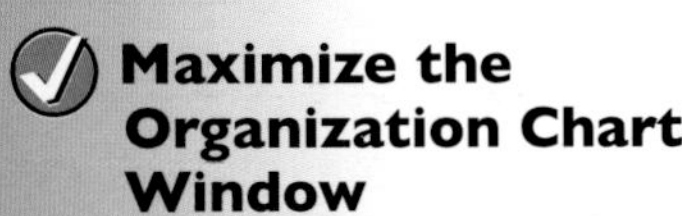

### Maximize the Organization Chart Window

When working in the Organization Chart program, it is easier to see everything if you maximize the Organization Chart window.

1. To change the font in a group of boxes, first select the boxes you want to format. See Task 5 if you're not sure how to select boxes. Then choose **Text, Font** from the menu bar.

2. In the Font dialog box, choose a font type, font style, and font size. The sample box shows you what the text will look like. Choose **OK** to apply the changes to the text.

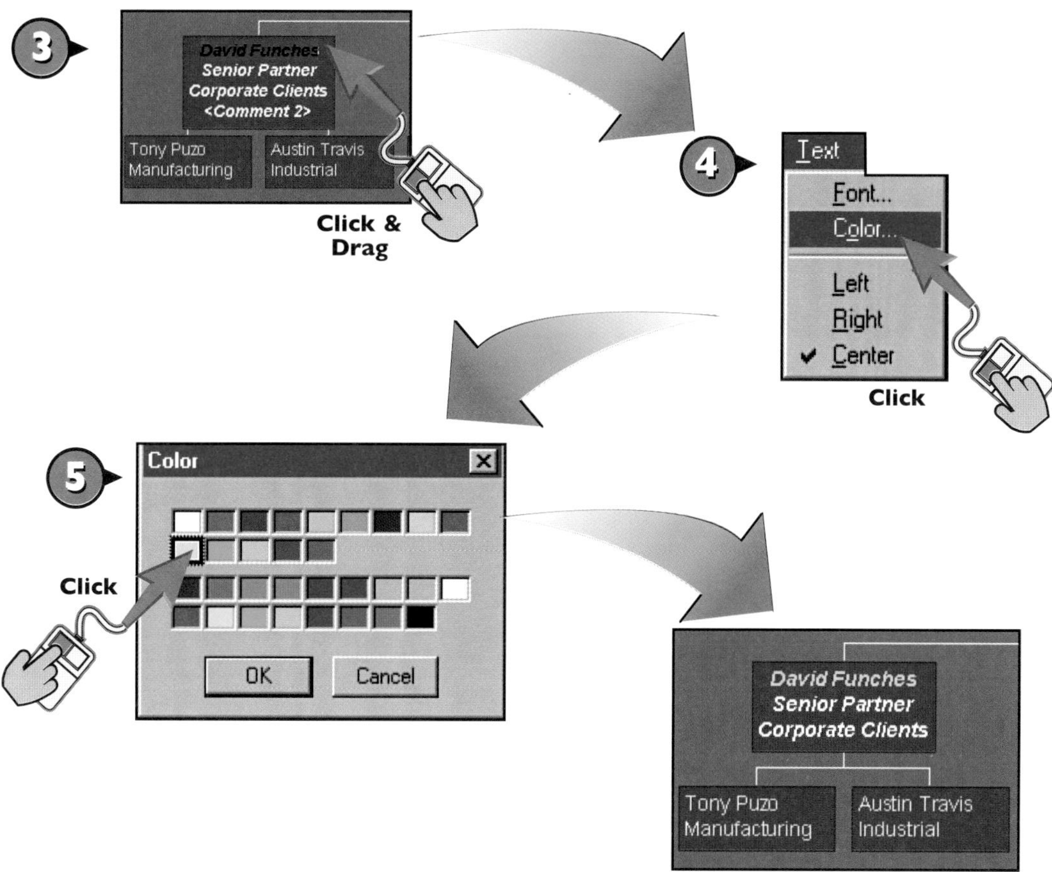


3 To format a single line of text in a box, drag the mouse pointer across the text to highlight it.

4 To change the color of the text, choose **Text, Color**. The Color dialog box appears.

5 Click the color you want; a dark border appears around the selected color. Choose **OK** to apply the color to the text.

**Selecting Specific Text in a Box**
When you want to change only one line of text in a box, select it by dragging the mouse pointer (a thin capital "I") across the text.

**Changing Text Alignment**
You can also change the alignment of the text in the boxes by choosing the Text menu (see step 4) and selecting Left, Right, or Center.

# Task 8: Formatting Boxes in an Organization Chart

## Changing the Background and Border Attributes of the Chart Boxes

You can format all or just a group of boxes in the organization chart. The box attributes include color, drop shadows, and border styles.

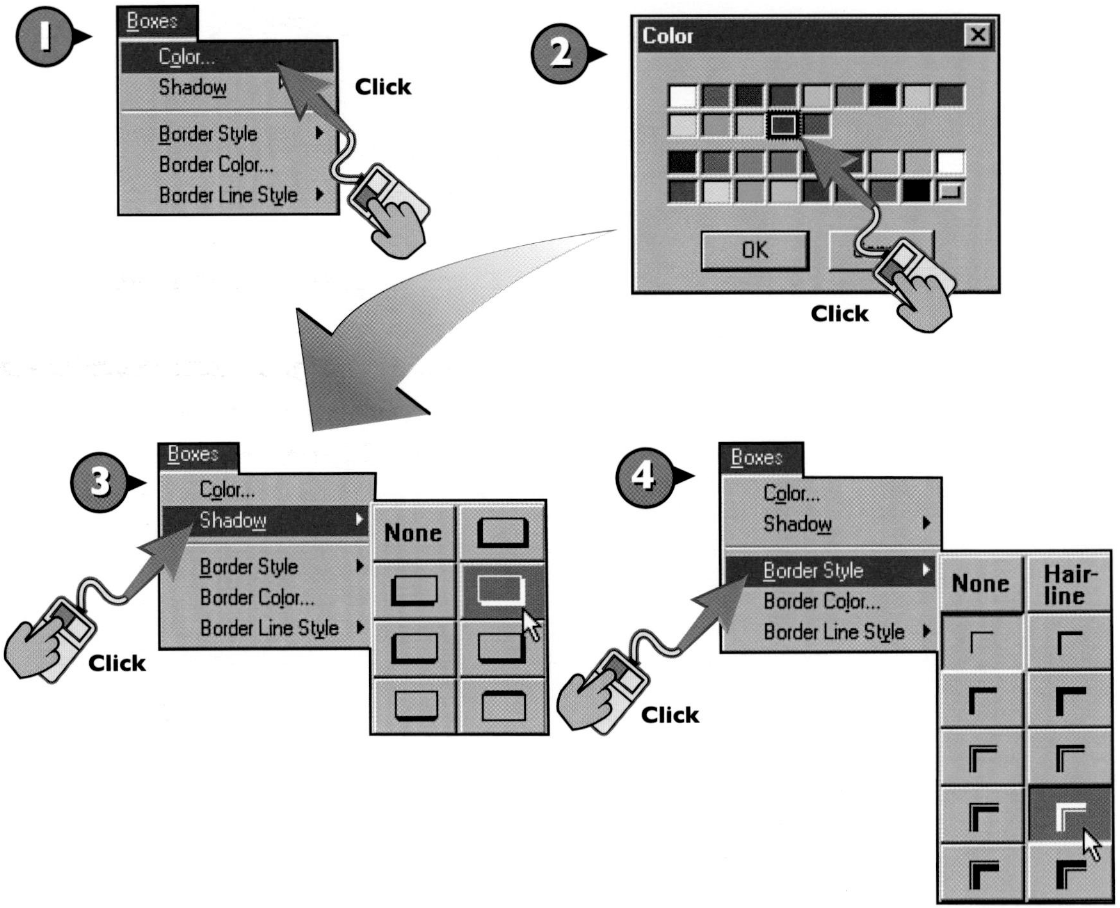

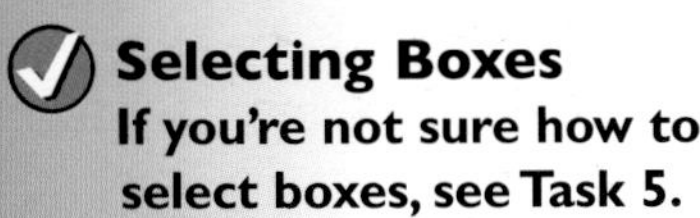

**Selecting Boxes**
If you're not sure how to select boxes, see Task 5.

Start Here



1. To change the box background color, first select the boxes you want to format. Then choose **Boxes, Color**.
2. From the Color dialog box, choose a color and click **OK**.
3. To apply a drop shadow to a box, first select the box(es). Then choose **Boxes, Shadow** and select the shadow position.
4. To change the box border appearance, first select the boxes. Then choose **Boxes, Border Style** and select a style.

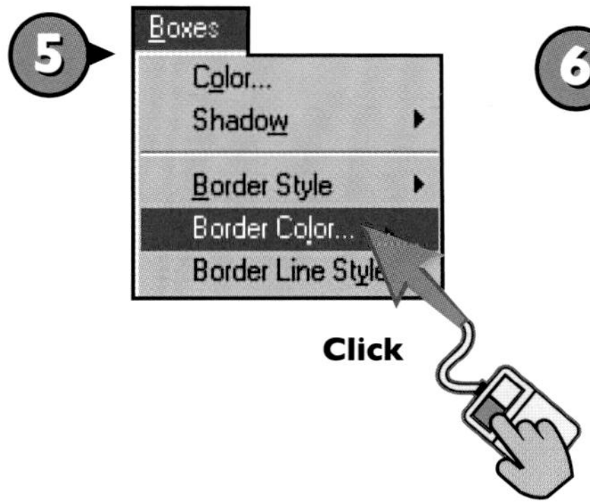

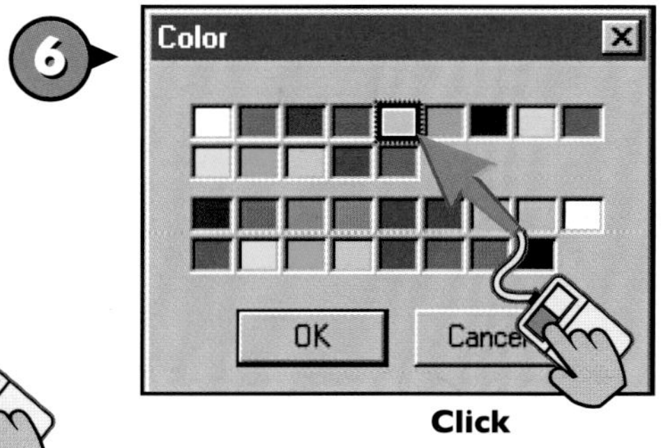

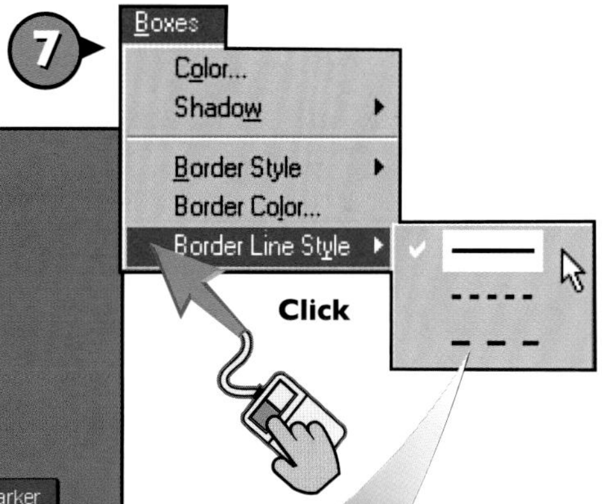

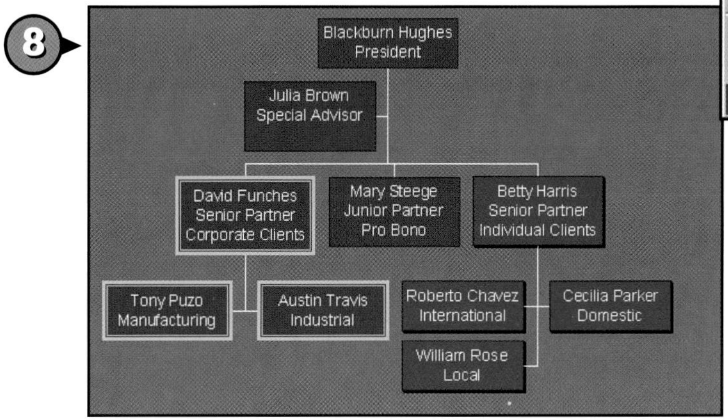

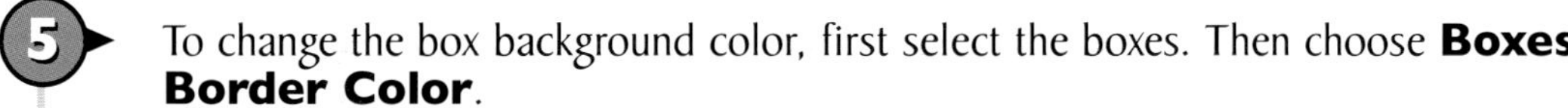

5. To change the box background color, first select the boxes. Then choose **Boxes, Border Color**.

6. From the Color dialog box, choose a color and click **OK**.

7. To change the type of line used on the box border, select the boxes. Then choose **Boxes, Border Line Style** and select a style.

8. This figure illustrates the border and background options discussed in this task.

### Use Contrasting Colors

**When selecting a box background color, make sure it contrasts with the text color. White (or light) text does not show up well on a yellow background. Black (or dark) text does not show up well on a blue background.**

# Task 9: Updating Your Presentation with the Organization Chart

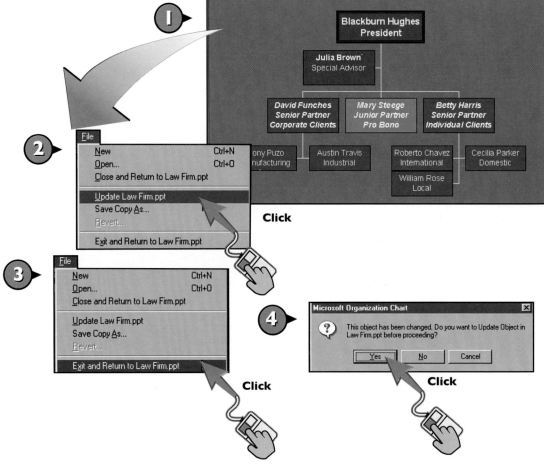

Start Here

## Exiting the Organization Chart Program

**Because organization charts are created in a separate program, you must exit the program to see the organization chart in your PowerPoint presentation.**

1. After you have created or modified an organization chart, you must update the PowerPoint presentation before you can see the organization chart.
2. To update your presentation with the changes made to the chart but remain in the Organization Chart program, choose **File, Update**.
3. To update your presentation and close the Organization Chart program, choose **File, Exit and Return**.
4. Choose **Yes** in the update dialog box.

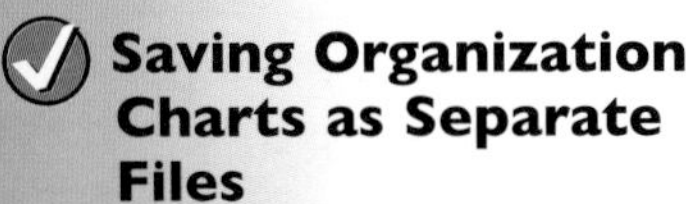

### Saving Organization Charts as Separate Files

**The File menu contains options to save (and subsequently open) organization charts you intend to use in several presentations, thus saving you the trouble of re-creating them.**

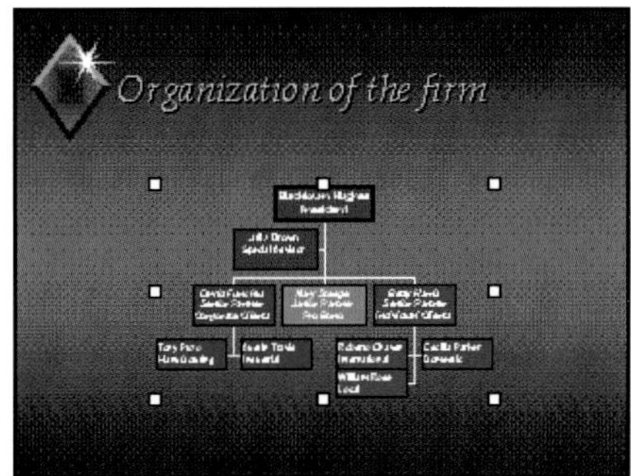

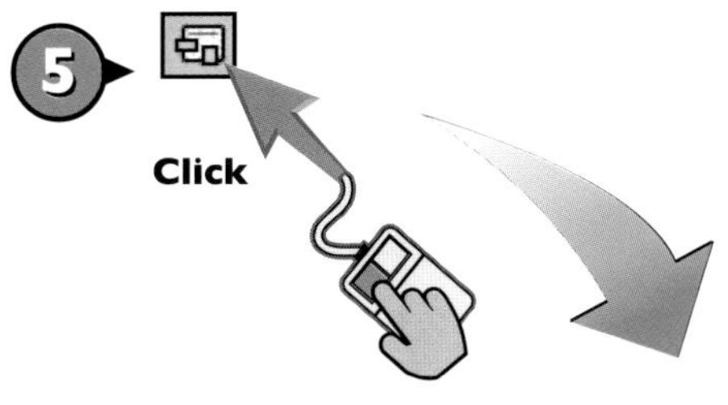


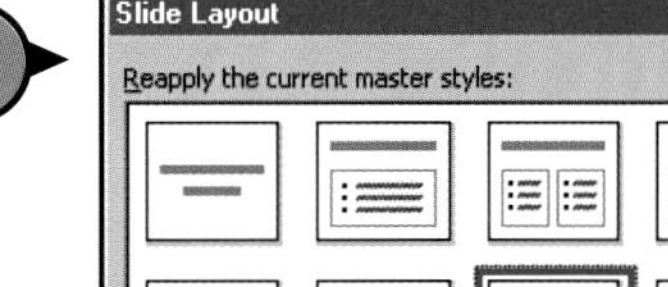

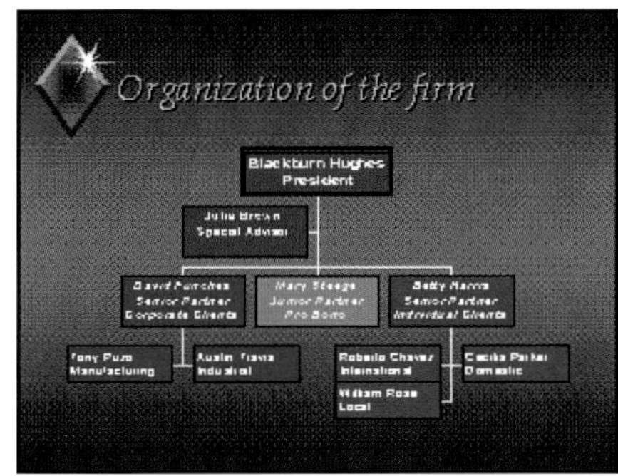

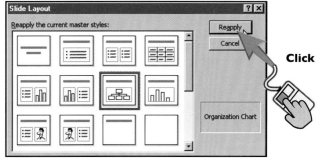

It is sometimes possible to enlarge the chart by simply reapplying the slide layout. Click the **Slide Layout** button on the Standard toolbar.

The Organization Chart slide layout is already selected. Click **Reapply**. The slide layout is updated and the slide is enlarged.

**Adjusting the Organization Chart Size**

**You can also enlarge an organization chart by dragging a selection handle. Be sure to drag a corner selection handle to avoid distorting the chart text.**

PART

# Working with Tables

A table is a particular type of slide in PowerPoint. Tables are especially useful for displaying a list of data or comparing two or more sets of data. For example, a list of product names and prices or a comparison of sales from this year and last year can be more clearly displayed in a table than in paragraphs of text.

When you create a table slide, you use the table features of Microsoft Word. Whenever you create or edit a table, the PowerPoint menu bar choices and toolbar buttons change to become Microsoft Word menus and toolbars.

# Tasks



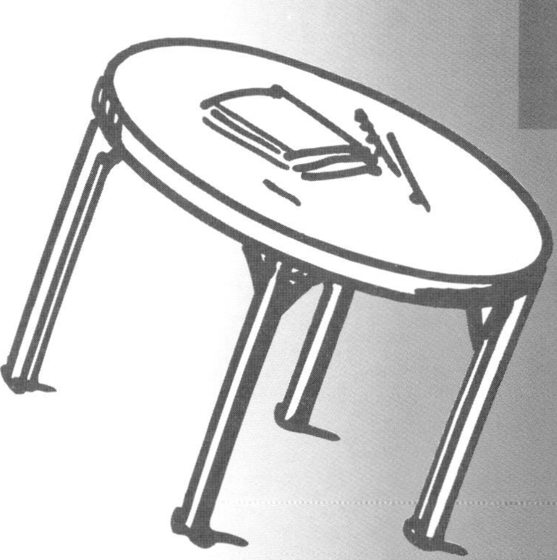

# Task 1: Creating a Table

## Using the Table Slide Layout

When you create a table in PowerPoint, you use the table features in Microsoft Word. The commands on the menu bar and the buttons on the PowerPoint toolbars become Microsoft Word commands and buttons.

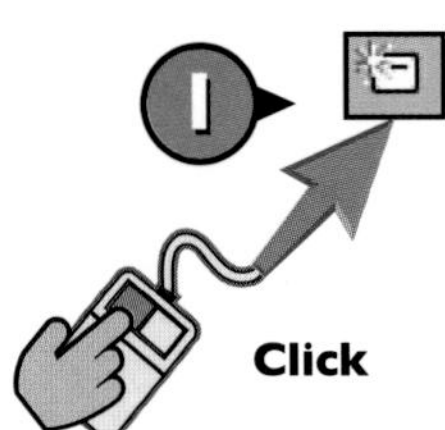

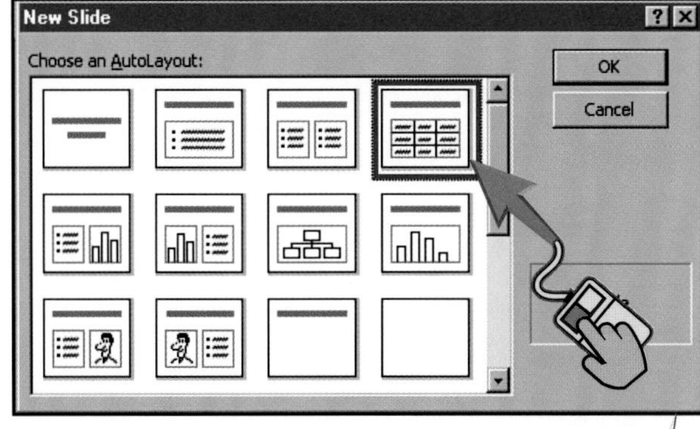

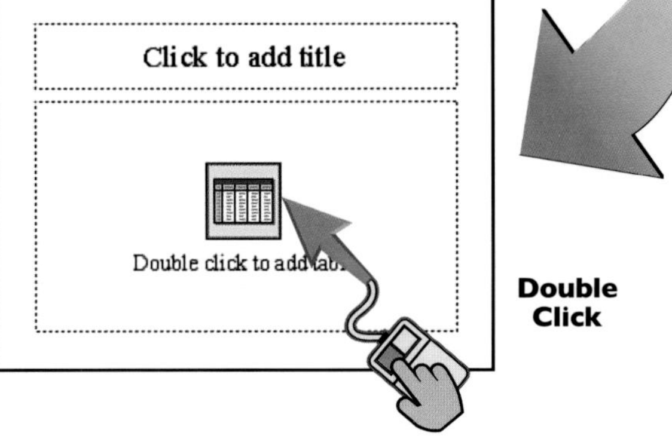


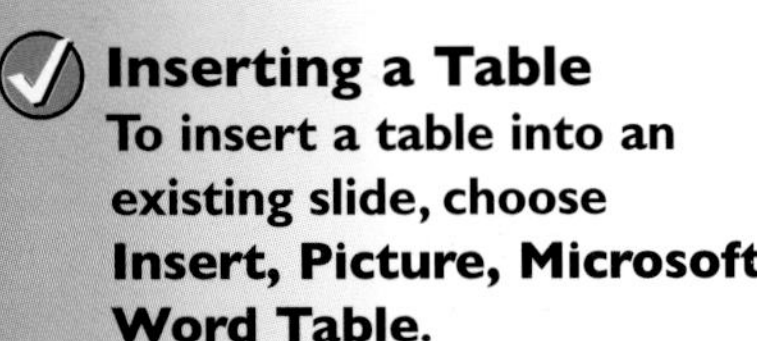

**Inserting a Table**
To insert a table into an existing slide, choose **Insert, Picture, Microsoft Word Table.**

1. Select the **New Slide** button on the Standard toolbar.

2. Double-click the Table layout in the New Slide dialog box.

3. The new slide appears, with the Table layout. Double-click the table placeholder to create the table.



Next Step

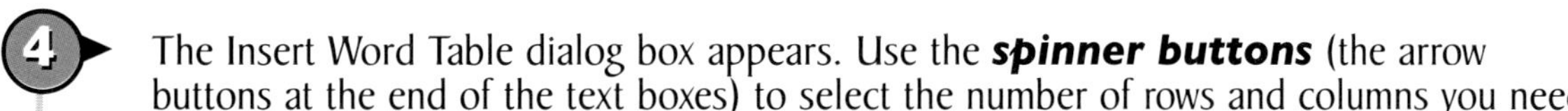

4. The Insert Word Table dialog box appears. Use the ***spinner buttons*** (the arrow buttons at the end of the text boxes) to select the number of rows and columns you need.

5. After you select the number of rows and columns, choose **OK**.

6. The table appears in the slide, ready for you to enter the data.

7. The Table menu on the menu bar includes many commands necessary for editing and formatting tables. Click **Table** to open the menu.

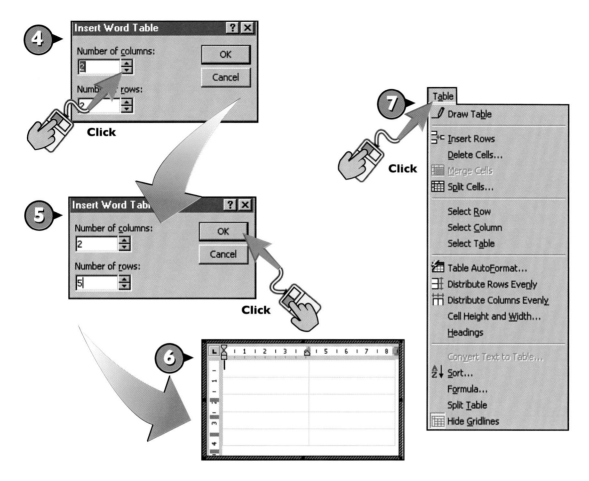

**Using Word Commands**
**Only when you are editing a table (indicated by the slash border and flashing cursor) do the menu commands and toolbars change to show Microsoft Word options.**

**Filling in the Table**
**See Task 2 for steps on entering or editing table data.**

# Task 2: Entering and Editing Text in a Table

## Inserting and Changing Table Data

**A flashing cursor indicates the *current cell*, or location, in a table. You enter and modify text in a table just as you do in any text object.**

Start Here

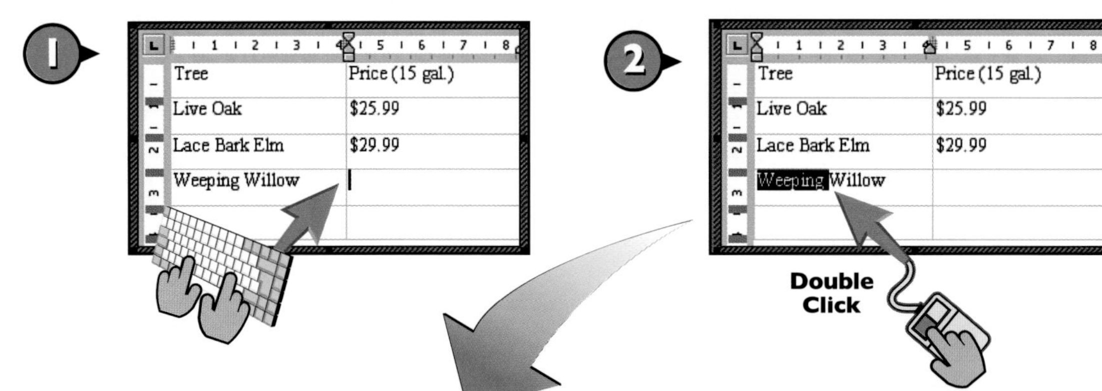


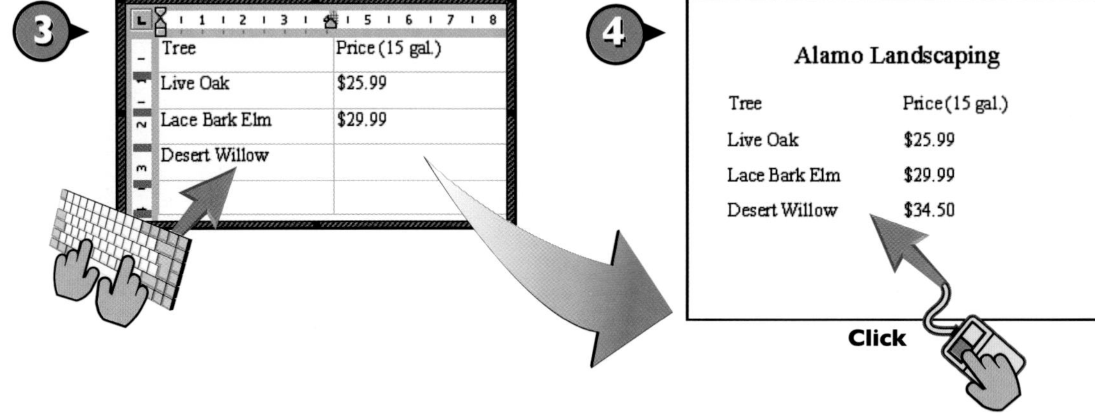


1. To enter text in a table, type an entry and press the **Tab** key to move to the next cell.
2. To edit text in a table, double-click to select a word or triple-click to select all the words in that cell.
3. As you type, the new data replaces the highlighted text.
4. Click outside the table to get out of the Edit mode and see the table in your slide.

**Formatting the Table**
**See Task 7 to learn how to format the borders and gridlines in a table.**

End Task

# Task 3: Changing Column and Row Size

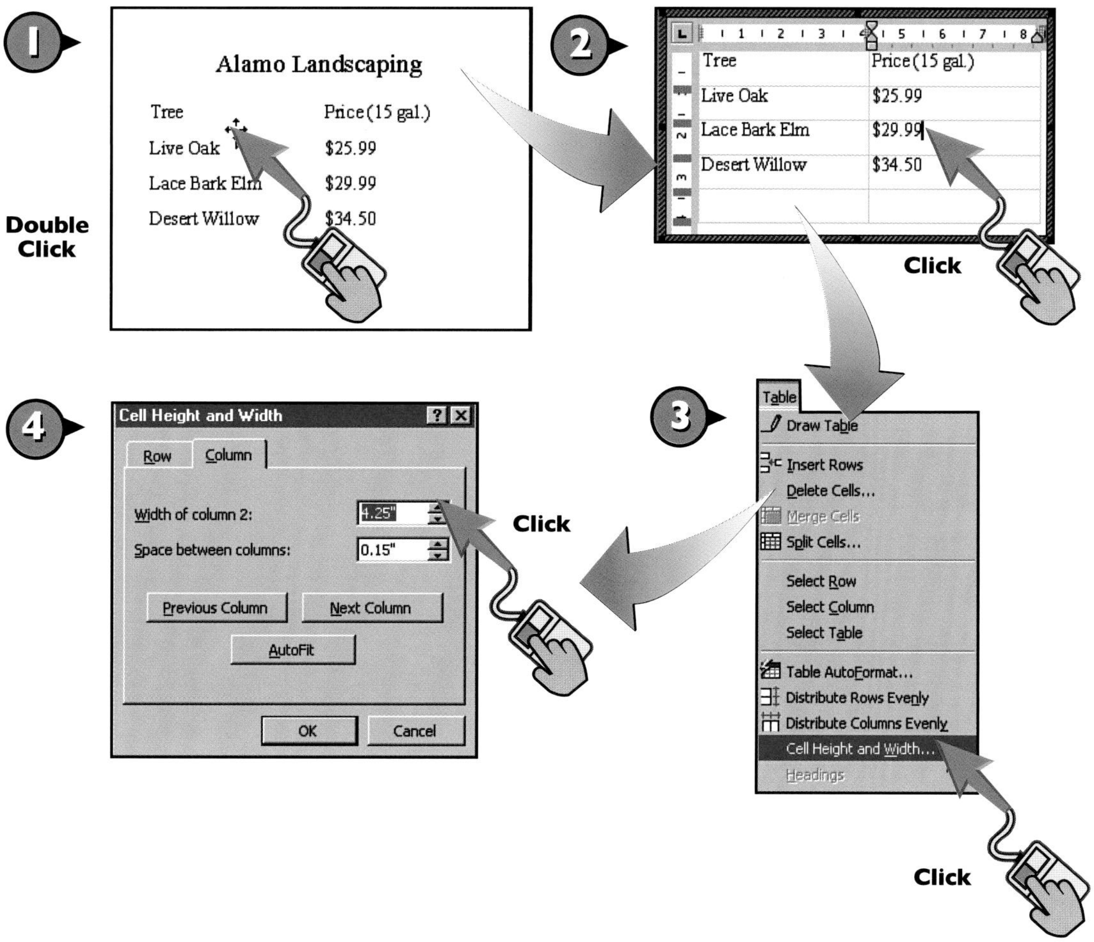

## Adjusting Column Width and Row Height

**Before you can adjust the column or row size, you must first get into the Edit mode by double-clicking on the table. Then use the Cell Height and Width dialog box to change the table.**

1. Double-click to edit the table.
2. Click anywhere in the row or column you want to adjust.
3. Choose **Table, Cell Height and Width** from the menu bar.
4. Choose the **Row** or **Column** tab in the Cell Height and Width dialog box, and use the spinner buttons to increase or decrease the height and width.

**Adjusting the Table Rows and Columns**
**The AutoFit option in the Cell Height and Width dialog box widens or shrinks the row or column to accommodate the longest entry.**

# Task 4: Inserting and Deleting a Column or Row

## Adding and Removing Columns or Rows in a Table

You must select an entire column or row before you can insert or remove it from the table. Use the Table menu to quickly select columns and rows.

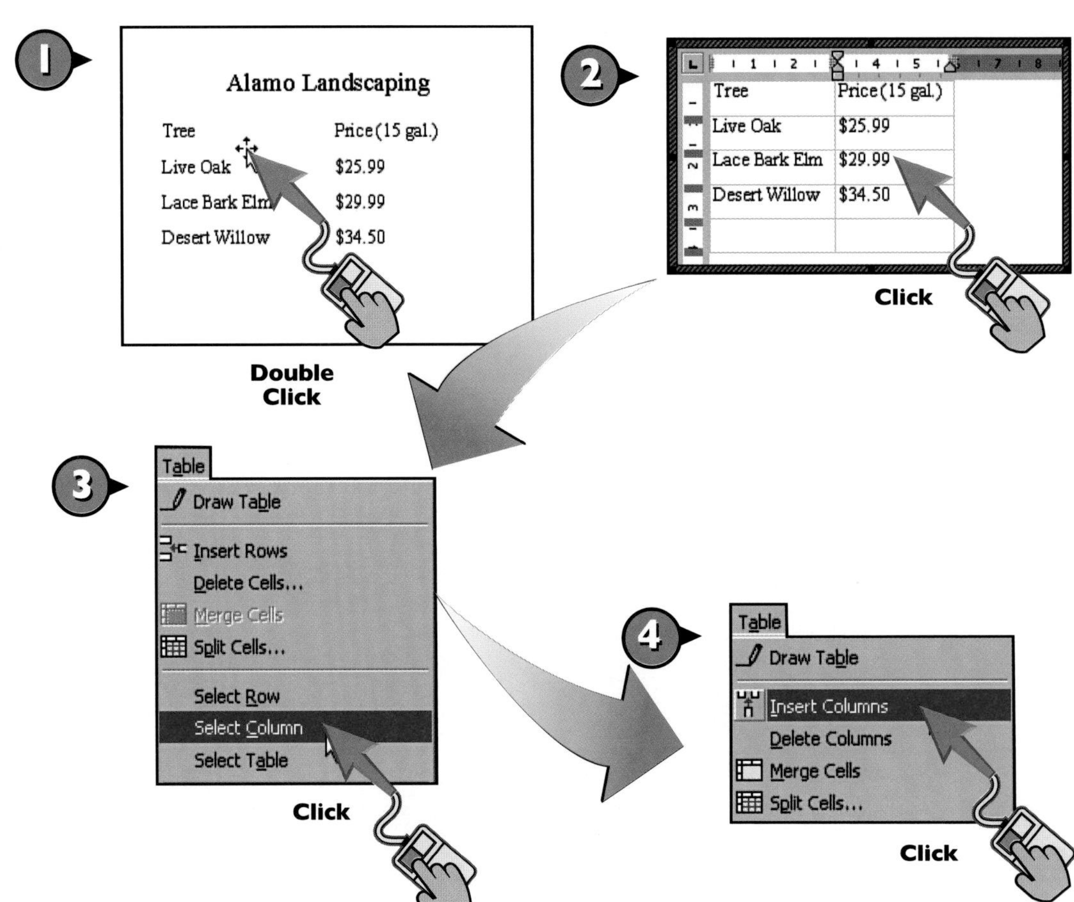


### Inserting Columns and Rows

When you insert a column or row, it is placed in the current (highlighted) location. The current column moves to the right. The current row moves down.

1. Double-click to edit the table.
2. To insert or delete a column, click in a cell where you want to insert or delete the column.
3. Choose **Table, Select Column** to highlight all the cells in this column.
4. Choose **Table, Insert Columns** to insert a column. Choose **Table, Delete Columns** to remove the selected column.

Next Step

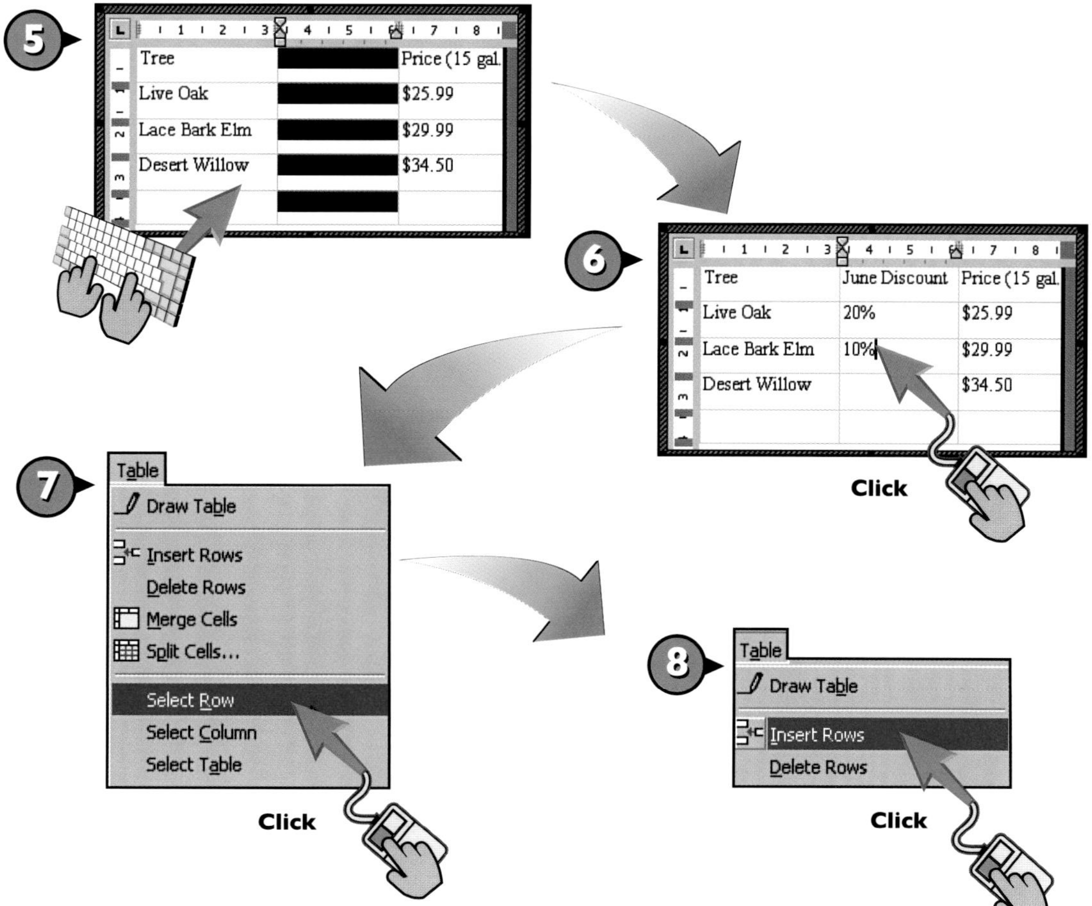

5 After you insert a column, you can begin typing data in the new column.

6 To insert or delete a row, click in a cell where a new row is to be inserted or deleted.

7 Choose **Table, Select Row** to highlight all the cells in this row.

8 Choose **Table, Insert Rows** to insert a row. Choose **Table, Delete Rows** to remove the selected row.

**Deleting Columns and Rows**

When you delete a column or row, the current (highlighted) one is removed. The remaining columns move to the left. The remaining rows move up.

**Selecting Multiple Columns or Rows**

To select more than one column or row, highlight the first one. Then press Shift and the keyboard arrow key that points in the direction you want to highlight.

# Task 5: Sorting Data in a Table

## Ordering the Table Data

**Reorder the rows of information in a table by sorting them. You can specify up to three separate criteria for your sort.**

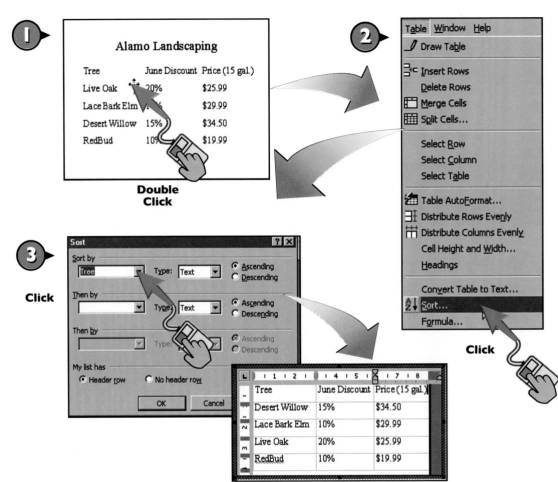

Start Here



1. Double-click to edit the table.

2. Choose **Table, Sort**; the Sort dialog box appears.

3. From the **Sort By** drop-down list, choose the column you wish to sort by. Then select **Ascending** or **Descending** and choose **OK**.

**Ascending versus Descending Sorts**
Use an ascending sort to arrange text alphabetically. Use a descending sort to list numbers from highest to lowest.

**Sorting Columns**
The text appearing in the first row of your table is assumed to be labels for each column.

End Task

# Task 6: Formatting Data in a Table

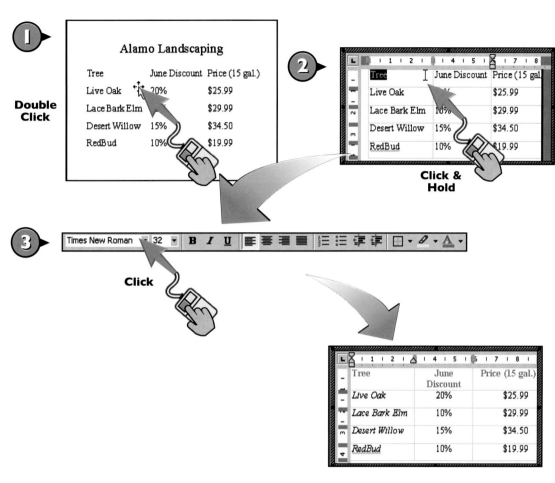

1 Double Click

| Alamo Landscaping | | |
|---|---|---|
| Tree | June Discount | Price (15 gal.) |
| Live Oak | 20% | $25.99 |
| Lace Bark Elm | | $29.99 |
| Desert Willow | 15% | $34.50 |
| RedBud | 10% | $19.99 |

2 Click & Hold

3 Click

Times New Roman 32 B I U

| Tree | June Discount | Price (15 gal.) |
|---|---|---|
| *Live Oak* | 20% | $25.99 |
| *Lace Bark Elm* | 10% | $29.99 |
| *Desert Willow* | 15% | $34.50 |
| *RedBud* | 10% | $19.99 |

1. Double-click the table to start editing.
2. Drag the mouse pointer (a capital "I") to select the data you want to change.
3. Use the Formatting toolbar to enhance the table. You can alter the ***font type*** and size; apply bold, italic, or underline; adjust the alignment; indent the data; or change the font color.

## Enhancing the Data in a Table

**You can quickly change the appearance of the data in a table by applying some simple formats from the Formatting toolbar.**

### Toolbar Button Descriptions

**If you're unsure what format you'll get by choosing a button on the toolbar, hold the mouse pointer over the button until the ScreenTip appears. And if you apply a format and decide you don't like it, undo it!**

# Task 7: Adding Borders and Shading to a Table

## Applying an Outline and Background Color to a Table

You can make a table stand out clearly from the rest of the slide by applying a few simple formats.

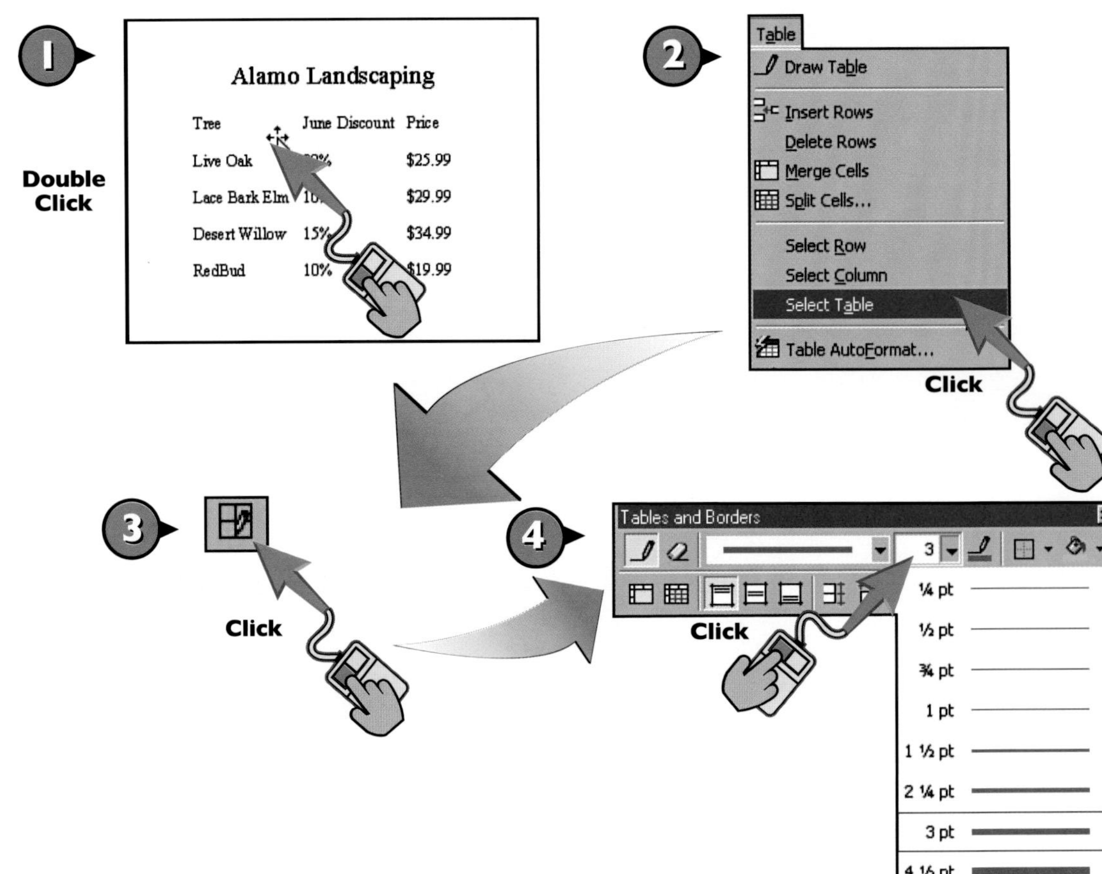


1. Double-click to edit the table.
2. To apply a border or shading to the entire table, you must first choose **Table, Select Table**.
3. Click the **Tables and Borders** button to display the Tables and Borders toolbar.
4. To add a border to a table, start by selecting a border thickness from the **Line Weight** drop-down list.

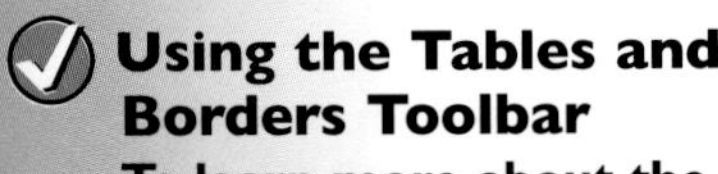

**Using the Tables and Borders Toolbar**
To learn more about the buttons on the Tables and Borders toolbar, hold the mouse pointer over the button until a ScreenTip appears.

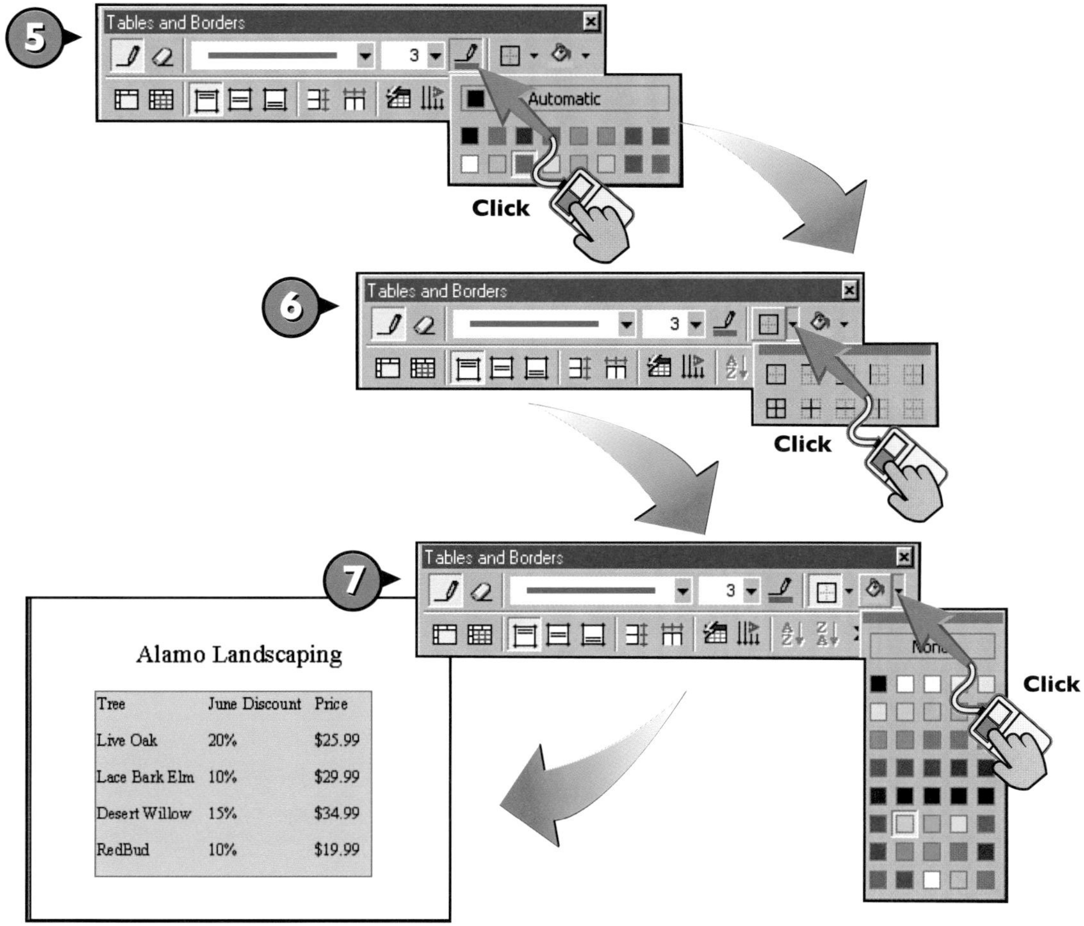

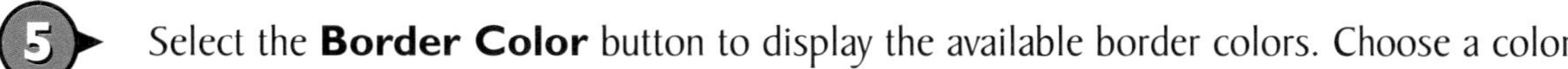

5. Select the **Border Color** button to display the available border colors. Choose a color.

6. Select the **Outline Border** button and choose a placement for the border.

7. To apply a background color, choose the **Shading Color** button. Choose a lighter color when you have a dark text color; choose a darker color to offset lighter text.

### WARNING

**Sometimes a newly added table border doesn't display properly. One way to avoid this is to optimize the row height and column width. After you select the entire table (in step 2), use the Distribute Rows Evenly and the Cell Height and Width commands to adjust the rows and columns.**

### Formatting Tables Quickly

**See Task 8 to learn about the Table AutoFormat feature.**

# Task 8: Using the Table AutoFormat Feature

## Formatting Tables Quickly

**The fastest way to enhance a table is to use the AutoFormat feature. You can choose from more than 35 different formats.**

Start Here

Double Click

Alamo Landscaping

| Tree | June Discount | Price |
|---|---|---|
| Live Oak | 20% | $25.99 |
| Lace Bark Elm | 10% | $29.99 |
| Desert Willow | 15% | $34.99 |
| RedBud | 10% | $19.99 |

Click

Table: Draw Table, Insert Rows, Delete Cells..., Merge Cells, Split Cells..., Select Row, Select Column, Select Table, Table AutoFormat..., Distribute Rows Evenly

Click

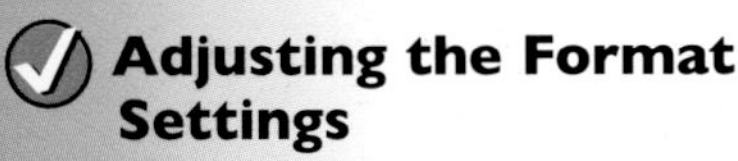

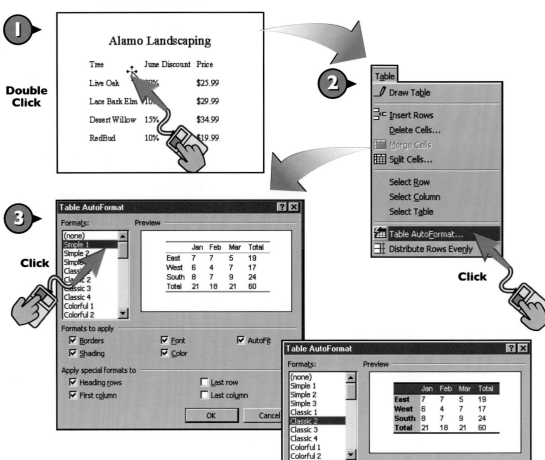

### Adjusting the Format Settings

**Adjust the format by turning off some of the Format To Apply options. Also, special formats can be applied to the first and last rows or columns.**

1. Double-click to edit the table.
2. Choose **Table, Table AutoFormat**.
3. In the Table AutoFormat dialog box, select a table format from the Formats list.

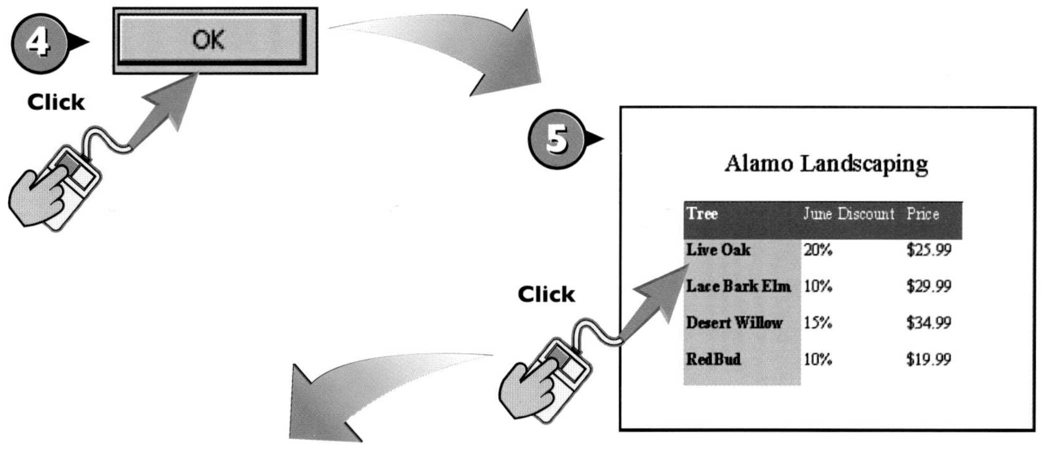


| Tree | June Discount | Price |
|---|---|---|
| Live Oak | 20% | $25.99 |
| Lace Bark Elm | 10% | $29.99 |
| Desert Willow | 15% | $34.99 |
| RedBud | 10% | $19.99 |

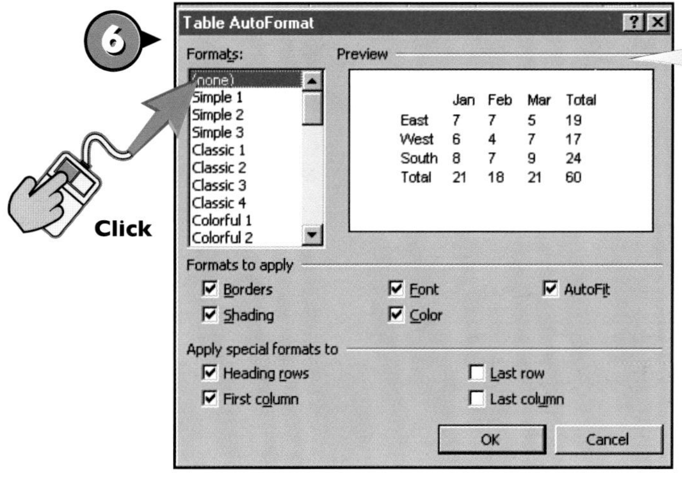


Alamo Landscaping

| Tree | June Discount | Price |
|---|---|---|
| Live Oak | 20% | $25.99 |
| Lace Bark Elm | 10% | $29.99 |
| Desert Willow | 15% | $34.99 |
| RedBud | 10% | $19.99 |

4. Choose **OK** to apply the formats to the table.

5. Click outside the table border to see the formats clearly.

6. To remove all formats from a table, follow steps 1 and 2 to display the AutoFormat dialog box again. Then select the **None** option in the Formats list and choose **OK**.

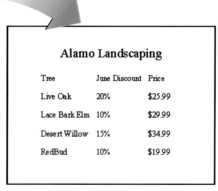

**WARNING**
**Any formats your table had before you applied an AutoFormat will be replaced with the formats in AutoFormat.**

**Exploring Other Format Options**
**After you apply an AutoFormat, you can use the format options discussed in Tasks 6 and 7 of this part to further customize the table's appearance.**

PART 9

# Sharing Data with Other Microsoft Office Programs

One of the most useful and timesaving features of Windows programs is the ease with which you can use the data from one program in another program. You can import a spreadsheet from Excel or a paragraph of text from Word into PowerPoint slides, eliminating the need to retype the data. You can also export a PowerPoint slide to be used in another program, such as Word.

This part concentrates on the most common types of importing and exporting tasks you will need to use. In most cases, you can create a link between the program where the data originated (the source) and the program the data is to be shared with (the target). The advantage of creating a link is that when the data changes in the source program, it is automatically changed in the target program.

# Tasks

## Displaying Excel Data in PowerPoint Slides

Data you have in an Excel spreadsheet can be imported into PowerPoint. You can *link* the PowerPoint slide to the original Excel data so the information on the slide automatically updates when you change the data in Excel.

# Task 1: Importing Data from an Excel Spreadsheet

Start Here

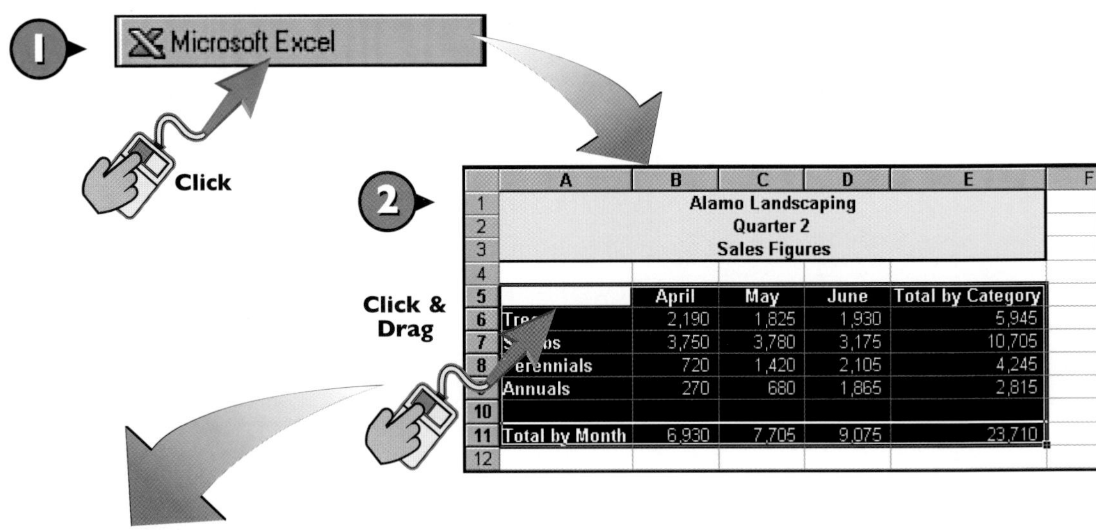


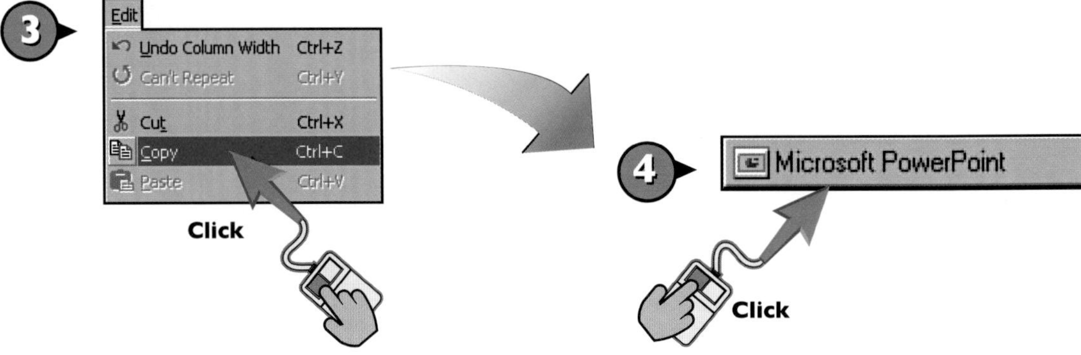


1. Open or switch to Excel.
2. Select the data you want to copy into PowerPoint.
3. Choose **Edit, Copy**.
4. Switch back to PowerPoint.

**Format of Excel Data**
The cell formatting in Excel impacts the appearance of the data when it is copied into PowerPoint. Change formats such as background or text appearance in Excel before you copy the data.

See Part 6, "Working with Graphic Charts," for steps on importing Excel data into a PowerPoint graphic chart.

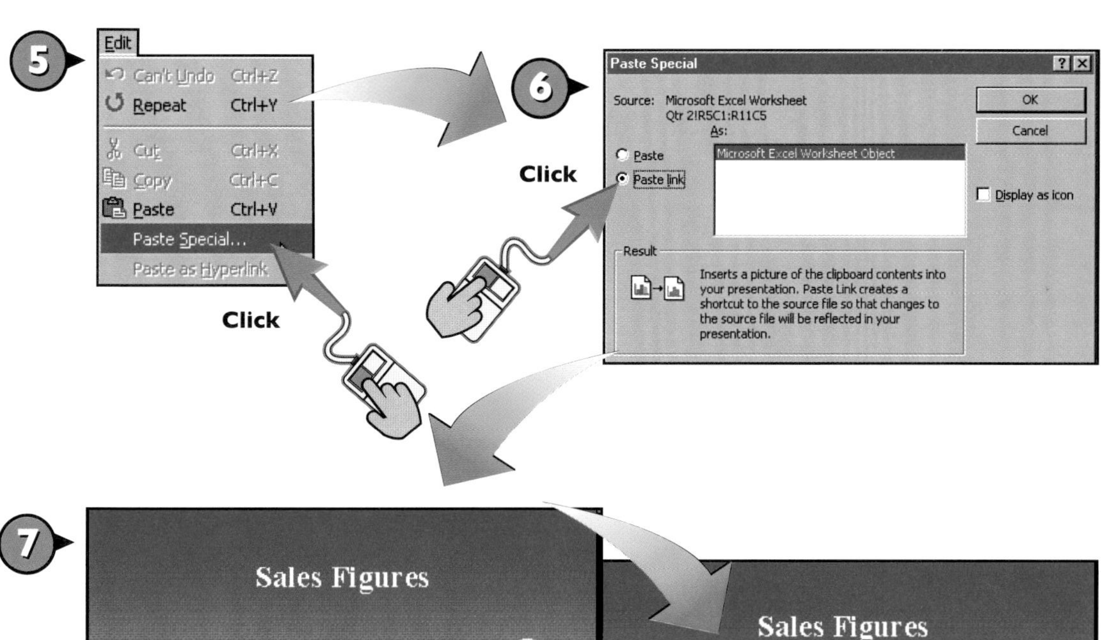


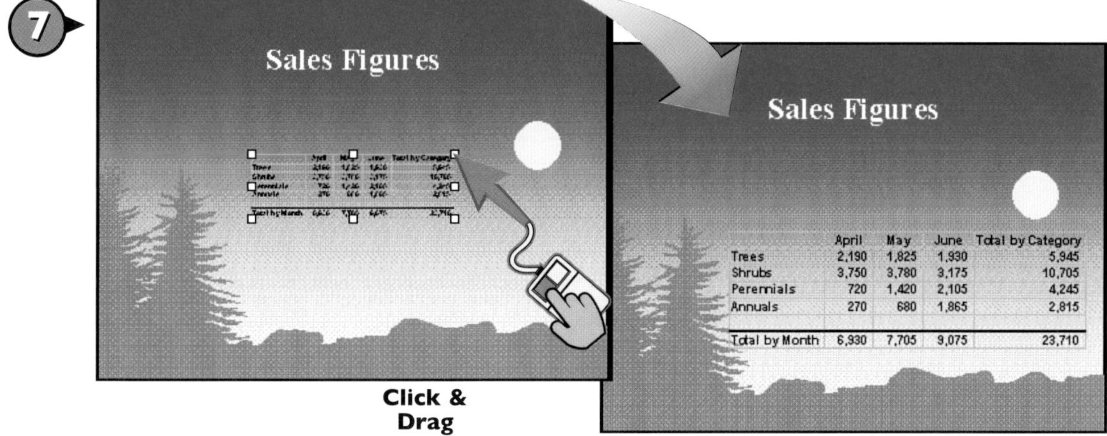


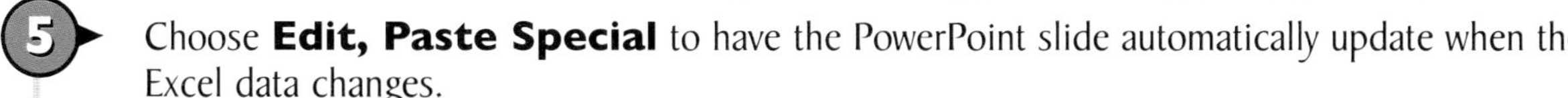

5 Choose **Edit, Paste Special** to have the PowerPoint slide automatically update when the Excel data changes.

6 Choose **Paste Link**; then choose **OK**.

7 The Excel data displays in the PowerPoint slide. Click and drag the ***selection handles*** to move and resize the Excel spreadsheet object.

**Paste versus Paste Special**

**If you choose Paste instead of Paste Special (or Paste Link), the data in the PowerPoint slides does not change when you update the data in Excel.**

# Task 2: Importing an Outline from Word

## Converting a Word File into a PowerPoint Presentation

**Before you can create a PowerPoint presentation from a Word outline, the outline must be formatted in a way PowerPoint can understand.**

**If you simply want to copy data from Word into PowerPoint, use the Edit, Copy and Edit, Paste commands.**

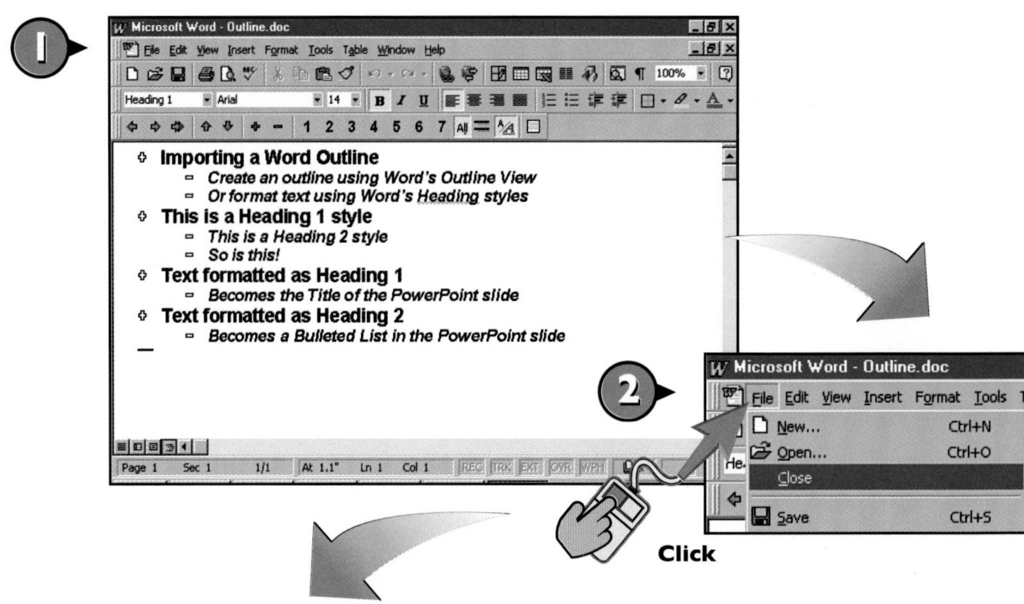


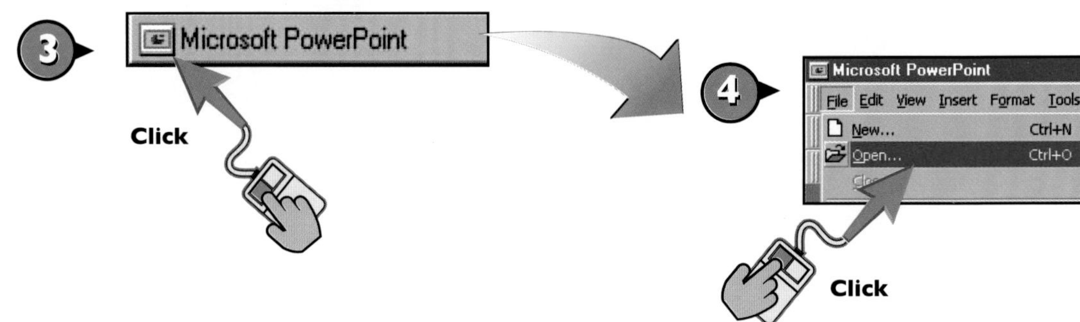


1. Create the Word outline by using the Outline View in Word or by applying Heading styles to each level in the outline.
2. Choose **File, Close**. The Word file must be closed before you can import it into PowerPoint.
3. Open or switch to PowerPoint.
4. In PowerPoint, choose **File, Open**.

Next Step

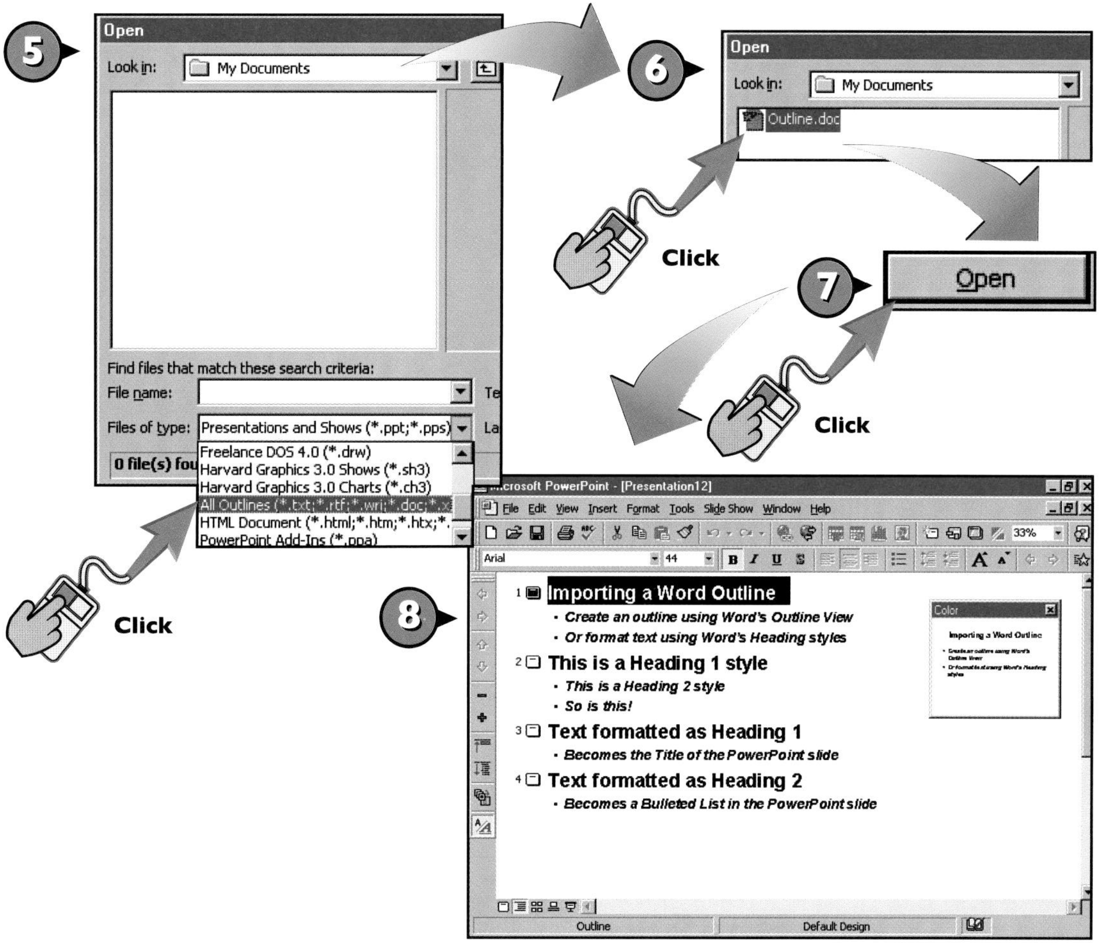

5 In the **Open** dialog box, choose **All Outlines** from the **Files of Type** drop-down list.

6 Locate and select the Word file.

7 Click **Open** to import the Word outline into PowerPoint.

8 A new PowerPoint presentation is created from the text in the Word file and displayed in the Outline View.

**Locating the Word Document**

**If the Word file is not in the My Documents folder, use the Look In drop-down box to locate the Word file.**

# Task 3: Importing a Table from Word

## Bringing a Word Table into PowerPoint

**Copying a table from Word and pasting it into a PowerPoint slide is accomplished with just a few mouse clicks!**

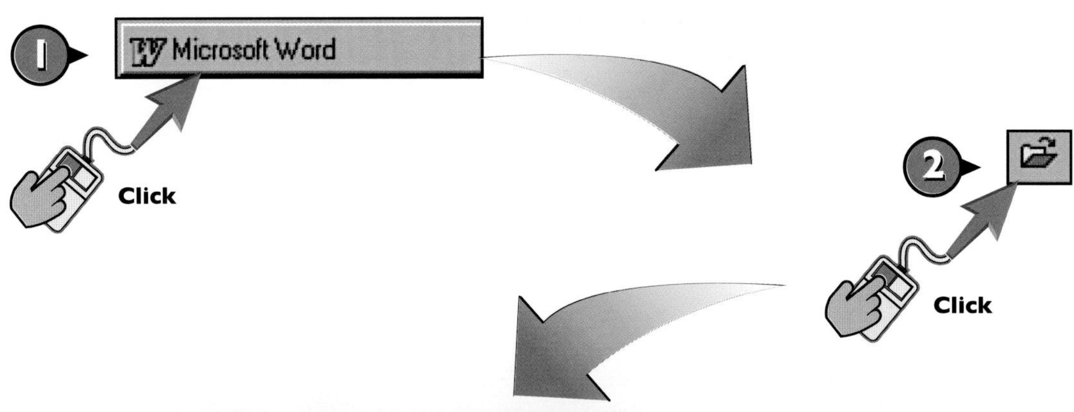


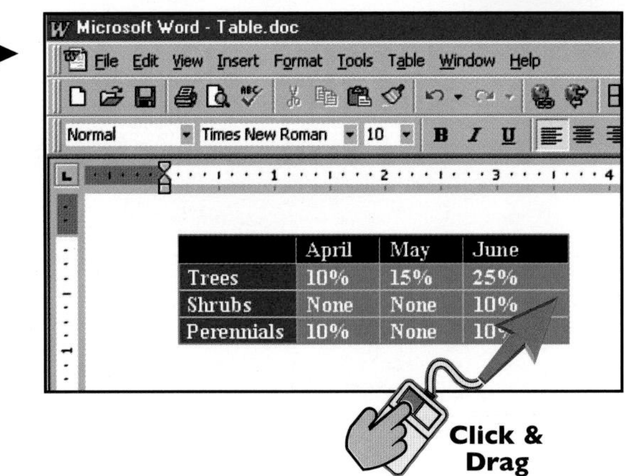


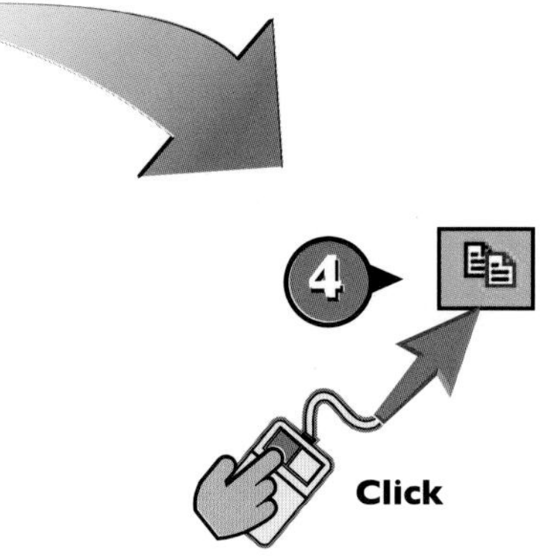


### Creating Tables in PowerPoint

**Instead of creating a table in Word and copying it into PowerPoint, you can create a Word table directly in PowerPoint. See Part 8, "Working with Tables," for steps on creating and formatting tables.**

Open or switch to Word.

Click the **Open** button and display the file containing the table to be imported into PowerPoint.

Select the data you want to copy into PowerPoint.

Click the **Copy** button.

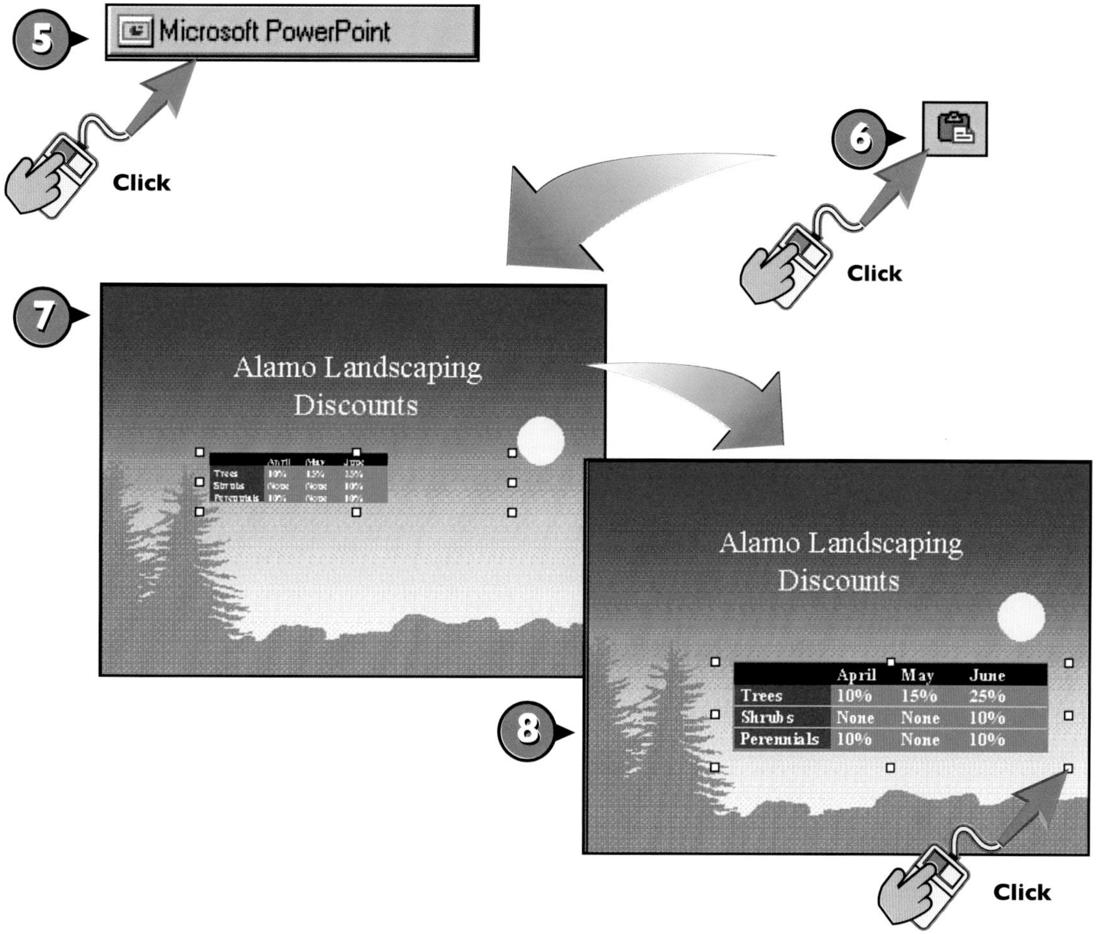

5. Switch back to PowerPoint.

6. Click the **Paste** button.

7. The Word table displays in the PowerPoint slide.

8. Click and drag the selection handles to move and resize the Word table.

### Linking the Table to PowerPoint

**Alternatively, you can use the Edit, Paste Special command to link the Word table to PowerPoint. When the data in the Word table changes, the copy of the table in PowerPoint will immediately reflect those changes.**

### Cropping the Word Table

**Sometimes it is necessary to *crop* the Word table object. Right-click the object and display the Picture toolbar. The Crop button is the seventh tool from the left. An object can be cropped from a corner or side selection handle. Press the Alt key when cropping from the side of an object.**

# Task 4: Exporting a PowerPoint Slide into a Word Document

## Copying a PowerPoint Slide into a Word Document

You can incorporate a PowerPoint slide into a Word document by using the **Copy** and **Paste** commands.

Start Here

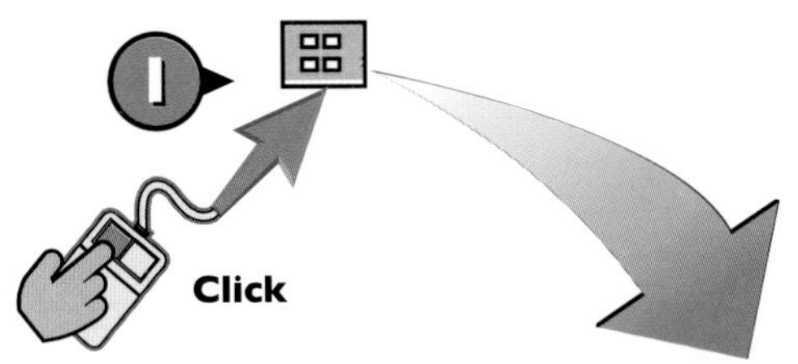


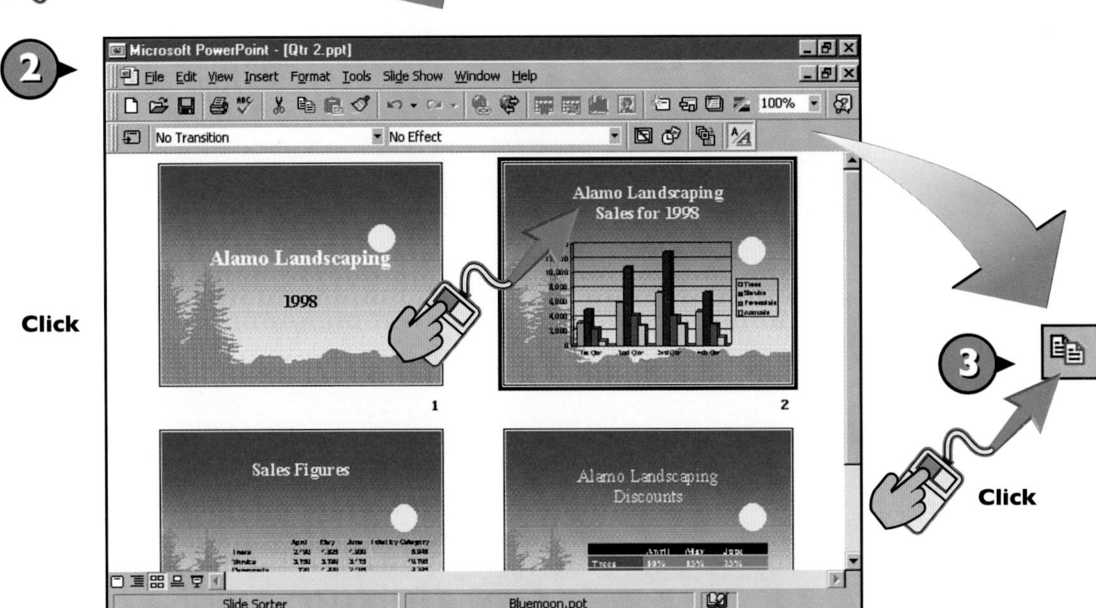

**Copying PowerPoint Slides**
These same steps can be used to copy a PowerPoint slide into other programs besides Word.

1. Click the **Slide Sorter View** button in the lower left corner of the PowerPoint screen.

2. Click the slide you want to copy. A heavy, dark border appears around the selected slide.

3. Click the **Copy** button.

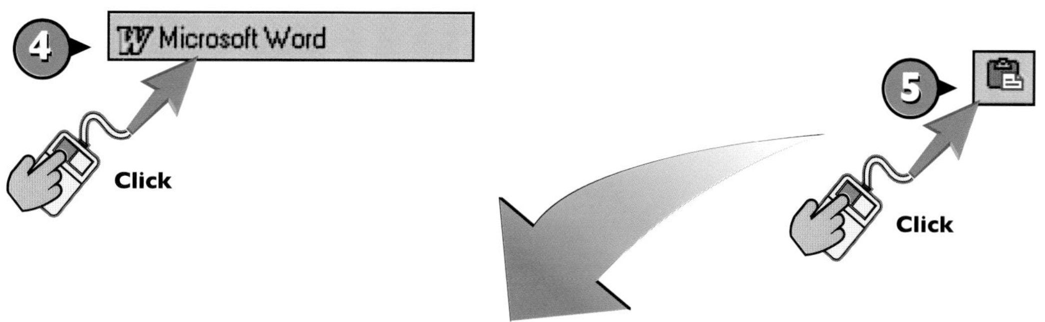


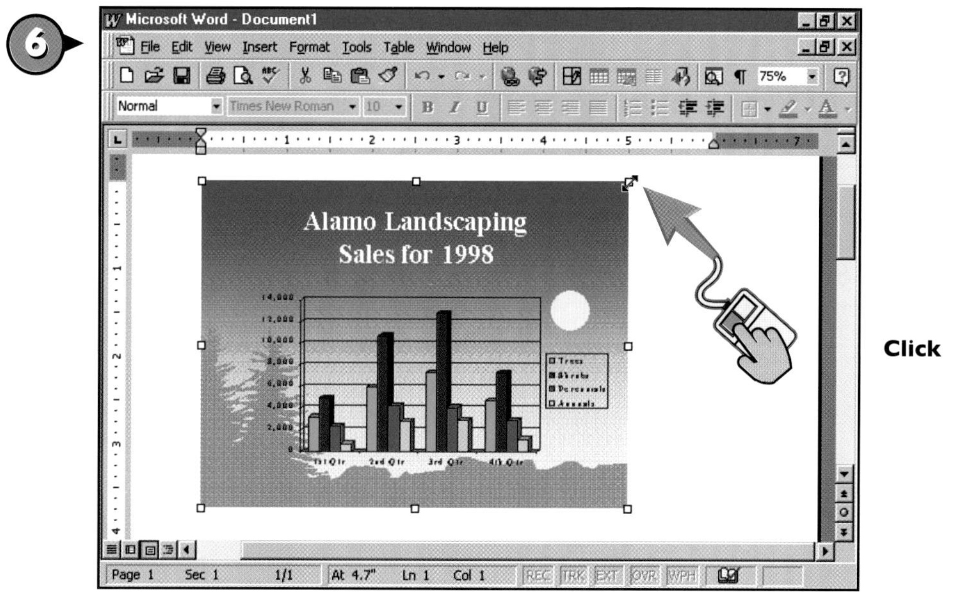


4. Open or switch to Word.

5. Click the **Paste** button.

6. Click the slide object and resize it by using the corner selection handles.

**Linking the PowerPoint Slide**
If you want to link the PowerPoint slide to Word, use **Edit, Paste Special** to create the link. When the slide is changed in PowerPoint, it will be updated in the Word document automatically.

PART 10

# Printing Your Presentation

PowerPoint enables you to print your presentation slides, just as they appear in the Slide Show. You can also print the text displayed in the Outline View, notes created in the Note Pages View, or audience handouts showing miniatures of your slides.

To save time, you can choose to print multiple copies of your slides, handouts, outline text, or notes pages. Draft copies can be printed in black and white, saving color for your final printouts.

The Print dialog box is where you select what you want to print. This dialog box can only be accessed through the File menu; it does not display when you select the Print button on the Standard toolbar.

# Tasks

# Task 1: Printing Slides

## Setting Options to Print a Copy of Your Slides

**Through the Print dialog box, you can print all or only a few of the presentation slides, choose the number of copies to print, and print draft copies in black and white.**

Start Here

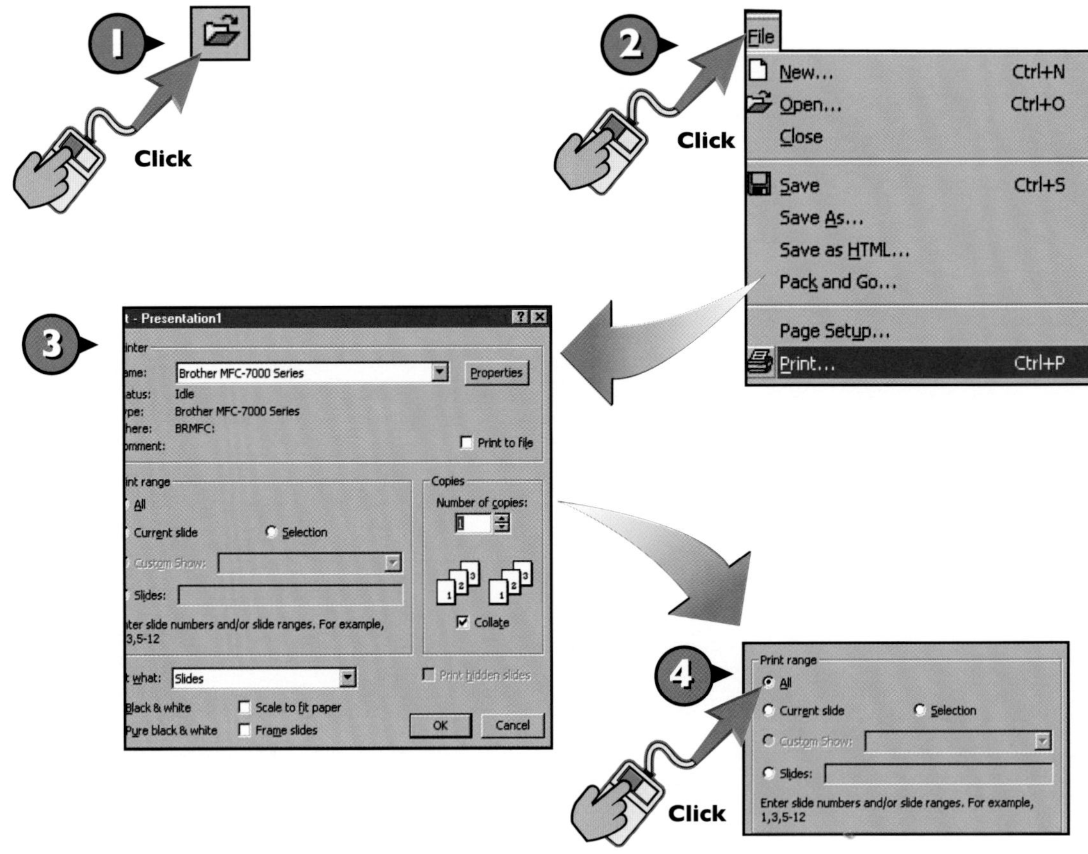


1. Open or switch to the presentation you want to print.
2. Choose **File, Print**.
3. The Print dialog box contains the options for selecting what you want to print. The default options are shown.
4. The Print Range area contains print options for printing slides.

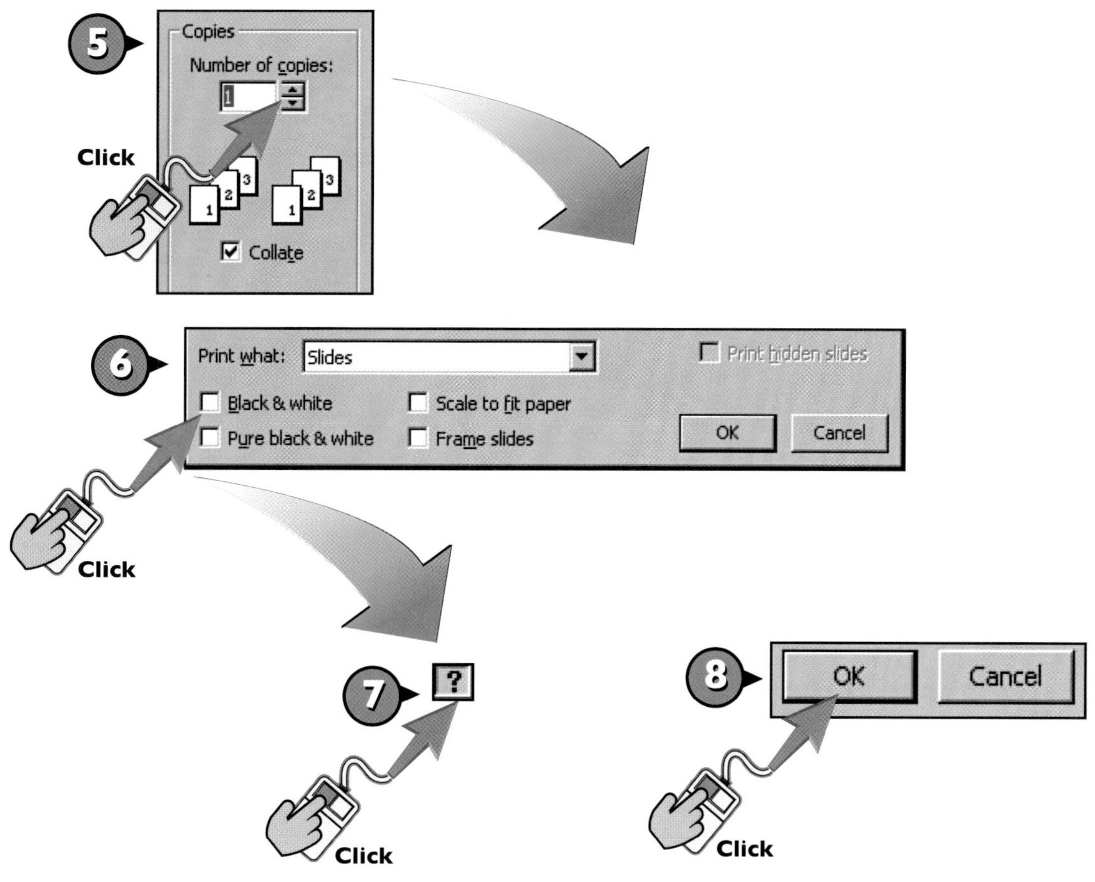


**WARNING**
**If you click the Print button on the Standard toolbar, your slides are printed immediately using the default settings. The Print dialog box does not appear.**

5 Select the number of Copies. Choose whether to have the copies Collated or not.

6 Click to choose options in the Print What area. By default, the Print What option is set to print slides. The Black & White option prints in shades of gray.

7 You can choose the **Help** button in the upper right corner of the Print dialog box to learn more about the options in the dialog box.

8 Choose **OK** to print the slides.

**Printing Black and White Slides**
**The Black & White setting also prints in shades of gray. Pure Black & White prints in only black and white, with no gray shading.**

# Task 2: Printing Handouts for Your Audience

## Choosing Options for Printing Handout Pages

You can print handouts that display two, three, or six slides on each printed page.

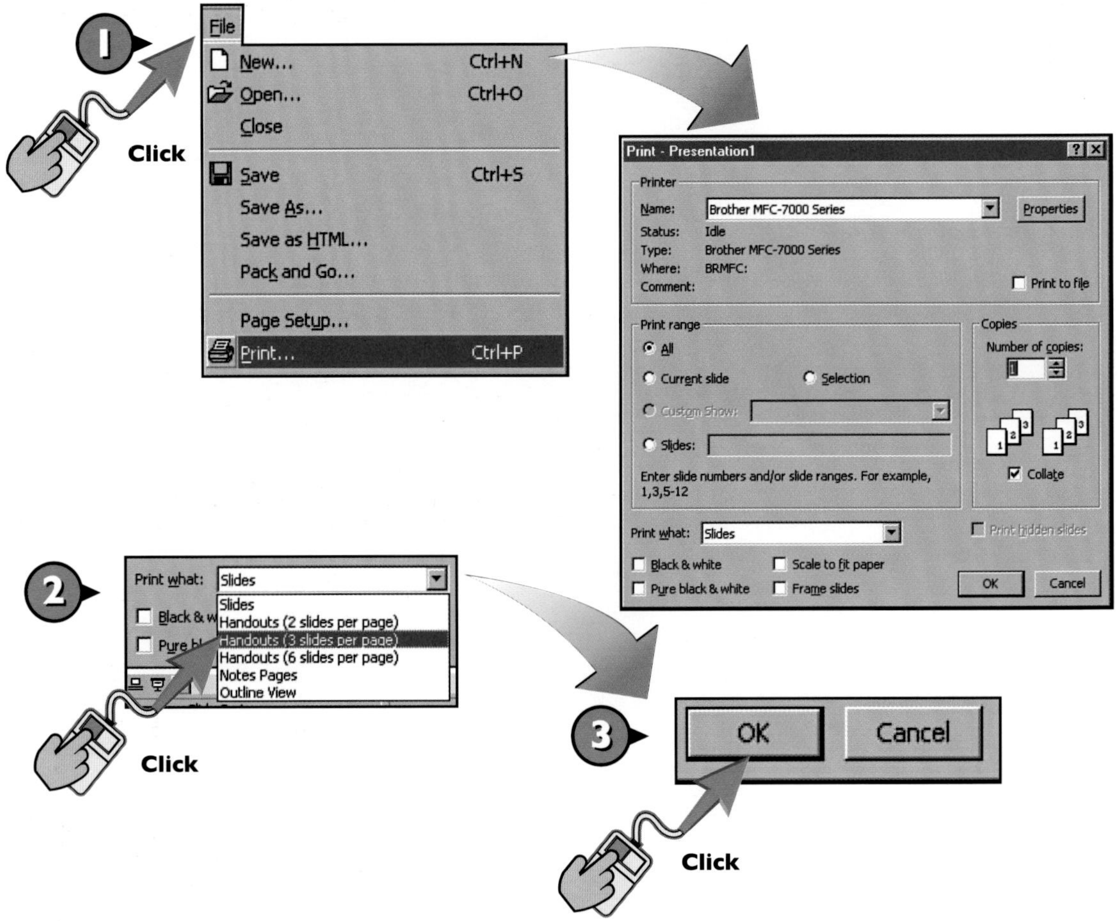

Start Here

**Must Use Dialog Box to Print Handouts**
You cannot print handouts by using the Print button or the Ctrl+P keyboard shortcut. You must use the Print dialog box.

Choose **File, Print**. The Print dialog box appears.

Choose a handout option from the Print What drop-down list.

Choose **OK** to print the handouts.

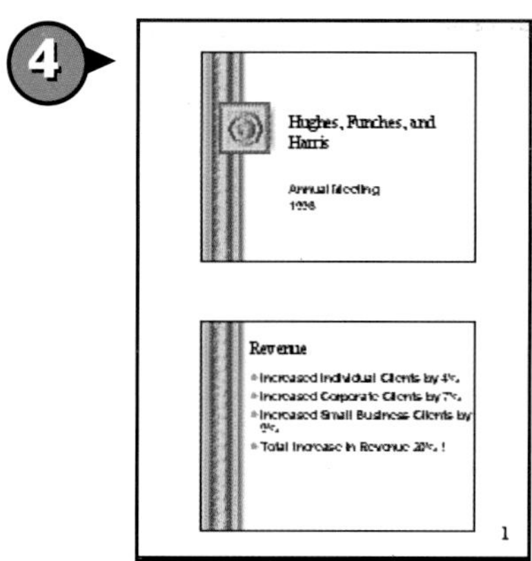

4
Hughes, Punches, and Harris
Annual Meeting
Revenue
Increased Individual Clients by 4%
Increased Corporate Clients by 7%
Increased Small Business Clients by
Total Increase in Revenue 20%!
1


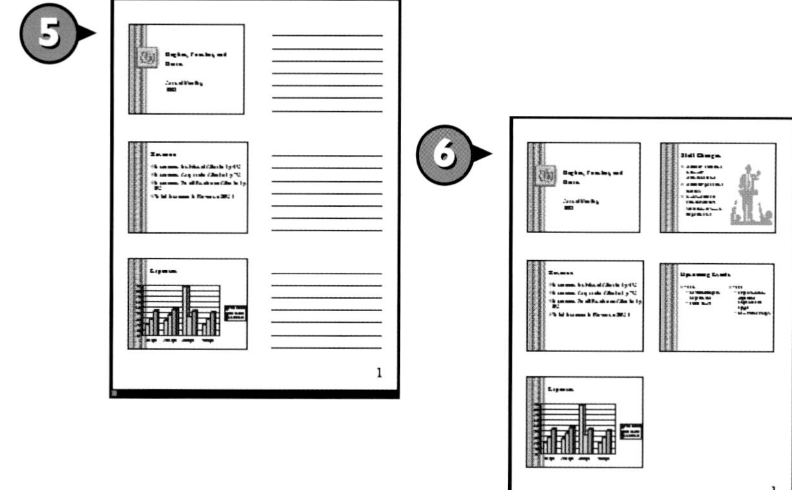


## Adding Headers and Footers to Handouts

Choose **View, Master, Handout Master** to add headers and footers such as the date the handout was printed, the name and phone number of the presenter, or to set the page number to include the total page count (for example, Page 1 of 5).

## Choosing a Handout Option

The **Handouts (3 slides per page)** option is a favorite among audiences. These handouts print three slide miniatures down the left side of each page and lines for taking notes down the right side.

4. An example of a printed handout with two slides per page.

5. An example of a printed handout with three slides per page. This option includes lines for taking notes.

6. An example of a printed handout which can display six slides per page.

# Task 3: Printing the Presentation Outline

## Printing the Outline View

The text displayed in the Outline View represents the bulk of most presentations. Having a printout of this view provides an easy way to review the presentation's flow and tone.

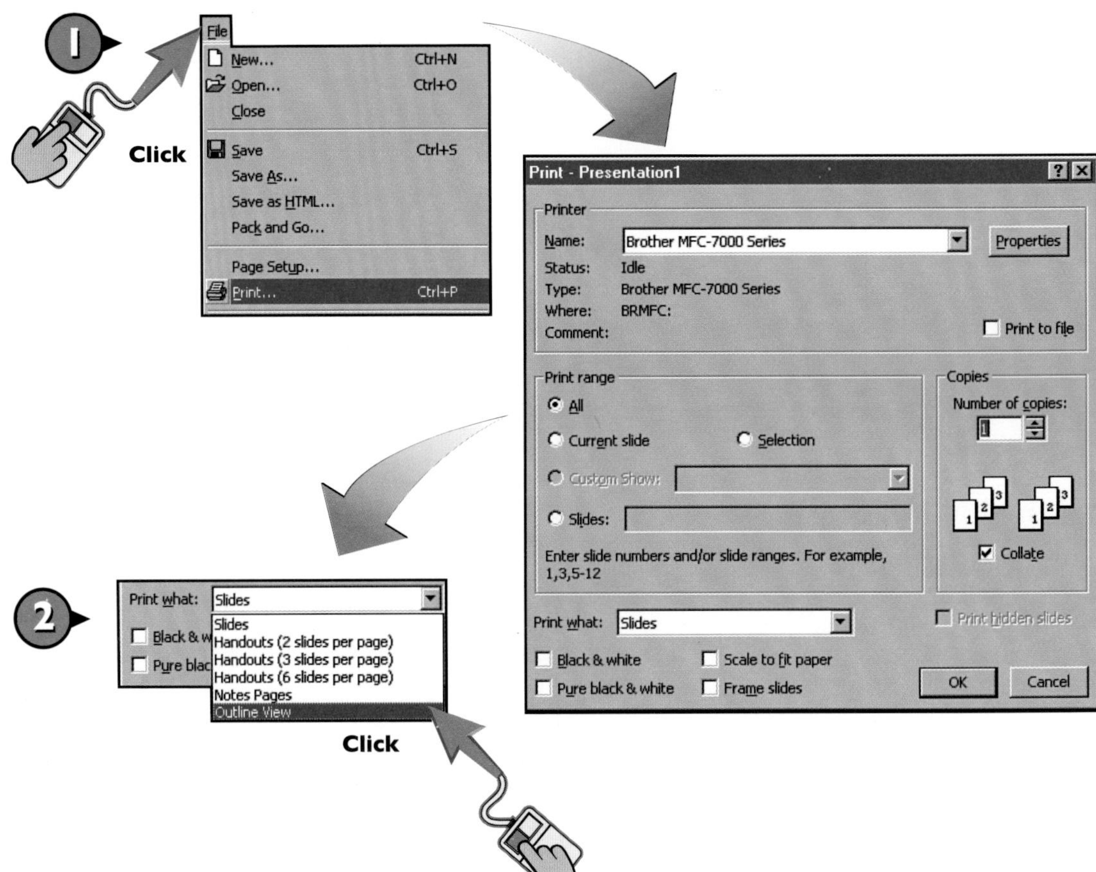

**Printing the Collapsed Outline**
You can print the full outline or collapse the outline to just the slide titles. Refer to Part 2, "Working in the Other Views," Task 8, for information on how to hide or display data in the Outline View.

Choose **File, Print**. The Print dialog box appears.

Choose the **Outline View** option from the Print What drop-down list.

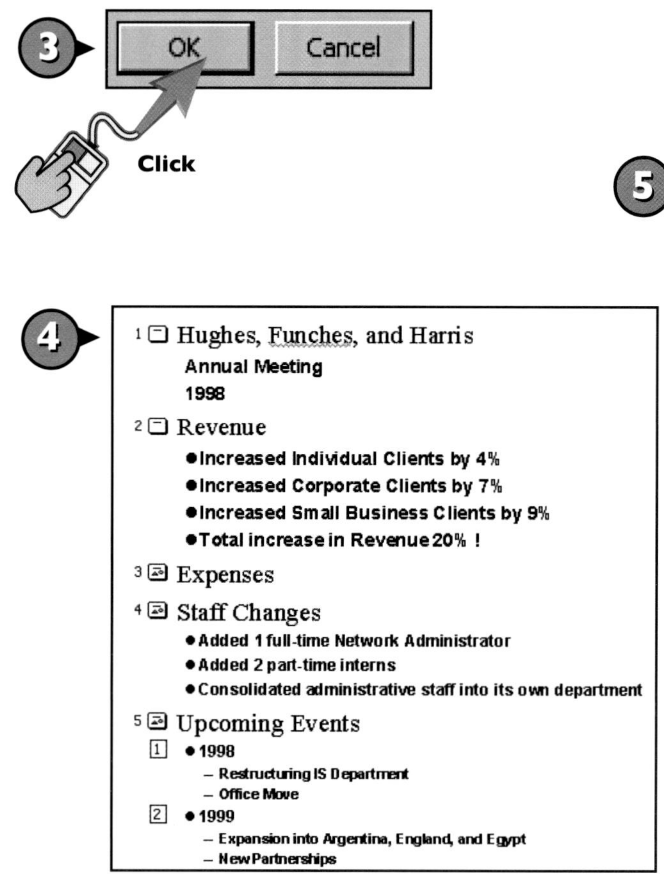

OK
Cancel
Click
1 Hughes, Funches, and Harris
Annual Meeting
1998
2 Revenue
●Increased Individual Clients by 4%
●Increased Corporate Clients by 7%
●Increased Small Business Clients by 9%
●Total increase in Revenue 20% !
3 Expenses
4 Staff Changes
●Added 1 full-time Network Administrator
●Added 2 part-time interns
●Consolidated administrative staff into its own department
5 Upcoming Events
1 ●1998
– Restructuring IS Department
– Office Move
2 ●1999
– Expansion into Argentina, England, and Egypt
– New Partnerships


1 Hughes, Funches, and Harris
2 Revenue
3 Expenses
4 Staff Changes
5 Upcoming Events

3. Choose **OK** to print the outline.
4. An example of a complete outline.
5. An example of a collapsed outline.

**Outline View Text**
**Remember, the only text you see in the Outline View is text that is part of a "click" placeholder. Independent text, graphic charts, tables, and clip art do not appear in the Outline View.**

**Must Use Dialog Box to Print the Outline**
**You cannot print the outline by using the Print button or the Ctrl+P keyboard shortcut. You must use the Print dialog box.**

# Task 4: Printing Speaker's Notes

## Printing the Notes Pages

**It is useful to have a set of notes you can refer to when giving a presentation.**

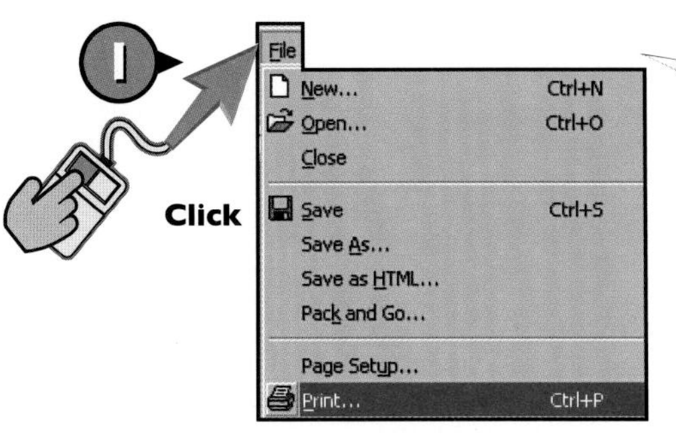


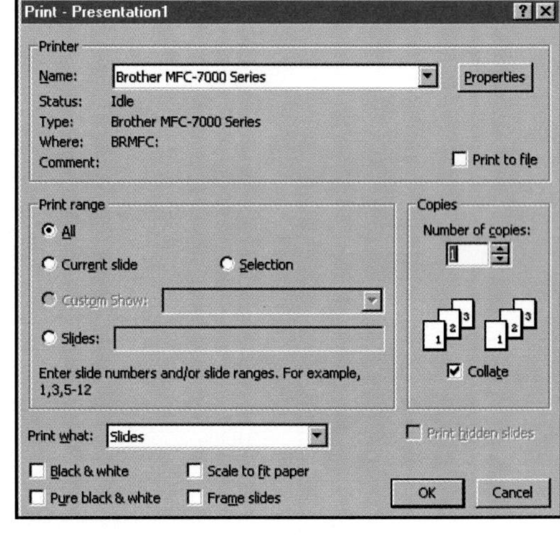

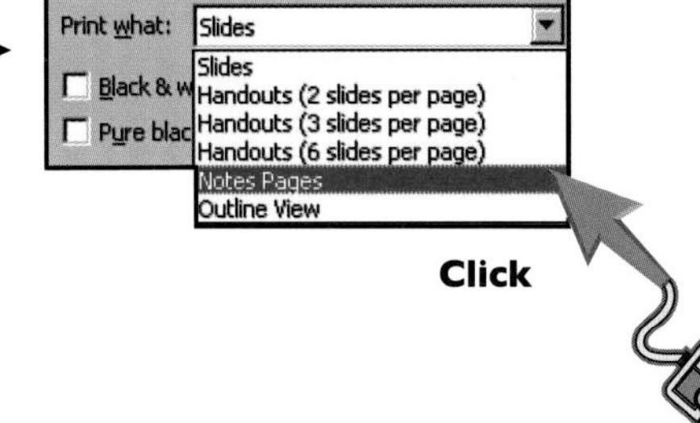

### Creating Speaker's Notes

**See Part 2, Task 9, for the steps to create a set of speaker's notes.**

1. Choose **File, Print**. The Print dialog box appears.

2. Choose the **Notes Pages** option from the Print What drop-down list.

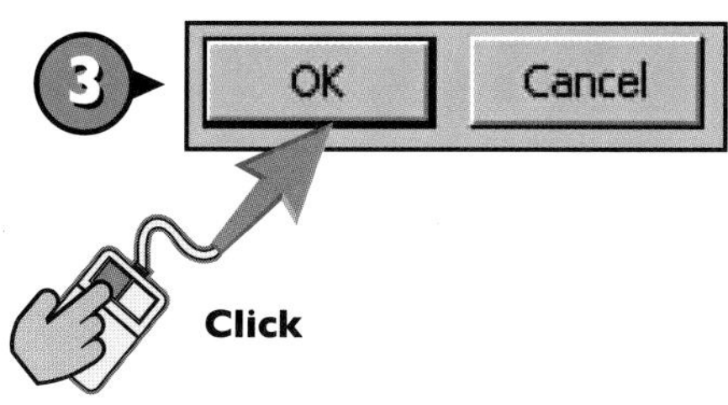


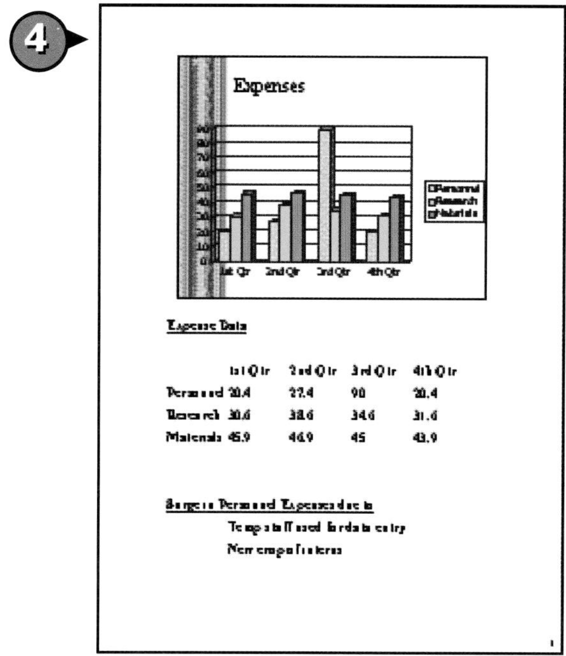


3. Choose **OK** to print the speaker's notes.

4. An example of a speaker's note.

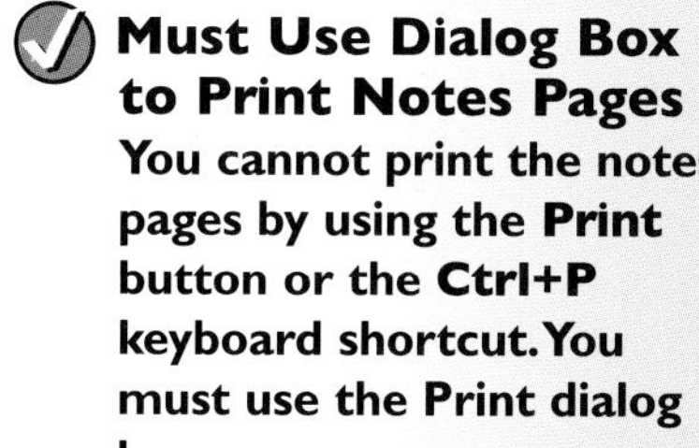

**Must Use Dialog Box to Print Notes Pages**
You cannot print the notes pages by using the **Print** button or the **Ctrl+P** keyboard shortcut. You must use the Print dialog box.

# Selecting Presentation, Animation, and Sound Settings

You can improve your presentation greatly by adding a few simple enhancements. Choose the way your slides transition (appear) on screen and how long each slide displays. Have a sound (such as applause or screeching tires) play when a specific slide appears. You can also select the order and way slide objects appear. Each bullet in a list can be displayed separately. Clip art, WordArt, and drawn objects can be animated to spiral or swivel as they appear on screen. Even graphic charts can be displayed one series or category at a time.

Video and sound clips available on the Microsoft Office 97 CD can be inserted and played as part of your presentation.

# Tasks

# Task 1: Previewing Your Presentation

## Running the Slide Show

As you add animation and sound to your slides, you'll want to be sure to preview your presentation to see how the settings will look and sound. Previewing a presentation is also known as *running* the slide show.

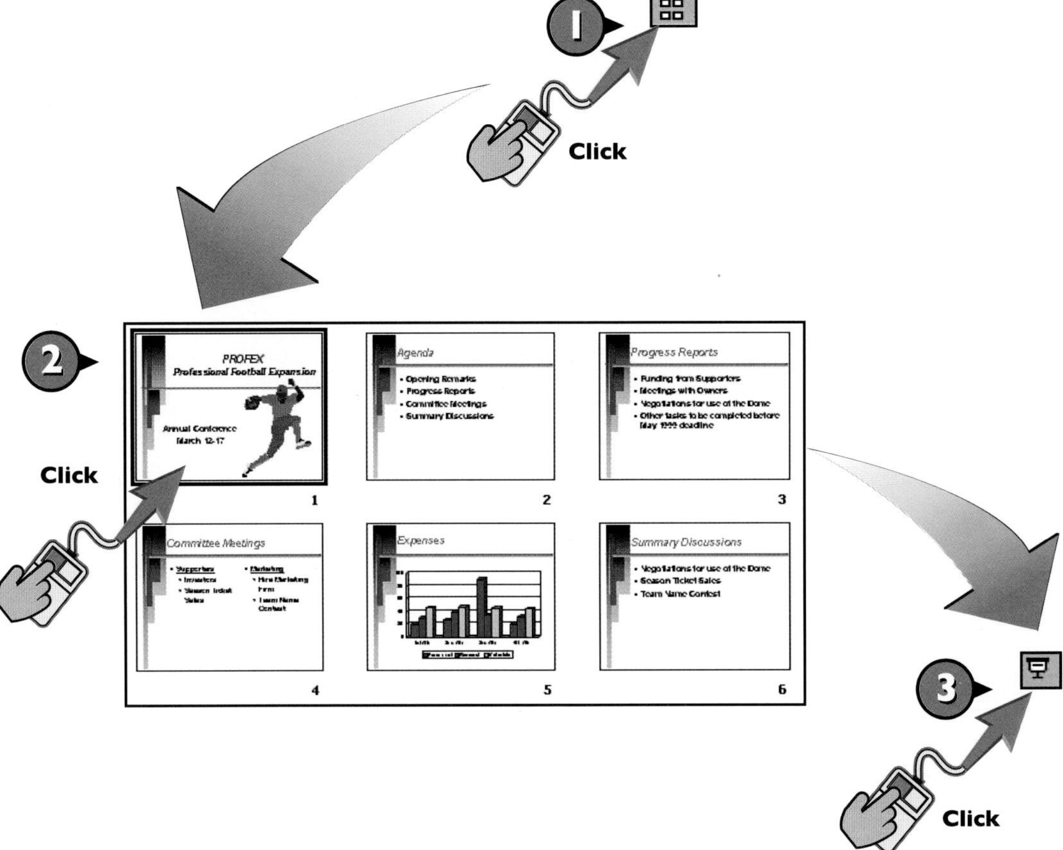

### Displaying Slide Show Settings

You can run the slide show from any view in PowerPoint. The Slide Sorter view, however, is the only view in which you can display slide show settings (which are discussed later in this part).

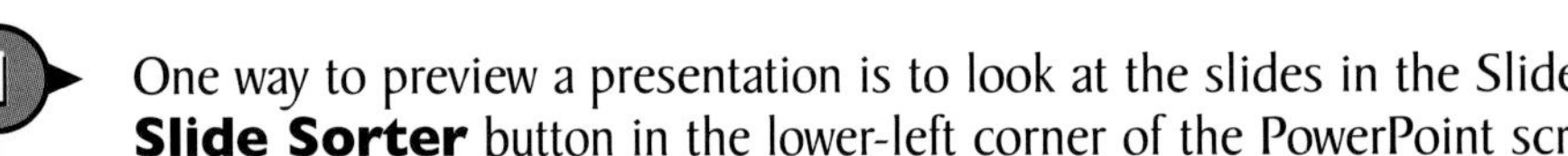

1. One way to preview a presentation is to look at the slides in the Slide Sorter view. Click the **Slide Sorter** button in the lower-left corner of the PowerPoint screen.

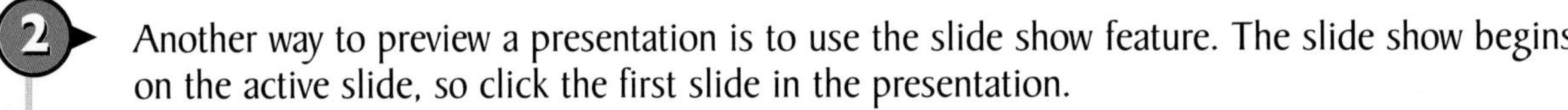

2. Another way to preview a presentation is to use the slide show feature. The slide show begins on the active slide, so click the first slide in the presentation.
3. Then click the **Slide Show** button in the lower-left corner of the PowerPoint screen to preview the presentation.



Next Step

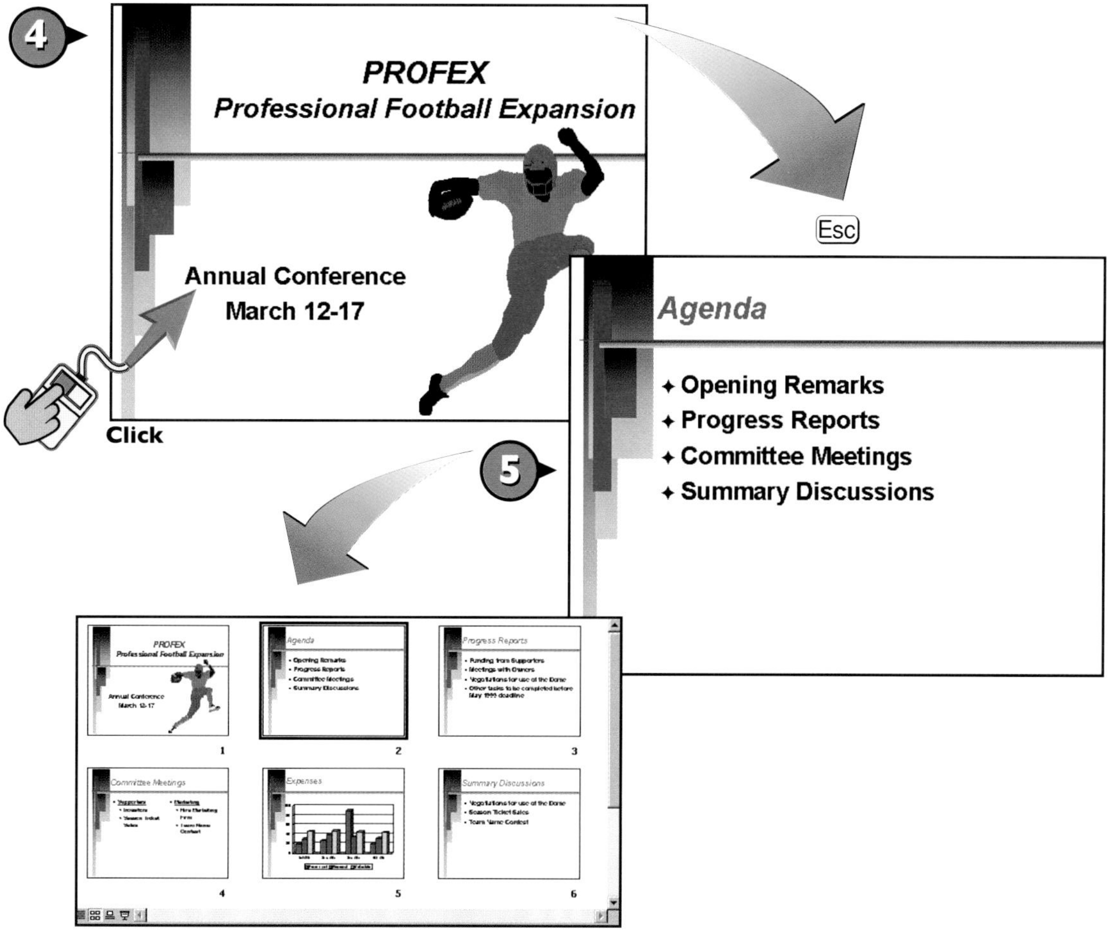

4 Click to display the next slide in the presentation.

5 To stop the presentation before you reach the end, press **Esc**. You return to the view from which you started the preview, and the last slide you looked at is the active slide.

**Why Use the Slide Show?**

**Use the slide show feature to preview your presentation before printing, to preview animation settings, and to rehearse your presentation.**

# Task 2: Adding Transitions Between Slides

## Selecting How Slides Appear When You Run a Slide Show

**One way to make your presentation more interesting is to add slide transition effects. Slide *transitions* are the way each slide appears as you advance through a presentation.**

### Using Transitions Effectively

**When faced with a lengthy presentation, try applying a different transition to each major topic in your presentation. This provides a subtle way of letting the audience know you are discussing a new topic.**

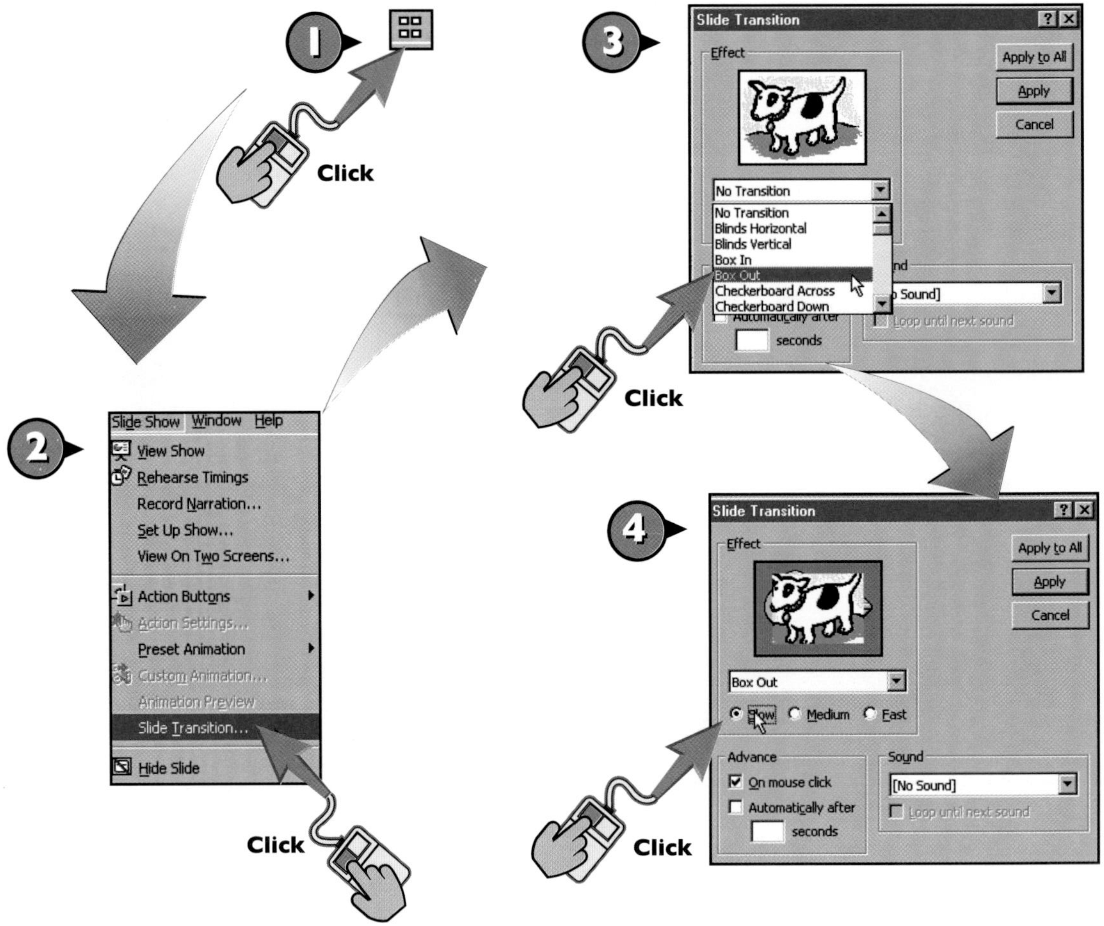

Switch to the Slide Sorter view.

To apply a slide transition, choose **Slide Show, Slide Transition**. The Slide Transition dialog box appears.

Choose a transition from the Effects drop-down list. The transition is displayed in the preview sample.

Click on **Slow**, **Medium**, or **Fast** to set the speed of the transition. The sample changes to illustrate the speed.

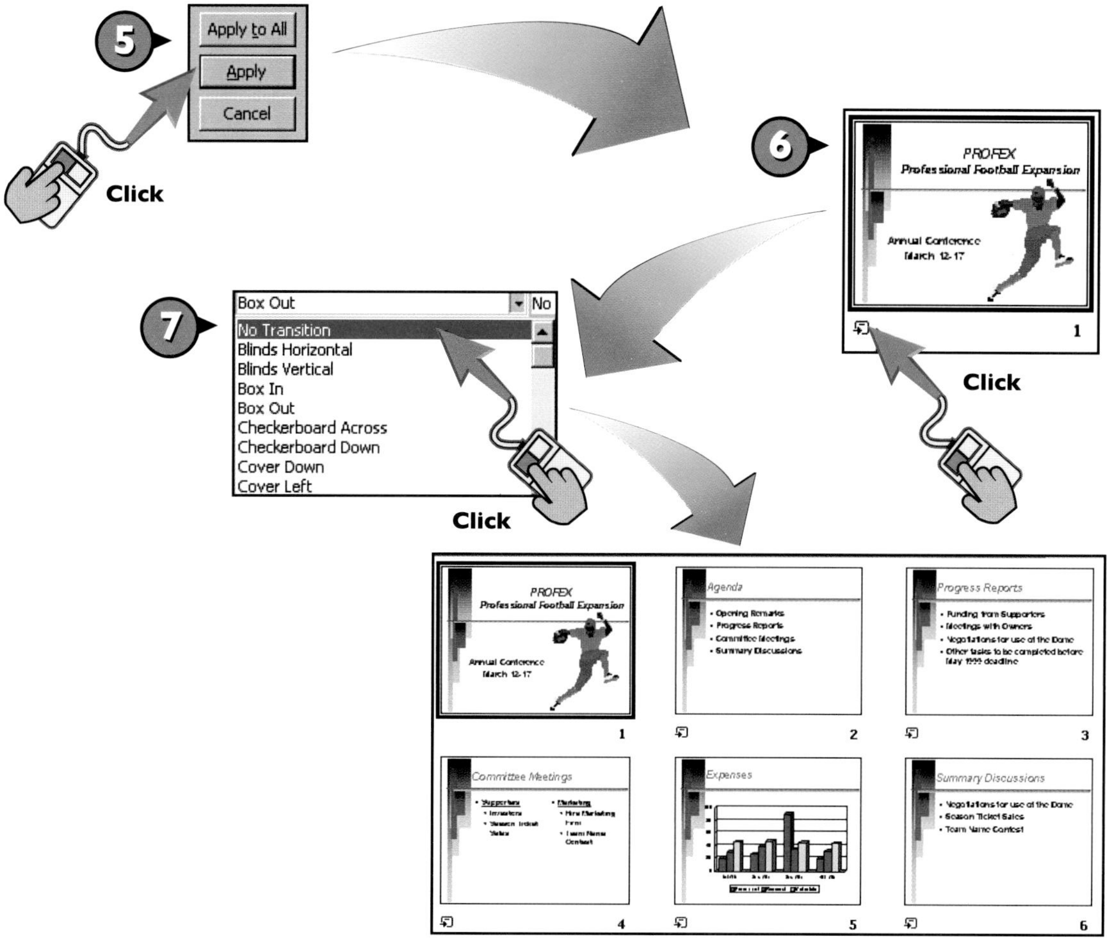

5
Apply to All
Apply
Cancel
Click
6
PROFEX
Professional Football Expansion
Annual Conference
March 12-17
1
Click
7
Box Out
No
No Transition
Blinds Horizontal
Blinds Vertical
Box In
Box Out
Checkerboard Across
Checkerboard Down
Cover Down
Cover Left
Click
Agenda
Progress Reports
Committee Meetings
Expenses
Summary Discussions
1
2
3
4
5
6

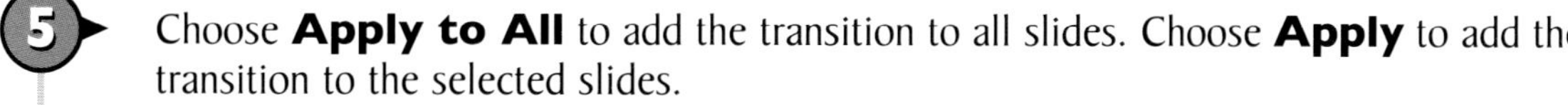

5 Choose **Apply to All** to add the transition to all slides. Choose **Apply** to add the transition to the selected slides.

6 A slide transition symbol appears below each slide miniature. Click the transition symbol to preview the transition.

7 To remove the transition from a slide, select the slide. Then click on the transition drop-down list on the Slide Sorter toolbar and choose **No Transition**.

### Selecting Multiple Slides

**You can select several slides in the Slide Sorter view by clicking on the first slide and then pressing Shift and clicking on each additional slide.**

### No Transition on the First Slide

**Your first slide does not need a transition. It should already be displayed as the audience comes into the room before you begin the presentation.**

End Task

# Task 3: Adding Sound to the Slide Transitions

## Using Transition Sounds

In addition to applying a transition effect, you can attach a sound to a slide. As the slide transitions onto the screen, the sound plays. So your audience can hear the transition sounds, make sure the machine you are using to give your presentation is capable of playing sound and has a set of speakers.

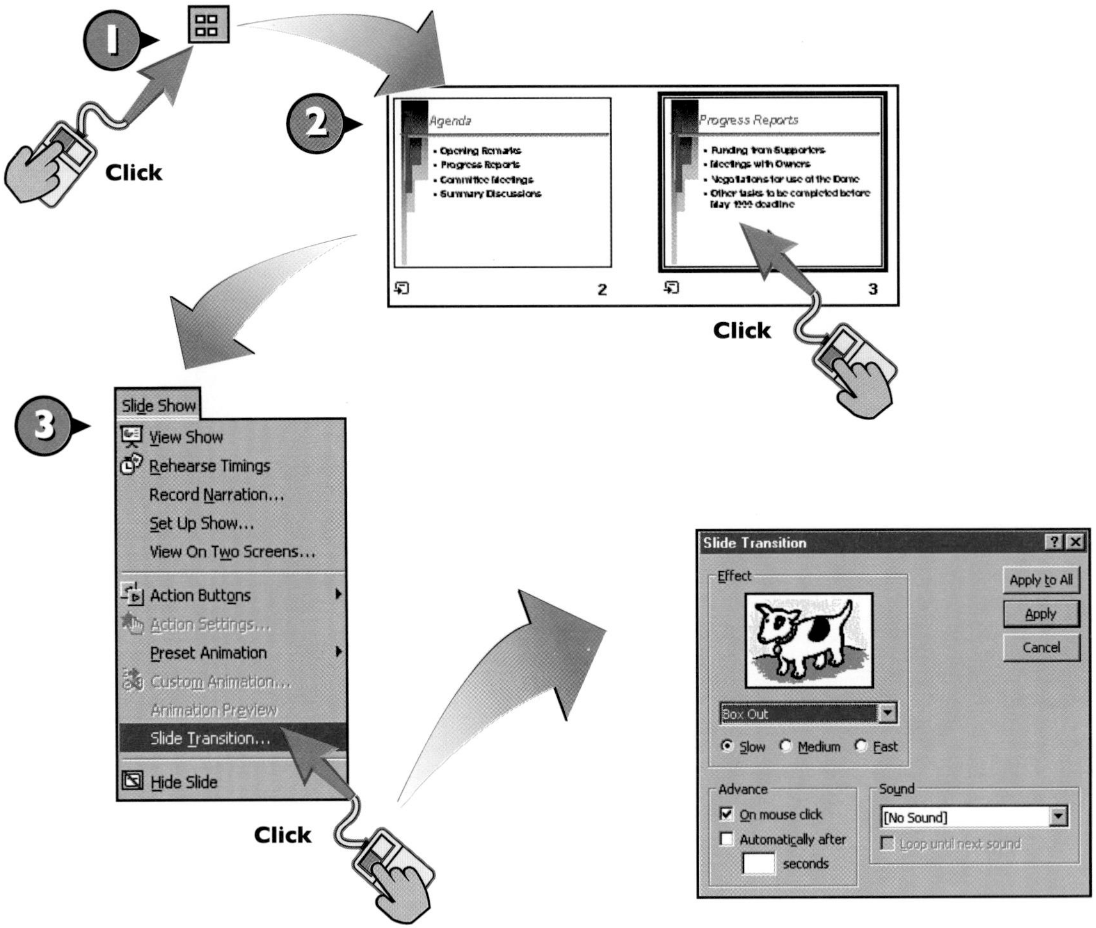

### Adding Sound Clips to Slides

Sounds (or music) can also be added to your slides to play when you click on or move your mouse pointer near an object. See Task 8.

1. Switch to the Slide Sorter view.

2. Select the slide to which you want to add the sound. A thick border appears around the slide.

3. Choose **Slide Show, Slide Transition**. The Slide Transition dialog box appears.

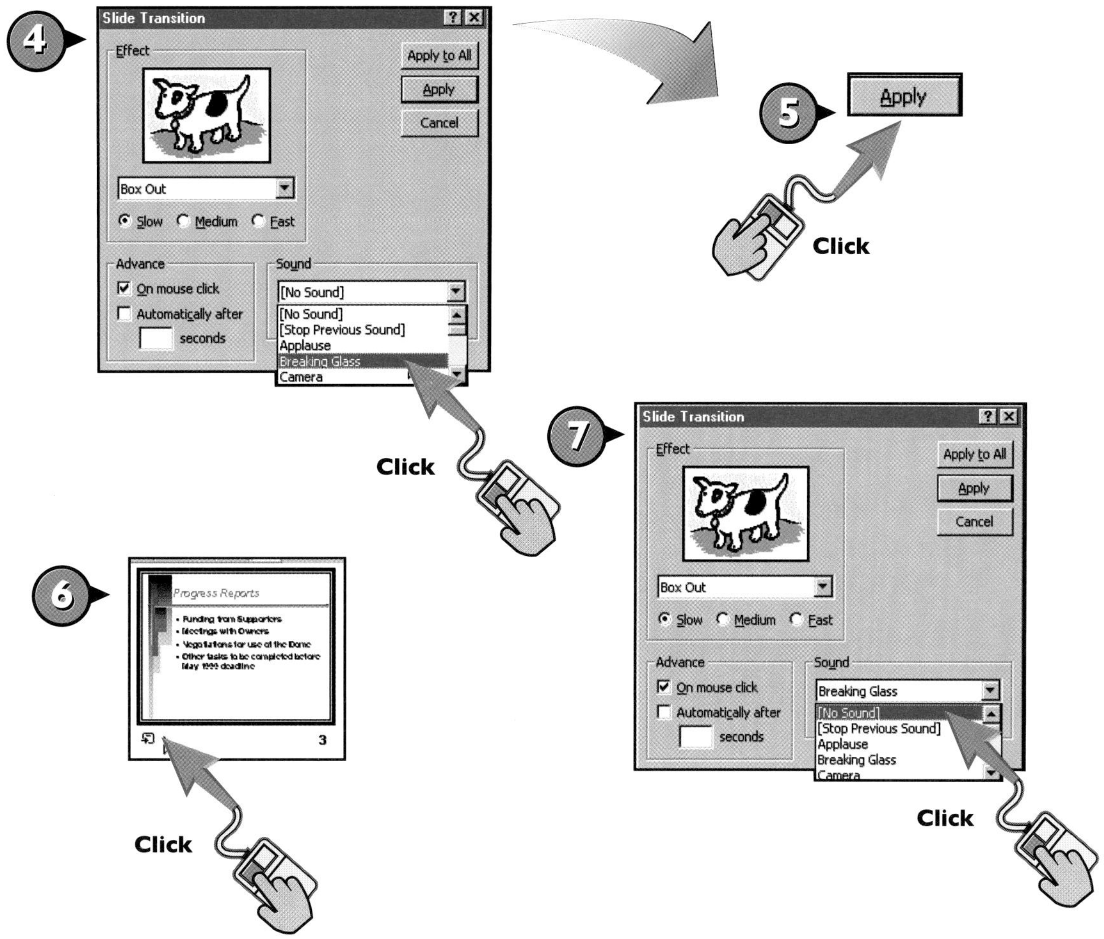

4. Select a sound from the Sound drop-down list.

5. Choose **Apply**; the sound is attached to the selected slide.

6. Click the transition symbol to see the transition and hear the sound.

7. To remove a transition sound, choose **Slide Show, Slide Transition** and select **No Sound** from the Sound drop-down list. Then choose **Apply**.

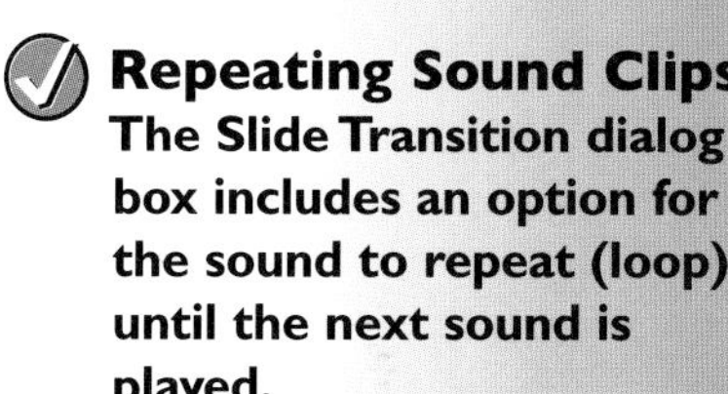

**Repeating Sound Clips**
**The Slide Transition dialog box includes an option for the sound to repeat (loop) until the next sound is played.**

**WARNING**
**It is easy to get carried away attaching sounds to slide transitions. Be sure you have a good reason for adding sound. Audiences might be distracted when too many sounds are used in a presentation—less is better!**

# Task 4: Setting a Display Time on Slides

## Using Slide Timings

**You can set up your presentation to advance through the slides automatically by adding a display time to each slide. This is particularly useful for standalone presentations at conventions, conferences, and kiosks.**

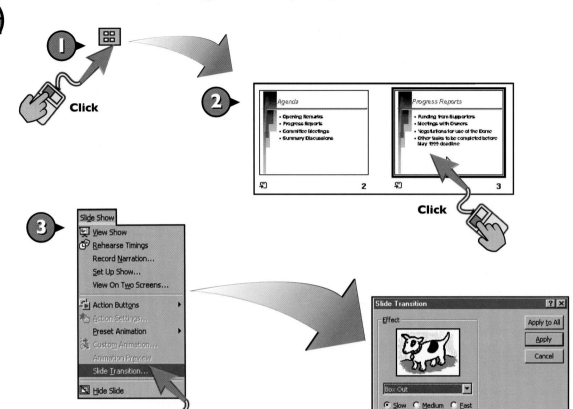

Start Here

1. Switch to the Slide Sorter view.
2. Select the slide to which you want to apply a display time. A thick border appears around the slide.
3. Choose **Slide Show, Slide Transition**. The Slide Transition dialog box appears.

### Pausing a Slide Show

**You can pause (and resume) a timed presentation by pressing the letter S on the keyboard.**

Next Step

Type the seconds you want the slide to be displayed. Choose **Apply to All** to add the same time to all slides. Choose **Apply** to add the time to the selected slides only.

Before you can run the presentation with the new slide timings, you must make certain the slide show options are set up correctly. Choose **Slide Show, Set Up Show**.

Make sure the **Using Timings** if Present option is selected.

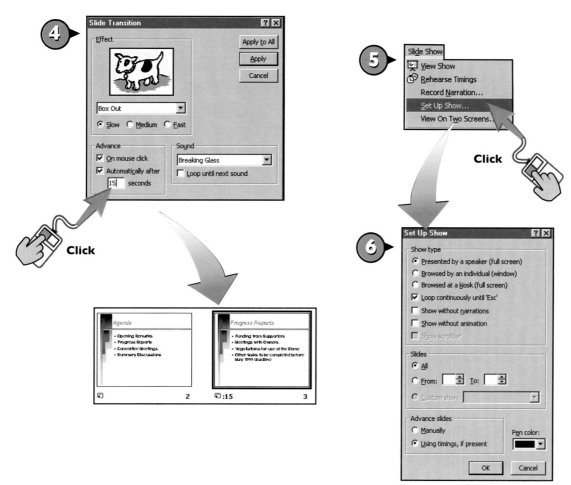

**Running the Presentation in a Continuous Loop**
See Part 12, "Running Your Presentation," Task 4, to learn how to set up the presentation to run continuously.

**Rehearsing a Presentation**
You can practice a presentation to determine how long it will take you to give it. Choose **Slide Show, Rehearse Timings.**

# Task 5: Animating Text

## Building the Slide Text

When you run a slide show, you have the option of "*building*" slides by setting up the objects to display sequentially. For example, each bullet in a list can appear individually, one after the other. When the text builds, the audience stays focused as you display and discuss each point. Building slide objects is called *animation*.

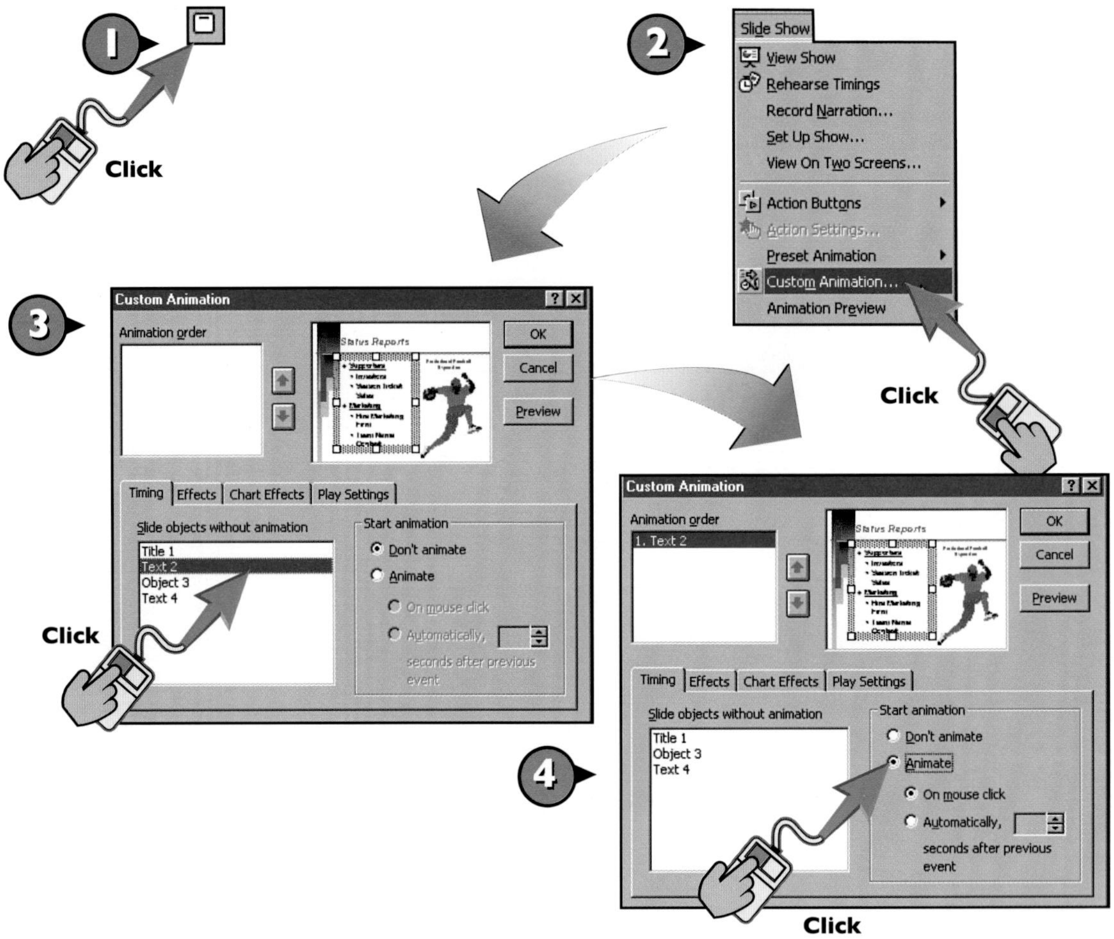

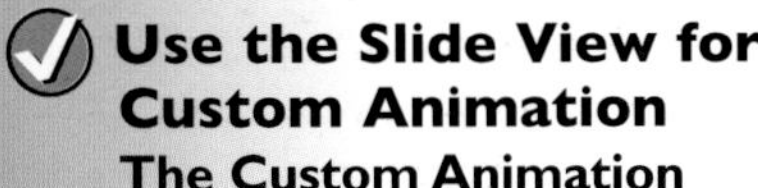

**Use the Slide View for Custom Animation**
The Custom Animation feature is only available in the Slide view.

1. Switch to the Slide view and display the slide you want to animate.

2. Choose **Slide Show, Custom Animation**.

3. A list of slide objects appears on the Timing tab. Click the object you want to animate. The miniature shows the selected object.

4. Click **Animate**. The object now appears in the Animation Order list.

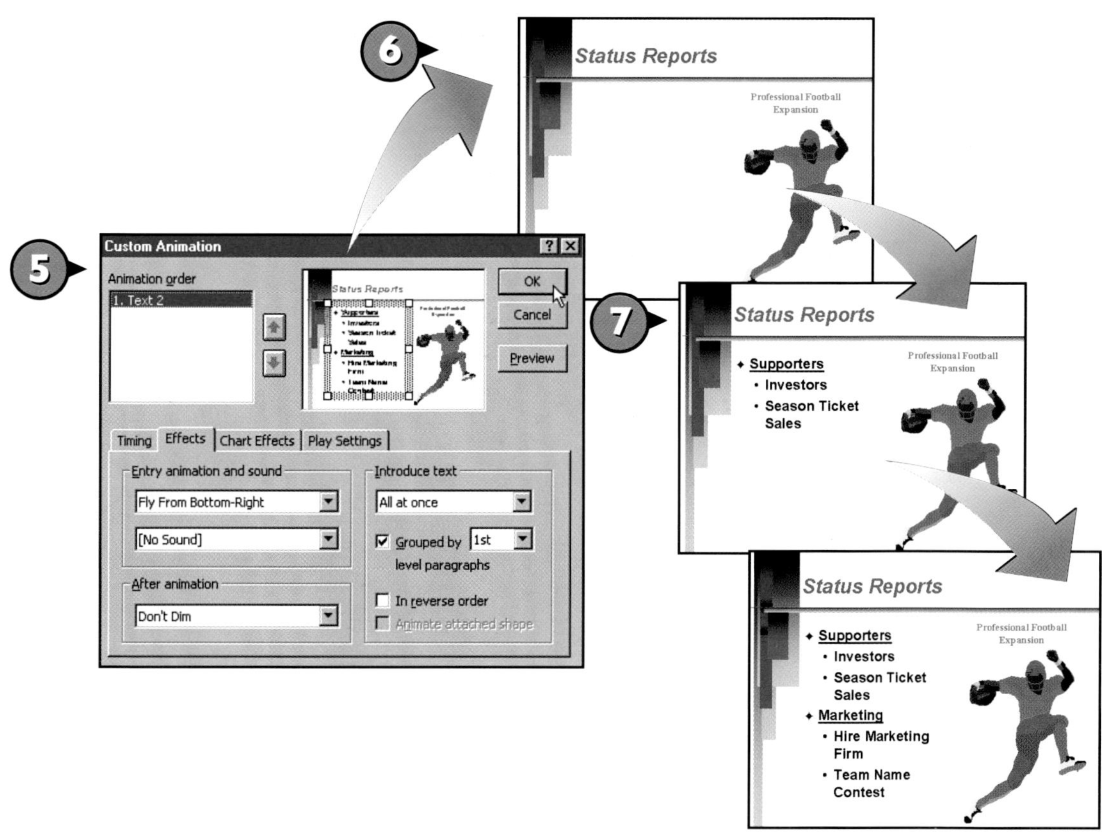


5 Click the **Effects** tab in the Custom Animation dialog box. Select an effect from the Entry Animation and Sound drop-down list.

6 With bulleted lists, you can select the bullet level where you want to group the animation, so select a level from the Grouped By drop-down list.

7 Choose **OK** to apply the animation. Finally, run the slide show to see how it looks.

**Animating Charts and Image Objects**
**You can animate any slide object—not just the text. See Tasks 6 and 7 for steps on animating clip art, WordArt, drawn objects, and graphic charts.**

**Previewing Animation Settings**
**Click the Preview button in the Custom Animation dialog box to see the animation effects in the slide miniature.**

**Preset Animation Adds Sound**
**The Slide Show, Preset Animation feature is not recommended because it also adds sound.**

# Task 6: Animating Clip Art, WordArt, and Drawings

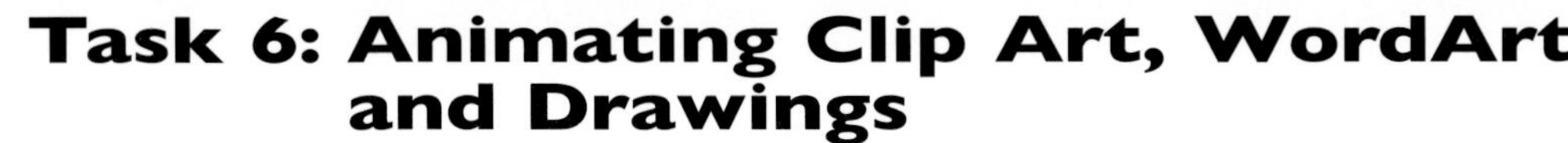

## Applying Animation Effects to Slide Objects

In addition to text, other objects can be animated when you run a slide show. For example, a WordArt or clip art object can spin or spiral in as it appears on the screen, or a sound can play.

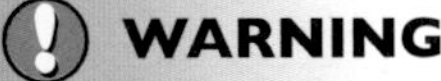

Start Here

**WARNING**
While animation can liven up any presentation, if you animate every object on a slide the audience might find it distracting.

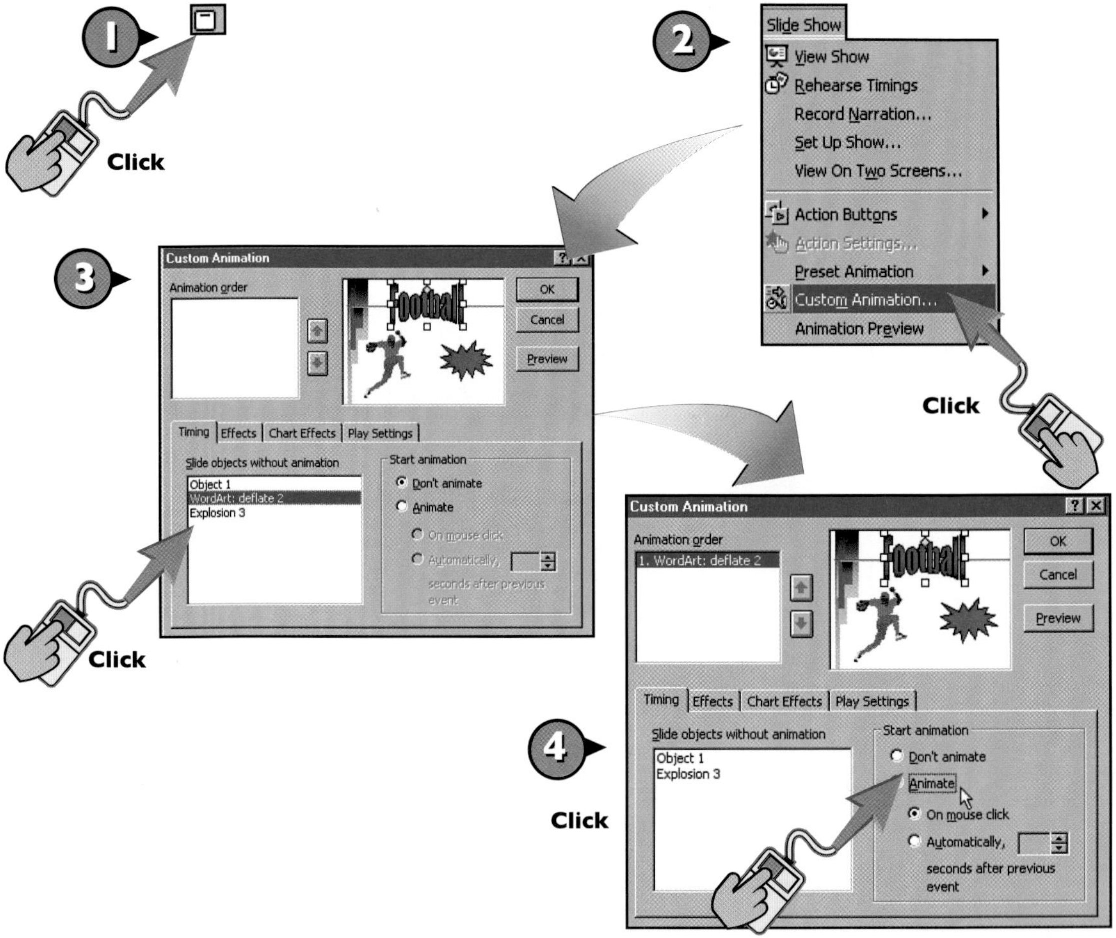

1. Switch to the Slide view and display the slide you want to animate.
2. Choose **Slide Show, Custom Animation**.
3. A list of slide objects appears on the Timing tab. Click the object you want to animate. The miniature shows the selected object.
4. Click **Animate**. The object appears in the Animation Order list.

Next Step

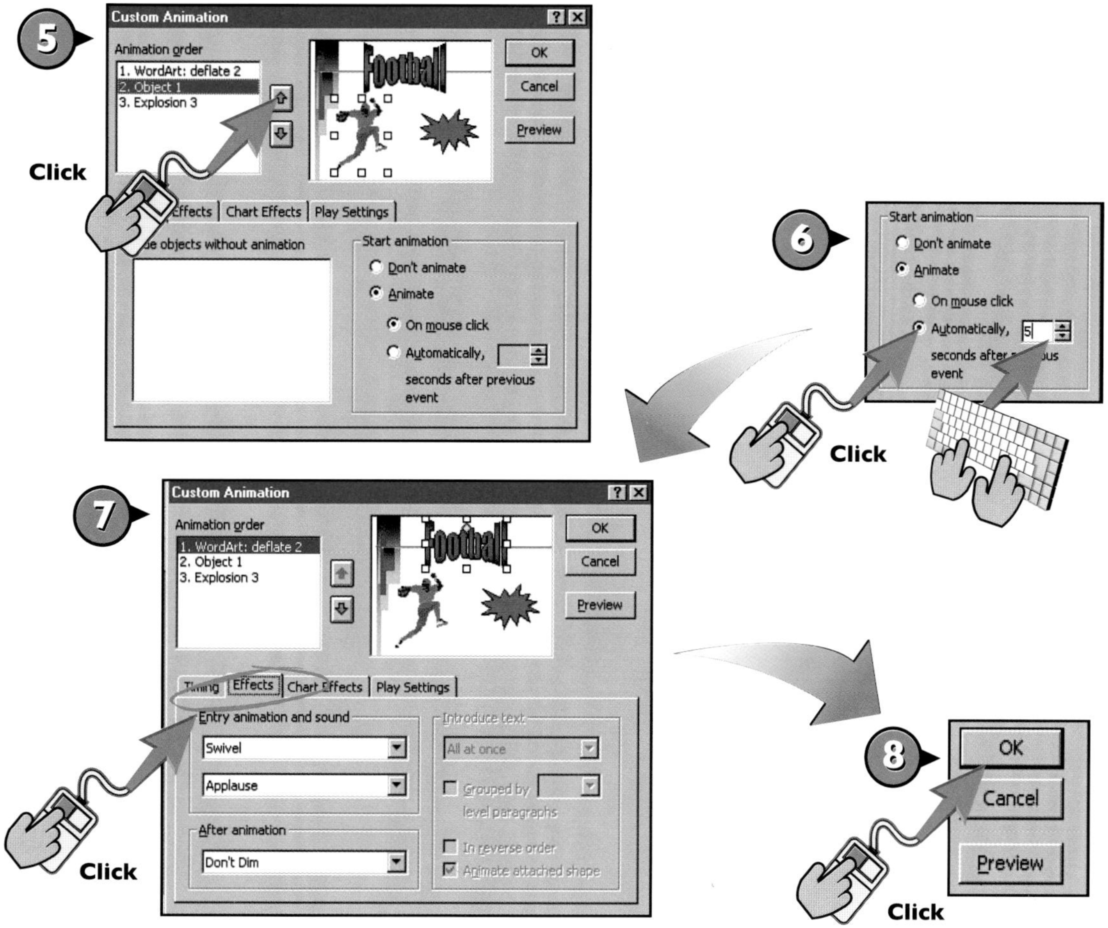

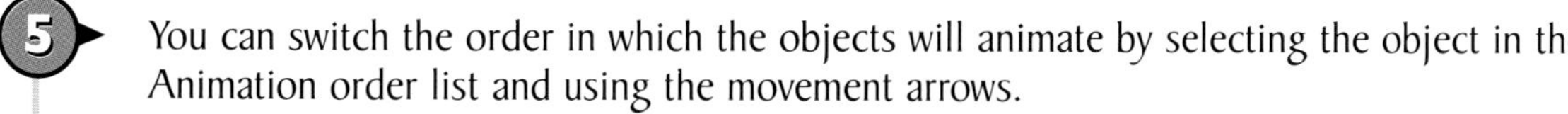

5. You can switch the order in which the objects will animate by selecting the object in the Animation order list and using the movement arrows.

6. You can choose **Automatically** and type a delay time to automatically time the animation of the object.

7. On the Effects tab, choose animation and sound effects from the Entry Animation and Sound drop-down lists.

8. Choose **OK** to apply the animation settings to the objects.

**Preview Animation Settings**
Click the **Preview** button in the Custom Animation dialog box to see the animation effects in the slide miniature.

**Hiding Objects after They Animate**
On the Effects tab of the Custom Animation dialog box is an option to hide the object after it has animated. Open the After Animation drop-down list and choose **Hide After Animation.**

# Task 7: Animating Charts

## Building Graphic Charts

**Animating charts is especially useful when you want to discuss the chart in detail. By displaying the data sequentially, you can be certain of the audience's attention.**

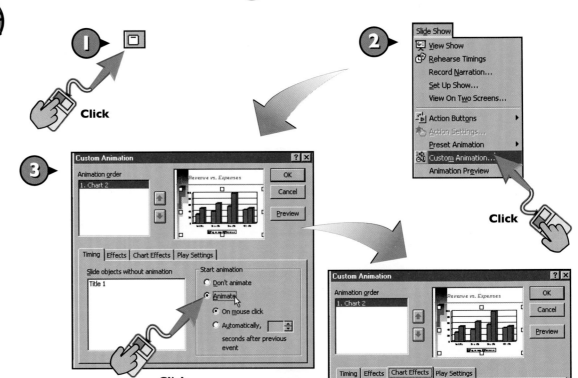

Start Here

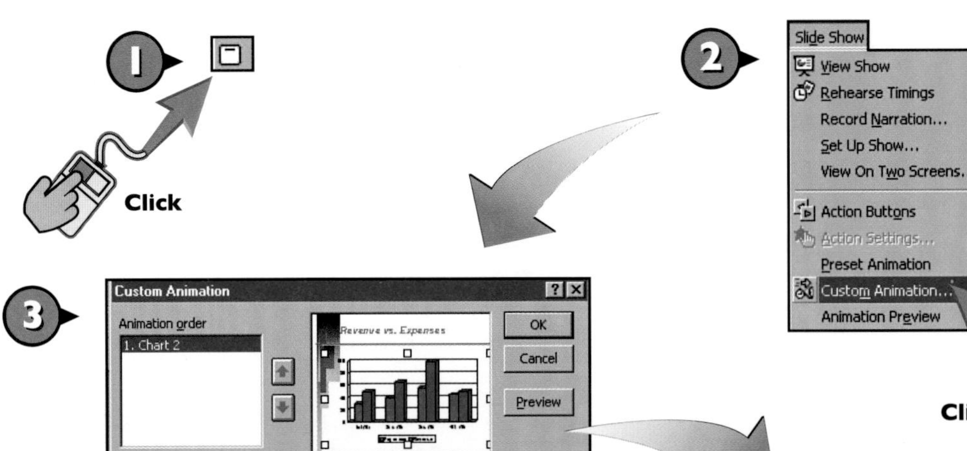


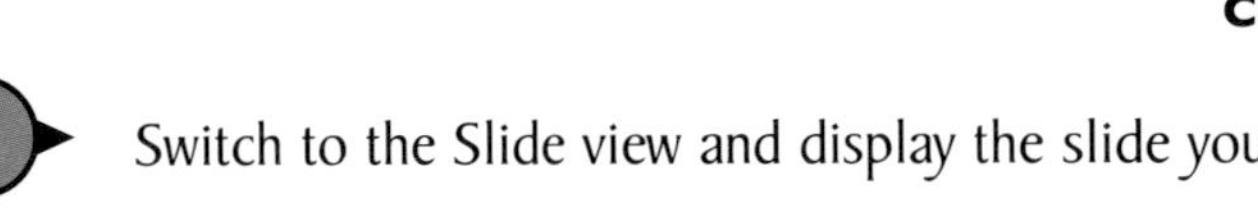

### Animating Slide Titles and Text

**In addition to animating the chart, you can animate the slide title and any other objects in the Slide Objects Without Animation list. You'll find this list on the Timing tab of the Custom Animation dialog box.**

1. Switch to the Slide view and display the slide you want to animate.
2. Choose **Slide Show, Custom Animation**.
3. A list of slide objects appears on the Timing tab. Click the chart object and choose **Animate**. The chart object moves to the Animation Order list.
4. Click the **Chart Effects** tab.

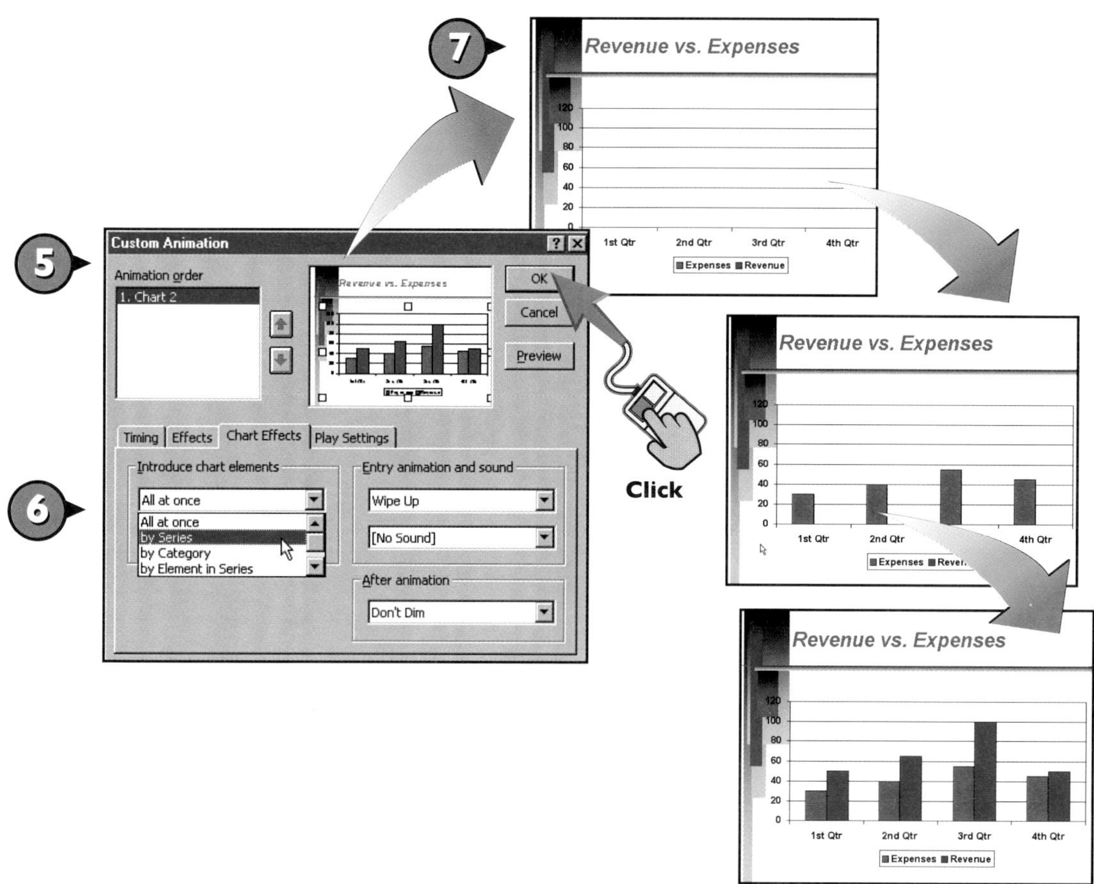


**5** From the Introduce Chart Elements drop-down list, choose how the chart will be animated.

**6** Then select the animation and sound effects from the Entry Animation and Sound drop-down lists and choose **OK** to apply the animation.

**7** Run the slide show to see the animation.

**Chart Animation Choices**
**With graphic charts, you can animate by series, by category, or by each data point.**

**Avoid Sound Effects with Chart Animation**
**Reserve sound effects for text, clip art, WordArt, or drawn objects. If you want to play a music clip during the animation of the chart,** **see Task 8.**

# Task 8: Adding Sound and Video Clips to Slides

## Inserting Sound and Video Clips from the Microsoft Office 97 CD

The Microsoft Office 97 CD comes with a set of sound and video clips. These clips are not loaded on your machine when PowerPoint is installed, so you must have the CD to access them.

Start Here

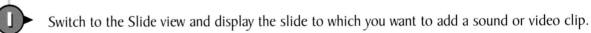

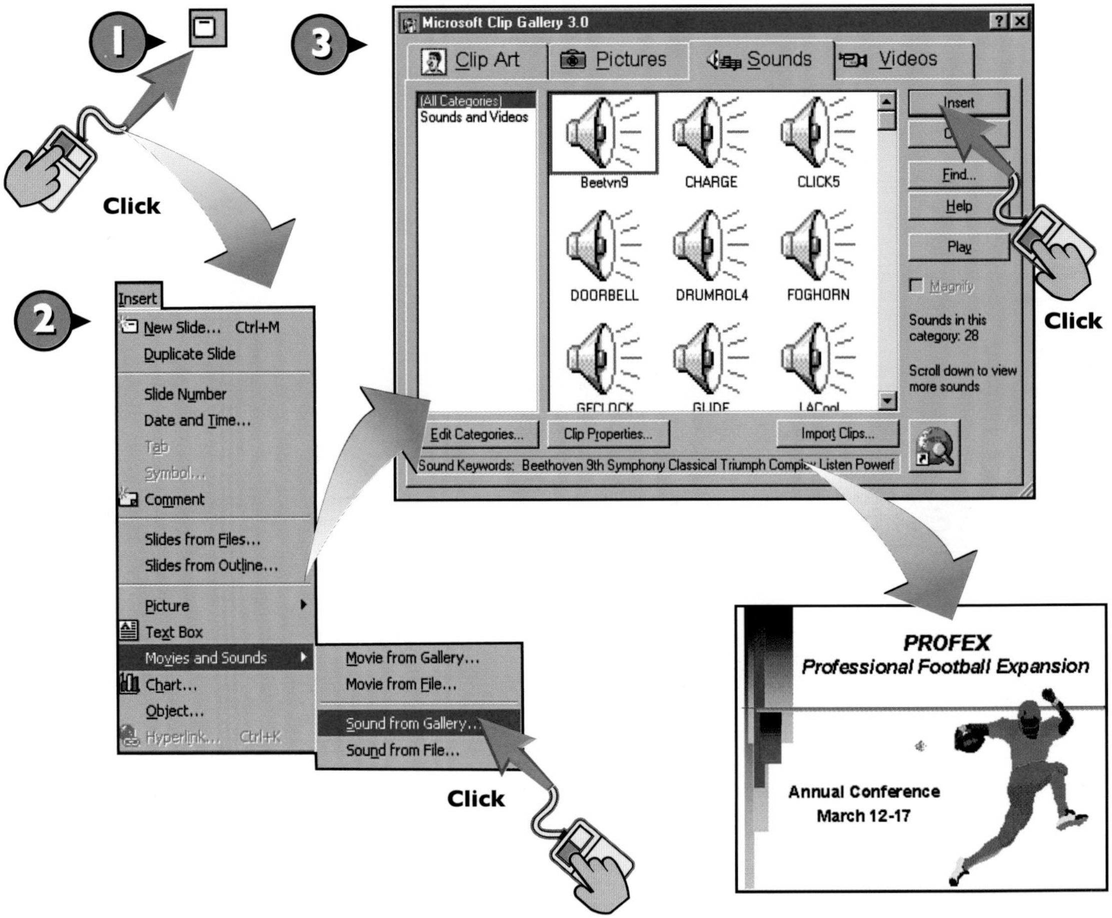

### Sound Clips on the Office 97 CD

The Office 97 CD includes 28 sound clips. Clip names in all uppercase are simply sounds. Clip names in mixed case are parts of music recordings, such as *Beethoven's 9th Symphony*.

1. Switch to the Slide view and display the slide to which you want to add a sound or video clip.
2. Select **Insert, Movies and Sounds, Sound from Gallery** to see the sound clips available on the Microsoft Office 97 CD.
3. Select a clip and choose **Play** to hear the sound. Choose **Insert** to insert the clip on the slide.

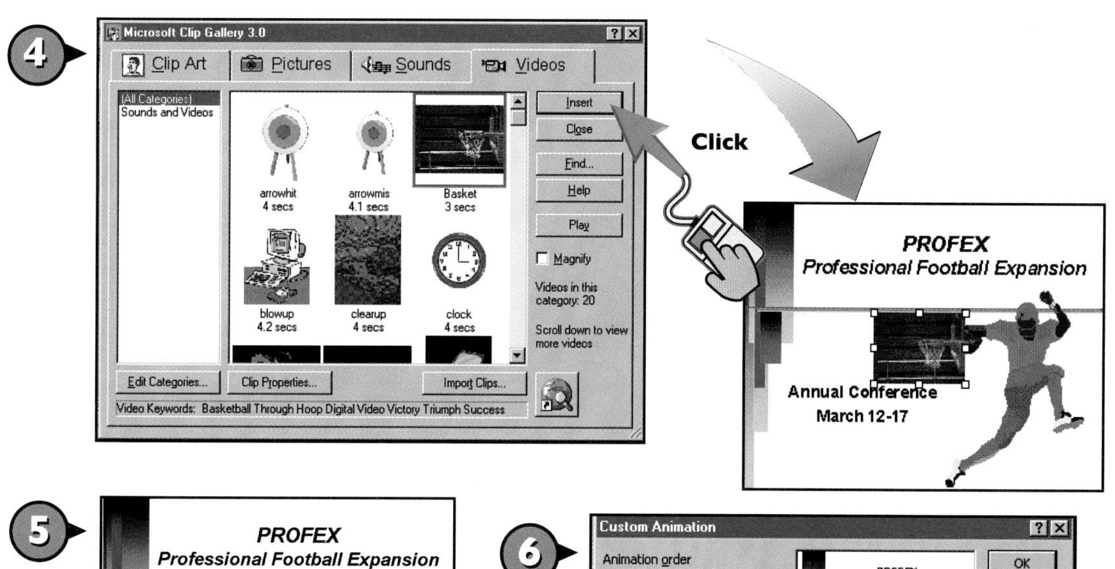

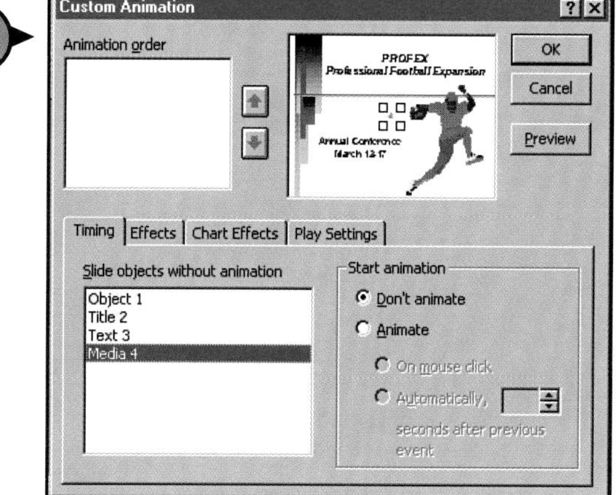


4 Select **Insert, Movies and Sounds, Movie from Gallery** to see the videos. Select a clip and choose **Play**. Choose **Insert** to insert the clip on the slide.

5 When you run the slide show, position your mouse pointer on the clip and click to play it.

6 You can also animate the sound or video clip through the Custom Animation dialog box. These clips are referred to as "media objects."

### Video Clips on the Office 97 CD

**The Microsoft Office 97 CD includes 20 video clips. Some of the clips are animated, and some are true video clips.**

### WARNING

**Sound and video clips are very large files. The *Beethoven's 9th Symphony* clip is 620KB and the 3-second Basket clip is 667KB. These two clips alone take up two-thirds of a floppy disk.**

PART 12

# Running Your Presentation

After you develop a presentation, you can print it or run it as a slide show. A ***slide show*** is simply a presentation you can run on a monitor or overhead projection for viewing by an audience. You can set options for your presentation so you can loop the presentation continuously or run it with set display times for each slide.

While running the slide show, you can easily skip slides or go back to an earlier slide. Additionally, you can take minutes (or notes) and assign action items as the presentation progresses. These minutes and assignments can be exported into Word or Outlook.

# Tasks

# Task 1: Running a Slide Show

## Selecting Slide Show Settings and Running the Slide Show

**Before running the slide show, you might want to confirm or change the slide show settings.**

Start Here

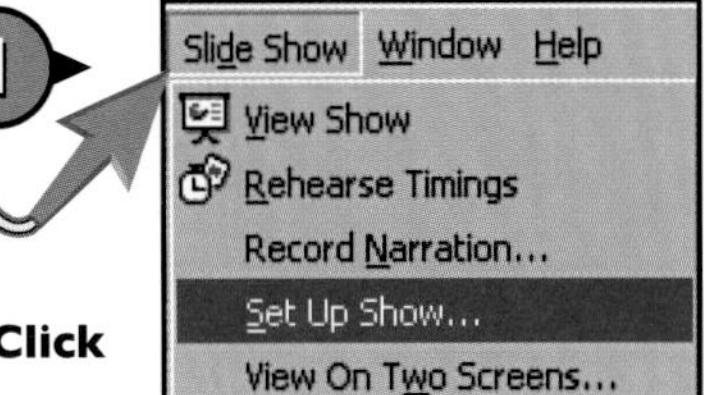

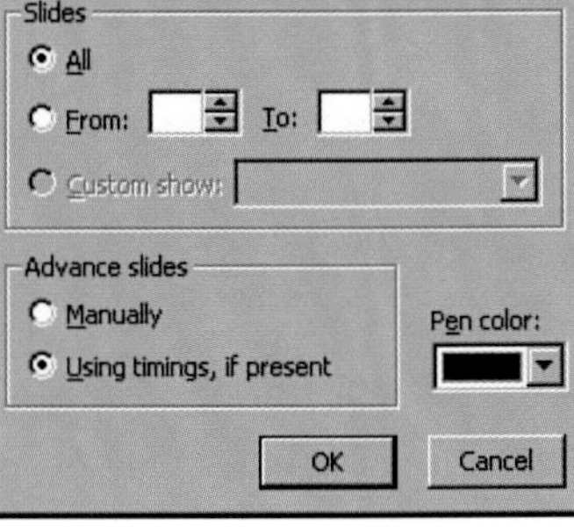


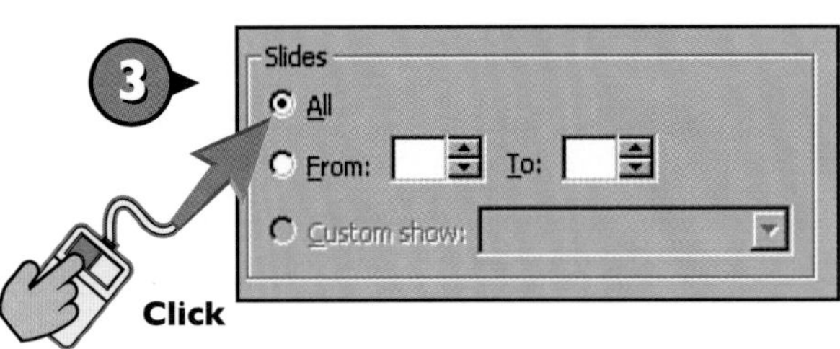


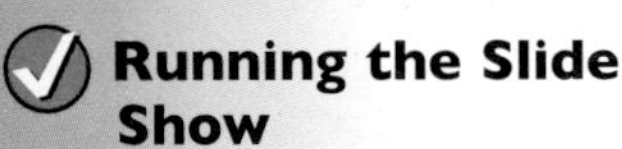

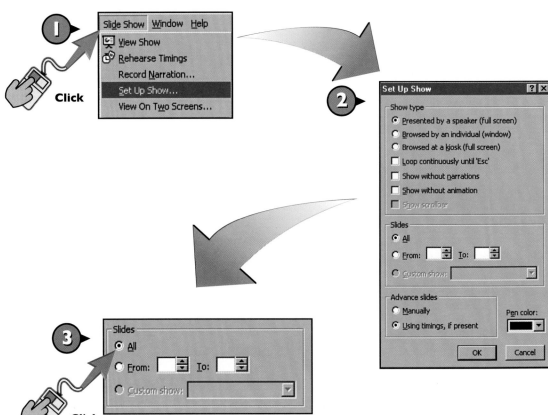

**Running the Slide Show**
**If you run the slide show without first validating the settings, the default settings are used.**

1. Choose **Slide Show, Set Up Show**.

2. The Set Up Show dialog box contains several options you can set before running the slide show.

3. By default, all slides in the presentation are seen when you run the slide show. You have the option of displaying a designated range of slides, if you prefer.

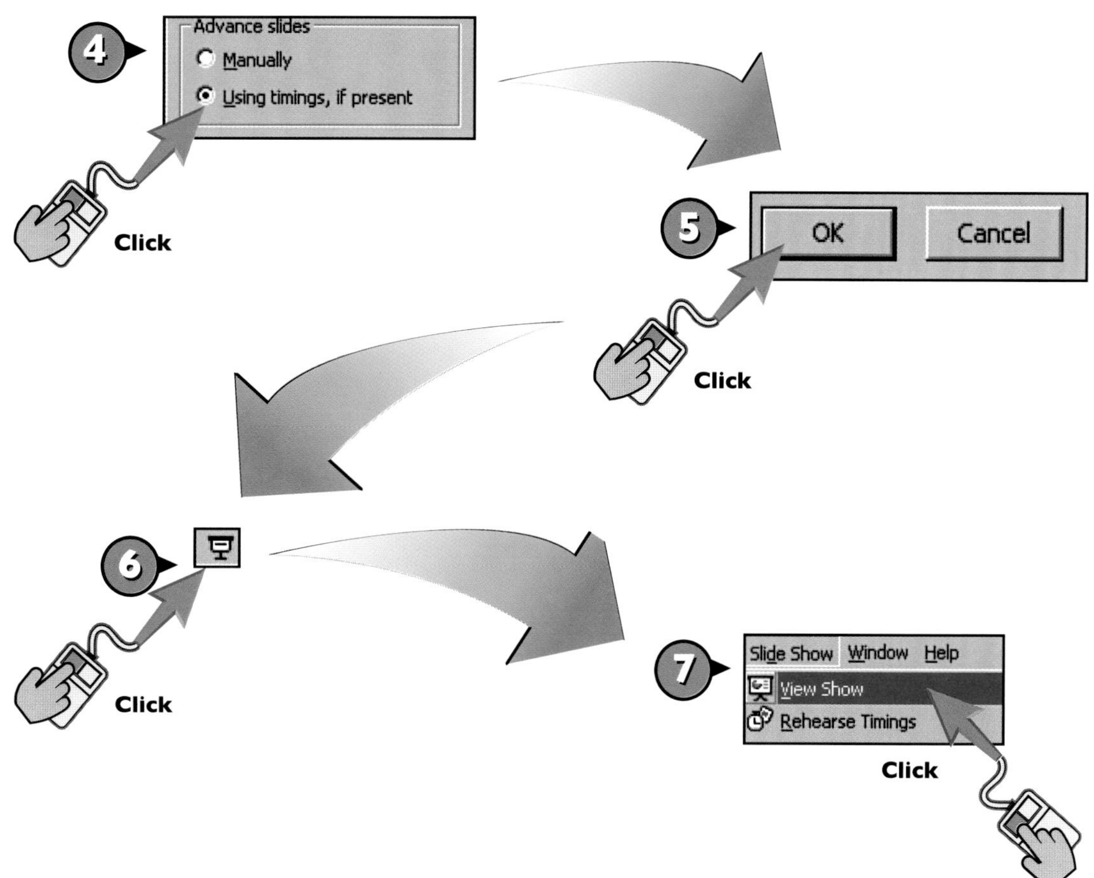

## Rehearsing the Slide Show

**If you have a limited amount of time to give your presentation, consider rehearsing it. Time yourself or add a display time to each slide; the slide show runs, using the timings and automatically changing to the next slide.**

**To rehearse your presentation, choose Slide Show, Rehearse Timings.**

**See Part 11, "Selecting Presentation, Animation, and Sound Settings," Task 4, to set a display time on each slide.**

4. Make sure the **Using Timings, if Present** option is selected if you have set a display time on the presentation slides.

5. Choose **OK** to accept the slide show settings.

6. To run the slide show from the active slide, click the **Slide Show** button in the lower-left corner of the screen.

7. To run the slide show from the first slide in the presentation, choose **Slide Show, View Show**.

# Task 2: Navigating Through a Presentation

## Moving Around in the Presentation While Running the Slide Show

While running the slide show, it is sometimes necessary to skip forward or jump back to a particular slide. If the slides have predefined timings, you might want to pause the show as you (or the audience) discuss a slide topic in more depth. The Slide Navigator provides a method for moving around during a slide show and keeps track of the last slide you looked at.

Start Here

1. After establishing the Slide Show settings (described in Task 1), start the Slide Show.
2. When you move the mouse during the Slide Show, the Slide Show control appears in the lower-left corner of the slide.
3. Click the **Slide Show** control to display a list of commands available while the show is running.
4. Display a specific slide by choosing **Go, By Title** from the Slide Show menu and selecting the slide you want to display.

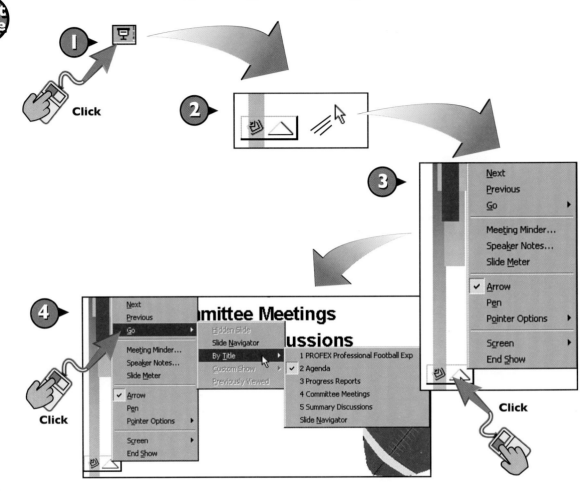

### Shortcut to Display the Slide Show Control Menu

The Slide Show control menu also displays if you right-click on any part of the slide while running the show.

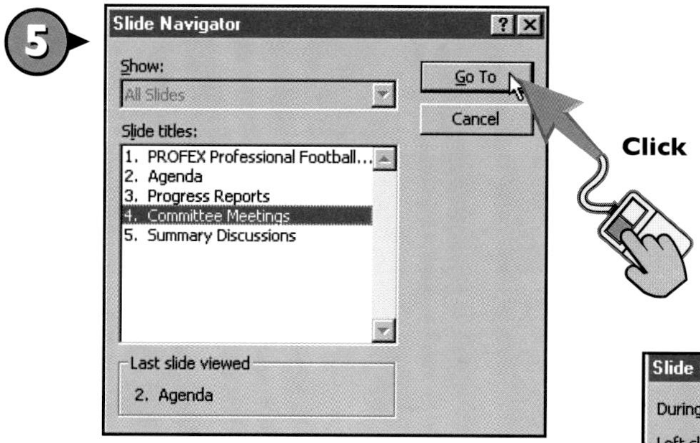

5

Slide Navigator

Show:

All Slides

Slide titles:

1. PROFEX Professional Football...
2. Agenda
3. Progress Reports
4. Committee Meetings
5. Summary Discussions

Last slide viewed

2. Agenda

Go To

Cancel

Click

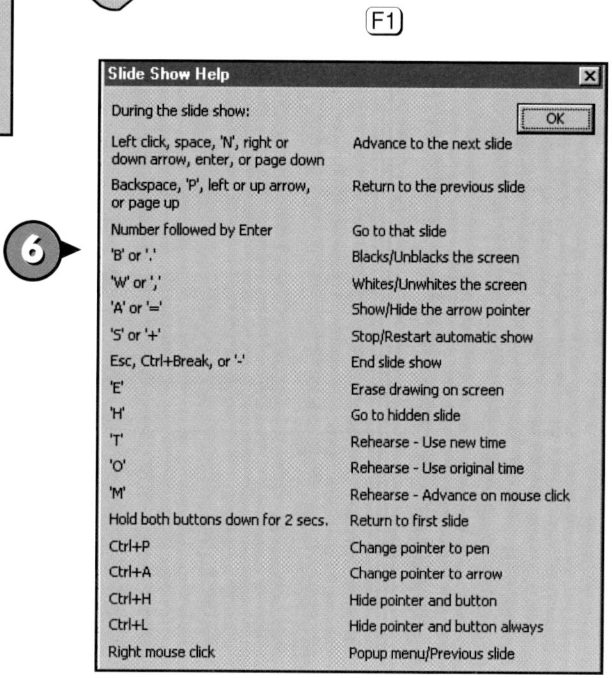

F1

6

Slide Show Help

During the slide show:

OK

| | |
|---|---|
| Left click, space, 'N', right or down arrow, enter, or page down | Advance to the next slide |
| Backspace, 'P', left or up arrow, or page up | Return to the previous slide |
| Number followed by Enter | Go to that slide |
| 'B' or '.' | Blacks/Unblacks the screen |
| 'W' or ',' | Whites/Unwhites the screen |
| 'A' or '=' | Show/Hide the arrow pointer |
| 'S' or '+' | Stop/Restart automatic show |
| Esc, Ctrl+Break, or '-' | End slide show |
| 'E' | Erase drawing on screen |
| 'H' | Go to hidden slide |
| 'T' | Rehearse - Use new time |
| 'O' | Rehearse - Use original time |
| 'M' | Rehearse - Advance on mouse click |
| Hold both buttons down for 2 secs. | Return to first slide |
| Ctrl+P | Change pointer to pen |
| Ctrl+A | Change pointer to arrow |
| Ctrl+H | Hide pointer and button |
| Ctrl+L | Hide pointer and button always |
| Right mouse click | Popup menu/Previous slide |

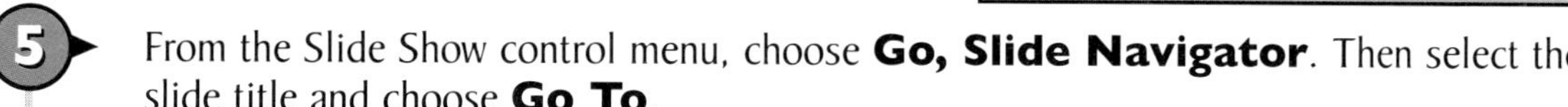

5 From the Slide Show control menu, choose **Go, Slide Navigator**. Then select the slide title and choose **Go To**.

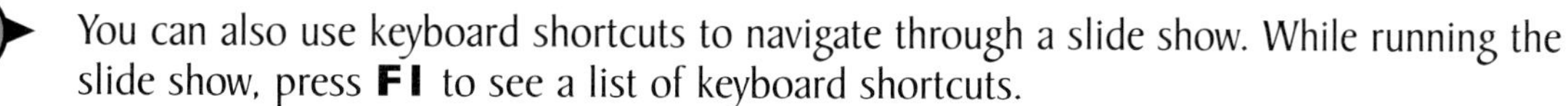

6 You can also use keyboard shortcuts to navigate through a slide show. While running the slide show, press **F1** to see a list of keyboard shortcuts.

**Print the Keyboard Shortcuts**

To print the list of keyboard shortcuts, choose **Help, Contents and Index.** Click on the **Index** tab, type **slide show,** and double-click on **Keyboard Shortcuts.**

With the keyboard shortcut list displayed, choose **Options, Print Topic.**

# Task 3: Using the Meeting Minder

## Taking Notes and Assigning Tasks During a Slide Show

**You can use the *Meeting Minder* while running the Slide Show to document minutes and action items and to export the minutes and action items to Word or Outlook.**

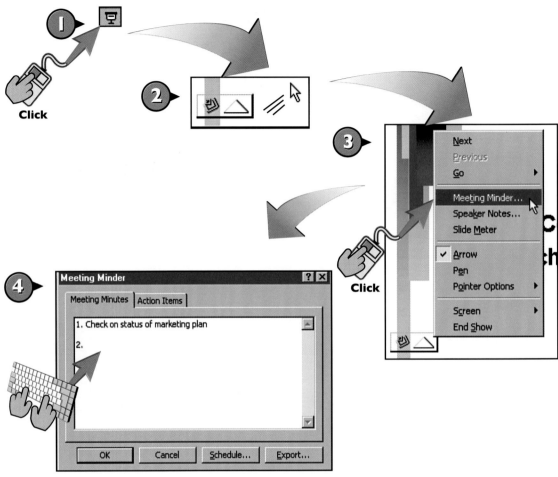

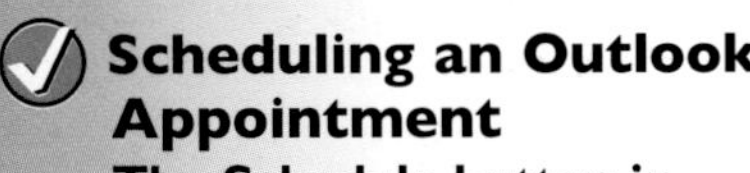

**Scheduling an Outlook Appointment**
**The Schedule button in the Meeting Minder starts Outlook and displays an appointment window.**

1. After establishing the Slide Show settings (described in Task 1), start the Slide Show.

2. When you move the mouse during the Slide Show, the Slide Show control appears in the lower-left corner.

3. Choose **Meeting Minder** from the Slide Show control menu.

4. To create minutes or notes during slide show discussions, type the minutes in the Meeting Minutes box.

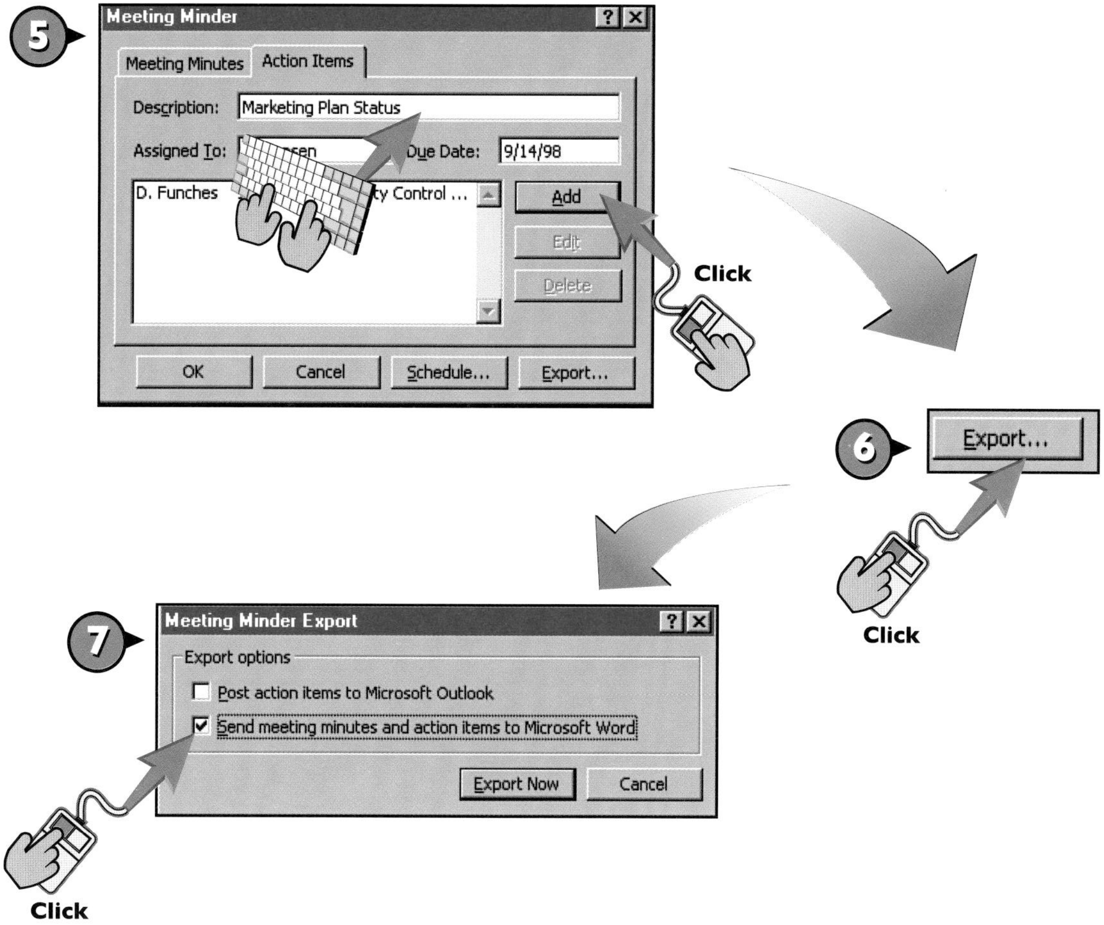

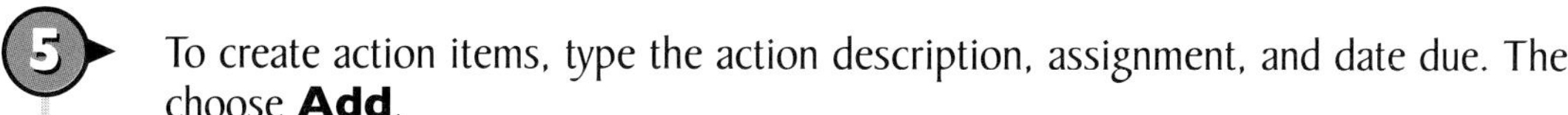

**5** To create action items, type the action description, assignment, and date due. Then choose **Add**.

**6** Choose the **Export** button.

**7** After choosing one or both of the Export Options, choose **Export Now**.

### Assigned To Text Limitation

The maximum number of characters allowed in the Assigned To box is 10.

### Export to Outlook or Word

The Export button enables you to export the action items to Outlook, export the minutes and action items to Word, or export to both programs.

# Task 4: Setting the Presentation to Run Continuously

## Running the Slide Show in an Automatic Loop

In some situations, it is useful to have a slide show run automatically, without the need to restart the show each time. This is especially useful at conferences, trade shows, and kiosks.

Start Here

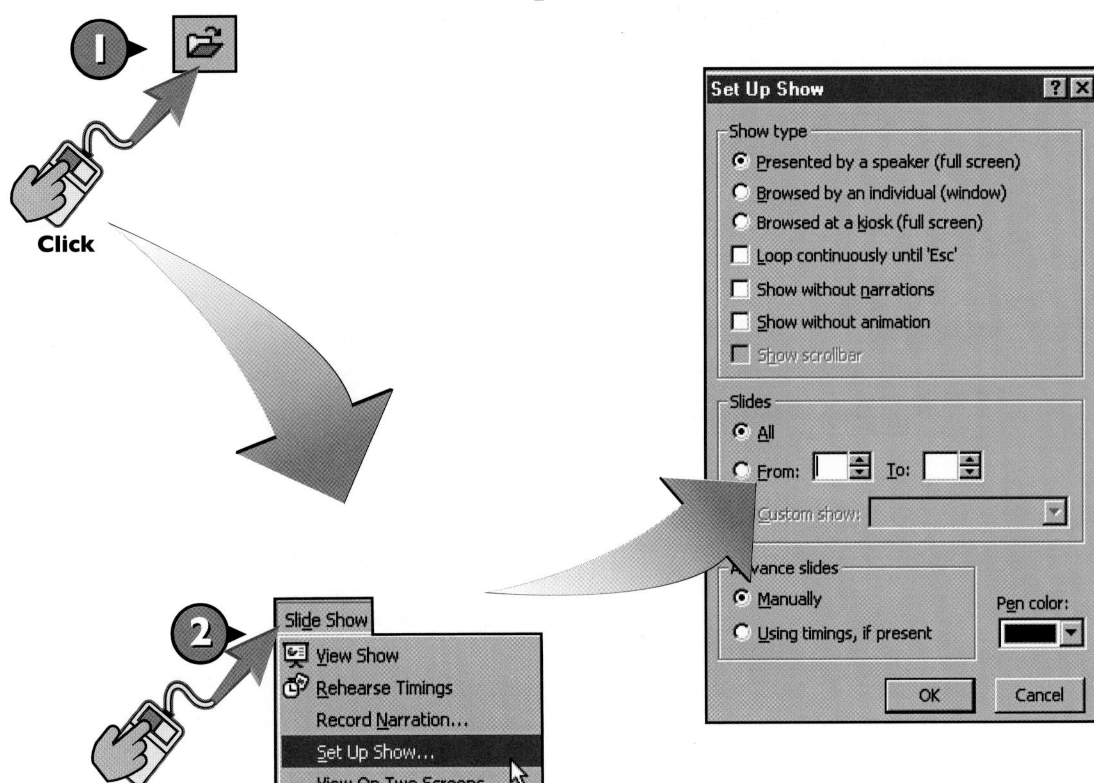


**WARNING**
**When you're running a presentation in a continuous loop, you must have display times assigned to each slide. See Part 11, Task 4 for steps on adding automatic display times to slides.**

1. Open or switch to the presentation you want to run continuously.
2. Choose **Slide Show, Set Up Show**. The Set Up Show dialog box appears.

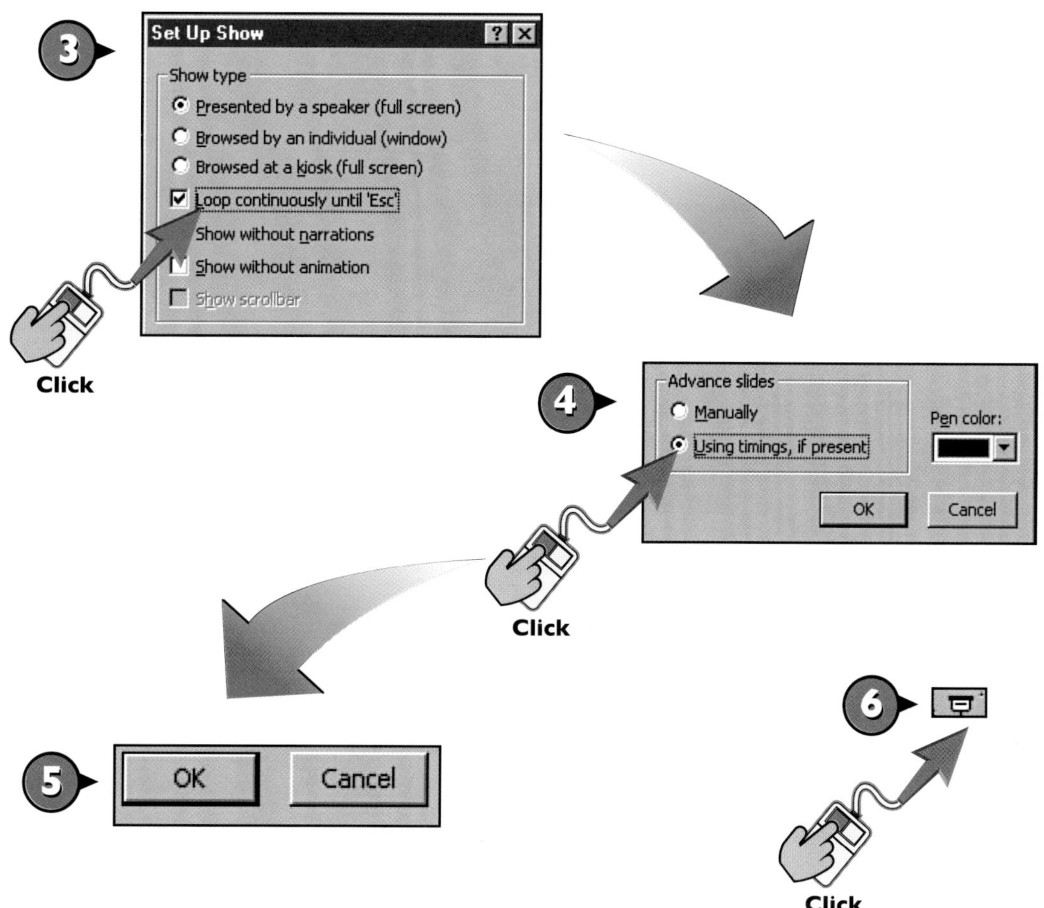


3. Choose **Loop Continuously Until 'Esc.'**

4. Make sure the **Using Timings, if Present** option is selected.

5. Choose **OK**.

6. When you are ready to run the show continuously, click the **Slide Show** button. Press **Esc** to stop the show.

**Slide Show Settings**
**These settings remain assigned to the slide show until you change them.**

**Advancing the Slide Show**
**You must set the slides to advance by using the slide timings; otherwise, the person viewing the show has to press Enter or click with the mouse to advance the show.**

# Glossary

**Animation** Displaying objects sequentially to "build" a slide or to add fancy entry or sound effects to slide objects.

**Branch (organization charts)** A manager box and all the subordinate boxes.

**Bullets** A list of individual text topics or points, where each point is preceded by a symbol.

**Cell** In PowerPoint, the intersection of a row and column in the datasheet or a table.

**"Click" placeholder** A predefined object in a PowerPoint slide, such as a title, a list of bullets, or a graphic chart.

**Clip art** Predesigned drawings or cartoons. PowerPoint contains dozens of clip art objects for you to choose from.

**Current cell** The active cell in the Datasheet or a table. Typically, a flashing cursor appears in the current cell.

**Data point** One number plotted on a graphic chart.

**Data series** A group of numbers plotted on a graphic chart. Data series are displayed in the legend in a graphic chart.

**Data category** A group of data points, one from each data series. Data categories are displayed on the x-axis in graphic charts.

**Drag and drop** A mouse technique that enables you to move or copy objects.

**Edit mode** In PowerPoint, designated by a slash-mark border. Clicking a bulleted list or other text object places you in the Edit mode, ready to modify the text. The mouse pointer is a thin capital "I", and a flashing cursor appears next to the text. Double-clicking a graphic chart, organization chart, or table also places you in the Edit mode.

**Font type** The text appearance. Examples of font types include Arial, Courier, Times New Roman, and Desdemona.

**Group (organization charts)** All the boxes on one level, under one manager.

**Indenting** In a list of bulleted text, a bullet can be made into a sub-bullet by moving it farther from the left margin. Also called "demoting."

**Layering** Each object on a PowerPoint slide exists on its own level, including all text and drawn objects. You can bring objects forward or send them backward by using the Drawing toolbar.

**Level (organization charts)** A row of boxes within an organization chart that represents one level within the reporting structure of an organization.

**Link** A copy of an object (or data) formatted so that a change in the original object (or data) is reflected in the copy. Links are often used between Excel data and PowerPoint charts; when the Excel data is changed, the PowerPoint chart changes.

**Master** Each PowerPoint presentation has four master templates: Title Master, Slide Master, Handouts Master, and Notes Pages Master. Masters are the "blueprints" for placement and formatting of objects on PowerPoint slides or printed materials.

**Microsoft Graph** A program used by PowerPoint (and other Microsoft Office programs) to create graphic charts such as column, pie, and line charts.

**Microsoft Organization Chart** A program used by PowerPoint to create organization charts.

**Objects** Any item on a slide is considered an object. This includes "click" placeholders for bulleted lists, charts, and tables as well as independent text, clip art, WordArt, and drawings.

**Outdenting** In a list of bulleted text, a bullet can be made into a main bullet by moving it toward the left margin. Also called "promoting."

**Placeholder** See *"Click" placeholder*.

**Plotting (data)** The graphical representation of numbers in a chart. For example, a set of revenue numbers can be plotted as a set (or series) of columns in a chart.

**ScreenTip** A pop-up that describes a part of the screen. ScreenTips display when you rest the mouse pointer over a toolbar button or when you are editing a graphic chart.

**Scroll** Moving the screen display to see additional data. Most windows have scrollbars. Only the mouse can be used to scroll a window display.

**Selection handles** The set of small boxes that appear at strategic positions around an object when you click on it. An object must be selected before it can be formatted. Selection handles are used to resize objects.

**Slide show** Running a presentation on a monitor or overhead projection system.

**Slide Master** A specific type of Master used for all slide layouts except the Title Slide layout. See also *Master*.

**Spinner buttons** A type of button found in dialog boxes. Two arrows or triangles, one pointing up and the other pointing down. Click the up arrow to increase the value or the down arrow to decrease the value. For example, in the Print dialog box, spinner buttons are used to select the number of copies to be printed.

**Subscript** Displaying letters or numbers offset below normal text. For example, the scientific designation for water, $H_2O$.

**Superscript** Displaying letters or numbers offset above normal text. For example, a copyright symbol, Microsoft©, or a number, $C^3$.

**Transitions** The way a slide appears onscreen. Used with slide shows to move from slide to slide.

**WordArt** An option to display text in curves, waves, and angles with special color formatting.

**X-axis** The horizontal axis in a graphic chart; lists the chart categories. Examples of typical categories are months, quarters, and years.

Index

## A



## B

# C

# D

# E



# F

## G - H



## I - J



## K - L

## M



## N - O

# P - Q

## R



## S

## T

# U - V



# W - Z